Johannine Ethics

Johannine Ethics

The Moral World of the Gospel and Epistles of John

SHERRI BROWN AND CHRISTOPHER W.
SKINNER, EDITORS

FORTRESS PRESS
MINNEAPOLIS

JOHANNINE ETHICS
The Moral World of the Gospel and Epistles of John

Cover design: Alisha Lofgren

Print ISBN: 978-1-4514-9646-8
eBook ISBN: 978-1-5064-3846-7

The paper used in this publication meets the minimum requirements of American National Standard for Information Sciences — Permanence of Paper for Printed Library Materials, ANSI Z329.48-1984.

Manufactured in the U.S.A.

This book was produced using Pressbooks.com, and PDF rendering was done by PrinceXML.

*For our colleagues and students at Creighton University
and Loyola University Chicago*

Contents

Part II. Implied Ethics in the Johannine Literature

Part III. Moving Forward

Contributors

Cornelis Bennema
Senior Lecturer in New Testament, Union School of Theology, UK and Research Fellow, Department of Old and New Testament Studies, Faculty of Theology and Religion, University of the Free State, Bloemfontein, South Africa

Sherri Brown
Assistant Professor of New Testament, Department of Theology, Creighton University, Omaha, Nebraska

Jaime Clark-Soles
Professor of New Testament, Altshuler Distinguished Teaching Professor, Perkins School of Theology, Southern Methodist University, Dallas, Texas

Raymond F. Collins
Visiting Scholar, Department of Religious Studies, Brown University, Providence, Rhode Island

R. Alan Culpepper
Dean and Professor of New Testament Emeritus, McAfee School of Theology, Mercer University, Macon, Georgia; Research Fellow, Department of Old and New Testament Studies, Faculty of Theology and Religion, University of the Free State, Bloemfontein, South Africa

Toan Do
Post-Doctoral Research Fellow, Institute for Religion and Critical Inquiry, Faculty of Theology and Philosophy, Australian Catholic University, Melbourne, Victoria, Australia

Michael J. Gorman
Raymond E. Brown Chair in Biblical Studies and Theology, St. Mary's Seminary & University, Baltimore, Maryland

Dorothy A. Lee
Frank Woods Professor of New Testament, Trinity College, University of Divinity, Parkville, Victoria, Australia

Francis J Moloney, SDB
Senior Professorial Fellow, Catholic Theological College, University of Divinity, Melbourne, Australia

Alicia D. Myers
Assistant Professor of New Testament and Greek, Campbell University Divinity School, Buies Creek, North Carolina

Adele Reinhartz
Professor, Department of Classics and Religious Studies, University of Ottawa, Ottawa, Ontario, Canada

Christopher W. Skinner
Associate Professor of New Testament & Early Christianity, Loyola University Chicago, Chicago, Illinois

Lindsey Trozzo
Lecturer in Rhetoric and Biblical Heritage, Baylor Interdisciplinary Core, Honors College, Baylor University, Waco, Texas

Preface

This project unfolded in dribs and drabs over several years in conversations at professional meetings, numerous emails, and random text messages before we finally sat down and said to one another, "Let's get serious about this thing!" Once we finally "got serious" we were surprised to find that others were equally interested in exploring the moral world of the Johannine literature. At the outset, we wanted to put together a substantive discussion of ethics in the Gospel and Epistles of John, and the finished product is significantly better and more fully developed than either of us imagined in the early stages of the project. This is no doubt due, in large part, to our outstanding group of contributors. We are thankful both for their contributions and for their attentiveness to our deadlines.

Both of us have had major life changes since beginning this project, including changes in institutional affiliation. In 2014, Sherri moved from Niagara University in New York to Creighton University in Omaha, Nebraska. In 2016, Chris moved from Mount Olive College in North Carolina to Loyola University Chicago. Both of these cross-country moves affected our productiveness and altered the timeline of the book. We want to thank Fortress Press and, in particular, Neil Elliott for their sensitivity to these and other influential life situations over the past three years.

In bringing forth a volume such as this, there are always people to thank whose names might not otherwise show up in the pages of the book. We would both like to thank Fr. Paul Adaja, who, while serving as Chris's research assistant in the fall of 2016, helped compile and organize the bibliography. Portions of our research were also presented at various meetings of the Catholic Biblical Association of

America and the Society of Biblical Literature. We are appreciative of the many friends, colleagues, and other scholars who raised questions, provided helpful suggestions, or listened as we made our argument for the presence and value of ethics in the Johannine writings.

Sherri: I would like to thank the ethics faculty in the Department of Theology here at Creighton, including Julia Fleming, Todd Salzman, Gail Risch, and Christina McRorie. Conversations with them in the hallway, over drinks, and in more formal office meetings have greatly assisted me in the development of my understanding of the study of ethics as well as of current discussions in the field. My chair, Julia Fleming, has been particularly supportive in all my many and varied endeavors over the past several years, even when she is patiently trying to teach me to say no. In addition, the biblical studies faculty here at Creighton have also been a constant font of sustenance, debate, and fun. I love working everyday with Ron Simkins, Sue Calef, Nicolae Roddy, Gordon Brubacher, and Dulcinea Boesenberg. I would also like to thank my family, in all its various forms, for its undying encouragement to seek new horizons. In October 2015, my father passed away, and I feel the loss of him daily and in innumerable ways. Nonetheless, I would not be where I am without him. His unassuming good nature and humor have always buoyed me even when the waves of life's stresses threatened. To love both life and God's good creatures the way he did will always be my goal.

Chris: I would like to express my appreciation to Dr. Hollis Phelps, my colleague for six years at Mount Olive College in North Carolina. Numerous conversations during that period, and particularly over the past three years, have helped me think more critically and more honestly about how "ethics" function in ancient texts and in modern societies. I would also like to express appreciation for my new colleagues at Loyola University Chicago, not only for their warm reception, but also for all they have done to help me get acclimated to a new life and unfamiliar surroundings. Conversations with Edmondo Lupieri, Tom Wetzel, Teresa Calpino, Devorah Schoenfeld, Emily Cain, Aana Vigen, Colby Dickinson, and Bob DiVito have been particularly helpful in a myriad of ways and are deeply appreciated. Finally, I want to acknowledge that there are four other people who form the foundation of my life and consistently remind me that I am a part of something much bigger than myself. My wife, Tara, and our three kids, Christopher, Abby, and Drew, infuse every day with significance and meaning that would otherwise be absent. I am thankful that they continue to love me when I am unlovable and encourage me to undertake projects like this one, even when it means that I will occasionally be preoccupied.

Finally, we would like to dedicate this book to our colleagues and students at Creighton University and Loyola University Chicago. We are both so pleased with and so thankful for where we have landed. Our new situations have provided us with daily encounters and challenges that spur us ever onward in our chosen vocations.

Introduction:
(How) Can We Talk About Johannine Ethics? Looking Back and Moving Forward

CHRISTOPHER W. SKINNER

Scholars in search of ethical material in the New Testament[1] have long overlooked or downplayed the potential contribution of the Gospel and Epistles of John.[2] Noting that the Fourth Gospel in particular lacks the same sort of ethical emphases as the Letters of Paul or the Synoptic Gospels, commentators have been quick to dismiss the Gospel as having little value for discussions of New Testament ethics. Expressing what has been a common view, one Johannine scholar has flatly asserted that "the Fourth Gospel meets none of our expectations about the way ethics should be constructed."[3] Others have gone so far as to deny that ethics can be found in the Johannine literature.[4] Fortunately, however, recent years have seen numerous attempts to revisit this discussion by shining a light on the "problem" of Johannine

1. I would like to thank Dr. Lindsey Trozzo for reading an earlier draft of this chapter and providing a number of insights and suggested readings.

2. For the purposes of this volume, we are focusing on the Fourth Gospel and the three epistles bearing the name of John. Since there are numerous questions about how the book of Revelation fits within the corpus traditionally known as the Johannine literature, we have intentionally left it out of our considerations here. Throughout this volume, our discussion will limit the Johannine literature to the Gospel and Epistles.

3. Wayne A. Meeks, "The Ethics of the Fourth Evangelist," in *Exploring the Gospel of John: In Honor of D. Moody Smith*, ed. R. Alan Culpepper and C. Clifton Black (Louisville: Westminster John Knox, 1996), 320.

4. J. L. Houlden expresses this perspective: "Even when [John] speaks of the command to love and of doing what Jesus commands, John's real concern is not primarily ethical at all. His concern is with the new condition of life conferred on the believers through Christ" (*Ethics and the New Testament* [Harmondsworth, UK: Penguin, 1973], 36).

ethics.[5] There is little doubt that previous commentators were correct in their assessment that the Johannine literature lacked the same explicit ethical instructions as the Letters of Paul (e.g., Gal 5:16–26; 1 Cor 13:1–13), or the teachings of the Matthean (e.g. 5:1–7:29) or Lukan Jesus (e.g., 6:17–49). But isn't this understanding of ethics necessarily narrow and shortsighted? Doesn't such an approach prejudice the discussion from the outset? Could it be that the Johannine literature has a rich understanding of what constitutes ethics, and that our problem is ultimately one of restricted definition and limited imagination? This volume operates under the conviction that the answer to each of the foregoing questions is yes.

As a way of situating this volume within the wider context of scholarship on New Testament ethics, this chapter considers the related questions, Can we talk about Johannine ethics? and if so, How can we talk about Johannine ethics? Specifically, we will explore the three most commonly articulated views on the presence or value of ethics in the Johannine literature: (1) the Johannine literature is essentially devoid of ethical material; (2) the ethics of the Johannine literature are limited, often being described as exclusive, sectarian, negative, or oppositional; (3) the ethics of the Johannine literature are inclusive or valuable for incorporation into broader schemes of Christian ethics or moral theology. Since this book is aimed primarily at students, this survey is not meant to be an exhaustive history of recent scholarship on the subject but rather representative of the most important conversations.[6] Our concern here is with tracing the major

5. See, e.g., Johannes Nissen, "Community and Ethics in the Gospel of John," in *New Readings in John: Literary and Theological Perspectives; Essays from the Scandinavian Conference on the Fourth Gospel in Aarhus 1997*, ed. Johannes Nissen and Sigfred Pedersen, JSNTSup 182 (Sheffield: Sheffield Academic, 1999), 199, 210; Jey J. Kanagaraj, "The Implied Ethics of the Fourth Gospel: A Reinterpretation of the Decalogue," *TynBul* 52 (2001): 33–60; D. Moody Smith, "Ethics and Interpretation of the Fourth Gospel," in *Word, Theology, and Community in John*, ed. John Painter, R. Alan Culpepper, and Fernando F. Segovia (St. Louis: Chalice, 2002), 109–22; Hans Boersma, "A New Age Love Story: Worldview and Ethics in the Gospel of John," *CTJ* 38 (2003): 103–19; János Bolyki, "Ethics in the Gospel of John," *ActAnt* 44 (2004): 99–107; Jan G. van der Watt, "The Gospel of John's Perception of Ethical Behaviour," *IDS* 45 (2011): 431–47; van der Watt, "Ethics through the Power of Language: Some Explorations in the Gospel according to John," in *Moral Language in the New Testament: The Interrelatedness of Language and Ethics in Early Christian Writings*, ed. Ruben Zimmerman, Jan G. van der Watt, and Susanne Luther, WUNT 296 (Tübingen: Mohr Siebeck 2010), 139–67, and from the same volume, Kobus Kok, "As the Father Has Sent Me, I Send You: Towards a Missional-Incarnational Ethos in John 4," 168–96. See especially the essays in Jan G. van der Watt and Ruben Zimmerman, eds., *Rethinking the Ethics of John: "Implicit Ethics" in the Johannine Writings*, WUNT 291 (Tübingen: Mohr Siebeck, 2012).

6. For a recent comprehensive survey of this subject, see Jan G. van der Watt, "Ethics and

categories for speaking about ethics that have developed within contemporary research. After exploring these three approaches, we will then briefly introduce our integration of these approaches through the individual contributions to this volume and their potential for developing new proposals and categories for conceiving of Johannine ethics.

JOHANNINE ETHICS: WHAT ARE THEY SAYING?

THERE ARE NO ETHICS IN
THE JOHANNINE LITERATURE

The notion that the writings of John are devoid of ethical material has been a strongly held position for decades. Only recently has that near consensus been seriously challenged. As has already been mentioned, scholarly engagement with New Testament ethics has long suffered from a restricted definition of what constitutes ethical instruction, and this has no doubt set the lines for understanding John's contribution (or lack thereof) to the discussion. As a means of illustrating this we turn to a quotation from the well-known New Testament scholar John P. Meier. On the issue of John's ethics, Meier opines:

> Apart from the love that imitates Jesus' love for his own, *John's Gospel is practically amoral*. We look in vain for the equivalents of Jesus' teaching on divorce, oaths and vows, almsgiving, prayer, fasting, or the multitude of other specific moral directives strewn across the pages of Matthew's Gospel. Everything comes down to imitating Jesus' love for his disciples; *what concrete and specific actions should flow from this love are largely left unspoken.*[7]

Note that Meier's critique of John includes a seemingly fixed definition of ethics. He provides specific categories (Jesus must discuss *moral issues* like divorce or *religious issues* like prayer) and modes of

Ethos in the Gospel according to John," *ZNW* 97 (2006): 147–75; and Ruben Zimmerman, "Is There Ethics in the Gospel of John?," in van der Watt and Zimmermann, *Rethinking the Ethics of John*, 44–80. See also, Richard B. Hays, "Mapping the Field: Approaches to New Testament Ethics," in *Identity, Ethics, and Ethos in the New Testament*, ed. Jan G. van der Watt, BZNW 141 (Berlin: de Gruyter, 2006) 3–19.

  7. John P. Meier, "Love in Q and John: Love of Enemies, Love of One Another," *Mid-Stream* 40 (2001): 47–48 (emphasis added).

instruction (what he terms "specific moral directives"). Further, his definition excludes anything implicit in the narrative that those without a preconceived notion of ethics might consider useful in evaluating the moral world of the Fourth Gospel.

Meier's negative assessment is one among many similar examples that we could introduce as evidence here.[8] If we approach the Johannine literature looking for an ethics that consists of explicit references to moral conduct, the observation of a set of rules, or the development of a series of virtues, there is a good chance that we will come away from our search disappointed. There is an equally good chance of our concluding that John has nothing to contribute to a conversation about New Testament ethics.[9] Thus before we are able to analyze the Johannine literature in new and potentially constructive ways, we must move beyond the standard definition of ethics that has long been applied to other New Testament literature. Noting the patristic proclivity for holding the Fourth Gospel in high regard for the development of moral character, Bernd Wannenwetsch asserts that there are "powerful and *specifically modern biases* that trigger the suspicion that with John we cannot do the sort of ethics we think we should be doing today."[10] It behooves us to think more broadly and across different historical, social, and theological contexts in our evaluation of the potential value of the Johannine literature for doing ethics.

In a recent comprehensive overview of the field, Ruben Zimmerman has sought to challenge the "outdated consensus" that the Gospel of John contains no ethics. Concluding his survey, he writes:

> The fact that research into New Testament ethics has concentrated on paraenetic text segments, which are not found in the Gospel of John and very infrequently in the Letters of John, has led scholars to disregard the fact that ancient ethical discourse was much less interested in the clarification of individual questions than has been perceived within the scope of New Testament research. *The separation of theology and ethics does not*

8. See the exhaustive survey of this particular judgment in Zimmerman, "Is There Ethics in the Gospel of John?," 44–57.

9. Boersma notes that we "must beware of the pitfall of simply combing his gospel in search for statements indicating a concern for broader moral or social issues. Such a search can only end up in disappointment. One looks in vain for explicit statements on the environment, on the treatment of the economically marginalized, or on Christian involvement in politics" (Boersma, "A New Age Love Story," 104–5).

10. Bernd Wannenwetsch, "Political Love: Why John's Gospel Is Not as Barren for Contemporary Ethics as It Might Appear," in *"You Have the Words of Eternal Life": Transformative Readings of the Gospel of John from a Lutheran Perspective*, ed. Kenneth Mtata (Minneapolis: Lutheran University Press, 2012), 93–94 (emphasis added).

correspond to ancient thinking, but instead reflects a structure of perception that was introduced by Rudolf Bultmann in order to describe Pauline ethics as an indicative-imperative schema.[11]

I find myself in substantial agreement with Zimmerman's observation, though I think it could be stated more forcefully: Our obsession with Paul's Letters and their consistent emphasis on explicit ethical instruction has not merely influenced but rather tainted our ability to see other material in the New Testament as ethical. Contrary to this modern tendency, most of the essays in this volume work from the assumption that there are ethics in the Johannine literature.[12] Against that backdrop, we turn now to the remaining two perspectives from which our contributors will be working.

THE ETHICS OF THE JOHANNINE LITERATURE ARE SECTARIAN, EXCLUSIVE, NEGATIVE, OR OPPOSITIONAL

For the past five decades, scholars have paid particular attention to the sectarian nature of the Johannine literature. Beginning in the late 1960s and throughout the 1970s, a handful of scholars began setting forth serious historical reconstructions of the Johannine community. In particular, the groundbreaking work of J. Louis Martyn (along with important contributions from Raymond E. Brown, Wayne Meeks, D. Moody Smith, and R. Alan Culpepper) revolutionized contemporary readings of the Fourth Gospel; their work continues to be foundational for modern understandings of Johannine sectarianism.[13]

Martyn's argument for a two-level reading of the Fourth Gospel was a watershed moment in contemporary Johannine studies, shaping the way scholars have understood the *Sitz im Leben* of the

---

11. Zimmerman, "Is There Ethics in the Gospel of John?," 61–62 (emphasis added).

12. In her chapter, Adele Reinhartz takes issue with the current emphasis on finding ethics in the Johannine literature, preferring instead to locate herself in the camp of those who do not think John has much to say about a normative ethics.

13. See in chronological order, J. Louis Martyn, *History and Theology in the Fourth Gospel* (Nashville: Abingdon, 1968); Wayne A. Meeks, "The Man from Heaven in Johannine Sectarianism," *JBL* 91 (1972): 44–72: D. Moody Smith, "Johannine Christianity: Some Reflections on Its Character and Delineation," *NTS* 21 (1974–1975): 222–48; R. Alan Culpepper, *The Johannine School*, SBLDS 26 (Missoula, MT: Scholars Press, 1975); and Raymond E. Brown, *The Community of the Beloved Disciple: The Lives, Loves and Hates of an Individual Church in New Testament Times* (New York: Paulist, 1979).

community.[14] Martyn argued that the Johannine community was embroiled in a theological controversy with the local synagogue, a claim he attempted to validate through an examination of three passages in which the term *aposynagōgos* (out of the synagogue) is used (John 9:22; 12:42; 16:2).[15] There is no need to rehearse the finer points of Martyn's theory here, as it has been a topic of nearly continuous conversation in Johannine studies.[16] Suffice it to say that while there remains debate over the details of Martyn's proposal, along with a growing group of scholars who attempt to refute it altogether,[17] there is still fairly wide acceptance of the two-level hypothesis.

Related to the claim that Johannine ethics are sectarian and exclusive is the observation that the Johannine literature is negative or oppositional inasmuch as it is rooted in the pitting of different groups against one another. In the Gospel a group known simply as "the Jews" (Greek: *hoi Ioudaioi*)[18] is consistently at odds with Jesus, while the Epistles portray a conflict within the community that has led to a departure of some Jesus followers who hold a different christological point of view.[19] These observations have led some to conclude that the ethics of the Johannine literature do not reflect the

14. John Ashton has written that Martyn's book was "the most important single work on the Gospel since Bultmann's commentary" (*Understanding the Fourth Gospel* [Oxford: Clarendon, 1991], 107).

15. Among those who doubt the existence of a Johannine community are Richard Bauckham ("For Whom Were the Gospels Written?," in *The Gospels for All Christians: Rethinking the Gospel Audiences*, ed. Richard Bauckham [Grand Rapids: Eerdmans, 1998], 9–48), and his former student Edward W. Klink III (*The Sheep of the Fold: The Audience and Origin of the Gospel of John*, SNTSMS 141 [Cambridge: Cambridge University Press, 2007], Klink, *The Audience of the Gospels: The Origin and Function of the Gospels in Early Christianity*, LNTS 353 [London: T&T Clark, 2010]). See also the recent proposal of Urban C. von Wahlde, *Gnosticism, Docetism, and the Judaisms of the First Century: The Search for the Wider Context of the Johannine Literature and Why It Matters*, LNTS 517 (London: Bloomsbury T&T Clark, 2015).

16. Most recently, Jonathan Bernier (*Aposynagōgos and the Historical Jesus in John: Rethinking the Historicity of the Johannine Expulsion Passages*, BibInt [Leiden: Brill, 2013]) argues for the plausibility that the *aposynagōgos* passages reflect an experience of expulsion that took place during Jesus's lifetime.

17. The dissent of Adele Reinhartz on this question is particularly noteworthy; see e.g., "Judaism in the Gospel of John," *Int* 63, no. 4 (2009): 382–93.

18. Much has been written on this subject. For an accessible introduction to the issues that is accessible to students, see Jaime Clark-Soles, "The Jews in the Fourth Gospel," in *John*, vol. 1, *Chapters 1–9*, ed. Cynthia A. Jarvis and E. Elizabeth Johnson, Feasting on the Word Commentary (Louisville: Westminster John Knox, 2014), xi–xiv.

19. These two discussions are obviously much more complex than we can cover here. The translation and identity of *hoi Ioudaioi* have been topics of seemingly endless discussion, as has the unfortunate legacy of Christian anti-Judaism spawned by particular readings of the Fourth Gospel. Also, the debate over the opponents in the Johannine epistles continues.

universal quality of Jesus's teaching elsewhere in the New Testament. For example, Luke's Jesus encourages his followers to love their neighbors (10:25–37), while Matthew's Jesus commands his followers to love their enemies (5:43–45), both of which can be applied universally. However, both the Johannine Jesus and the author(s) of the Epistles encourage love for "one another."[20] In the context of the Johannine community's ongoing conflicts, is this the same sort of inclusive love we see in Matthew and Luke, or is there an inherent tribalism embedded in this love?

In his analysis of the love relationships in the Gospel and 1 John, Fernando Segovia examined Johannine love language against the backdrop of the community's proposed history. Segovia grouped John's love commands into seven distinct categories: (1) the Father's love for Jesus, (2) the Father's love for the disciples, (3) Jesus's love for the Father, (4) Jesus's love for the disciples, (5) the disciples' love for the Father, (6) the disciples' love for Jesus, and (7) the disciples' love for each other.[21] Notice that there is no specific command that love be for all. Segovia's broader interest in the study was to better understand the redaction of the Fourth Gospel vis-à-vis 1 John, though he also argues for the sectarian character of the love commands expressed in these writings.[22] In this same vein, Wayne Meeks has commented that the "only rule [of the Johannine Jesus] is 'love one another,' and that rule is both vague in its application and narrowly circumscribed, being limited solely to those who are firmly within the Johannine circle."[23] Ernst Käsemann has written that there "is no indication in John that love for one's brother would also include love toward one's neighbour."[24] Similarly, Frank Matera wonders, "What is the content of this *love*? How do disciples exercise this *love* in real life situations? Whom does this *love* include? Is this a universal love such as is found in the Gospel of Luke, or has love become exclusive and sectarian in

20. E.g., John 13:34-35; 15:12, 17; 1 John 3:11, 14, 16, 23; 4:7, 11.

21. Fernando F. Segovia, *Love Relationships in the Johannine Traditions: Agapē/Agapan in 1 John and the Fourth Gospel*, SBLDS 58 (Chico, CA: Scholars Press, 1982).

22. In a related study, Segovia notes that "a number of recent exegetical studies on the different levels of the Johannine tradition have adopted the position that the community behind that tradition was consistently 'sectarian' in nature" (Fernando F. Segovia, "The Love and Hatred of Jesus and Johannine Sectarianism," *CBQ* 43 [1981]: 258).

23. Meeks, "Ethics of the Fourth Evangelist," 318.

24. Ernst Käsemann, *The Testament of Jesus: A Study of the Gospel of John in Light of Chapter 17*, trans. Gerhard Krodel (London: SCM, 1968), 59. Similar descriptions abound; see Mary E. Clarkson, "The Ethics of the Fourth Gospel," *AThR* 31 (1949): 112–15; Victor Paul Furnish, *The Love Command in the New Testament* (Nashville: Abingdon, 1972), 144–48.

the Fourth Gospel?"[25] Thus one serious implication from observations about the various community conflicts is that while there are ethics in the Johannine literature, they are not suitable within the broader context of what could be termed "Christian" instruction.

In a well-known denunciation of John's "moral bankruptcy," Jack T. Sanders has written:

> Precisely because such [fundamentalist] groups, however, now exist in sufficient abundance to be visible, *perhaps the weakness and moral bankruptcy of the Johannine ethics can be seen more clearly.* Here is not a Christianity that considers that loving is the same as fulfilling the law (Paul) or that the good Samaritan parable represents a demand (Luke) to stop and render even first aid to the man who has been robbed, beaten, and left there for dead. Johannine Christianity is interested only in whether he believes. "Are you saved, brother?" the Johannine Christian asks the man bleeding to death on the side of the road. "Are you concerned about your soul?" "Do you believe that Jesus is the one who came down from God" "If you believe, you will have eternal life," promises the Johannine Christian, while the dying man's blood stains the ground.[26]

While there is some truth to this rhetorically powerful caricature, we can confidently say that Sanders has substituted one contemporary appropriation of the Gospel of John with the Gospel itself. The same sort of criticism Sanders raises against fundamentalist readings of John could also be raised against the egregious examples of anti-Judaism that have been justified by some readings of the Fourth Gospel over the centuries. While there is no doubt that many illegitimate actions have been justified by specific contextual readings of the New Testament, as we move forward here we will keep our reflections on the nature of Johannine ethics in the context of the history of the Johannine community rather than specific appropriations of Johannine texts.[27]

---

25. Frank J. Matera, *New Testament Ethics: The Legacies of Jesus and Paul* (Louisville: Westminster John Knox, 1996), 92 (emphasis added). It is important to note that Matera has a largely sympathetic reading of John's ethics, despite the way he has framed the question excerpted above.

26. Jack T. Sanders, *Ethics in the New Testament* (Philadelphia: Fortress Press, 1975), 99–100 (emphasis added).

27. A conspicuous example of using NT texts to justify illegitimate behavior can be found by looking at the arguments of American slaveholders against those advocating for the abolition of slavery. Slaveholders commonly used Pauline statements about "slaves obeying their masters" (Eph 6:5–8; Col 3:22; Titus 2:9) to justify slavery as a God-ordained institution.

The recent history of research has produced countless similar denunciations of Johannine ethics. While the most prominent arguments in favor of recognizing ethics in the Johannine literature have also argued that those ethics are negative, sectarian, or inward looking, more recent treatments have argued that the ethics of the Johannine literature are positive and potentially viable within broader schemes of Christian ethics. We turn now to those arguments.

THE ETHICS OF THE JOHANNINE LITERATURE ARE BROAD, INCLUSIVE, OR VALUABLE FOR THE CONSTRUCTION OF CHRISTIAN ETHICS OR MORAL THEOLOGY

The third and final position we will consider in our survey is the claim that Johannine ethics are suitable for incorporation into broader schemes of Christian ethics or moral theology.[28] This position has received little attention until very recently, though constructive conversations have given rise to new ways of conceiving of Johannine ethics. The South African scholar, Jan van der Watt has been particularly important to this movement, as he has helped bring forth three different volumes in the series Contexts and Norms of New Testament Ethics, a wider project on various ethical concerns in the New Testament (two of these have been coedited with the German scholar Ruben Zimmerman).[29]

One of the three volumes in this series focuses primarily on *Johannine* ethics, exploring "how the narrated text reveals an underlying

28. "Christian ethics" and "moral theology" are essentially the same enterprise with different names. Typically those working within the Protestant traditions are said to engage in the study of Christian ethics, while Roman Catholic scholars do moral theology. While there is some truth to this dichotomy, a more careful distinction should be made. Among Protestant theologians, there is no standard, widely accepted definition of Christian ethics. Stanley Hauerwas, one of the most recognizable mainline Protestant theologians, argues that "ethics is theology," and that as such it is quite naturally an enterprise of the church (see *The Peaceable Kingdom: A Primer in Christian Ethics* [Notre Dame: University of Notre Dame Press, 1983], xv–xxvi). In Roman Catholic circles, moral theology is a subdiscipline within Catholic theology that addresses ethical issues, including those related to social justice, sexual and medical ethics, and moral virtue. For more on the history and practice of moral theology, see James F. Keenan, *History of Catholic Moral Theology in the Twentieth Century: From Confessing Sins to Liberating Consciences* (London: Continuum, 2010).

29. See van der Watt, *Identity, Ethics, and Ethos*; Zimmerman, van der Watt, and Luther, *Moral Language in the New Testament*; van der Watt and Zimmerman, *Rethinking the Ethics of John*.

value system and ethical reflection *sui generis,* which can retrospectively be classified as 'ethics' or better as 'implicit ethics.'"[30] Seeking to challenge the contention that the Johannine literature has no ethics, van der Watt notes that "by means of narration, there is a coherent reflection on values and behavior" embedded within the Johannine literature.[31] Such an approach constitutes a step beyond traditional approaches that sought to identify ethical concerns apart from sustained exegetical treatments. In other words, more detailed engagement with the wider narrative of the Gospel or underlying narrative of the Epistles has the potential to offer new insights and provide a fuller understanding of John's implicit ethics. Several contributions within these three volumes argue for a largely favorable understanding of the ethics implied in the Johannine writings.

For example, in his chapter from the second volume in the series, Kobus Kok argues for a "missional-incarnational ethos" in the Fourth Gospel. He uses Jesus's interaction with the Samaritan woman (John 4) as the basis upon which to describe the Gospel as a "narrative of moral language."[32] He writes, "As Christians, the basis or motivation of our being is built on the basis of a particular understanding of God, the world and God's story of the world."[33] After a detailed exegesis of John 4, Kok wonders whether this particular story can be connected at the macro-level to the sending of the disciples and wider notion of "mission" in the narrative. He ultimately concludes in the affirmative:

> It could thus be argued that those who seek to speak of moral language in John (at least on the textual level) should probably also include the reality of a missional-incarnational ethos that will transcend all boundaries (cultural, social, economical, racial, etc.) to show love and be accepting of everyone. From the investigation above, it becomes clear that the narrative of Jesus and the Samaritan woman should be integrated not only with the sending motive and ethos of the Son, but also with the imperative of the missional ethos of the followers of Jesus (see John 20:21). Together these elements form an inclusive moral language or ethical paradigm of mission and give the reader a *full and integrated picture of the essence of behavior in following the way of Jesus.*[34]

30. van der Watt, preface to *Rethinking the Ethics of John,* x.
31. Ibid.
32. Kok, "As the Father Has Sent Me, I Send You," 169.
33. Ibid., 171.
34. Ibid., 193 (emphasis added).

Other studies, emerging from what might be called a "broadly evangelical" outlook, have sought to draw on a wider Christian theological framework. Building upon the work of N. T. Wright, Hans Boersma prefers to focus on what he calls "the biblical story," rather than mining the pages of the Fourth Gospel for explicit moral teaching. Boersma argues that the authority of the Gospel (or "story authority") comes from its place in the wider narrative of God's work in the world. On that basis he argues that John's worldview is not "sectarian and introspective in character," and that the Gospel makes "significant contributions to a Christian worldview."[35] Such claims stand in stark contrast to the decades-long emphasis on the inward looking perspective of the Johannine writings. In another study arising from this broadly evangelical background, Jey Kanagaraj argues that John roots his understanding of ethics in the Decalogue. He meticulously works through various passages of the Gospel, attempting to demonstrate how each of the Ten Commandments is implicitly embedded in the narrative. Arguing that this reinterpretation of the Decalogue is intentional, Kanagaraj avers that such "a narrative style is an evidence of the *positive approach that John takes in his presentation of the Gospel*. We have seen how John reinterprets the Decalogue *in its positive, redemptive, and practical dimension*."[36] It is also important to note here the work of Richard Burridge, who has sought to articulate an understanding of Johannine ethics in the Fourth Gospel in terms of "imitating Jesus."[37] Burridge's monograph treats the Fourth Gospel in the wider context of New Testament ethics, though he also has an essay in which he focuses exclusively on how this approach relates to John's ethics.[38] For Burridge, our understanding of the gospel genre is directly related to our understanding of the ethics embedded there. Since the gospels are widely held to be Greco-Roman biographies, which by their very nature are concerned with demonstrating the virtue of a given individual, Burridge

35. Boersma, "A New Age Love Story," 118.

36. Kanagaraj, "Implied Ethics of the Fourth Gospel," 61 (emphasis added).

37. See Richard A. Burridge, *Imitating Jesus: An Inclusive Approach to New Testament Ethics* (Grand Rapids: Eerdmans, 2007). See also Richard B. Hays (*The Moral Vision of the New Testament: A Contemporary Introduction to New Testament Ethics* [San Francisco: HarperSanFrancisco, 1996], 138–57), who treats John as a positive contribution within the wider context of the NT ethics.

38. Richard A. Burridge, "Imitating Jesus: An Inclusive Approach to the Ethics of the Historical Jesus and John's Gospel," in *John, Jesus, and History*, vol. 2, *Aspects of Historicity in the Fourth Gospel*, ed. Paul N. Anderson, Felix Just, and Tom Thatcher (Atlanta: Society of Biblical Literature, 2009), 281–90.

argues that we should stop approaching the gospels as ethical treatises and instead read them with a view to imitating the actions of Jesus. With respect to the Fourth Gospel, Burridge argues that even though John's Jesus seems quite different from the Synoptic portraits, he is ultimately a model of imitable behavior in that he calls others to follow God and be part of an inclusive community.

Other studies have utilized a narrative-exegetical approach to suggest potentially positive prospects for speaking about John's ethics. Since many judgments about the presence or value of Johannine ethics are made outside the context of sustained narrative readings of the Gospel, an exegetically oriented approach has the potential to yield fresh contributions to this discussion.[39] This approach contrasts with that of Boersma mentioned above insofar as it is explicitly concerned with John's story world rather than the broader "Christian" story of Jesus.

After an assiduous examination of Johannine "love" language, Jörg Frey similarly concludes that John's love is universal rather than sectarian. Throughout his article he seeks to establish a "semantic network" of John's love language that connects the accounts of Jesus's public ministry (John 1–12), the Farewell Discourses (John 13–17), and the passion narrative (John 18–20). When this semantic network is appreciated through reading the Fourth Gospel in its entirety, he argues, the positive elements of John's ethical presentation organically emerge.[40]

In his recent volume, *Love in the Gospel of John*,[41] Francis J. Moloney raises the question of how to understand the various types of love discussed in the Fourth Gospel. Moloney's contributions in this volume are not limited to the discussions covered by this survey, but his methodology is important for analyzing our three approaches

---

39. The discussions of Johannine love commands discussed earlier (e.g., Meeks, Segovia, Sanders) were presented in the contexts of source- and redaction-critical arguments and showed a distinct concern to uncover the *Sitz im Leben* of the Johannine community. Moloney's approach is different insofar as it consists of a sustained narrative exegesis while also being squarely situated in the context of historical discussions about the Johannine community.

40. "The complete 'movement' of love, the 'cascade' of love relations from God to the world and to Jesus and the disciples to the communal love of the disciples (to be perceived by everybody) and backwards, including the possible perception or even belief by 'the world' can only be seen if the Gospel is read and interpreted in its entirety" (Jörg Frey, "Love-Relations in the Fourth Gospel: Establishing a Semantic Network," in *Repetitions and Variations in the Fourth Gospel: Style, Text, Interpretation*, ed. Gilbert Van Belle, Michael Labahn, and Peter Maritz, BETL 223 [Leuven: Peeters, 2009], 171–98 [198]).

41. Francis J. Moloney, *Love in the Gospel of John: An Exegetical, Theological, and Literary Study* (Grand Rapids: Baker Academic, 2013).

to John's ethics. While showing a primary concern for interpreting the text as a complete utterance in its final form, Moloney is also at pains in this book to situate the Gospel in its historical and theological contexts. This results in a nuanced treatment that appreciates the inner workings of the Johannine community and its history, but also the universalizing role John has played throughout its reception history. After a helpful discussion of the failures of John's community, Moloney comments,

> If John's Gospel were a sectarian tract, an "inner secret" written for the private mutual exhortation of a secret enclave that failed—we would not have it as part of the Christian canon. . . . But in fact the Gospel of John is a story of Jesus that has been publicly proclaimed for almost two thousand years. It continues to ask readers and hearers to "remember Jesus" and to put their lives where their words are.[42]

In the context of this discussion, Moloney seems particularly annoyed by the "arrogance" of certain sectarian theories and their failure to consider the history of interpretation.[43] He closes the book by succinctly expressing the Fourth Gospel's positive, though admittedly limited, contributions to our understanding of love as a category within New Testament ethics: "The Gospel of John does say *something* about an understanding of Christian love, even though it must not be claimed that it says *everything*."[44] This recognition is a helpful safeguard against the all-too-common practice of insisting that each text in the New Testament is as robustly developed as the next for our contemporary understanding of theology or ethics. We know that this is very often not the case. As was the case with Frey's treatment, the virtue of Moloney's work is that it draws conclusions about specific themes (viz., love) only after sustained exegetical consideration. In many ways, this approach, irrespective of one's ultimate judgment

42. Ibid., 210. See also my own judgment regarding the potentially universal quality of John's love language in "Virtue in the New Testament: The Legacies of Paul and John in Comparative Perspective," in *Unity and Diversity in the Gospels and Paul: Essays in Honor of Frank J. Matera*, ed. Christopher W. Skinner and Kelly R. Iverson, ECL 7 (Atlanta: Society of Biblical Literature 2012), 313–15.

43. He writes, "There is a sense of arrogance in the claim that for two thousand years the Gospel of John has enjoyed favor and had influence because it has been misinterpreted. . . . At last, it appears, with the arrival of the social science reading of the text, true light has dawned" (Moloney, *Love in the Gospel of John*, 201n45).

44. Ibid., 214 (emphasis in original).

on the value or presence of ethics in John, is a roadmap for how such research should be conducted.

It goes without saying that numerous other studies could be introduced into our survey as a means of illustrating all three perspectives I have chosen to highlight here. However, as indicated at the outset of this survey, my intent has been to be representative rather than exhaustive in my coverage of the subject. I have now considered the major categories and some of the important conversation partners in the broader discussion of Johannine ethics. This survey has shown that the field is open for ongoing dialogue about the presence, nature, and value of ethics within the Johannine literature. It is our hope that this book can facilitate those conversations by providing substantive discourse about the various positions mentioned above, while suggesting constructive prospects for the future.

JOHANNINE ETHICS: WHAT CAN *WE* SAY?

Since this book is dedicated to exploring the moral world of the Johannine literature—an undertaking that assumes the existence of ethical material—it naturally follows that many of the essays in this volume fit within the latter two categories covered by our brief survey of scholarly opinion. Each contributor takes their own approach to discussing the role of ethics in the Johannine literature, and there is great diversity of opinion about the presence, tone, extent, or value of that material. Therefore, their studies take different routes within those three categories, and this is intentional. The result of this open inquiry is a volume divided into three major sections that represent broad perspectives on both the foundational and applied ethics of the literature as well as directions for the future.

PART 1: THE JOHANNINE IMPERATIVES

The first part of the book consists of three chapters and focuses on the Johannine imperatives: believe, love, and follow. Insofar as explicit imperatives and prohibitions have played a foundational role in the development of both Jewish and Christian ethics, it seems prudent to consider how direct commands in the Gospel and Epistles contribute to our understanding of *Johannine ethics*.

In the first chapter of part 1, Sherri Brown argues that the core proclamation of the Prologue to the Fourth Gospel (1:1–18) is that those who receive the Word are given the power to become children of God (1:12), and since the prologue is the gateway into the narrative, this is also the heart of the gospel message. In Brown's view, the establishment of childhood in God through Jesus Christ is the culmination of all God's dealings with the world, and is the *telos* of both creator and creation. Her argument explores how one receives and believes in the Word, what it means to become "children of God," and how this could be construed as the goal of the entire Gospel. The journey of believing thus becomes the foundation of the ethical life in the community of the Beloved Disciple.

In chapter 2, I undertake an examination of love—the most overtly ethical imperative in the Johannine literature. With an emphasis on both the historical development of the Fourth Gospel and the narrative in its final form, I attempt to demonstrate that the seemingly limited audience of John's commands to "love one another"—which we will come to understand as "sacrificial self-giving"—should be understood in a broader sense than the sectarian critique allows. With specific attention to the Farewell Discourse (John 13–17), I argue that the radical and countercultural vision of Johannine spirituality calls followers to reject sin and imitate Jesus's own example, and it is therefore not necessary to understand this call in a sectarian or exclusive manner. Rather, we should understand an implicit universality in the love commands of the Johannine Jesus.

In the final chapter of part 1, Raymond F. Collins considers the Johannine imperative to follow. In the Fourth Gospel, only two persons are said to receive the imperative invitation "follow me" from Jesus. Gathering his first disciples, Jesus says to Philip, "follow me" (John 1:43). In the Gospel's epilogue, the risen Jesus twice tells Peter to "follow me" (John 21:19). Nevertheless, Collins contends that the command embraces the Johannine story *in its entirety*. The intervening narrative describes many disciples following Jesus, and while these characters follow Jesus in a nondescript fashion, two *logia* uttered by Jesus point to the ultimate significance of the imperative to follow. On the one hand, following Jesus is a matter of hearing his voice (John 10:4–5), and on the other, it is a matter of receiving the light of life (John 8:12), rooted in a personal relationship with Jesus.

PART 2: IMPLIED ETHICS IN
THE JOHANNINE LITERATURE

The second part of this book consists of seven chapters and is dedicated to exploring various angles on the implied ethics of the Johannine literature. R. Alan Culpepper begins part 2 by providing a close reading of the Fourth Gospel, focusing on the role of the Prologue in developing John's creation ethics. The Prologue establishes the theme of life so prominent in the rest of the Gospel, and grounds it in God's creative work through the Logos. Culpepper aims to draw out the implications of this narrative opening for the ethics of John. In particular, the wisdom background and the context of creation give the theme of life a universal rather than sectarian dimension. The sacredness of life is also deeply rooted in Jewish ethics, which recognizes both creation and covenant as ethical foundations. When these associations are clarified, John's ethics can be seen in a much richer, textured perspective: Jesus restores and points to the completion of human life. The love command is set in a universal rather than sectarian context, and distinctions of ethnicity, gender, and social standing are diminished.

Incarnation is a crucial theme in the Gospel's Prologue and is foundational to all of our thinking about Johannine Christology. In the next chapter, Jaime Clark-Soles uses this affirmation as a starting point to examine the relationship between ethics and incarnation, with specific emphasis on disability studies. Drawing on insights from social and cultural models, Clark-Soles explores numerous texts with a view to answering the question: From a disability perspective, what are the promises and pitfalls of these texts with respect to ancient audiences and later interpreters? She recognizes that, with respect to persons with disabilities, the Gospel of John has both liberative and problematic potential. She is concerned to uncover the ways in which the text possesses liberative potential and in the ways in which it presents obstacles for those seeking abundant life (John 10:10). She argues that through the insistence on material creation as the locus of God's attention and activity, the Fourth Evangelist emboldens the audience to interpret the text in ways that promote the flourishing of all, even when that entails resisting some of the text's own contextually bound perspectives.

In the next chapter, Adele Reinhartz evaluates arguments that the

Gospel implies an ethical system and presents Jesus as an ethical model, and aims to challenge the more recent, optimistic view about finding moral precepts beneath the surface of the Gospel. Focusing on John 7, the text in which Jesus secretly goes up to Jerusalem for a Jewish festival after informing his brothers that he does not intend to go, Reinhartz argues that John's implied author is not concerned to show Jesus as an ethical actor but rather is entirely focused on the Gospel's central message: the importance of belief in Jesus as the Messiah and Son of God. Reinhartz thus regards this presentation of the Johannine Jesus as duplicitous.

The next two chapters in part 2 are devoted to examining the difficult issue of Jesus's enemies in the Fourth Gospel. First, Michael J. Gorman explores John's implied ethic of love toward enemies. As noted above, the Fourth Gospel has been criticized for its restriction of love to the believing community or, in a more extreme form of criticism, for its "moral bankruptcy" with respect to its apathy toward, and even hatred of, outsiders. Gorman proposes that in spite of these criticisms, the Gospel has an implicit ethic of enemy-love, grounded in the divine act of sending the Son into a hostile world to save it and implied in the Son's similar sending of the disciples into a hostile world to live missionally and peacefully by means of the Spirit.

In the next chapter, Alicia Myers provides the second sustained reflection on Jesus's potential opponents in the Fourth Gospel. She begins by noting that of all the ethical categories at play in the Gospel, the presentation of "the Jews" (*hoi Ioudaioi*) ranks among the most fraught. Given the negative ethics that the Gospel has been used to justify against Jewish people, John's often negative portrayal of the Jews in his narrative requires continued study and reflection. Recognizing both the enduring argument of a two-level drama (Martyn) and the significant work of problematizing the ease of the two-level reading (Reinhartz), Myers focuses on the ethics of John's presentation of the Jews in terms of the Gospel's literary and rhetorical aspects, rather than positing a possible historical reconstruction. In particular, she examines the "character" (*ēthos*) and characterization of the Jews in John according to rhetorical categories and constructions of identity common to the ancient Mediterranean world. Myers concludes that the rhetoric of the Gospel ultimately creates empathy between the Gospel audiences and the Jews who struggle within the text, rather than necessitating the antipathy and condemnation that has unfortunately so often resulted.

Toan Do next seeks to draw out a connection between the Johannine request to "come and see" with John's ethic of love. In a recent study, Peter J. Judge links the invitation "come and see" with Johannine Christology.[45] The imperative "come and see" occurs several times in the Gospel of John, with different inviters to different invitees: one from Jesus to the two disciples of John the Baptist (1:39), one from Philip to Nathanael (1:46), one from the Samaritan woman to her villagers (4:29), and finally from the Bethany villagers to Jesus (11:34). Do poses a simple question in his study: Is Christology sufficient in the Johannine invitation "come and see," especially in the case of Philip's invitation to Nathanael? John 14:8–14 seems to prove negatively the christological aspect of this invitation; then in John 14:15 Jesus rightly places an ethical aspect of seeing and knowing Jesus, namely, "If you love me, you will keep my commandments." Do concludes that in the end, *love for Jesus* will sufficiently sustain and preserve the Johannine invitation to "come and see."

In the final chapter of part 2, Francis J. Moloney raises a crucial question: is love the only substantive element in Johannine ethics? Within the Johannine literature, God's action of loving has initiated the presence of Jesus in the world (John 3:16–17). Moloney uses this observation as a basis for his exploration of the God who sends, the task of the Johannine Jesus who makes God known, and the request that disciples and followers of Jesus manifest love in a certain way. In the first place, little consideration is given to the enduring presence of a traditional eschatology in John (e.g., 5:28–29; 6:40, 54), and the importance of "deeds" or "works" in John (e.g. 3:19–21). Against the all-too-common focus on using imperatives as the primary basis for ethics, this chapter tests the hermeneutical intuition that Johannine ethics have their basis in God's love, but are best articulated in the narrative expression and experience of love, rather than in the love commands. The Johannine Jesus points out that good and evil deeds performed between the now of Christian life and the future judgment lead to life or condemnation (5:27–29).

45. Peter J. Judge, "Come and See: The First Disciples and Christology in the Fourth Gospel," in *Studies in the Gospel of John and Its Christology*, ed. Joseph Verheyden, Geert van Oyen, Michael Labahn, and Reimund Bieringer, BETL 265 (Leuven: Leuven University Press, 2014), 61–69.

PART 3: MOVING FORWARD

The final section of this volume consists of three chapters that attempt to advance our discussions of John's moral world beyond what has already been proposed in contemporary scholarship. In the first chapter of part 3, Lindsey Trozzo combines genre analysis and rhetorical criticism to consider how the Fourth Gospel's participation in the *bios* genre and incorporation of the encomiastic topics might shed light on Johannine ethics. Through a comparative examination of Plutarch's *Lives*, Trozzo seeks to demonstrate that though it is not a straightforward ethical commentary, John's complex biographical narrative delivers implicit moralism and carries significant ethical force. Without expecting every episode within the Fourth Gospel to offer ethical content, she argues that within the overall rhetorical trajectory of the *bios*, each episode plays a part in establishing the ethical force of the text. Since the text incorporates certain rhetorical features, rhetorical analysis can be utilized to provide a new way of reading and a new set of questions that can be applied to the pursuit of Johannine ethics.

In the second chapter of part 3, Dorothy Lee explores a heretofore-untapped area of potential ethical inquiry in the Johannine literature. She begins by noting that the theology of the Fourth Gospel has tended to be interpreted within a human-centered framework, focusing exclusively on the relationship believers have to God and to one another. As a consequence, little emphasis has been placed on the place of creation in the Gospel. Seen from a wider perspective, however, the Johannine worldview presents the Word made flesh in divine solidarity not only with humankind but also with the life of creation. The echoes of the creation stories in Genesis 1–3, along with the language of "flesh" found throughout the Fourth Gospel, imply God's commitment to the flourishing and transforming of all created things. This transformation has ethical as well as spiritual implications. Lee argues that the flesh of Jesus, radiant with divine glory, bridges in every sense the gulf that divides creation from God. This is the basis of John's ethical understanding, in which God's re-creation embraces the material world in all its variety and complexity. It implies a corresponding ethical responsibility for the well-being of creation on the part of the community of faith. From this viewpoint, the Johannine love command has the potential to extend not only to human beings but also to all living things ("all flesh") created by the divine-human Word.

Cornelis Bennema closes out part 3 with a chapter on virtue ethics and the Gospel of John. Virtue ethics, deontology, and consequentialism constitute the three major approaches in normative ethics. Virtue ethics have played an important role in the Western philosophical tradition, from the early Greek philosophers—most notably Aristotle—to the medieval Christian period, finding their fullest Christian expression in the writings of Thomas Aquinas. The basic concept behind virtue ethics is that virtues are morally valuable character traits or dispositions firmly entrenched in a given individual. While virtue ethics is the oldest of the three, it became marginalized during the Enlightenment, and was only revived in the late twentieth century. In contrast to duty, rules (deontology), or the outcomes of actions (consequentialism), virtue ethics stresses moral character and the virtues that a character embodies as the basis for determining or evaluating ethical behavior. Bennema argues that virtue ethics is the most conducive approach for exploring Johannine ethics going forward. For John a virtuous life of allegiance to Jesus, guided by the Spirit, leads to and expresses the ultimate moral good of participation in the divine life. Since a number of characters in the Fourth Gospel display aspects of such a virtuous life, an agent-focused approach such as virtue ethics proves useful in discussions of Johannine ethics.

JOHANNINE ETHICS IN PROSPECT

In the final chapter, Sherri Brown and I conclude this volume with a discussion of Johannine ethics in prospect. The first part of the present introductory chapter has concentrated on the three common approaches to grappling with Johannine ethics in an attempt to set the stage for the essays that follow. In our concluding chapter, we will reflect on the findings of our contributors and suggest prospects for the future. While varying approaches to understanding the moral world of the Johannine literature will likely persist, the implications for a way forward offer insight into the understanding of right action as revealed in the life and ministry of the Johannine Jesus and the life of the Johannine community. It is incumbent upon the future of Johannine scholarship to reckon with this important and long-neglected aspect of the Gospel and Epistles of John.

PART I

The Johannine Imperatives

1.

Believing in the Gospel of John: The Ethical Imperative to Becoming Children of God

SHERRI BROWN

Take the first step in faith. You don't have to see the whole staircase, just take the first step.

—Rev. Dr. Martin Luther King, Jr.

To open our contribution proper to the growing discussion of both an expanded notion of ethics and the ethical material of the Johannine literature, we intend to grapple with the concept of ethical imperatives.[1] As the title of this chapter suggests, my own contribution is the proposal that the summons to believe is not only an ethical imperative but also the foundational human component of John's story of the good news of the Christ event. The argument begins as follows.

The core proclamation of the Prologue to the Gospel of John is that the Word become flesh is the gift of truth that empowers those who receive and believe in him to become children of God (1:1–18).[2] Much like the prologues in ancient Greek dramas, John's Prologue gives audiences a synthesis of events to come. It tells audiences the

---

1. See the discussion in the Introduction, especially n4, for bibliographic information.

2. See below for detail. For a fuller treatment of my understanding of the structure and content of the prologue, see Sherri Brown, *Gift upon Gift: Covenant through Word in the Gospel of John*, Princeton Theological Monograph Series (Eugene, OR: Pickwick, 2010), 78–95; and Sherri Brown and Francis J. Moloney, *Interpreting the Gospel and Letters of John: An Interpretation* (Grand Rapids: Eerdmans, 2017), 163–77. This argument is drawn largely from the work of R. Alan Culpepper, "The Pivot of John's Prologue," *NTS* 27 (1980): 1–31; and Francis J. Moloney, *Belief in the Word: Reading John 1–4* (Minneapolis: Fortress Press, 1993), 36–45.

who and the *what* of the events at hand, but leaves open the *how*. The subsequent drama *shows* what the Prologue *tells* since the story itself is necessary to understand how the events play out. In other words, the Prologue is the gateway into the narrative, and this core proclamation is, therefore, also the heart of the gospel message. The establishment of childhood in God through the Word of God incarnate in Jesus the Christ is the culmination of all God's dealings with the world, the goal of the Creator and creation. The claim is that those who receive the Word (v. 12a) will be given the power to become children of God (v. 12b). But how does one go about this receiving? By believing in his name (v. 12c).

But is this summons to childhood through faith solely a component of the evangelist's christological claims? Jesus famously claims, "I am the way, and the truth, and the life. No one comes to the Father except through me" (14:6).[3] Is the concept of faith restricted to the nature of the personal relationship between God and the believer? The narrative is also often noted to be a Gospel of encounters as Jesus interacts with people in the midst of their celebrations (2:1–12), their questioning (3:1–21), their daily lives (4:1–42), their ritual lives (5–10), and their suffering (11:1–44). We can also notice that "belief" as a noun (*pistis*) does not occur in the Fourth Gospel, but forms of the verb "to believe" (*pisteuein*) occur regularly and often (ninety-eight times). Thus faith in the Gospel of John is always dynamic and rightly described in terms of an action, or better, an active journey powered by encountering others along the way. The journey of believing could, therefore, be multifaceted, reflecting both the evangelist's christological claims of how relationship with God is achieved *and* how the children of God interact with the world around them. Believing, therefore, is also an ethical imperative of the evangelist and the foundation of the ethical life in the community of the Beloved Disciple.

SOME PRESUPPOSITIONS

In order to explore these claims, it will be helpful to lay out several presuppositions in how I interpret the Gospel. We will begin with

---

3. Unless otherwise indicated, all translations are the author's from the Nestle-Aland 28th ed. Greek New Testament.

structure and move to content. The Fourth Evangelist has woven an intricate and carefully crafted narrative.

THE FLOW OF THE GOSPEL OF JOHN

The Prologue (1:1–18) provides the clear words of an insider—the narrator who communicates to the audience everything he believes they need to know to begin the Gospel. John 1:19 starts the story itself, yet at John 13 something different happens. The audience is provided with what can be regarded as a new direction at 13:1. It opens the period of private ministry and departure that flows through to 20:29, with the final verses (20:30–31) serving as a conclusion to the body of the Gospel—a first ending. Then we read John 21, an epilogue to this story that looks to the future of the community formed by the narrative. In John 1:1–20:31, therefore, the evangelist writes a powerful and cohesive narrative to show audiences *that* Jesus is the Messiah and Son of God and *how* a community of believers can find life in his name. In John 21 the evangelist provides a continuation of the community and an indication for how it is to go on in an ever-changing and challenging world.

In this unfolding of John's story of the good news, the Prologue becomes the key to interpreting the narrative. I will discuss this more in a moment, but for now will note that the Prologue is the key to unlocking the door through which audiences encounter not only John's Christology but also his theology and moral world.[4] The body of the narrative is broadly made up of two parts, and I am happy to use Raymond Brown's language of the Book of Signs to character-ize Jesus's public ministry and the Book of Glory to indicate his final teaching to his own, his passion, and his resurrection.[5] The epilogue provides a basis for leadership and community that is not addressed in chapters 1–20.[6] This structural summary leads to the following fairly standard, though by no means universal, understanding of the flow of the narrative:

---

4. Morna D. Hooker, *Beginnings: Keys that Open the Gospels* (London: SCM, 1997), 64–83.

5. Raymond E. Brown, *The Gospel according to John I–XII*, AB 29 (Garden City, NY: Dou-bleday, 1966); Brown, *The Gospel according to John XIII–XXI*, AB 29a (Garden City, NY: Dou-bleday, 1970).

6. Francis J. Moloney, *Glory Not Dishonor: Reading John 13–21* (Minneapolis: Fortress Press, 1998), 182–92.

1:1–18   The Prologue

            • Introduction to the Nature and Mission of the Word

1:19–12:50 The Book of Signs

            • The Word Reveals Himself to the World and his Own through a
            Public Ministry

            1:19–51   The Revelation of Jesus—the Opening Days

                         • The Calling of the First Disciples

            2:1–4:54   Jesus's Instruction on Faith—From Cana to Cana

                         • The Educational Journey of Belief in the Word

            5:1–10:42   Jesus and the Jewish Festivals

                         • The Perfection of Jewish Traditions of Worship

            11:1–12:50   Jesus Moves toward the Hour of Death and Glory

                         • The Arrival of the Hour

13:1–20:31 The Book of Glory

            • The Word Makes God Known and Is Glorified in Death and
            Resurrection

            13:1–17:26   Jesus's Last Discourse

                         • The Footwashing, Betrayal, and Jesus's Final Teaching
                         to His Disciples

            18:1–19:42   Jesus's Passion

                         • The Arrest, Trial, Crucifixion, Death, and Burial of
                         Jesus

            20:1–31   Jesus's Resurrection

                         • The Empty Tomb and Jesus's Appearances to His
                         Disciples

            21:1–25   The Epilogue

                         • Conclusion of the Mission of the Word That Leads the
                         Community into the Future

THE SUBSTANCE OF THE GOSPEL OF JOHN

The theme of covenant is woven through the storytelling fabric of John's Gospel.[7] The Old Testament authors use the metaphor of covenant to express the special relationship between God and God's creation in general, and God's chosen people Israel in particular. Both the texts that narrate the story of Israel and its relationship with God and the prophetic literature that communicates God's will and summons Israel to live rightly in this relationship are replete with accounts of and references to God's covenantal activity in the world.[8] In addition to detailed recounting of covenant-making and covenant-renewing rituals and ceremonies, this literature preserves the broader imagery and themes of the covenant metaphor. These storytellers and prophets integrate this language into their larger works in order to share their message of life in unique relationship with God, even when the term *covenant* does not appear. The prophets in particular rarely use the word itself, even as they infuse their works with calls to covenant relationship and ethical behavior.[9] Likewise, this term does not appear in the Johannine literature. Nonetheless, like his scriptural predecessors, this evangelist incorporates the metaphor of covenant in the telling of his message. The Fourth Evangelist weaves the thematic language and symbolism of covenant throughout his story of God's activity in the world in and through Jesus as a literary technique to draw his readers into his sacred narrative of true relationship with God.

For the evangelist, the good news is that God has fulfilled all his prior covenantal activity in the incarnation and redeeming sacrifice of his Son and put in place a new covenant available to all humankind. Further, this new covenant seems to have two primary commandments: to believe and to love.[10] The commandment to believe is introduced in the Prologue and illustrated primarily, though not completely, across the Book of Signs. The commandment to love is encapsulated in the new opening at 13:1, "Now before the festival of the Passover, when Jesus knew that his hour had come to depart out

7. Sherri Brown, *God's Promise: Covenant in John* (Mahwah, NJ: Paulist Press, 2014).

8. See Genesis 1–3, 6–9, 12–17; Exodus 19–24; 2 Samuel 7; Jeremiah 31.

9. For a discussion of the classical prophets with examples that yield concepts such as "knowing God," "truth," and "love/loving-kindness," as covenantal, see Brown, *Gift upon Gift*, 54–62.

10. This is not to say that these are the only ethical imperatives present in the Gospel. In this volume, Raymond Collins also explores the command "to follow" (see esp. John 1:43; 21:19, 22).

of this world to the Father, having loved his own who were in the world, he loved them to the end." The theme takes hold in 13:34, when Jesus expressly presents the "new commandment that I give to you, that you love one another; even as I have loved you, that you also love one another" and continues in both discourse and deed across the Book of Glory. Audiences can then reflect on the public ministry and see this modeled in Jesus's teaching about his relationship to the Father even as Jesus commits the ultimate act of love through his self-sacrifice. The commandment to believe is more of an undercurrent in the Book of Glory, as this part of the narrative is directed to Jesus's own, those who have stuck out the public ministry and believe. Their task now is to let this faith take root and "abide" or "remain" (the Greek verb *menein*) by loving one another through the coming crises. Once we get to the close of the body of the narrative, however, the commandments come together in the postresurrection appearances as the disciples struggle to grasp the reality of the risen Jesus. The resurrected Jesus teaches, "Blessed are those who have not seen and yet believe," and the narrator shares that the entirety of the narrative "has been written that you may believe that Jesus is the Christ, the Son of God, and that believing you may have life in his name" (20:29–31). The epilogue then responds to lingering questions on believing and loving as the new community forges its way into the future.

The current project attempts to study the summons to believing as a call to action in community based in the Prologue, actualized across the Book of Signs, and affirmed in the concluding sounds of the Gospel.

THE PROLOGUE AND THE FOUNDATIONAL CALL TO THE ACTION OF BELIEVING IN JOHN 1:1–18

In her work on the New Testament narratives, Morna Hooker notes that there is often a literary and thematic connection between the beginning and ending of a composition. Strong endings often take us back to where we began, and skillful storytelling techniques often remind us that it was the writer's purpose all along to lead us to precisely this point.[11] Much like the chorus in ancient Greek dramas,

11. Morna D. Hooker, *Endings: Invitations to Discipleship* (Peabody, MA: Hendrickson, 2003), 3; see also Hooker, *Beginnings*, 64–83.

the Prologue gives audiences a synthesis of events to come. Further, this becomes information that most characters in the story *don't* have. Audiences are thus put in a privileged position as we participate in the action of the story, identifying with this or that character and waiting, even hoping, for them to catch on and begin to grasp the fullness of what is at stake. In ancient Greek tragedy, the prologue was the first component of the play that set forth the subject and protagonists of the drama when the chorus entered the stage. The prologue would typically give the mythological background necessary for understanding the events of the play. Likewise in the case of the Gospel of John, we learn how God interacts with God's creation. The Prologue introduces the setting, previews the main characters, and establishes the primary themes for the work. Although audiences may not fully understand the enigmatic ideas and motifs of the Prologue, they create the tension that invites the question of the *how* of God's action in the world. As I suggested in the introduction, the subsequent narrative *shows* what the Prologue *tells*.[12] The story itself is necessary to understand how it all happens. The Fourth Evangelist's use of the poetic prologue as a foundation for his Gospel that suddenly and definitively breaks into prose narrative can also be understood as a reflection of his theological perspective.[13] The incarnation of the Word suddenly and definitively turns the custom and "truth" of the world on its ear. John 1:1–18 is therefore a carefully composed prologue that is essential to understanding the rest of the narrative.

The structure of these eighteen verses is elusive. Numerous attempts have been made to capture the fullness of this poetic prelude.[14] For the purposes of this study, the work of R. Alan Culpepper

---

12. "Showing" and "telling" are the two means by which narratives reveal character. See Wayne C. Booth, *The Rhetoric of Fiction* 2nd ed. (Chicago: University of Chicago Press, 1983), 3–9. Tom Thatcher elaborates: "'Telling' occurs when the narrator makes direct evaluative statements or gives information not normally available in the readers' experience. 'Showing' occurs when the narrator offers selective information about the actions of the characters and allows readers to draw conclusions from them. By combining 'telling' and 'showing' the author enables readers to develop 'both intrinsic and contextual knowledge' of the characters." Tom Thatcher, "Jesus, Judas, and Peter: Character by Contrast in the Fourth Gospel," *BSac* 153 (1996): 435. See also W. J. Harvey, *Character and the Novel* (Ithaca, NY: Cornell University Press, 1965), 32.

13. Robert Alter, *The Art of Biblical Narrative* (New York: Basic Books, 1981), 23–46, esp. 26.

14. For several recent scholarly claims, as well as her own complex mapping, see Mary L. Coloe, "The Structure of the Johannine Prologue and Genesis 1," *ABR* 45 (1997): 40–55. See also Charles H. Giblin, "Two Complementary Literary Structures in John 1:1–18," *JBL* 104 (1985): 87–103; J. Irigoin, "La composition rythmique du prologue de Jean (I, 1–18)," *RB* 98 (1991): 5–50.

on the Prologue proves most insightful.[15] Recognizing the complexity of these verses, Culpepper acknowledges that more than one structuring technique may well be in play.[16] Nonetheless, he is convinced that the underlying framework of the Johannine Prologue is a chiasm that turns on the pivot of verse 12b (H).[17] He suggests the evangelist begins with cosmic assertions of the eternal nature of God and God's Word and moves to more specific claims of the interaction of the Word of God in creation in terms of a familial relationship (vv. 1–11). The crux of the Prologue is that Jesus gives those who receive and believe in him "power to become children of God" (v. 12). John is then able to proclaim the incarnation of the Word in Jesus Christ as God's promised gift of truth to humankind who, in turn, reveals God to all who receive him (vv. 13–18).[18] If verse 12 is indeed the central thesis of the Prologue, this proclamation also indicates the aim of the entire mission of both Christ and the narrative that shares this good news. The crux of the Prologue, and thus the focus of the narrative the Prologue introduces, is the mission of the Word of God, who gives "power to become children of God" as well as the necessary response-in-action of receiving and believing.

15. Culpepper, "Pivot," 1–31. D. A. Carson likewise sees Culpepper's as the most persuasive structure of the Prologue presented to date (D. A. Carson, *The Gospel according to John*, Pillar New Testament Commentary [Grand Rapids: Eerdmans, 1991], 13).

16. Thus any diagram should be open to the fluidity of the evangelist's style since "perfect symmetry or adherence to the identifiable pattern" should not be expected and various literary techniques are often not mutually exclusive (Culpepper, "Pivot," 8). In n. 35, Culpepper then defers to the work of Charles H. Talbert: "Imperfections of form are the rule in antiquity. . . . It was, moreover, a stated rule that perfect symmetry was to be avoided (e.g., Horace, *On the Art of Poetry*, 347ff.; Longinus, *On the Sublime*, 33, I; Demetrius, *On Style*, 5, 250)." For detail, see Charles H. Talbert, "Artistry and Theology: An Analysis of the Architecture of Jn 1,19–5,47," *CBQ* 32 (1970): 341–66.

17. Culpepper, "Pivot," 8. His analysis is based on three overarching criteria: (1) language—primarily the occurrence/repetition of catchwords; (2) conceptual parallels; and (3) content—in terms of the theme or themes of each passage. See ibid., 9–17 for the analysis and 16 for a diagram of the criteria and evidence for the chiasm. The rest of the study (17–31) focuses on the significance of the pivot (v. 12b).

18. Ibid., 7–31.

THE STRUCTURE OF THE PROLOGUE, JOHN 1:1–18

A   vv. 1–2   The Word in the Beginning with God
  B   v. 3   What Came to Be through the Word
    C   vv. 4–5   Life and Light in the Darkness
      D   vv. 6–8   John, Sent from God for Testimony
        E   vv. 9–10   The Light in the World
          F   v. 11   His Own Did Not Receive Him
            G   v. 12a   Receiving Him
              H   v. 12b   Becoming Children of God
            G′   v. 12c   Believing Him
          F′   v. 13   His Own of Born of God
        E′   v. 14   The Word Became Flesh in the World
      D′   v. 15   John's Testimony
    C′   v. 16   Gift upon Gift
  B′   v. 17   The Gift of Truth in Jesus Christ
A′   v. 18   The Son Reveals the Father[19]

THE SUMMONS TO BELIEVING FOR BECOMING CHILDREN OF GOD AT THE CRUX OF THE PROLOGUE

Werner Kelber aptly remarks that "both in life and in literature beginnings are consequential, but risky undertakings" that often create the central predicament of the coming story.[20] Morna Hooker further suggests that beginnings are the manners by which the evangelists present the key to understanding all that follows.[21] To home in on the ethical imperative to believe, I will focus on the central verses of the Fourth Evangelist's "beginning," verses 9–14.

John, the first human being (*anthrōpos*) introduced to the story, is "sent from God" (*apestalmenos para theou*) "as a witness to testify to the light" (vv. 6–8).[22] By announcing John and his role, the

19. This structure follows Culpepper's argumentation and adds my titles to the sections.

20. He then goes on to discuss the Fourth Gospel's beginning in this way: "Transcendental and earthly beginnings, this double gesture of centering and decentering, constitute the prologue's program which creates the central predicament for the subsequent narrative." Werner H. Kelber, "The Birth of a Beginning: John 1:1–18," *Semeia* 52 (1990): 121–44, here 121.

21. Hooker, *Beginnings*, xiii. For discussion of the Prologue as the key to the Gospel, see 64–83.

22. These verses, along with their counterpart in v. 15, interject a striking prose style into the fluid hymnlike poetry of the rest of the Prologue, leading many to argue they are interpolations

evangelist also introduces the concept of "believing" in the Word. He carefully notes the distinction between John the human witness and the light, but John's purpose is crucial to point to the light and thus facilitate the process of believing (*hina pantes pisteusōsin di' autou*, v. 7). Verses 9–10 flow from the final words of verses 6–8 and return focus to the light, further characterized by way of truth (*to phōs to alēthinon*, v. 9). The true light whose enlightening reign reaches everyone was coming into the world. The incarnation foreshadowed here comes to pass in the counterpart to these verses, verse 14. The imminent conflict of the Gospel story is also reaffirmed, this time in terms of knowledge (v. 10; see v. 8). Verse 11 provides powerful parallelism to this disconnect between the light and the world through the intimate language of "his own." The *logos*, instrumental giver of life and light in intimate relationship with God, comes into what is his own and is not received by these own people. Giving, receiving, and rejecting in relationship thus become the operative interactivity of the incarnation of the Word.

At verse 12 the audience arrives at the pivot of the Prologue (v. 12b, marked H) and the hinges upon which the pivot turns (vv. 12a and 12c, marked G and G').[23] Put another way, the force of the entire Prologue is poised on the fulcrum of the mission of the Word to give "them power to become children of God."[24] The balance of the three phrases of verse 12 can be lost in English translations.[25] In effect, however, the evangelist's syntax allows the central assertion of the Word's giving action to be framed by the introduction (v. 12a) and

to the *Vorlage* of the Prologue. John A. T. Robinson, e.g., has bluntly referred to these verses as "rude interruptions" (John A. T. Robinson, "The Relation of the Prologue to the Gospel of John," *NTS* 9 [1963]: 120–29). For a brief discussion as well as her own contrasting argument that these verses are an integral connection to the body of the narrative to follow, see Morna D. Hooker, "John the Baptist and the Johannine Prologue," *NTS* 16 (1970): 354–58. Culpepper concurs and argues that the double articulation of John and his role is further evidence of the chiastic presentation of the Prologue ("Pivot," 12–13).

23. The discussion of this verse is based on the position detailed in Culpepper, "Pivot," 15–17.

24. In delineating the "laws of chiastic structures," Nils Wilhelm Lund (*Chiasmus in the New Testament: A Study in the Form and Function of Chiastic Structures* [Peabody, MA: Hendrickson, 1992], 46) claims that the "very core of the message is found in the central line." It is notable that, although Käsemann's analysis of the Prologue takes a very different approach, he too identifies this verse as the climax: "Verse 12 specifies the gift which is his to bestow and the goal of his redeeming effectiveness." See Ernst Käsemann, "The Structure and Purpose of the Prologue to John's Gospel," in *New Testament Questions of Today* (London: SCM, 1969) 151–52.

25. The RSV, NRSV, and NIV, e.g., present v. 12c in apposition to v. 12a and thus directly following it, reading v. 12acb: "but to all who received him, who believed in this name, he gave power to become children of God."

description (v. 12c) of the potential recipients of the gift of the Word. These verses are thus corresponding phrases that hinge the core assertion of verse 12b, and this is the crux of the Prologue's message to the audience.[26] Therefore, it also profoundly affects the corresponding elements that balance the Prologue.[27] The claim is those who receive the Word are given the power to become children of God, and one goes about receiving him in order to achieve this by *believing in his name* (v. 12c). The remainder of the Prologue can thus be studied in terms of how it sheds light on what it means to become "children of God" by believing in his name and how this could be the *telos* of John's Gospel.

Verse 13 (F') stands in apposition to verse 12 and also corresponds antithetically to verse 11 (F). If verse 12c describes the role of "receivers" in this relationship, then verse 13 describes the role of God and the "how" of becoming God's children. Spiritual birth comes from above.[28] As a result of the Word's coming into the world and the rejection by his own, the "privilege of becoming the covenant people of God" changes forever.[29] Concluding this initial characterization of the children of God, the evangelist returns to what God did to make this possible.

Corresponding to the proclamation in verses 9–10 (E), verse 14 (E') announces how the true light came into the world, who the *logos*

---

26. Although he does not identify a chiasm, Brown (*Gospel according to John I–XII*, 10) also correlates these phrases.

27. The correspondence of receiving the Word to becoming children of God also suggests "while Israel, which had been given the Torah, nevertheless rejected the Logos, some others, not necessarily Israel by virtue of flesh-and-blood parentage, became children of God via their receiving of the *Logos Asarkos*" (Daniel Boyarin, "The Gospel of the Memra: Jewish Binitarianism and the Prologue to John," *HTR* 94 [2001]: 278). See also C. H. Dodd, *The Interpretation of the Fourth Gospel* (Cambridge: Cambridge University Press, 1960), 271. Ernst Käsemann asserts that v. 12 "could be regarded as the culmination of the whole . . . [of] what was achieved by the manifestation of the Revealer" (see Käsemann, "Structure and Purpose of the Prologue," 152). Although I do not concur with his assessment of the Prologue as an example of early Christian Gnosticism, his insights on v. 12 are striking and extend beyond this perspective.

28. Carson, *John*, 126. Raymond Brown questions the use of *haimatōn* in the plural to mean natural descent. Lacking a better interpretation, however, he concludes this must have been the evangelist's intention. He notes that *thelēmatos sarkos* must indicate "lust" and *thelēmatos andros* refers to the culturally accepted role of the husband in such family matters (Brown, *Gospel according to John I–XII*, 11). Frank Kermode, in his study of the axioms of "being" and "becoming" in the Prologue, notes: "we meet in v. 13 a paradoxical style of becoming (of birth) which is actually a form of being: being born not of the stuff of becoming, being born into being" (see Kermode, "St. John as Poet," *JSNT* 28 [1986]: 3–16 [here 10]).

29. John W. Pryor, "Covenant and Community in John's Gospel," *RTR* 47 (1988): 48. Heritage and ethnic identity have become irrelevant to birth from God.

becomes, and what is given in the process: "And the Word became flesh." With regard to the Prologue's flow, these words announce an event long coming, made possible by the plan of God to reenvision the covenant people as children of spiritual, not human, birth. Just as God's action in the covenantal giving of Torah changed the nature of God's relationship with creation, the incarnation of the Word, while very much in accord with that history, once again decisively alters the manner by which creation can relate to God. The mission of the Word that has become human in Jesus the Christ is to give the gift of truth that empowers those who receive and believe in him to become children of God. The remainder of the Gospel will narrate the "how" of the covenantal claim that the Prologue introduces.

THE CHALLENGE OF BELIEVING FOR POTENTIAL CHILDREN OF GOD IN JOHN 1:19–51

After the Prologue, there is a continuous narrative from John 1:19 to 12:50 through which Jesus emerges and conducts his public ministry. The bridge from the Prologue to the action of the body of the Gospel is manifested in the human witness sent from God named John. He becomes the embodiment of the Prologue as he continues to give valuable information about the person of Jesus as well as about the story to come, now in the form of dialogues with other human characters. John 1:19–51 occurs over the course of four consecutive days through which John points to Jesus as the "Lamb of God" who is coming into the world to take away its sin. John points his disciples to Jesus, who then begins to collect followers who themselves wonder aloud whom they have found. Once the spotlight shifts to Jesus, it remains there for the rest of the narrative.

These opening days culminate as Jesus responds to Nathanael with his first major teaching of the Gospel, which also challenges the fledgling disciples' understanding of what it means to believe. Nathanael is "wowed" by Jesus and heaps traditional titles upon him: "Rabbi," "Son of God," "King of Israel" (v. 49). Jesus stops him short, "Do you believe because I told you that I saw you under the fig tree?" (v. 50). Jesus goes on to identify the title that will be his preferred self-designation for his ministry: the Son of Man (v. 51). In so doing, Jesus underscores that he, in all of his humanity, is the point of communication between heaven and earth (v. 51; see Dan 7:13–14).

The nature of Jesus's promise in response to Nathanael's confession in verses 49–50 is significant. Jesus indicates that greater "believing" than that manifested by Nathanael will be required. Being "wowed," or what some call "signs-faith," is an important first step, but it is not the whole journey. If only the disciples are able to reach another depth of believing, they will see greater things. This vision of "greater things" points to the future. The vision of the open heavens, and God communicating with humankind through his Son, Jesus, the Son of Man, lies before the disciples, and the audience. Both the disciples and audience are now ready for the revelation of God in Jesus, the Son of Man.

THE CALL TO BELIEVE IN THE WORD IN JOHN 2–4

Across the Book of Signs, believing becomes the fundamental commandment by which Jesus calls people to live. He then goes on to teach, however, that this believing must not be based on signs alone, but must be founded in the word of Jesus—both his being as the Word of God and the words of his teaching. As an audience to John 2–4, we participate in Jesus's travel from Cana in Galilee, south into Jerusalem and the environs of Judea, north through Samaria, and finally back into Galilee and Cana, but also have the discipleship-oriented episodes of 1:19–51 at the forefront of our consciousness. At the close of those first days, we cannot help but feel that the disciples are coming to authentic faith and understanding of Jesus and that we are grasping the Christology of the Gospel. But then we encounter Jesus's semi-reprimand of Nathanael. This is part of the teaching strategy of the Gospel: whenever people (characters in the Gospel and/or audiences of the Gospel) seem to come to a solid articulation of faith, Jesus engages them in dialogue and challenges them to go further. But if the disciples need to go further, where must they go? The evangelist answers this question across the narrative journey from Cana to Cana, providing an early Christian catechesis, or "education," on authentic faith.

The two signs at Cana in Galilee that form the beginning and ending of this teaching are the literary frames of the journey of faith. The physical movement between these two events mirrors the theological journey through which Jesus brings himself and his message as the Word of God to people, first in a Jewish setting then in a non-Jewish setting. This portion of the Gospel thus offers the universal possibility of a journey of believing. Jesus encounters different people or groups of people and challenges them to move out of their comfort zones and religious preconceptions and move into a new relationship with God the Father through himself, the Son. This relationship then necessitates a fundamental ethical stance in the world. John 2–4 can be structured as a series of encounters as follows.

FROM CANA TO CANA—JESUS'S INSTRUCTION ON FAITH, 2:1–4:54

- 2:1–12 Encounter with Jesus's Mother and the First Sign at Cana in Galilee

- 2:13–25 Encounter with the Jewish Leaders in the Temple Area in Jerusalem

- 3:1–21 Encounter with Nicodemus in Jerusalem

- 3:22–36 Encounter with John the Baptist and His Final Witness in Judea

- 4:1–3 Transition—Jesus Leaves Judea and Moves into Non-Jewish Territory

- 4:4–15 Encounter with the Samaritan Woman at Jacob's Well (Part 1)

- 4:16–30 Encounter with the Samaritan Woman at Jacob's Well (Part 2)

- 4:31–44 Encounter with the Samaritan Villagers

- 4:45–54 Encounter with the Royal Official and the Second Sign at Cana in Galilee

In this structure, we see examples of different types of responses to Jesus's challenge both from within Judaism and from the broader non-Jewish, or Gentile, world. Each encounter provides a model for a belief response, some positive, some negative, and some, like Nicodemus, try to ride the fence between both worlds. Although this may be acceptable for the meantime, Jesus in this Gospel will ultimately push all those he encounters to make a firm decision about believing precisely because this believing leads to action. And one's action in the world, especially in the face of doubt and challenge, determines their quality of life. Each of these encounters will also move the plot of the story forward as Jesus reveals more about himself, and audiences move toward his inevitable arrest, passion, and glorification. Therefore, we can also diagram the flow of this narrative like so:

JESUS'S INSTRUCTION ON FAITH—THE JOURNEY: THERE AND BACK AGAIN, 2:1–4:54

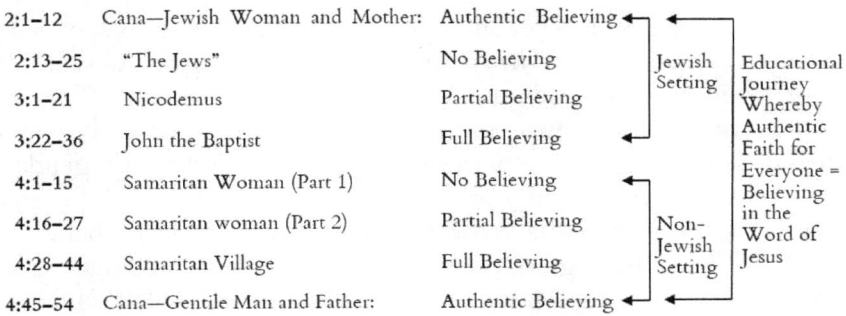

Reference	Encounter	Believing	Setting	
2:1–12	Cana—Jewish Woman and Mother:	Authentic Believing		
2:13–25	"The Jews"	No Believing	Jewish Setting	Educational Journey Whereby Authentic Faith for Everyone = Believing in the Word of Jesus
3:1–21	Nicodemus	Partial Believing		
3:22–36	John the Baptist	Full Believing		
4:1–15	Samaritan Woman (Part 1)	No Believing		
4:16–27	Samaritan woman (Part 2)	Partial Believing	Non-Jewish Setting	
4:28–44	Samaritan Village	Full Believing		
4:45–54	Cana—Gentile Man and Father:	Authentic Believing		

The Cana-to-Cana narrative is thus an educational journey through which the evangelist teaches the nature of authentic believing. As we arrive at 4:54, the ministry of Jesus has come a long way. All those he has encountered have been affected by his word and deed, some changed forever (John the Baptist, the Samaritan villagers), others resolutely unchanged ("the Jews"[30]), and still others slowly making the first steps along their own journeys of faith (Nicodemus, the Samaritan woman). Jesus, too, has been affected by these encounters. His interactions with people along the way are marked by his human experience of them and with them. As his renown spreads he is brought into contact with more and more people. Yet, in these ensuing encounters, he pushes harder for those he meets to believe in his word, *despite* that renown. His disciples, too, are journeying, watching, and remembering. This is a dynamic process of ever-

---

30. As scholars often note, this term, from the Greek *hoi Ioudaioi*, is loaded and difficult to unpack in this Gospel. Later in this volume, Alicia Myers grapples with the issue in more detail. John uses it in different ways across his narrative. Here I am indicating those, particularly of the authorities, who find themselves on the opposing side of Jesus in the central christological debate of the Gospel.

challenging and deepening belief in the word, based in relationship. Audiences, likewise, are making this journey along with them.

The theological focus of this narrative unit, therefore, is on believing and its role in uniting people with God in relationship through Jesus. This new commandment of believing has emerged strongly over the course of these early chapters. Jesus is open to everyone he encounters, but he is also provocative and challenging. By approaching Jew and Gentile, man and woman, Samaritan and royal official alike, Jesus welcomes all even as he makes strong christological claims about his relationship to God his Father. At the same time, Jesus also pushes people to a new openness both to God and to each other. In this way, believing also becomes part of the ethic of the Gospel. The evangelist teaches that right action involves believing in the word of Jesus, which reveals God and God's welcome to everyone. This, in turn, must lead those who receive and believe in Jesus to be open to and welcoming of all others, regardless of race, ethnicity, gender, socioeconomic class, or any other potential division. We might refer to this call to believe as a vertical commandment between believers and God that is theological, christological, and ethical such that it also leads to a horizontal summons to accept all others as fellow children of God. John 2–4 therefore fully establishes believing in the word of Jesus as foundational to the new relationship offered by God through Christ.

THE ACTIVITY OF BELIEVING IN JOHN 5–10

The dialogues of the rest of the Book of Signs, particularly those across the often-called "Feasts Section" of John 5–10, further illustrate how believing is lived through action. During the Feast of Tabernacles, for example, Jesus challenges those he encounters to abide in the truth and to see the presence of the Father in him, the Son. Rather than asking simply for an expression of belief, Jesus calls people to abide (*meinēte*) in his word (*tō logō tō emō*) to establish the existential state (*este*) of true discipleship (8:31). Abiding in the word of Jesus allows those who are his disciples to come to know the truth (*gnōsesthe tēn alētheian*), which will in turn set them free (*hē alētheia eleutherōsei hymas*, 8: 32).[31] He verbalizes the role and mission with which he was characterized in the Prologue: the gift of truth that can

31. Francis J. Moloney (*The Gospel of John* [SP 4. Collegeville, MN: Liturgical Press, 1998],

be received by all (1:14, 16–17).[32] Here, Jesus explains how this happens. While the initial criterion for becoming disciples is believing Jesus's word, the feast exchanges establish the criterion for identifying authentic children of God in the line of Abraham's covenantal response: conduct.[33] Action, specifically one's response to the word of God, is the criterion for identifying paternity and thereby authentic childhood, as opposed to physical descent alone. The gulf separating Jesus and many of "the Jews" that he encounters is the result of a profound *closedness*. Jesus, by contrast, challenges them to the *openness* of the very figures of their religious history to which they appeal.[34]

THE CONSEQUENCES OF BELIEVING FOR JESUS IN JOHN 11–12

John 11–12 is crucial to the theological flow of this good news because this passage moves the narrative out of the ministry and into the cross. In the words and actions of Jesus, the evangelist culminates the themes of life and light that have permeated his gospel from their introduction in the Prologue (1:3–5). The entrance into a new segment in the story is indicated by the introduction of a different setting (Bethany, 11:1) and fresh characters (the siblings Mary, Martha, and Lazarus, whom Jesus loves, vv. 1–3). The story begins strangely. The narrator offers a flash forward (what literary critics call a prolepsis) that Mary is the one who anointed Jesus (v. 2), as if that bit of information is something we know. But it has not yet happened. These words raise a note of tension about the events that are to come. When Mary does eventually anoint Jesus, his

227) notes the particle *hina* followed by the aorist subjunctive indicates Jesus's desire that an action already begun come to fruition. See BDF §373.

32. For the connection of these verses to the "truth" of the "eternal existence and saving mission of Jesus" established in the Prologue, see C. K. Barrett, *The Gospel according to St. John: An Introduction with Commentary and Notes on the Greek Text*, 2nd ed. (Philadelphia: Westminster, 1978), 344.

33. Culpepper, "Pivot," 28.

34. Moses is the focus of Jesus's teaching following the healing on the Sabbath in John 5 as well as in his Bread of Life Discourse in John 6, while Abraham comes to the fore in the Tabernacles Discourse of John 7–8. Moses returns in the trial scene of John 9, which leads into the Good Shepherd metaphor of John 10, which is particularly prevalent for God and his Messiah in the Prophets and Psalms (e.g., Isa 40:11; Jer 3:15; 23:4; 50:7; Ezek 34:11–24; 37:24; Mic 5:4; 7:14; Zech 10:2–3; 11:16; Pss 23:1–6; 28:9; 78:70–72; 79:13; 80:1; 95:7; 100:3). All this leads to question of Jesus as Messiah in the Dedication teaching of John 10, which has further Davidic undertones.

impending death has already been established by the Jewish authorities (see 11:45–54; 12:1–8). Although it is Lazarus whose physical life is at stake, the intricately constructed narrative that unfolds across 11:1–12:8 emphasizes the faith journeys of Jesus's friends Mary and Martha as he challenges them to see in him not the culmination of a historical religious system but the perfection of life in the Spirit through believing in God. In the midst of this story of friendship and believing, the arrival of the final Jewish festival of this story is announced at 11:55. The Passover is at hand, and the many who have arrived in Jerusalem are abuzz with what might occur. The tension is high and the crisis is at hand. This is confirmed as John 12 begins with the narrative that reports Mary's anointing of Jesus with perfumed oil. What was announced in 11:2 comes to pass in 12:1–8. Defending her actions, Jesus confirms its purpose: "so that she might keep it for the day of my burial. . . . You do not always have me" (12:7–8). Believing in the word of Jesus means taking action, even in small ways that counter the status quo and reveal childhood in God sometimes in the face of skepticism from one's allies.

THE CONSEQUENCES OF BELIEVING
FOR DISCIPLES IN JOHN 13–17

Audiences of the Gospel have the Prologue resonating in their ears as they listen to Jesus's teaching and experience his encounters. They have heard about the glory of God's action in the world through the gift of truth manifest in Jesus. Thus, when audiences experience Jesus verbalizing what God is doing through him in the tenor of his own voice, there is room for his word. Once we reach the Book of Glory, Jesus has reconstituted "his own" in all those who have accepted the challenge to believe in his word. These disciples, too, have opened themselves to Jesus's call. In John 13–17, the last discourse, Jesus can change prepare "his own," those who believe in him, for the further challenge to abide in this truth in the face of his coming death and its aftermath (John 18–19).

Jesus's last discourse in John 13–17 provides the symbolic rituals of a footwashing and a last meal followed by a final teaching for his fledgling and often confused disciples. Through these actions, Jesus likewise both reflects on their time together and prepares his disciples not only for his coming arrest and death but also for the reality of his future physical absence and their new mission as shepherds of the community he has forged (see esp. 16:1–4). He proclaims, "Amen, amen, I say to you, the one who believes in me will also do the works that I do and, in fact, will do greater works than these because I am going to the Father" (14:12). Believing leads to action, and this action imitates the activity of Jesus. As he wraps up his discourse to "his own," he queries, "Do you now believe?" and prepares them for the task ahead (16:31–33). As he closes his final prayer, Jesus prays not only for the disciples with him "but also on behalf of those who will believe in me through their [the first disciples'] word, that they may be one . . . so that the world may believe that you have sent me" (17:20–21). He is now ready to face this last task of his earthly mission and depart.

THE CULMINATION: LIFTING UP THE SON OF MAN AS CHRIST AND SON OF GOD IN JOHN 18–19

Christian tradition has long identified Jesus's willing acceptance of these events to come as his "passion." Although we use this word in many ways in contemporary parlance, from hunger for success or accomplishment to sexual desire, the term comes into English from the Latin word for "suffering" (*passio*). Christians understand Jesus's willing suffering, even to the point of the sacrifice of his life, to be foundational for understanding him as the Christ. And yet, in the Jewish tradition from which the Gospels arose, messiahs do not get crucified. The expectation for a king like David who rises to put in place a sovereign nation, or a prophet like Moses who brings about an eschatological in-breaking of God's reign, do not allow for the scandal of capital execution as a common criminal. Thus the earliest Christians had to struggle with this historical fact both to make sense of their experience of Jesus, as well as to form their own identity as a community of believers. The preservation and telling of this story must, therefore, have had its beginnings in the earliest development of the church. But if this is the story of a traditional messiah-king, it is the most stunning political failure in the history of the world. Something else must be going on.

John's passion narrative is indeed the climax of the story of the Christ's mission on earth, and a careful reading shows the evangelist intricately weaving the threads of his larger understanding of the good news into a rich fabric that redefines what it means to be the Christ. Jesus is the promised heir of the Davidic covenant (2 Samuel 7), but his messiahship is only fully realized also in terms of the Sinai covenant (Exodus 1–35). That covenant, put in place by God through Moses following the exodus of the Israelites from Egypt, gave the Ten Commandments and the ensuing laws of the Torah as a gift that guides the people in right relationship with God and in ethical interaction with one another. The Torah also prescribed sacrifice as the means for atonement and reconciliation with God. John 18–19 presents Jesus as the Christ who is Son of Man and Son of God, not by coming down from the cross and living as an earthly king in splendor, but by remaining *on* the cross to become the one ultimate redeeming sacrifice that atones for all sin for all time.

In John's Gospel, therefore, the cross is presented as Jesus's most significant human experience. God exalts Jesus in this "lifting up" on the cross. This same phenomenon of circumventing human understanding and expectation appears in the evangelist's use of the term "glory" across the Gospel.[35] The glory of God, and the means by which Jesus is glorified (through his crucifixion), flows from the evangelist's understanding of revelation. John has taught that God so loved the world that he handed over his only Son (3:16). This handing over is an incredible act of love. Further articulation of this self-gift in love was presented in the last discourse as the revelation of God that Jesus brings. Jesus, the Son given to the world, loved his own to the end (13:1). The glory of God and God's glorification of Jesus lies in this gift of the Son that begins with the incarnation (1:1–18), but is not complete until he is lifted up on the cross and hands over his spirit, "It is finished" (19:30).

Jesus is not, it turns out, a political messiah who revels in victory; rather, the evangelists teach that he is a covenantal messiah whose kingdom *is not* of this earth, who *is* the gift of truth that fulfills the promises of God's prior covenants and puts in place a new covenant open to all humankind by his very loss (John 1:12–18; 3:16–17; 18:33–38). This new covenantal relationship is built on believing—the faith of Jesus the Christ, who, like the good shepherd, will lay down his life for his own, and the faith of human beings who go forth in this world in courage by living a life formed by that same sacrificial service. That loss, however, is not the end of the story.

---

35. See esp. 1:14 (2×); 2:11; 8:50–55; 12:28 (2×), 38–43; 13:32; 16:14; 17:1–5, 22–24.

God's plan continues to defy human expectations, and there is always the hope of the empty tomb.

THE COMMANDMENT TO BELIEVE AND THE ACTIVITY OF "HAVING LIFE IN HIS NAME" IN JOHN 20–21

In John 20, those who believe encounter Jesus anew, now as the risen Christ, and are challenged once again to a more deeply rooted abiding in a life of believing. Moving seamlessly from several disciples' encounters with the risen Christ, through Jesus's words to Thomas about his faith in the one he can see, the evangelist addresses his audience, telling them that he has written a book so that, even though they do not see Jesus, they can believe (20:30–31). The book has been written that, through believing, they have life. These encounters present the evangelist's story of the resurrection of the Word of God through the lens of his concern for the members of the early Christian community. They continue to abide in this world even as they strive to abide in Christ's word.

CONCLUSION: BELIEVING AS AN ETHICAL IMPERATIVE

Thomas needed to see in order to believe, despite the word of his brothers and sisters in community. He embodies human nature—he is every person, including those in the early Christian community and beyond. Jesus thus teaches that believing without seeing is blessed. How is the Christian community to do this? Here we circle back to the Prologue, but now through the lens of the encounters of Jesus's own with the risen Christ. The Christian community continues to receive Christ, the Word of God, through each other, activating their ongoing believing by cultivating their love for one another and responding both to each other's needs and each other's teaching. The Fourth Evangelist teaches that in the ongoing lives of the community, believing is practiced by receiving the Word of God, *by receiving one another*. This is the means to having life in Christ's name—the purpose of the good news—and therefore a foundational ethical imperative of the Gospel.

We, too, can now circle back to the words of the paradigmatic person of believing in action, the Rev. Dr. Martin Luther King Jr.:

> By opening our lives to God in Christ, we become new creatures. This experience, which Jesus spoke of as the new birth, is essential if we are to be transformed nonconformists. . . . Only through an inner spiritual transformation do we gain the strength to fight vigorously the evils of the world in a humble and loving spirit.[36]

---

36. From the sermon titled "Transformed Nonconformist" by Martin Luther King Jr. in *Strength to Love*, gift ed. (Minneapolis: Fortress Press, 2010), 11–20 (here 17).

2.

Love One Another: The Johannine Love Command in the Farewell Discourse

CHRISTOPHER W. SKINNER

A cursory reading of the Johannine literature makes it immediately clear that love is an abiding theme across the entire corpus. The various terms for love (*agapaō*, *phileō*, and their cognates) appear over one hundred times in the Fourth Gospel and Johannine Epistles.[1] Though there is little dispute among scholars as to the importance of this theme for appreciating the message(s) of the Johannine literature, there is significant debate over how John's vision of love is to be understood. In the opening chapter, I presented the various scholarly approaches to the question of John's ethics, and there I discussed the dispute over whether John's ethics are to be understood as sectarian and exclusive or having universal implications. Nowhere is that debate more important than in an examination of John's love command.

Amid the sea of voices that have dismissed the Johannine love command as of little concern for the broadest of Christian audiences, Ernst Käsemann has written that "there is no indication in John that love for one's brother would also include love toward

---

1. The noun *agapē* appears seven times in the Gospel and twenty-one times in the Epistles, while the verbal form appears thirty-seven times in the Gospel and thirty-one times in the Epistles. The noun *philos* appears six times in the Gospel and three times in the Epistles, while the verbal form appears thirteen times in the Gospel.

one's neighbour."[2] Rather, he avers, love in the Fourth Gospel is directed only to members of the inward-looking group. Such assertions require that we either ignore seemingly universal statements about God's love for the world (e.g., John 3:16–17), or that we reinterpret such statements in light of form- and redaction-critical speculations about the development of the text. For his part, Käsemann engages in the latter approach, insisting that such universal statements belong to an earlier stratum of the tradition and fail to reflect authentic Johannine thinking. The current chapter proceeds under the assumption that the text of the Fourth Gospel reached its final form at a point in time for numerous reasons—among them is certainly the belief that the text had a coherent and unified message to relay to early Christians.[3] Thus Käsemann's approach requires some refutation, though it is neither my aim to provide, nor is there space here to discuss, each instance in which the love command arises in the Fourth Gospel.[4] Instead, I wish to undertake a more particular task with a more specific focus. While I grant that sectarian elements are present within the Fourth Gospel, the evangelist also uses cosmic language throughout to speak of Jesus and the implications of his descent, mission, vocation, and glorification. We will focus here on the narrative rhetoric that arises from an analysis of the *final form* of text rather than assigning certain statements within the Gospel to other strata or stages in the development of the Johannine tradition.[5] This will allow us to consider everything within the Gospel as an expression of genuine Johannine thought (contra Käsemann). Before we begin, it is also important to note that a great deal has been written about the role of love in the Johannine literature. This chapter

2. Ernst Käsemann, *The Testament of Jesus: A Study of the Gospel of John in the Light of Chapter 17*, trans. Gerhard Krodel (London: SCM, 1968), 59.

3. My concern in critiquing Käsemann, and those who accept his argument, is one of methodology. Like the early narrative critics who rejected the endless speculations of redaction criticism, I prefer to start with what we have (the final form of the text) rather than what we do not have (various hypothetical editions with differing theological assumptions). An approach that engages in such speculation necessarily engages in a type of special pleading that erases or, at the very least, ignores all the evidence that does not seem to fit the theory of composition. This is exactly the sort of move Käsemann makes when considering seemingly universal texts like John 3:16–17.

4. For a recent, comprehensive treatment of the subject, see Francis J. Moloney, *Love in the Gospel of John: An Exegetical, Theological, and Literary Study* (Grand Rapids: Baker Academic, 2013).

5. I do not intend this comment as a rejection of the valuable insights provided by form and redaction criticism; I merely want to highlight the differences involved in treating the text as a complete utterance vis-à-vis treating only specific passages in isolation.

does not purport to be the final word on the subject, but rather an interaction with the text of the Fourth Gospel in light of the history of reception. In what follows, I will consider Jesus's words and actions throughout the so-called Farewell Discourse (John 13–17); this includes a consideration of the footwashing in John 13, Jesus's directions to his disciples in John 15, and the "high priestly prayer" of John 17. Understanding John as a narrative Christology, we will read these passages with a view to examining the unfolding narrative rhetoric to demonstrate the universality and normativity of John's love command.[6]

THE EXTENT OF THE FAREWELL DISCOURSE
(13:1–17:26)

Before I begin my analysis of three passages from the Gospel's Farewell Discourse, it will prove important to establish briefly the literary parameters of this section of the narrative, since I will contend that the unit makes important contributions to our understanding of Jesus's love command in John. There is no little debate about the extent of the Farewell Discourse,[7] though it is widely recognized that some or all of John 13–17 constitutes a coherent farewell address meant to prepare the disciples for Jesus's departure.[8] This sort of

6. This term was first used by Robert Tannehill, "The Gospel of Mark as Narrative Christology," *Semeia* 16 (1979): 57–95. Understanding the Gospels as narrative Christologies forces us to engage the text as a whole utterance with greater attention to narrative dynamics; only through the unfolding story are we able to understand how major themes are developed and presented from beginning to end.

7. Some see the entirety of 13:1–17:26 as constituting John's Farewell Discourse; see, e.g., Leon Morris, *The Gospel according to John*, NICNT (Grand Rapids: Eerdmans, 1995), 542; Craig S. Keener, *The Gospel of John: A Commentary*, 2 vols. (Peabody, MA: Hendrickson, 2003), 1:893; Francis J. Moloney, *The Gospel of John*, SP (Collegeville, MN: Liturgical Press, 1998), 370. Among those who see the discourse beginning at 13:31, see Jerome H. Neyrey, *The Gospel of John*, NCB (Cambridge: Cambridge University Press, 2007), 240; Rudolf Schnackenburg, *The Gospel according to St. John*, 3 vols. (New York: Crossroad, 1990), 3:6–89; and D. A. Carson, *The Gospel according to John*, Pillar New Testament Commentary (Grand Rapids: Eerdmans, 1990), 476; see also Bruce Woll, "The Departure of 'The Way': The First Farewell Discourse in the Gospel of John," *JBL* 99 (1980): 225–39. Both Robert Kysar, *John*, ACNT (Minneapolis: Augsburg Publishing House, 1986), 219; and Herman Ridderbos, *The Gospel of John: A Theological Commentary* (Grand Rapids: Eerdmans, 1997), 481; see the discourse beginning in 14:1 and extending through v. 17. Other proposals include 13:31–16:33; see Scott E. Kellum, *The Unity of the Farewell Discourse: The Literary Integrity of John 13:31–16:33*, JSNTSup 256 (Sheffield: Sheffield Academic, 2004).

8. "Readers of John 13–17 quickly learn that this seemingly disorganized assemblage of materials makes excellent sense when viewed as a farewell address" (Neyrey, *Gospel of John*, 238).

farewell address is not uncommon in ancient literature.[9] Jerome Neyrey outlines the nine elements of a typical farewell address, all of which are present in John 13–17: (1) announcement of death or departure, (2) review of the patriarch's life, (3) relationships to be maintained, (4) revelations of beneficial things to come, (5) predictions of future hard times, (6) exhortation to practice a group-specific virtue and to avoid a group-specific vice, (7) successor named, (8) legacy bestowed, and (9) occasionally a final prayer or blessing.[10] It is also critical to note Neyrey's clarification that these nine elements *do not follow a specific chronology* in any given farewell address. In fact, his reconstruction of Jesus's farewell address locates these common elements in a very different order from what is listed above.

We need to acknowledge that some commentators exclude the first two units of chapter 13 (vv. 1–17; vv. 18–30) from the Farewell Discourse, insisting that they do not represent true *discourse material*. This essay will treat all of chapters 13–17 (with specific emphasis on 13:1–17; 15:1–17; 17:1–26) as part of the same literary unit; I will argue that this choice makes sense, especially in light of the common elements from Neyrey's list. In particular—and since some exclude the unit from the Farewell Discourse—Jesus's behavior in 13:1–17 amounts to both an exhortation to practice a group-specific virtue (number 6) and the bestowal of a legacy (number 8). Thus I will argue that 13:1–17 is an integral part of the wider unit, consisting of 13:1–17:26.[11]

JESUS'S "EXAMPLE" (*HYPODEIGMA*) IN JOHN 13:1–17

Those who have been dismissive of the Fourth Gospel's value for constructing normative Christian ethics have consistently pointed to the absence of clear imperatives like those we see in the Pauline literature. However, at the outset of Jesus's Farewell Discourse, the narrator describes a scene in which Jesus is said to love his disciples "to the end" (*eis telos*, v. 1) and provides for them an enduring example

9. There are two examples of such discourses in the Pentateuch—the farewell addresses of Jacob in Genesis 49 and Moses in Deuteronomy 32. The Testament of the Twelve Patriarchs is a helpful example of this type of farewell speech, and may be an ideal paradigm for understanding the genre.

10. Neyrey, *Gospel of John*, 239.

11. On the literary unit of 13:1–38, see Francis J. Moloney, "The Literary Unity of John 13,1–38," *ETL* 91 (2015): 33–53.

(*hypodeigma*, v. 15). In this section of the discourse, we will see that this *hypodeigma*, though not an imperative in the purest sense, functions within the narrative as an implicit command to Jesus's disciples, and one that extends beyond the particular behaviors associated with footwashing.[12]

The scene is set just before the Passover (v. 1a), when Jesus knows his hour (*hōra*) is approaching.[13] We read that Jesus loved his own who were in the world "to the end" (*eis telos*, v. 1d). This phrase, like many throughout the Gospel, likely carries several different shades of meaning.[14] It can be used to suggest that Jesus's love endures to the very end (viz., his crucifixion). However, *eis telos* can also indicate the ultimate "goal" or "aim" of an activity and can thus be understood to describe Jesus loving his own "fully" or "completely." Taken in this way, the phrase indicates that the proleptic activity this statement anticipates—Jesus's washing of his disciples' feet—is an embodiment of the fullest or most complete expression of his love for them. This is an important point insofar as it lays the groundwork for our appreciation of the overarching christological and ethical significance of the footwashing.

Knowing that his departure is near, Jesus demonstrates the extent of his love toward the disciples while providing them with a model on which to base their future service of others in his name. The narrator provides an internal view here, particularly by providing details related to the thoughts and perceptions of both Judas and Jesus, and thus looking forward to the impending battle between light and darkness as the events of the evening move forward.[15] First, the narrator reports that the devil (*diabolos*) has already put it in mind that Judas Iscariot should betray Jesus. This statement is meant to recall Jesus's earlier comment to his disciples: "Have I not chosen you, the Twelve? But one of you is a devil" (*kai ex hymōn heis diabolos estin,*

---

12. In my discussion of John 17, I will connect the claim that the *hypodeigma* is an implicit imperative for Jesus's disciples to the claim that all disciples of all future time periods are in view.

13. Jesus's "hour" (*hōra*) is a particularly important theme in John. It is often a proleptic reference to his crucifixion and resurrection. Jesus has previously spoken about his "hour" in 2:4; 4:21, 23; 5:25, 28; 7:30; 8:20; 12:23, 27.

14. See Christopher W. Skinner, "An Alien Tongue: The Foreign Language of the Johannine Jesus," in *Reading John*, Cascade Companions (Eugene, OR: Cascade, 2015), 68–95.

15. For more on light/darkness, see the chapter titled "Light and Darkness" in Craig Koester, *Symbolism in the Fourth Gospel: Meaning, Mystery, Community*, 2nd ed. (Minneapolis: Augsburg Publishing House, 2003), 141–74.

6:70).[16] Commentators recognize a Semitic idiom in verse 2 ("to put in mind"),[17] which is best expressed in C. K. Barrett's translation: "the devil had already *made up his mind* that Judas should betray him."[18] R. Alan Culpepper points out that the heart of the devil rather than the heart of Judas is the object of "put it into" (*ballō eis*).[19] At the same time, the audience learns that Jesus knows "everything has been handed over to him by the Father," and that just as he has come from the Father (see 1:1–2) he will soon return to him. This sets up a critical contrast between the heart/mind of the devil (v. 2) and the heart/mind of Jesus (vv. 1, 3).[20] Later, in verse 20, Satan will enter into Judas and the two worlds will clash. God's design is being worked out in Jesus while Satan's design is worked out in the actions of Judas.

In verse 4 Jesus rises from the meal, removes his outer garments (*tithēsin ta himatia*), and takes a towel (*labōn lention*) to wrap around his waist. The narrator's use of *tithēmi* and *lambanō* (here and in v. 12) calls attention back to the image of the Good Shepherd in 10:11–18. There, Jesus announced that the Good Shepherd lays down his life (*tēn psychēn autou tithēsin*, 10:11, 15, 17, 18) in order to take it back up again (*hina palin labō autēn*, 10:17, 18). The use of *tithēmi* also recalls the words of Jesus in 11:34, when he inquires about the burial place of Lazarus: "Where have they put him?" (*pou tetheikate auton*). These linguistic cues here in verse 4 link to the Good Shepherd discourse (where there is veiled reference to the "laying down" and "taking up" of life) and the encounter with Lazarus (where death and burial are explicit) and looks forward to the crucifixion and resurrection of Jesus, thus signaling his actions here as *symbolic and prophetic*, and

16. All translations of ancient texts in this chapter are mine unless otherwise specified.

17. We see this construction in Job 22:22 (LXX): *kai analabe ta rhēmata autou en kardia sou* (and lay up these words in your heart); the corresponding Hebrew phrase in the MT is *wəśim bilbābekā*. Another example from the LXX that does not have a counterpart in the MT is 1 Sam 29:10: *kai logon loimon mē these en kardia sou* (and do not put an evil word in your heart).

18. C. K. Barrett, *The Gospel according to St. John: An Introduction with Commentary and Notes on the Greek Text*, 2nd ed. (Philadelphia: Westminster, 1978), 439. See also Schnackenburg, *Gospel according to St. John*, 3:6–17; Morris, *Gospel according to John*, 614; Francis J. Moloney, *Glory Not Dishonor: Reading John 13–21* (Minneapolis: Fortress Press, 1998), 1n39; See also R. Alan Culpepper, "The Johannine *hypodeigma*: A Reading of John 13," *Semeia* 53 (1991): 136. Brown translates the idiom as "*The devil had already induced Judas*, son of Simon, the Iscariot, to betray Jesus" (Raymond E. Brown, *The Gospel according to John XIII–XXI*, AB 29a (Garden City, NY: Doubleday, 1970), 548) (emphasis added).

19. Culpepper, "Johannine *hypodeigma*," 136.

20. Here I take the terms "to know," *eidōn* (used in reference to Jesus in vv. 1, 3) and "heart," *kardia* (used in reference to the devil in v. 2) to imply perception or cognition.

highlighting the ultimate extent of his service. On this point, Barrett comments, "When Jesus lays aside his garments in preparation for his act of humility and cleansing he foreshadows the laying down of his life."[21] This is a point which must be emphasized. The footwashing is *symbolic* in that it provides a depiction of sacrificial self-giving, and *prophetic* in that it anticipates *Jesus's ultimate act* of sacrificial self-giving—his death on behalf of the world.

Jesus begins in earnest to wash and dry the disciples' feet (v. 5), which leads to a brief exchange with an incredulous and uncomprehending Peter (vv. 6–9). In the course of their conversation, Jesus comments that though Peter fails to understand now, he will understand in the future. This present-future schema appears in numerous passages throughout the Gospel, where the audience is invited to reflect on the narrated events from two perspectives: one related to the real-time narration of events and one from a distinctly post-resurrection perspective. When Jesus tells Peter that he will understand *in the future*, he is pointing forward to a time when all that has happened will be explained by and interpreted through the lens of resurrection. Peter's misplaced literalism, and in fact initial rejection of the footwashing (see vv. 6, 8a), misses the larger point that this symbolic and prophetic action has consequences beyond a particular time and a particular type of service. Emphasis should not be placed on the "here and now" but on the future; likewise, emphasis should not be placed on a particular type of service (viz., the literal practice of footwashing), but rather on various forms of sacrificial self-giving. This will become clearer only in a future, post-resurrection perspective.

Jesus's explanation and instruction at the close of the footwashing reinforce our understanding of this event as both symbolic and prophetic (vv. 12–17). It is somewhat ironic that Jesus asks his disciples—who are often represented by the voice of Peter—if they understand what he has just done for them. It seems unlikely that they have understood, given Peter's protestations and requests during his dialogue with Jesus in verses 6–9. Jesus, their Lord (*kyrios*) and Teacher (*didaskolos*), instructs them to continue washing one another's feet (v. 14b),[22] but if we stop there in our interpretation of Jesus's actions

---

21. Barrett, *Gospel according to St. John*, 439. Brown (*Gospel according to John XIII–XXI*, 551) also sees potential parallels between the present text and 10:11, 15, 17, 18.

22. On the suggestion that this *hypodeigma* is to be regarded as a literal command to continue the footwashing, see the discussion in J. Ramsey Michaels, *The Gospel of John*, NICNT (Grand Rapids: Eerdmans, 2010), 735–36.

we will be guilty of the same type of misplaced literalism displayed by characters throughout the Fourth Gospel.[23] An agenda of outward behavior that is characterized by sacrificial self-giving—beyond the simple behavioral parameters associated with footwashing—is at the heart of this command. "Jesus' instruction is a call to his disciples to repeat in their lives what he has done for them. He has given them the example of a loving gift of self in love, symbolized by the footwashing, which they must now repeat."[24] This point becomes clearer in verse 15: "I have given you an example [*hypodeigma*], in order that, just as I have done for you, you should also do."

The term *hypodeigma*, translated variously as "example" and "model," appears in several contexts associated with noble death and righteous behavior, and provides for the disciples and the audience a link between the sacrificial self-giving of the footwashing and that of the death of Jesus.[25] That Jesus's death should be connected to the example of footwashing as the premier display of sacrificial self-giving is not a new suggestion, and it fits neatly within the cumulative narrative rhetoric of the Gospel to this point. Having learned of Jesus's "arrival" through incarnation (see 1:14), the audience is now being systematically prepared for the departure of Jesus in his return to the Father. This departure is the telos of Jesus's ministry, which will result in the sending of the Paraclete, who will further prepare the disciples to live as Jesus instructed and as the Father commands. The footwashing is not to be regarded as an end unto itself but as a prophetic and symbolic event that anticipates and invites the disciples into the mode of sacrificial self-giving realized in the crucifixion. Barrett's comment here is instructive:

> There stands first a symbolic narrative, the washing of the disciples' feet, which prefigures the crucifixion itself, and in doing so points the way to

23. On this and other elements of distinctly Johannine speech, see the classic work Paul D. Duke, *Irony in the Fourth Gospel* (Atlanta: John Knox, 1985); see also my chapter, "An Alien Tongue: The Foreign Language of the Johannine Jesus," in *Reading John*, 68–95.

24. Moloney, *Glory Not Dishonor*, 16.

25. 2 Macc 6:28: "I will leave the young with a noble example [*hypodeigma*] of how to die willingly and nobly for the revered and holy laws"; 4 Macc 17:22–23: "And through the blood of the devout ones and their death as an atonement, divine providence preserved Israel, which has previously been afflicted. For the tyrant Antiochus, when he saw the courage of their virtue and their endurance under torture, proclaimed them to his soldiers as an example [*hypodeigma*] for their own endurance"; Sir 44:16: "Enoch pleased the Lord, and was translated, since he was an example [*hypodeigma*] of repentance to all generations." For more on these parallels, see Culpepper, "Johannine *hypodeigma*," 142–43.

the interpretation of the crucifixion. The public acts of Jesus on Calvary, and his private act in the presence of his disciples, are alike in that each is an act of humility and service, and that each proceeds from the love of Jesus for his own.[26]

While I will not examine the remainder of John 13 here, I do want to highlight several verses that help to reinforce the interpretation advanced above. Having both provided an example for his disciples (vv. 1–17) and celebrated a final meal with them (vv. 18–30), Jesus will begin to speak in detail about his departure. In verses 34–35 he says, "I give you a new commandment: love one another. As I have loved you, so you must love another. By this everyone will know you are my disciples, if you love one another." Three times in the span of these two verses Jesus instructs his disciples to love another, and in that same context he notes, "as I have loved you." There can be little doubt that this hearkens back to the image of 13:1, where Jesus loves his disciples *eis telos*. By imitating the manner in which he has demonstrated his own love toward them—what I have termed sacrificial self-giving—the disciples will be a light to all humanity. Their outward displays of love will have potentially universal implications, causing all to take notice. This is the first indication in the Farewell Discourse that the implications of such love extend beyond the insider group of the Twelve. We will see this emphasis again in John 17. For now, I will close this section with a brief summary of my argument:

1. The footwashing symbolizes a service to others and points forward to the crucifixion, Jesus's definitive act of sacrificial service.

2. Against that backdrop, Jesus's command that his disciples "do as I have done for you" (v. 15) extends beyond the literal act of footwashing and implies ongoing service and sacrifice.

3. Thus the love Jesus displays and commands his disciples to display—what I have consistently termed "sacrificial self-giving"—is the foundational expression of the oneness he shares with the Father and wishes to share with them (see 15:1–5).

26. Barrett, *Gospel according to St. John*, 346.

BEARING FRUIT BY SHOWING LOVE IN JOHN 15

This section of the Farewell Discourse is largely concerned with the oneness of the Father and Son and the concomitant interconnectedness of Jesus's followers to both Father and Son. In my consideration of John 13:1–17 I placed particular emphasis on the term *hypodeigma* (example, v. 15) as a way of helping us come to terms with some of the ethical implications of the Farewell Discourse. Here in 15:1–17, I will again single out specialized Johannine vocabulary.

As this new section of the discourse begins, Jesus utters the first of his final two predicated "I am" statements, which is often rendered: "I am the true vine" (*egō eimi hē ampelos hē alēthinē*; similarly in v. 5, *egō eimi hē ampelos*).[27] Jesus uses the images of an *ampelos* (often rendered "vine"), *geōrgos* ("gardener"), and *klēmata* (usually rendered "branches") to explain further the relationship between himself and the Father as well his own oneness with his disciples. The Father is the gardener who prunes the tree. This image is clear. However, though almost universally rendered as "vine" and "branches" respectively, Chrys Caragounis makes a compelling argument that *ampelos* more properly denotes a "vineyard," while *klēma* denotes "vine" in pre-Christian Hellenistic Greek.[28] The image of Israel as vineyard is a common one in the related literature, and Caragounis's understanding likely comports better with what we know of ancient viticultural practices.[29] Irrespective of the specific nuance we apply to each term, the relationships are the same: the Father is the gardener, and Jesus is the entity in which his followers are rooted.

Perhaps the most important term in these first few verses is the distinctively Johannine verb *menō* (abide, remain).[30] This verb is the unifying element across verses 1–11, a unit that consists of three sub-sections: verses 1–5a (abiding in Jesus), verses 5b–8 (implications of abiding in Jesus), and verses 9–11 (abiding in Jesus's love). What does it mean to "abide" in Jesus? Craig Keener notes that the "image of

27. Previous statements have appeared in 6:35, 41, 48, 51 ("bread of life"/"living bread"), 8:12 ("light of the world"), 10:7, 9 ("the door"), 10:11, 14 ("good shepherd"), 11:25 ("resurrection and the life"), and 14:6 ("the way, the truth, and the life").

28. Chrys C. Caragounis, "Vine, Vineyard, Israel, and Jesus," *SEÅ* 65 (2000): 201–14.

29. See the helpful discussion of the conceptual background behind John 15 in Keener, *Gospel of John*, 2:988–98.

30. The term appears fifty-three times in the Johannine literature: thirty-three times in the Fourth Gospel, eighteen times in 1 John, and twice in 2 John. *Menō* appears only forty-nine times total across the remainder of the NT.

organic union works well for (and even goes beyond) the idea of intimate relationship. . . . As they continued in this union, [the disciples] would know Jesus better (15:15; 16:13–15) and hence begin to reflect the 'fruit' of his character (15:8–9)."[31] An organic oneness exists between Jesus and the Father. They "abide" in one another. This same relationship is being offered to the disciples, but they *must choose to abide* in order that they will bear fruit.

There is a shift from the indicative in verses 1–3 to the imperative in verses 4–17. Clear implications flow from the positional relationship the disciples have with Jesus. This is not a relationship of sheer privilege; there are responsibilities involved. Verses 4–8 are explicitly focused on the bearing of fruit. We see another reference to the manner in which Jesus has loved his disciples in verse 9: "as the Father has loved me, so have I loved you." The oneness shared by the Father and Son is offered to the disciples if they remain in his love. That "bearing fruit" in this context is ultimately about the expression of love becomes clearer in verses 12–17, where love is the primary emphasis, and the mode of expression is through sacrificial self-giving. It seems clear that verses 12–17 form a coherent subunit as the two framing verses form an *inclusio* with the explicit statement "love one another."

Jesus again instructs the disciples to "love one another as I have loved you" (v. 12). This immediately recalls the words of 13:1, 34–35. How has Jesus demonstrated love for them? He has loved them, *eis telos*—fully and completely. Above, I argued that in the footwashing we saw a symbolic and prophetic action that anticipates the crucifixion. Here, Jesus makes that teaching explicit: "Greater love has no one than this, that he lay down [*thē*] his life for his friends." Notice again the use of *tithēmi*, as in 10:11–18, 11:34, and 13:4. Jesus calls directly for the sort of sacrificial self-giving that was previously only implied in the *hypodeigma* of 13:1–17.

The relationship between the disciples and Jesus is one of friendship, but only insofar as they continue to do what he has commanded (v. 14). Such behavior is the expression of the oneness shared both by Father and Son and by the disciples and Jesus. By virtue of this behavior and their standing before the Father, the disciples are no longer to be called servants, but friends of God (v. 15). Jesus has revealed the Father to them, as was promised in the Prologue (see 1:18, *ho ōn eis ton kolpon tou patros ekeinos exegēsato*), and has chosen them to bear

---

31. Keener, *Gospel of John*, 2:999.

fruit (v. 16). That fruit, as I discussed above, is displaying love, and not just any type of love but an ultimate gift—a willingness to lay down one's life. Their fruit must be that of sacrificial self-giving. Jesus punctuates this section with a concise restatement of his overall point: "This is my commandment, that you love one another" (v. 17).

The following summary enumerates the highlights from my study of John 15:1–17:

1. The same oneness shared by the Father and Son is available to those who "abide" in Jesus.

2. This "abiding" in Jesus is the means by which the disciples bear fruit.

3. Bearing fruit is primarily actualized by showing love to one another (viz., "their friends"; *hoi philoi autou*).

4. And finally, love, as defined here by Jesus, is the willingness to lay down one's life for one's friends—a picture of the same sacrificial self-giving displayed by Jesus (in the *hypodeigma* of 13:1–7, and in the crucifixion).

JESUS'S PRAYER IN JOHN 17

Even a casual reading of the so-called high priestly prayer of John 17 leads to the recognition that the prayer is easily divided into three parts: (1) Jesus's prayer for himself (vv. 1–5), (2) Jesus's prayer for his disciples (vv. 6–19), and (3) Jesus's prayer for the disciples of all ages (vv. 20–26).[32] I am concerned here chiefly with the third part of the prayer insofar as it bears on my contention that there is an underlying universality in the love language used in the Fourth Gospel and specifically in the Farewell Discourse. I will look very briefly at verses 1–5 and verses 6–19 before moving on to a more in-depth consideration of verses 20–26.

The first two portions of Jesus's prayer rehearse themes that have already appeared in the rest of the Gospel and in the Farewell Discourse. These themes include the glorification of the Son, Jesus's return to the Father, the intimacy and oneness of Father and Son,

---

32. In his treatment, Moloney (*Love in the Gospel of John*, 122–33) departs from the more traditional structure: Jesus prays to the Father (17:1–8); Jesus prays to the "Holy Father" (17:9–19); Jesus prays to the Father (17:20–26).

and the potential for persecution. The first part of the prayer reflects Jesus's awareness that his hour—the time of his "glorification"—is approaching (v. 1). Armed with this knowledge, he prays that he would be granted glory in the presence of the Father in the same way he has glorified the Father by completing his work on earth (vv. 4–5).

The second part of the prayer is focused on the Twelve. While it is not possible here to be certain whether Jesus is referring to his immediate band of followers or all of those who are currently regarded as "disciples" in the story, I am more persuaded by the former.[33] Jesus "reminds" the Father that he has revealed God to the disciples and prays that the disciples be protected as they continue in the world after his departure. If the disciples are to remain in the world and continue abiding (15:1–5), they will need a special enablement from the Father. They have been sent by Jesus, just as Jesus was sent by the Father. After Jesus departs, the disciples will now be the revealers of Father and Son in the same way Jesus has been the revealer of the Father (see 1:18).

Before moving on to a consideration of the final part of Jesus's prayer, I want to pause briefly to focus on several statements in this middle section that may seem to contradict the larger point I have been advancing in this chapter—that there is an inherent and underlying universality in Jesus's love commands across the Farewell Discourse. While Jesus prays for his disciples he makes the following statements about "the world":

17:9: I am praying for them [the disciples]. I am not praying for the **world**, but for those you have given me, for they are yours.

17:14: I have given them [the disciples] your word and the **world** has hated them, because they are not of the world just as I am not of the **world**.

17:16: They [the disciples] are not of the **world**, even as I am not of the **world**.

---

33. For most of the Gospel, Jesus's followers are called *mathētai*. John appears to have no knowledge of a tradition of the "apostles" (*hoi apostoloi*), which is Luke's preferred term, and little concern for the tradition of "the Twelve" (*hoi dōdeka*), which is one of Mark's preferred terms. In John 6, however, many disciples (*polloi mathētai*) depart after Jesus's "hard word" (6:60), at which point Jesus turns to "the Twelve" (6:67). I am persuaded that the Twelve are in view here in 17:6–19.

These three statements seem to indicate Jesus's disdain for or hostility toward the world, but is this really the case? Perhaps the best-known verse in the Gospel of John announces God's love *for* and Jesus's role in bringing eternal life *to* the world (3:16–17). But there does seem to be some ambiguity in Jesus's various statements about "the world." For instance, in the context of this same prayer, Jesus references "the world" in the following verses:

> 17:11: And I am no longer in the **world**, but they are still in the **world**, and I am coming to you.

> 17:13: I am coming to you now, but I say these things while I am in the **world**, so that they may have the full measure of my joy within themselves.

> 17:15: I do not ask that you take them out of the **world** but that you keep them from the evil one.

Within these two sets of verses, the term "world" (*kosmos*) appears to have at least two different meanings, one related to an outward disposition and the other related to a spatial sphere. Commentators have long recognized that multiple meanings for *kosmos* are operative within the Fourth Gospel, creating a complex picture of John's understanding of "the world."[34] As I have noted elsewhere,[35] *kosmos* carries a range of meanings, several of which the evangelist employs.[36] The term is used to refer to the material reality of the created world,[37] the physical realm into which Jesus has entered,[38] and the object of God's affection and salvific intentions.[39] In John, the world is both a place of beauty—a realm of human existence created and loved by God—and a metonymical term symbolizing humanity. Further, the *kosmos*, as a symbol of humanity, is characterized by its

---

34. See the very helpful coverage of the semantic range of the term in Stanley B. Marrow, "*Kosmos* in John," *CBQ* 64 (2002): 90–102.

35. See Christopher W. Skinner, "The World (Kosmos): Promised and Unfulfilled Hope," in *Character Studies in the Fourth Gospel: Narrative Approaches to Seventy Figures in John*, ed. Steven A. Hunt, D. Francois Tolmie, and Ruben Zimmerman (Grand Rapids: Eerdmans, 2016), 61–70.

36. BDAG, s.v. *kosmos* (561–63).

37. Notably 1:10: "the world did not know him" (*ho kosmos di' autou egeneto*).

38. In John, Jesus has come "from above." He is constantly speaking of his departure in the Farewell Discourse. His descent from the Father represents his entrance into "the world," the realm of "below." His departure to the Father represents his exit from "the world" to the realm of the "above." On this, see 1:9, 10a; 3:17ab, 19; 6:14.

39. See, among others, 1:29; 3:16, 17c; 4:42; 6:51.

waywardness and recalcitrance; the world is fundamentally opposed to the things of God (see e.g., 1:10–11).[40] Both of these nuances are operative in John 17, and it is necessary for us to be precise when discussing Jesus's comments about the world in the middle section of the high priestly prayer; otherwise, we may be guilty of claiming that Jesus's disposition toward the *kosmos*—in the sense of wayward humanity—is negative or oppositional. These observations relate to a spatial dualism present within the Gospel. For the evangelist, there are two spheres—the realm above and the realm below. The realm above is the heavens, where the Father resides and from which the Son has been sent. That realm is characterized by the things of God. The realm below is the *kosmos*, which is characterized by opposition to and rejection of both Father and Son. When Jesus prays for his disciples in verses 6–19, he asks for their protection from those who oppose the things of God (*kosmos* as metonymy for humanity) while they remain on earth (*kosmos* as spatial realm). However, neither statement should be read, as some have suggested, as the Johannine Jesus's hatred for the world or insular perspective on love.

As we move to the final portion of Jesus's prayer, we see Jesus beginning to pray for the unity and protection of disciples of all future periods: "I do not pray concerning them [viz., the Twelve] only, but also *for all of those who will believe* in me through the word" (v. 20). Like earlier cosmic statements in the Gospel, this prayer clearly reveals an emphasis beyond the parochial realm of the Johannine sect. Verse 21 continues the idea from the previous verse, expressing a desire for all future disciples to experience the oneness that characterizes the relationships between the Father and Son, and between the Son and the Twelve.

Oneness between Father, Son, and disciples includes an impartation of glory (*doxa*, v. 22). *Doxa* is an incredibly important theme throughout the Fourth Gospel, making its first appearance in the Prologue. In 1:14 we read, "And we beheld his glory; glory as of the

---

40. The Prologue (1:1–18) is the interpretive lens through which to read the entire Gospel. Thus 1:10–11 presents foundational claims about the nature of the *kosmos* as both a place and a symbol for humanity, and the role of the world vis-à-vis Jesus, which inform our reading of the rest of the narrative. Jesus has come into the world (as place) and the world (as humanity) has not received him (v. 10). The substance of this claim is reiterated in v. 11, only with different terminology: "he came to his own place [*ta idia*] and his own people [*hoi idioi*] did not receive him." A close reading of the text yields an audience expectation that humans throughout the Gospel will resist and oppose Jesus, which is exactly what happens.

unique son of the Father." On this verse, Rudolf Bultmann helpfully comments that the *doxa*

> consists in what [Jesus] is as *Revealer* for men, and he possesses the *doxa* really—as becomes clear toward the end of the Gospel (12.28; 13.31f; 17.1ff.)—when that which he himself is has been *actualised* in the believer. Correspondingly it is those who, as believers, allow him to be for themselves what he *is*, who see his glory. The vision of faith takes place in the process of upturning of all man's natural aims in life, a process which is described in v. 12 as *tekna theou genesthai* [becoming children of God].[41]

What Bultmann calls "man's natural aims" correspond to my understanding of the world as a metonymy for recalcitrant humanity. By virtue of his status with and as God (1:1) and his descent from heaven (1:11, 14), Jesus is already conformed to the things above rather than the things of this world. He must now transform his followers into such a state by sharing with them his glory. Just as the Father gave glory to Jesus, he will impart glory to his followers, though this reality is stated here in the form of a prolepsis: "I have given them the glory that you gave to me, in order that they might be one as we are one" (v. 22).

Jesus goes on to express his desire for all disciples to be with him and the Father and to experience the oneness they share, about which the world is ignorant (vv. 23–24). The prayer concludes with a major theme that was originally introduced in the Gospel's Prologue: the role of Jesus in revealing the Father. In what is probably the most important role of Jesus unveiled in the Prologue, the audience learns that Jesus makes the Father known (*ekeinos exegēsato*, 1:18). In revealing "the Father," what has Jesus made manifest? Here in the Farewell Discourse we have seen him reveal a model for how to love—through sacrificial self-giving—as well as an abiding concern both for the oneness and protection of his disciples and the world. These concerns are at the very heart of the Father. Going forward, we will witness the full consummation of Jesus's glory and the fulfillment of each proleptic announcement given in the Farewell Discourse. Having completed our examination of the high priestly prayer, here is what we have learned

41. Rudolf Bultmann, *The Gospel of John: A Commentary*, trans. G. R. Beasley-Murray, R. W. N. Hoare, and J. K. Riches (Philadelphia: Westminster, 1971), 68–69 (italics in original).

1. Jesus's love for "his own" extends beyond the parochialism associated with "one another" (13:34–35) or "your friends" (15:13) to all those who will believe.

2. Thus Jesus demonstrates his love fully and completely through his sacrificial self-giving on the cross, and this love will be universally available.

THE NORMATIVE INTENT OF SACRIFICIAL
SELF-GIVING

As we conclude this chapter, it is important to reiterate one common reason why we so often come to the Fourth Gospel with unrealistic expectations. When we look at the portraits of Jesus in the Synoptic Gospels, we see remarkable similarities in those accounts that are missing in John. Jesus is more fully developed in *different ways* across the Synoptics than in the Fourth Gospel, and the Johannine Jesus often falls short in the eyes of those who prefer the conflated Jesus of the Synoptic tradition. As I pointed out in the first chapter of this book, if we look at (or for) Johannine ethics through a Pauline or Matthean or Lukan lens, we are bound to be disappointed. However, when we read the Fourth Gospel on its own terms, we find ethics—while underdeveloped in comparison with other early Christian treatments—that need to be taken seriously as an expression of unified and coherent thinking about the legacy of Jesus. John does not give us the fullest or most comprehensive expression of universal or normative Christian ethics, but this does not mean that John fails to show *any universality* in the ethics of the Johannine Jesus.

Readers commonly approach the four gospels in light of one another, in light of the rest of the New Testament, or even in light of certain theological systems or confessions. However, the Gospel of John is a story about Jesus with the power to stand on its own without the assistance of other interpretations of Jesus's life and vocation. Only after we have appreciated John's unique message about Jesus should we introduce other interpretive voices. Against that backdrop, we must keep in mind Francis Moloney's implicit admonition to readers excerpted in the opening chapter of this book: "The Gospel of John does say *something* about an understanding of Christian love, even though it must not be claimed that it says *everything*."[42] We must therefore be cautious in examining the expectations we bring to the text, and we must let the authentic voice(s) of the Johannine literature speak on their own terms. When we approach the Fourth Gospel attempting to ask specific questions about its implications for normative Christian ethics, we run into several obstacles. At the end of the day we are left with a historically situated text that raises numerous problems for any system of ethics, the most notable of which are contentious interrelationships posited by contemporary reconstructions of the Johannine community.[43] Does this, however, necessitate our understanding of everything in the Gospel as sectarian? My answer here is no.

My examination of love imagery and love commands in the Farewell Discourse has attempted to show that John's vision of love is both local and universal. Throughout this chapter I have tried to make the point, through a close reading of crucial passages within the Farewell Discourse, that there is a trajectory from the more particular to the more universal across John 13–17, beginning with an emphasis on "one another," moving to an emphasis on "friends," and culminating in Jesus's prayer for all followers of all future time periods. Jesus says that true love—the love he commands his disciples to display—is most fully expressed in the willingness to lay down one's life for friends. By virtue of sharing oneness with Jesus and the Father, the disciples have become the friends of Jesus. His crucifixion on behalf of the world is the pathway by which *all can potentially become his friends*. What could be more universal, more normative than that?

42. Moloney, *Love in the Gospel of John*, 214 (emphasis original).

43. As mentioned in the first chapter of the book, see the various proposals set forth in the following works: J. Louis Martyn, *History and Theology in the Fourth Gospel* (Nashville: Abingdon, 1968); Wayne A. Meeks, "The Man from Heaven in Johannine Sectarianism," *JBL* 91 (1972): 44–72; D. Moody Smith, "Johannine Christianity: Some Reflections on Its Character and Delineation," *NTS* 21 (1975): 222–48; R. Alan Culpepper, *The Johannine School*, SBLDS 26 (Missoula, MT: Scholars Press, 1975); and Raymond E. Brown, *The Community of the Beloved Disciple: The Lives, Loves and Hates of an Individual Church in New Testament Times* (New York: Paulist Press, 1979). See also the recent work of Urban C. von Wahlde, *Gnosticism, Docetism, and the Judaisms of the First Century: The Search for the Wider Context of the Johannine Literature and Why It Matters*, LNTS 517 (London: Bloomsbury T & T Clark, 2015).

3.

"Follow Me": A Life-Giving Ethical Imperative

RAYMOND F. COLLINS

Half a century ago, Noël Lazure wrote that the Christian should act in accord with what he or she is.[1] He went on to say, "The moral demands flowing from such an understanding of Christian existence are summed up in the verb 'follow.'"[2] Since then little attempt has been made to unpack this statement. The present essay is an attempt to redress that lacuna.

THE FIRST FOLLOWERS

The Fourth Evangelist's description of day three at the beginning of Jesus's ministry provides his readers with a paradigmatic account of the first followers of Jesus (John 1:35–42).[3] As the evangelist tells the story, the day began with John, the witness par excellence, pointing to Jesus and, with a revelation formula characteristic of the jargon of the Fourth Gospel, saying "Look, here is the Lamb of God" (1:36) within earshot of two of his own disciples.[4] The next verse in the

---

1. See Noël Lazure, *Les valeurs morales de la théologie johannique (Évangile et Épîtres)*, EBib (Paris: Gabalda, 1965), 58.
2. Ibid. My translation.
3. See Raymond F. Collins, *These Things Have Been Written: Studies on the Fourth Gospel*, LThPM 2 (Louvain: Peeters; Grand Rapids: Eerdmans, 1990), 48–51; Collins, "First Disciples," in *John and His Witness*, Zacchaeus Studies: New Testament (Collegeville, MN: Liturgical Press, 1991), 33–45.
4. Michael de Goedt, "Un schème de révélation dans le Quatrième Évangile ," *NTS* 8, no.

evangelist's narrative captures the significance of the moment. Having heard what the Witness had to say, "they followed Jesus."

The visual contrast limned by the evangelist in that third-day scene is striking. The contrast is between the static and the dynamic. John was standing (*eistēkei*). With him were two disciples (*mathētai*), two students, pupils who listened to what John had to say. Jesus walked by (*peripatounti*). The pair of disciples became men on the move; they followed (*ēkolouthēsan*) Jesus. Later in his story, the evangelist will identify those who accompany Jesus as his disciples (*mathētai*), but not now. He wants his readers to know that the two who left John to follow Jesus had begun a journey, the journey of discipleship.[5]

At this point in his narrative, the evangelist leaves the pair in anonymity as he emphasizes their movement. Jesus seems to have heard the fall of their footsteps. He turned and saw the pair following him. As the evangelist had twice used the noun *mathētai*, "disciples," to characterize their relationship with John, so now he twice uses the verb *akoloutheō*, "follow," to speak of their relationship with Jesus (1:35, 37). In this picturesque little scene, the evangelist tells his readers that these two men were walking behind Jesus when he turned to them and asked, "What are you looking for?" Instead of replying directly, the pair responds to Jesus's question with a counterquestion, "Where are you staying?" In response to that question, Jesus offers an invitation, "Come and see." Following Jesus implies an invitation to see where it is that Jesus is staying.

This short exchange is no ordinary conversation. Its key words function on two levels in the Johannine story, the narrative and the symbolic. "Look" (*zēteite*), "stay" (*meneis*), and "see" (*opsesthe*) are among the most significant double entendres in the Fourth Gospel. On the narrative level, Jesus's "What are you looking for?" and "What do you want?" are virtually equivalent to "Why are you following me?" Their answer suggests that they were more than intrigued by John's identification of their interlocutor as "the Lamb of God."[6] Obviously Jesus had a unique relationship with God. In order to

2 (1962): 142–50. Throughout this essay, unless otherwise indicated, the English translation of the New Testament is from the NRSV.

5. von Wahlde suggests that in 1:37, 38, and 40—in a passage that he assigns to the earliest stratum of the Fourth Gospel—*akoloutheō* does not have the meaning of "being or becoming a disciple." The suggestion appears to be oblivious to the use of symbolic language in the passage of the Johannine gospel, in which these instances of *akoloutheō* presently appear. See Urban C. von Wahlde, *The Gospel and Letters of John*, ECC (Grand Rapids: Eerdmans, 2010), 2:61.

6. Jo-Ann Brant comments, "They seem to understand the messianic implications." See Jo-

probe this relationship further, the two who followed Jesus wanted to know where he was staying. On the narrative level, their question seems to imply no more than "Where are you staying tonight?" or "Is someone putting you up for the night?" but the present tense of the verb suggests that their question is more than a one-off query about where Jesus was to lay his head that night; it was a question about Jesus's permanent abode.

Jesus's response does not directly answer their question. His invitation directs them to come and see for themselves. The verb "see" (*opsesthe*) is in the future tense.[7] At some future moment these followers would see where it is that Jesus abides. For the time being their opportunity to see is on hold until more of the narrative has run its course. In the meantime these followers are left hanging. The real meaning of Jesus's invitation to them will unfold as the evangelist tells his story of the one enigmatically identified as the Lamb of God.

The evangelist continues to intrigue his readers as he brings his snippet of information on the third day to a close. He identifies one of those who followed Jesus as Andrew, Simon Peter's brother. The evangelist's silence as to the identity of the other follower has whetted the curiosity of scholars for decades. Many see in the anonymous follower the first appearance of the Beloved Disciple,[8] a major figure in the Fourth Gospel's narrative, who remains forever unnamed, a character whose identity has piqued the curiosity of biblical scholars for generations and still does.[9]

"FOLLOW": A JOHANNINE MOTIF

Some years ago I suggested that the evangelist's description of the third day, with its threefold use of the verb "follow," is a thesis

Ann T. Brant, *John*, Paideia Commentaries on the New Testament (Grand Rapids: Baker Academic, 2011), 50.

7. Surely 14:9 is not without interest for those who probe the meaning of Jesus's invitation. This essay on following Jesus is not the place to undertake an exhaustive study of the meaning of "see" in the Fourth Gospel. A half century ago, Raymond Brown offered a cursory introduction to the topic in his survey of Johannine vocabulary. See Raymond E. Brown, *The Gospel according to John I–XII*, AB 29 (Garden City, NY: Doubleday, 1966), 497–518 (here 501–3).

8. See, e.g., Brant, *John*, 51.

9. For a panoramic view of the possibilities, see James H. Charlesworth, *The Beloved Disciple, Whose Witness Validates the Gospel of John?* (Valley Forge, PA: Trinity Press International, 1995).

on following Jesus,[10] and "a paradigmatic narrative on Christian discipleship."[11]

After offering his audience a description of the first followers of Jesus in the first chapter of his narrative, the evangelist is not content to let the idea of following Jesus fade into the background of his story. He opens his account of the fourth day with a scene in which Jesus is again a man on the move. He is about to go to the Galilee, presumably accompanied by Andrew, the anonymous follower, and Simon Peter.[12] En route, Jesus found Philip and said to him, "Follow me" (*akolouthei moi*, 1:43). That Jesus found (*heuriskei*) Philip suggests that this was more than a chance encounter. Finding Philip was a deliberate act on Jesus's part.[13]

Having found the one for whom he was looking, Jesus says to him, "Follow me" (*akolouthei moi*). There is no initial get-acquainted conversation, just an immediate command, as from someone in authority. The present tense of the imperative suggests that following Jesus is a repetitive or continuous action. It is not to be a onetime activity of accompanying Jesus to Galilee. Writing about Philip later in the narrative, the evangelist portrays Philip as someone who did indeed follow Jesus (1:44–48; 6:5–7; 12:21–22; 14:810).

The terseness of the evangelist's ten-word description of the call of Philip contrasts sharply with what follows. Philip immediately springs into action, not by walking along behind Jesus but by doing what Jesus does.[14] Like Jesus himself, he finds someone (1:41)—the reluctant Nathanael, disinclined to go to Jesus. Then, like Jesus, Philip offers an invitation to Nathanael in the form of a command, "Come and see" (*erchou kai ide*, 1:48). Having called Nathanael, Philip then recedes into the background until he reappears in the episode of Jesus's feeding the five thousand.

Jesus's invitation to Philip is a onetime event in the body of the Fourth Gospel. The Johannine Jesus will not utter the words "Follow me" again until he twice addresses this charge to Simon Peter in the epilogue to the Gospel (21:19, 22). Only then, for just the second

---

10. Collins, *John and His Witness*, 48.

11. Collins, *These Things*, 98; see 100–101.

12. This suggests that Jesus was in Judea when he was followed by the two disciples of 1:36–39.

13. The REB's translation of *heuriskei* as "met" hardly does justice to the evangelist's word choice.

14. Commenting on the verb "follow," Lazure notes that imitating Christ is the first demand of discipleship. See Lazure, *Les valeurs morales*, 192.

time in the Gospel, does Jesus command a single individual to follow him. "Follow me," says Jesus to Simon Peter, and he does so twice. Coupled with the evangelist's narrative observation that the Beloved Disciple was following (*akolouthounta*, v. 20) Simon Peter and the risen Jesus, the after-breakfast scene (21:15–23) has a concentration of references to following Jesus equal to that of 1:37–40. It is as if "follow me" forms an *inclusio* encompassing the entire Gospel of John.

Between the call of Philip in 1:43 and that of Simon Peter in 21:19, 22, other people follow Jesus. Intrigued by Jesus's signs, a large crowd kept following him (*ēkolouthei*, 6:2), all the way to the shores of the Sea of Galilee. Simon Peter and another disciple, presumably the Beloved Disciple, followed Jesus (*ēkolouthei*, 18:15) to the courtyard of the high priest. The Beloved Disciple follows (*akoloutounta*, 21:20) Peter and Jesus after Jesus commanded Peter to "Follow me" for the first time.

Not only was Peter followed by the Beloved Disciple; Peter himself had once followed (*akolouthōn*, 20:6) the Beloved Disciple, lagging behind as the two of them ran to an empty tomb. Lazarus's tomb was, however, not empty when a group of Jews followed (*ēkolouthēsan*, 11:31) Mary of Bethany, expecting the bereaved woman to be on her way to weep at her brother's tomb.

In all these cases, following Jesus or someone else appears to be an almost banal activity. It is a matter of movement, in which the follower walks behind the one being followed. In these passages the verb *akoloutheō* has what Urban von Wahlde describes as a nontechnical meaning.[15] The Johannine narrator uses the verb in reference to an everyday kind of activity. People follow one another for all sorts of reasons.

FOLLOW ME

When, however, the Johannine narrator's Jesus *speaks* about "following," using the verb *akoloutheō*, the verb seems to have another connotation. It is no longer a matter of traipsing along behind Jesus for curiosity's sake or for some other reason. When the Johannine Jesus speaks about following him, he has something more in mind than a merely physical activity. For the most part, this something more

---

15. See von Wahlde, *Gospel and Letters*, 61.

includes accompanying Jesus, with Jesus in the lead. To "follow" is to come after someone else. The follower is not the leader. Nonetheless, the follower accompanies the leader along the way.

That this is so is clear in the way Jesus speaks to Philip in 1:43. Jesus has singled Philip out—he has found the one whom he wanted—and commanded him to follow him. "Follow me" (*akolouthei moi*), says Jesus, to the unsuspecting Bethsaidan. The language of Jesus's command to Philip echoes the language of Jesus's call of the tax collector described in the Synoptic accounts, but the call is, as it were, isolated by the evangelist (Matt 9:9; Mark 2:14; Luke 5:27).[16] While the tax collector was called when sitting at a toll-taker's collection booth and the pairs of brothers, Peter and Andrew, James and John, were called from their fishermen's tasks (see Matt 9:9–13; Mark 2:13–17; Luke 5:27–32; Matt 4:18–22; Mark 1:16–20), Philip is simply called; he is told to follow Jesus. The writer's focus is on the call itself. The Fourth Evangelist does not speak about how Philip earned his livelihood;[17] Philip's sole identity in the first part of the narrative in which he first appears is that of one who was told to follow Jesus. He is not called from; he is simply called—in fact, commanded—to follow Jesus.

The imperative mood of Jesus's words to Philip—Jesus's first spoken words about following him—identifies Jesus as one who has authority over Philip, commanding him as to what he should do. What he should do is follow Jesus. Philip responds to Jesus's command by following him—to the seaside locale in Galilee, apparently not so far from his home in Bethsaida, where Jesus will feed the crowd of five thousand people (see 6:5–7), to the festival in Jerusalem where Philip co-opts Andrew into joining him in telling Jesus that some "Greeks" wanted to see him (12:20–22), and to a supper in Jerusalem (14:8–10).

A close reading of these texts reveals that there was indeed more to following Jesus than merely accompanying him, following behind. Philip's looking for Nathanael (1:43–48) shows that to obey Jesus's command to follow him implies seeking out other disciples. It is surely illegitimate to attribute psychological motives to the characters in the Johannine narrative, but a commentator is tempted to observe that the Johannine Philip had an intuitive sense that following Jesus required some initiative on the part of the "follower." The narrative

16. See *deute opisō moi*, "follow me," in Mark 1:16 and Matt 4:19; Mark 1:16.

17. Nowhere in the Fourth Gospel is there any hint as to what Philip did for a living, either before or after his call.

gives no indication that Jesus told Philip to seek out another disciple, nor does it indicate that Philip had an example of some other disciple doing this to follow.[18] Without any external stimulus, Philip's discipleship is proactive rather than being sheepishly passive.

A reading of the other three Philip scenes in the Fourth Gospel (6:5–7; 12:20–22; 14:8–10) shows Philip in dialogue with Jesus. He entered into conversation with the one who had authoritatively said, "Follow me." His discipleship was not a silent following of Jesus; it was accompanied by pertinent and *ad rem* conversation.

TO FOLLOW JESUS IS TO POSSESS
THE LIGHT OF LIGHT

After the call of Philip, the Johannine Jesus does not speak again about following him until he says, "I am the light of the world. Whoever follows me [*ho akolouthōn emoi*] will never walk in darkness but will have the light of life" (8:12).

Jesus speaks these words during the seven-day Festival of Tabernacles (7:14), a feast noted for its magnificent light display. The Mishnah describes the erection of four golden candlesticks in the temple's Court of Women. Atop each candlestick was a bowl filled with oil and wicks. The light from these lamps was so legendary that the Mishnah says that there was not a courtyard in Jerusalem that did not reflect the light (*m. Sukkah* 5:3). Adding to the luminosity of the lamps were the men dancing around the candlesticks with as many as eight flaming torches in their hands. This torchlight ceremony was said to commemorate the pillar of fire in the wilderness (Exod 13:21; see Exod 14:24; 30:38; Ps 78:14; 105:39; Neh 9:12, 19).

This is the scenario in which the evangelist describes Jesus's uttering one of his memorable "I am" sayings (6:35, 41, 48, 51; 10:7, 9, 11; 14:11 25; 14:6; 15:1). "I am the light of the world" (*egō eimi to phōs tou kosmou*, 8:12a), proclaims Jesus.[19] Jesus is to repeat this auto-characterization on the occasion of his cure of a man born blind. Then,

18. The evangelist provides no indication that Philip was aware of what Andrew had done the previous day in Judea.

19. It may be that there was a touch of polemics in this characterization. Koester writes, "In Greco-Roman sources, the god Serapis was lauded as the 'light of all men' and the goddess Isis was 'light of all mortals.' Zeus could be called 'the light of men' and it was said of Jupiter that 'the whole world was filled with the light of his glory.'" See Craig R. Koester, *Symbolism in the Fourth Gospel: Meaning, Mystery, Community*, 2nd ed. (Minneapolis: Fortress Press, 2003), 159.

responding to the disciples' query about the cause of the man's congenital blindness, Jesus says of himself, "As long as I am in the world, I am the light of the world [*phōs eimi tou kosmou*]" (9:5).[20]

Given the plethora of references to light in the Jewish Scriptures,[21] it is impossible to identify any particular scriptural passage or passages that might maximally clarify Jesus's solemn utterance. Light is so much a part of human experience and so polyvalent a symbol that it is difficult to define. In the words of Craig Koester, the symbol calls forth "a host of varied and even contradictory associations on both the cognitive and affective levels."[22] Light is a major theme in the Fourth Gospel. Indeed, writes Koester, "Images of light and darkness pervade the Fourth Gospel, creating what is probably its most striking motif."[23] The word "light" (*phōs*) appears some twenty-three times in the evangelist's work (1:4, 5, 7, 8 [2×], 9; 3:19 [2×], 20 [2×], 21; 5:35; 8:12 [2×]; 9:5; 11:9, 10; 12:35 [2×], 36 [3×], 46). Use of the motif is concentrated in the so-called Book of Signs. The evangelist writes about light in seven chapters of the Gospel, all belonging to the Book of Signs (See John 1, 3, 5, 8, 9, 11, and 12).

The motif first appears in the Prologue (see 1:4, 5, 7, 8 [2×], 9). What the Prologue has to say about light not only highlights the importance of Jesus's self-identification as the light of the world (8:12a) but also anticipates this proclamation. In the Prologue we read that the Word "was the light of all people" (1:4) and, again, "The true light, which enlightens everyone, was coming into the world" (1:9). Verse 5 of the Prologue, "The light shines in the darkness and the darkness did not overcome it," foreshadows the contrast between light and darkness that appears in 8:12.

"By introducing the theme of light and darkness," Raymond Brown notes, "Jesus directs his discussion with the crowd from the intellectual realm to the moral realm."[24] We can only concur with Brown's opinion. The ethical component of the light-darkness symbolism is clearly seen in 3:19–22:

> And this is the judgment, that the light has come into the world, and people loved darkness rather than light because their deeds were evil.

20. In 9:2 the disciples are identified as *hoi mathētai*.
21. See, among others, "a light to the peoples" in Isa 51:4, arguably the closest biblical antecedent to Jesus's "light of the world."
22. Koester, *Symbolism*, 141.
23. Ibid.
24. Brown, *John I–XII*, 479.

For all who do evil hate the light and do not come to the light, so that their deeds may not be exposed. But those who do what is true come to the light, so that it may be clearly seen that their deeds have been done in God.

The narrative's account of Jesus speaking about evil deeds and of judgment introduces the evangelist's audience into the world of ethics. Evil deeds are shrouded in darkness. Deeds done in God are done in the light. In Jesus's day and at the time of the evangelist, many Jews believed that the majority of men and women lived in darkness (see 2 Baruch 18:1–2). Their conduct did not consist of deeds done in God. Early rabbis attributed this kind of behavior to the fact that gentiles lived without the Torah. In contrast, Israel lived in the light because of its possession of Torah. For the early rabbis, the Torah was a lamp or light (see Testament of Levi 14:4; Exodus Rabbah 33:3).

Having identified himself as the light of the world in 8:12, Jesus spells out the implications for those who follow him: "Whoever follows me will never walk in darkness but will have the light of life."[25] According to the Johannine Jesus, a person who walks in the darkness of night is likely to stumble (11:9). If someone walks in the darkness, that person does not know where they are going (12:35). This is only commonsense wisdom. Walking without the light of day puts any person in a precarious situation. They are liable to trip and fall; They can easily get lost.

Jesus is not really concerned about walking at night. He would have no need to remind his disciples that walking at night without a torch in hand or the moon shining strongly overhead means that one is running the risk of stumbling and/or getting lost. Jesus is pointing to something else. His language is metaphorical. His imagery recalls similar imagery in the Qumran writings; the Community Rule describes walking in the paths of darkness as a way of life characterized by all sorts of evil (see 1QS 4:9–11).

The lengthy catalogue of vices in 1QS 4:9–11 illustrates what is meant by walking the paths of darkness.[26] Those who walk in darkness are those whose lives are characterized by greed, sluggishness in the pursuit of justice, wickedness, falsehood, pride, haughtiness of

---

25. "Light of life" is an expression that also appears in 1QS 3:7.
26. The catalog of vices in 1QS 4:9–11 stands in sharp contrast with the catalog of virtues in 1QS 4:2–6.

heart, dishonesty, cruelty, much insincerity, impatience, much fool-ishness, impudent enthusiasm for appalling acts performed in a lustful passion, filthy paths in the service of impurity, blasphemous tongue, blindness of eyes, hardness of hearing, stiffness of neck, and hardness of heart. To walk the paths of darkness is to live a vile life of sin, and it will not go unpunished. Its consequence is affliction at the hands of the angels of destruction and eternal damnation by the wrath of God (See 1QS 4:11–13). The Qumran texts describe walking in darkness as a life of moral corruption whose end will be damnation.

In the Qumran texts, the antidote to walking in darkness is belong-ing to the covenanted community and submitting oneself, as a son of justice, a child of righteousness, to the Prince of Lights, to wit, "In the hand of the Prince of Lights is dominion over all the sons of justice; they walk on paths of light. And in the hand of the Angel of Dark-ness is total dominion over the sons of deceit; they walk on paths of darkness. From the Angel of Darkness stems the corruption of all the sons of justice, and all their sins, their iniquities, their guilts, and their offensive deeds" (1QS 3:20–22).[27]

The Dead Sea Scrolls' antithetical language concretized in the con-trast between light and darkness is similar to the language of the Johannine Jesus in 8:12. The Qumran texts state that submission to the rule of the Prince of Lights is what preserves a person from walk-ing in darkness, but the Johannine Jesus says that following him is what rescues a person from walking in darkness. The call of Philip shows that Jesus takes the initiative in inviting someone to follow him; John 8:12 points to the ethical implications of following Jesus. These ethical implications help to distinguish the Johannine notion of following Jesus from the Synoptic idea of following Jesus.

That following Jesus precludes walking in darkness calls for further ethical reflection. It is well known that "walk" is a common metaphor in Jewish ethical reflection. The manner in which a person "walks" serves as a figure of their good or evil behavior. The Qumran parallels cited above show that walking in darkness is different from walking in the shadows. Walking in darkness is a way of speaking about utterly immoral behavior.

The Dead Sea Scrolls have given scholars many new insights into the vocabulary of the Fourth Gospel; there are so many similarities

---

27. Martínez-Tigchelaar translation. Florentino García Martínez and Eibert J. C. Tigchelaar, *The Dead Sea Scrolls*, vol. 1, *1Q1–4Q273*, study ed. (Leiden: Brill; Grand Rapids: Eerdmans, 2000), 77.

between the words and expressions of the scrolls and those of the Fourth Gospel.[28] For the purposes of this study, "walking in darkness" must be singled out as a Johannine expression whose meaning is clarified by its appearance in the Dead Sea Scrolls.

The idea of walking in darkness recurs in 12:35, where the telling contrast between light and darkness is found once again (see 1 John 1:6). Jesus had repeatedly spoken of himself, using the image of light (3:19, 20, 21; see 1:4–5, 8–9). On the occasion of the Passover festival, he does so once again. He says to the crowd (*ho ochlos*, 12:34) gathered for the celebration, "The light is with you for a little longer. Walk while you have the light, so that the darkness may not overtake you [see 1:4]. If you walk in the darkness, you do not know where you are going." One final time—and the time is fleeting!—Jesus offers the crowd the opportunity to walk with him, to follow him.

The invitation comes with an ominous warning. The crowd should walk with Jesus so that it might not be overtaken by darkness and lose its sense of direction. The editors of the NRSV—and they are not alone in doing so—translate the clause *kai ho periptōn en tē skotia ouk oiden pou hypagei* of 12:35c as if the verbs were in the second person, "If you walk in the darkness, you do not know where you are going."[29] The words are, however, an expression of commonplace wisdom. They constitute a proverb, an adage.[30] Both the participle and the principal verb of this clause are in the third-person singular. The use of the second person applies the words to the audience, but such usage also deprives the adage of its common and universal meaning. Jesus uses the proverb to tell his audience that if they do

28. Specifically, with regard to the terminological and ideological relationship between 1QS 13–4:26 and the Fourth Gospel, Charlesworth comments, "It is difficult to overlook the probability that John was directly influenced by the Rule. These similarities, however, are not close enough nor numerous enough to *prove* that John directly *copied* from 1QS. But on the other hand, they are much too close to conclude that John and 1QS merely evolved out of the same milieu. John may not have *copied* from 1QS but he was strongly influence by the expressions and terminology of 1QS." See James H. Charlesworth, "A Critical Comparison of the Dualism in 1QS 3:13–4:26 and the 'Dualism' Contained in the Gospel of John," in *John and Qumran*, ed. James H. Charlesworth (London: Geoffrey Chapman, 1972), 76–106 (here 103, emphasis original).

29. See, e.g., Francis J. Moloney, *The Gospel of John*, SP 4 (Collegeville, MN: Liturgical Press, 1998), 347, 361.

30. Bultmann calls it a "perfectly typical figurative maxim." See Rudolf Bultmann, *The Gospel of John*, trans. G. R. Beasley Murray, R. W. N. Hoare, and J. K. Riches (Oxford: Basil Blackwell, 1971), 356.

not follow him, they will be lost. They will not know where they are going. They will have lost their way.[31]

Darkness, the adversary of light, represents sin and evil. What, then, can be said about Jesus, the light of the world? Jews and Samaritans alike considered the Torah to be a source of light (see *Testament of Levi* 14:4; *2 Baruch* 54:13–14; *Bar* 4:1–2; *Sir* 24:23; *Memar Marqah* 3.5; 4.2). Jews styled prophets, priests, and teachers as "lights" or "lamps" because they enlightened people by their teaching. This language was used of such luminaries as Moses, Aaron, Deborah, Samuel, Baruch, and Ezra.[32] Pseudo-Philo called Samuel "a light to the peoples" (*LAB* 51.6). Johanan ben Zakkai was called "the lamp of Israel" and "the lamp of the world" (*B. Bar* 28b; *'Abot. R. Nat.* 25).

Given this usage of the image of light, more or less contemporary with the composition of the Fourth Gospel, it is difficult to escape the conclusion that Jesus's self-designation as the light of the world points to—perhaps among other things as well—his role as a teacher, as one who conveyed divine wisdom for the benefit of the disciples. He was one who taught them how to walk in the light rather than in the darkness.

If walking in the darkness has an ethical connotation, the contrasting image of Jesus as the light with which the expression is conjoined in 8:12 has an ethical connotation as well. The follower who walks in his light will not walk in the darkness of sin and evil. To live in relationship with Jesus, to "follow" him, is to live in a way that is antithetical to a life of sin and evil. To follow Jesus is to walk the path of goodness.

THE SHEEP WHO FOLLOW

Rudolf Bultmann once wrote that the Fourth Gospel's use of follow in 8:12, along with its appearance in 10:4–5, 27, is a metaphorical use of the verb.[33] If the metaphorical use of *akoloutheō* in 8:12 has ethical implications, it may well be that the metaphorical use of the verb in 10:4–5, 27, also has an ethical nuance. Indeed, Lazure long

---

31. See 14:6, where Jesus speaks of himself as "the way" (*hē hodos*).

32. See Koester, *Symbolism*, 147nn20–21, for pertinent references.

33. Bultmann, *Gospel of John*, 344n1. Decades later, von Wahlde would write that the verb in this passage is used for being a disciple. See von Wahlde, *Gospel and Letters*, 61.

ago observed that the passages in the tenth chapter of the Gospel that employ "follow" bring out the ethical nuance of the verb.[34]

Jesus speaks of the sheep following the shepherd in his image of the Good Shepherd:

> When he has brought out all his own, he goes ahead of them, and the sheep follow [akolouthei] him because they know his voice. They will not follow [akolouthēsousin] a stranger, but they will run from him, because they do not know the voice of strangers. (10:4–5)

Incorporated into what the evangelist calls a *paroimia*,[35] a "figure of speech," the verbs have a figurative meaning. Jesus depicts a group of sheep walking behind a shepherd whom they have come to know. Commentators may suggest, as some do, that the shepherd would walk in front of the flock because he would have an "assistant" of some sort bringing up the rear, prodding recalcitrant sheep to follow the rest of the flock. That may well be, but the point of the story is that the sheep are following the shepherd.

The picturesque image is often interpreted allegorically. The flock that follows the shepherd symbolizes the church, the new community gathered together by Jesus.[36] Numerous biblical references to Israel as a flock of sheep with God or a human king as its shepherd facilitate this kind of allegorical interpretation. This interpretation merits further discussion, but my interest is more specific: what does it mean for the sheep to follow the shepherd?

The Johannine Jesus's *paroimia* says that the sheep follow the lead of the shepherd because they recognize his voice. Voice recognition in the situation at hand is what motivates the behavior of the sheep. They respond to the voice of the shepherd, whom they know, but they do not respond to the voice of strangers, whom they do not know. Were these "sheep" humans rather than domestic animals, we would say that their behavior is characterized by three elements of an ethical life. The first is discernment. They distinguish between the one whom they follow and those whom they do not follow. This process of discernment is a matter of distinguishing one voice from the voice of several others. Second, the sheep's discernment results in

---

34. See Lazure, *Les valeurs morales*, 59.

35. The Greek word, whose precise meaning has generated the use of much ink, appears in the LXX as a translation of the Hebrew *māšāl*.

36. So, Moloney, *John,* 308–9.

action. Discernment is not forever buried in the psyche. Appropriate action follows the process of discernment. Discernment is translated into action that involves their entire being. Third, the action of the sheep is a matter of following the leader. It is a matter of having an example to follow.

To these key observations one might add two others. First of all, there is a corporate dimension to the activity of the sheep. They are not isolated from one another but act in solidarity with one another.[37] They are together, as it were, establishing the ethos of the flock, recognizing the voice of one to be followed. Second, they act in concert in following their leader even though the shepherd's voice does not specifically indicate where they are going.[38] There is almost a reckless abandon in following the example of him whom they trust.

The discourse of John 10:1–30 is complex. In verses 26–27, the Johannine Jesus returns to the image of the sheep: "but you do not believe, because you do not belong to my sheep. My sheep hear my voice. I know them and they follow me." Jesus continues with, "I will give them eternal life, and they will never perish" (10:28a). With these words, Jesus reveals that the figure of speech in verses 4–5 was really about human beings.

The shepherd of the earlier vignette was not just any run-of-the-mill shepherd but Jesus himself as he revealed in another significant *Egō eimi* saying, "I am the good shepherd" (*egō eimi ho poimēn ho kalos*, 10:11a). The significance of Jesus's self-identification as the shepherd of the flock continues in 10:25–27. Belief in Jesus is the reality that enables people to be members of the flock that follows him. Intimacy exists between the followers and the shepherd. The shepherd knows his sheep, not simply in a (re)cognitional sense but also in an experiential sense.

John 10:28 adds to the Johannine author's reflections on following Jesus that Jesus will confer the gift of eternal life (*zōēn aiōnion*) on those who follow him. Eternal life is given as a gift (*didōmi*). Eternal life is not earned by living an ethical life, symbolized by the image of

---

37. Note the six plurals in this brace of verses: "all his own" (*ta idia panta*), "them" (*autōn*), "sheep" (*probata*), "know" (*oidasin*), "follow" (*akolouthēsousin*), "run from" (*pheuxontai*), and "know" (*oidasin*).

38. This element of the sheep's behavior deserves to be underscored. All too often the idea that the Fourth Gospel is lacking in ethical concern is predicated on the fact that the Fourth Gospel does not speak of specific behaviors, such as those encouraged in the Sermon on the Mount or those discouraged in the various catalogs of vices in the NT.

following Jesus; it is a gift. Following Jesus has its own intrinsic value; it does not need to be valorized by some external goal.

TO FOLLOW IS TO SERVE

In the Fourth Gospel, Jesus's first words about following him were addressed to Philip. As the evangelist's story about Jesus continues to unfold, the writer depicts a short scene in which a group of Greeks, gentiles in Jerusalem for the Passover festival, come to Philip, informing him about their desire to "see" Jesus (12:20–22).[39] Philip goes to get Andrew. Together, they go to Jesus and tell him about this strange request. Jesus responds to the news with a formal discourse which begins, "Very truly, I tell you."[40] The discourse appears to be addressed not only to Philip and Andrew but also to the group of Greeks.

Jesus begins by speaking about his forthcoming martyrdom and the fate of those who follow him, in words that are remarkably similar to logia found in the Synoptic sayings source.[41] Then, continuing to speak in the third-person singular, Jesus speaks more generally as he says: "Whoever serves me [emoi . . . diakonē] must follow me [emoi akoloutheitō], and where I am there will my servant [ho diakonos ho emos] be also. Who serves me [emoi diakonē], the Father will honor" (12:26).

These words do not directly imply suffering and martyrdom, but they would surely have served as a source of strength and consolation for a Johannine community that was facing opposition and perhaps martyrdom as the first century CE was coming to its close. The ultimate lot of this Johannine community would be similar to that of Jesus. Its members will be with Jesus. Their serving and following Jesus will culminate in their being with him and being honored by the Father. "There is a hint here," writes Moloney, "of the disciples' being swept up into the oneness that unites the Father and the Son."[42]

---

39. On the significance of the use of the verb *idein*, see Moloney, *John*, 359.

40. *Amēn, amēn, legō hymin*, "Amen, Amen, I say to you" (author's translation). See 5:19, 24, 25; 6:6, 32, 47, 53; 8:34, 51, 58; 10:1, 7; 13:16, 20, 21; 14:12; 16:20, 23. Also see 3:5, 11; 13:38; 21:18, where the second-person pronoun is in the singular.

41. Q 9:24 (Luke 9:24 // Matt 16:24–25). See also the discussion of the logion's relationship with the Synoptic tradition in J. Ramsey Michaels, *The Gospel of John*, NICNT (Grand Rapids: Eerdmans, 2012), 689–91.

42. Moloney, *John*, 359.

The Fourth Gospel does not often speak about service. To be sure there were servants working the wedding feast of Cana (2:5, 9) and Martha served a dinner after Lazarus had been raised from the dead (12:2), but this is the only time that the Johannine Jesus speaks about service, and the service is to him. Since service appears only once in the Fourth Gospel, the reader must ask what service to Jesus really means. Ernst Haenchen speaks of it as "a service, that must be carried out in selflessness and self-denial."[43] For J. Ramsey Michaels, "the unspoken implication is that 'serving' Jesus involves imitating his behavior, doing what he did by serving others, or each other. This will become explicit later on, when Jesus speaks privately to all his disciples about what discipleship means."[44]

Michaels's observation is apropos. What does Philip, the one found by Jesus (1:43), do after he has been told to "follow me"? He goes and finds Nathanael (1:45). John 6 describes a large crowd (*ochlos polys*, 6:2) following Jesus to the other side of the Sea of Galilee. Jesus appears to be concerned about this vast crowd becoming hungry. Jesus knew what he was going to do (6:6) but nonetheless draws Philip into his concern by asking him, "Where are we to buy bread for these people to eat?" (6:5). Philip is overwhelmed by the magnitude of the problem and replies with a non-answer, "Six months' wages would not buy enough bread for each of them to get a little" (6:7).[45]

Andrew, one of the first to follow Jesus (1:40), then enters into the picture. Although the number of hungry people is quite large and Andrew, too, is overwhelmed by the magnitude of the problem, he introduces a boy with five barley loaves and two fish (6:9a).[46] A few loaves and a couple of fish are not much. Together they constitute an utterly inadequate amount of food to be able to feed a large crowd. Nonetheless, they are a beginning. And then Jesus proceeds to feed the five thousand (6:10).

Details of the feeding are beyond the particular interest of this study. What is of interest are two considerations. The first is that two

43. Ernst Haenchen, *John 2: A Commentary on the Gospel of John Chapters 7–21*, trans. Robert W. Funk, ed. Robert W. Funk and Ulrich Busse, Hermeneia (Philadelphia: Fortress Press, 1984), 92.

44. To which Michaels adds, "See, for example, 13:14–15, 34–35, 15:12 (*John*, 692).

45. The Greek is *diakosiōn dēnariōn*, literally, "two hundred denarii." Since the denarius was the average worker's daily wage, two hundred denarii would represent more than half a year's wages for the average Galilean.

46. See 6:9b, "But what are they [the five loaves and two fish] among so many people?"

of Jesus's first disciples share Jesus's concern for the hungry crowd. The second is that, in different ways, they assist Jesus—"serve him" in the idiom of 12:36—in assuaging the hunger of the crowd. Not only were they servants to Jesus, but they also served those in need to whom Jesus ministered. Michaels appears to have been spot on in writing that "'serving' Jesus involves imitating his behavior, doing what he did by serving others, or each other."[47]

That this is so becomes explicit in the foot washing scene of John 13:1–7. In this scene, Jesus's disciples are students (*mathētai*) who learn a lesson from their teacher. The evangelist describes Jesus's lesson as follows:

> You call me Teacher and Lord—and you are right, for that is what I am. So if I, your Lord and Teacher, have washed your feet, you also ought to wash one another's feet. For I have set you an example, that you also should do as I have done to you. (13:13–15)

The vocabulary the evangelist uses to describe Jesus in this passage is of utmost importance in the common quest of this project, the probing of the ethical insights of the Fourth Gospel.

Jesus is "Teacher" (*didaskalos*).[48] He teaches by the example (*hypodeigma*) that he gives.[49] The example that Jesus gives at this critical moment in his life extends beyond the simple, servant-like gesture of foot washing.[50] The "example" must be seen broadly.[51] It is the example of service to others. That is the lesson that the "disciples" are to learn from their Teacher. Jesus is also "Lord" (*kyrios*). He has the authority to command his servants, to tell them what to do. And so

---

47. Michaels, *John*, 692.

48. See Raymond F. Collins, "'You Call Me Teacher and Lord—and You Are Right. For That Is What I Am' (John 13:13)," in *Studies in the Gospel of John and Its Christology: Festschrift Gilbert Van Belle*, ed. Joseph Verheyden et al., BETL 265 (Leuven: Peeters, 2014), 327–48.

49. A contemporary reader of the Fourth Gospel should recall not only the importance of "example" in Hellenistic rhetoric but also the great Greek philosophers Socrates, Plato, and Aristotle, who served as models and examples for their followers. Aristotle founded the Peripatetic school, the group of disciples who "walked with" their teacher.

50. Keener writes, "One who sought to wash another's feet normally took the posture of a servant or dependent. . . . In both early Jewish and Greco-Roman texts, foot washing frequently connotes servitude." See Craig S. Keener, *The Gospel of John: A Commentary* (Peabody, MA: Hendrickson, 2003), 2:904.

51. See Michaels, *John*, 735: "Nor should it be forgotten that the Gospel writer views Jesus as an example to his disciples on a rather wide front not just with reverence to the washing of feet."

he does: "you also ought [*opheilete*] . . . you also should do [*hymeis poiēte*]."⁵²

Arguably the evangelist has made use of a chiasm in 12:13–35 to clarify the meaning of the titles "Teacher" and "Lord."⁵³ Jesus is Teacher (and Lord) because he has given his disciples an example (13:13, 15). He is Lord (and Teacher) because he has told them what to do (13:14a, b).

"FOLLOW ME" IN THE FUTURE, THE PRESENT, AND THE FUTURE

During the meal described in John 13, Simon Peter, perhaps unwittingly, allows Jesus to speak about following him:

> Simon Peter said to him [Jesus], "Lord, where are you going?" Jesus answered, "Where I am going you cannot follow [*akolouthēsai*] me now; but you will follow afterward [*akolouthēseis de hysteron*]." Peter said to him, "Lord why can I not follow [*akolouthēsai*] you now?" (13:36–37a)

Three times this short dialogue uses the verb *akoloutheō* in reference to following Jesus, but it leaves Simon Peter and the contemporary reader in a state of abeyance as to what following Jesus means. To prove his loyalty and his readiness to "follow" Jesus, the impetuous Peter blurts out, "I will lay down my life for you" (13:37b). This intervention signals a turn in the dialogue. The discussion focuses on Peter's loyalty and readiness. Jesus responds, "Will you lay down your life for me? Very truly, I tell you, before the cock crows, you will have denied me three times" (13:38). This harsh reality check leaves Peter—and the reader/listener—hanging as to what Jesus means when he speaks about following him later. What is this mysterious "later" (*hysteron*)?

The answer is given in the evangelist's epilogue, John 21. Commentators almost unanimously interpret this chapter as the rehabilitation of Simon Peter. Jesus had said that Simon Peter would deny him three times (*tris*). Peter, the would-be follower, did so in grand style—to a female gatekeeper, to a group of people warming themselves around a charcoal fire, and to a relative of Malchus whose

---

52. Note the emphatic *hymeis*. The command is formally directed to the group of disciples.
53. Note the reversal of the sequence of the two titles in 13:14.

right ear Peter had impetuously severed (18:17, 25, 27). In John 21, with another charcoal fire nearby (21:9), Jesus interrogates Simon Peter about his love for him, not once, not twice, but three times (21:15–17). To Peter's thrice-repeated profession of love for Jesus, Jesus responds three times with a command that Peter take care of the flock. Jesus's second command is pertinent to my present inquiry. Jesus says to Peter, "Tend my sheep" (*poimaine ta probata mou*, 21:16c). With these words the resurrected Jesus entrusts responsibility for shepherding Jesus's flock to Peter. Peter is to become the shepherd in Jesus's stead.

The dialogue between the risen one and the rehabilitated one does not stop in 21:17. It begins again in verse 18, with a new solemn utterance that begins, "Very truly, I tell you."[54] Jesus's words are addressed directly to Simon Peter. The solemnity of the formal address recalls the solemnity of Jesus's rejoinder to Peter in 13:38, "Will you lay down your life for me? Very truly, I tell you, before the cock crows, you will have denied me three times." The discourse that follows the "Very truly, I tell you" of 21:18 focuses on Peter's death. Peter does not take the initiative in laying down his life; others will take him where he would rather not go (see 10:11, 15, 17–18).

Jesus sums up this little discourse on Peter's death with "follow me" (*akolouthei moi*, 21:19). The words echo those addressed to Philip by Jesus toward the beginning of the evangelist's narrative (see 1:43), but the words are uttered by a Jesus who has entered into a new phase of his existence. He has laid down his life and taken it up again. Jesus's words to Peter do not entail the latter's walking the paths of Palestine, following along after Jesus. Rather they have a figurative meaning;[55] they suggest that Peter, like Jesus, will die the martyr's death.[56] "The invitation," says Jo-Ann Brant, "is to follow a path to death."[57] Following that path lies in the future.

The evangelist's story is not over until it is over. What about now? What about the interim between Peter's death in the future and the present that begins with Jesus's third appearance to his disciples (see 21:14)? The final episode in the evangelist's story answers this question (21:20–23). The scene begins with Peter turning and seeing the

---

54. *Amēn, amēn, legō soi*, "Amen, Amen, I say to you" (author's translation). See 12:24; 13:38.

55. See Raymond E. Brown, *The Gospel according to John XIII–XXI*, AB 29a (Garden City, NY: Doubleday, 1970), 1108.

56. See Collins, *These Things*, 135; von Wahlde, *John*, 2, 61.

57. Brant, *John*, 285.

Beloved Disciple, following (*akolouthounta*) Jesus and himself.[58] Peter wants to know what's up. He asks Jesus, "what about him?" (21:21). Jesus tells Peter to mind his own business. The Beloved Disciple is going to be around for a while. In the meantime, Peter's business is to follow Jesus. The final words spoken by the Johannine Jesus are addressed to Peter, to whom Jesus says, "Follow me," (*akolouthei moi*).[59] Peter must follow the example of the shepherd by taking care of the flock.

To follow Jesus is to walk the path of discipleship. It is to have the attitude of Jesus and to the things that he does, even when these things are not reinforced with a specific command. What Jesus says to Peter in 21:22 projects the command from Jesus lifetime into the future to be lived by his disciples, his followers until the end.

THE ETHICAL PARADIGM

This overview of the Fourth Gospel's motif of following Jesus has revealed that following Jesus is not a theme unrelated to ethics. The length of the present essay does not allow for an in-depth analysis of the ethical nuances of following Jesus, but some points come quickly to the fore. Among them are the following:

1. To follow Jesus is to avoid the manifold forms of evil symbolized by the paths of darkness.

2. To follow Jesus is to hear his voice with discernment and to accept him as Teacher and Lord, the source of a new way of life.

3. To follow Jesus is to join his flock and adopt its ethos.[60]

4. To follow Jesus is to serve him and others.

5. To follow Jesus implies that one is drawn into Jesus's concern to feed the hungry—an ethical imperative of Jesus's day and ours.

---

58. The mundane use of "follow" in 21:20a stands in sharp contrast to the more theological use of the verb in vv. 19 and 22.

59. Verse 21c is an instance of indirect discourse, the evangelist's interpretation of what his main character, Jesus, had said to the Beloved Disciple.

60. Even in English, "ethical" is cognate with "ethos." "Ethos" connotes the standards or norms of a group. It requires another level of ethical discourse to determine whether these standards are ultimately "ethical."

More can be written about the singular Johannine ethical paradigm constituted by "Follow me." These five points are a good start. Others can follow.

PART II

Implied Ethics in the Johannine Literature

4.

The Creation Ethics of the Gospel of John

R. ALAN CULPEPPER

The Gospel of John is unique among the Gospels in that it opens with a cosmic Prologue that introduces Jesus as the incarnation of the Logos, through whom the world was created. This essay[1] explores the implications of this introduction for the ethics of the Gospel, as a contribution to recent narrative-critical study of the Gospel's "implied ethics." I will suggest that John is rooted in Jewish tradition that grounded ethics both in creation and in covenant, especially the Sinai covenant.

Obviously, there is more here than I can excavate in one essay, so it will necessarily be a fast tour, programmatic and suggestive for further exploration. As a point of departure, we may pose the question, What are the implications of starting the story of Jesus with the role of the Logos (Word) in creation? Our plan will be to assess briefly (1) the new approach to John's ethics, (2) the role of the Prologue as introductory exposition, (3) creation in Jewish tradition, (4) creation ethics and covenant ethics in Judaism, (5) the sacredness of human life in Jewish tradition, (6) the theme of life in John as an ethical principle, (7) John's ethic of divine love and its fulfillment, and (8) implications of creation ethics.

1. I wish to express my gratitude to Jan G. van der Watt and the Radboud University Nijmegen for the invitation to deliver the Radboud Prestige Lectures in April 2013. This essay originated in those lectures.

THE NEW APPROACH TO JOHN'S ETHICS

In his groundbreaking work on New Testament ethics, Richard Hays contended that the ethical significance of the New Testament narratives cannot be restricted to their didactic content. Moral instruction is communicated not only in *didachē* (teaching) but also in

> the stories, symbols, social structures, and practices that shape the community's *ethos*. A text such as the Gospel of John, for example, may have relatively little explicit teaching, but its story of a "man from heaven" . . . is fraught with ethical implications for the community that accepts the message and finds itself rejected by the world.[2]

Following Hays, several Johannine scholars have applied this insight to the Gospel of John. For example, Johannes Nissen shifts the focus from individual ethics to the community ethos and defines the early Christian communities as communities of character. Identity shapes action, being shapes seeing: "*Who we are* and *who we are becoming* as a result of the faith we hold determines in large part *what we see*."[3] Following this same line of thought, Richard A. Burridge sought to broaden the basis of New Testament ethics from its explicit instructions to its responses to the life and example of Jesus. Resisting the limitation of Johannine ethics to the new command, Burridge insists, consistent with his "principal argument" that "the full picture of what love means in the Fourth Gospel can be found only in its portrait of Jesus."[4]

The papers from a conference held at Nijmegen in 2009, collected in a volume appropriately titled *Rethinking the Ethics of John*, took up the challenge of interpreting John's implicit, narrative ethics.[5] In the introductory essays, Michael Labahn and Ruben Zimmermann

---

2. Richard B. Hays, *The Moral Vision of the New Testament: A Contemporary Introduction to New Testament Ethics* (San Francisco: HarperSanFrancisco, 1996), 4.

3. Johannes Nissen, "Community and Ethics in the Gospel of John," in *New Readings in John: Literary and Theological Perspectives, Essays from the Scandinavian Conference on the Fourth Gospel in Århus 1997*, ed. Johannes Nissen and Sigfred Pedersen, JSNTSup 182 (Sheffield: Sheffield Academic, 1999), 200; citing Bruce C. Birch and Larry L. Rasmussen, *The Bible and Ethics in the Christian Life* (Minneapolis: Augsburg Publishing House, 1976), 88–89.

4. Richard A. Burridge, *Imitating Jesus: An Inclusive Approach to New Testament Ethics* (Grand Rapids: Eerdmans, 2007), 327.

5. Jan G. van der Watt and Ruben Zimmermann, eds., *Rethinking the Ethics of John: "Implicit Ethics" in the Johannine Writings*, Kontexte und Normen neutestamentliche Ethik/Contexts and Norms of New Testament Ethics 3, WUNT 291 (Tübingen: Mohr Siebeck, 2012).

respond to the widely held view that in contrast to the Synoptic Gospels John offers no instruction in ethics because it does not contain explicit injunctions and prohibitions, or teachings on ethical issues, and does not present Jesus as a model to be imitated.[6] For example, there is no Sermon on the Mount in John, none of the parables we find in the other Gospels, nor any of the lists of virtues and vices we find in the rest of the New Testament. This does not mean that the Gospel of John has no ethical teachings. Michael Labahn contends that "the quest for a Johannine ethic cannot be limited to direct moral instructions such as the 'new commandment,' but must also consider the whole story and its underlying value system, which together lead the reader toward certain actions that are in accordance with the text's ideas."[7] Instead of presenting the traditional forms of ethical instruction, the Gospel draws the reader into a narrative world in which Jesus is characterized as a revealer sent from above to make known God's revelation for humanity—a revelation that has inescapable implications for ethics.

Rather than instructions related to various typical ethical situations, the Johannine Jesus gives the disciples an encompassing new commandment: "Love one another as I have loved you" (John 13:34–35; 15:12, 17). More than a code of specific instructions that his disciples should follow, Jesus lays down a principle that pervades the ethics of Johannine Christians. "Love one another" is a comprehensive, challenging basis for ethics. Of course, the love command occurs in other forms in Jewish and Christian teachings, other religious traditions, and now in secular humanism also. On the other hand, the injunction to "love one another *as* [*kathōs*] *I have loved you*" ties the love command to history, to the person of Jesus, and to the memory of his ministry. In John, moreover, it ties the love command to the incarnation and embeds it within the narrative of the Gospel. As John says in the Prologue, "the word became flesh and lived among us, and we have seen his glory, the glory as of a father's only son, full of grace and truth" (1:14).[8] This means, at a minimum, that when we seek to

6. See, e.g., Wayne A. Meeks, "The Ethics of the Fourth Evangelist," in *Exploring the Gospel of John: In Honor of D. Moody Smith*, ed. R. Alan Culpepper and C. Clifton Black (Louisville: Westminster John Knox, 1996), 317–26, esp. 318. Among others who take a similar view Burridge (*Imitating Jesus*, 291–92) cites Brian Blount, Wolfgang Schrage, and Frank J. Matera.

7. Michael Labahn, "'It's Only Love'—Is That All? Limits and Potentials of Johannine 'Ethics'—A Critical Evaluation of Research," in van der Watt and Zimmerman, *Rethinking the Ethics of John*, 16.

8. English translations follow the NRSV.

understand the meaning of the new command we are driven to the record of Jesus's ministry in the rest of the Gospel. There is a christo-logical context that defines and animates the ethics of this Gospel.

In addition, we should not miss the object or focus of the com-mand: "love *one another* as I have loved you." In contrast to the other Gospels and the love command in the Sermon on the Mount, the Johannine Jesus does not command love of one's enemy, or even one's neighbor. Just to sharpen this point for a moment, consider the following verses from Matthew:

> You have heard that it was said, "You shall love your neighbor and hate your enemy." But I say to you, Love your enemies and pray for those who persecute you. . . . For if you love those who love you, what reward do you have? Do not even the tax collectors do the same? (Matt 5:43–44, 46)

Similarly, in Luke Jesus responds to the lawyer's question, "And who is my neighbor?" (Luke 10:29) with the parable of the good Samari-tan. When set beside these texts, the new command in John appears to be limited, narrower, even sectarian.[9] Who is meant by "one another," and if it has the narrower meaning of fellow disciples rather than other human beings, as the words that follow suggest, namely, "By this everyone will know that you are my disciples, if you have love for one another" (13:35), does this mean that Jesus's disciples are to love only other disciples? The question already takes us into the world of the Fourth Gospel and to the Gospel as a whole.

Francis J. Moloney has recently given us a fresh reading of the nar-rative development of the theology of the Gospel, focusing on its portrayal of God's love.[10] Three facets of his argument reorient dis-cussion of the theme of love in John. First, Moloney argues that a full understanding of this theme requires attention not only to what Jesus *says* about love but also to what he *does*. Second, he interprets Jesus's actions as revelatory of what God does in and through his Son, cul-minating in Jesus's death. And third, Moloney connects Jesus's death, his "hour," to the theme of love. Jesus's mission, to complete or "per-fect" God's work (4:34; 5:36), reveals a God whose love for the world

9. Meeks, "Ethics of the Fourth Evangelist," 324; Robert H. Gundry, *Jesus the Word according to John the Sectarian: A Paleofundamentalist Manifesto for Contemporary Evangelicalism, Especially Its Elites, in North America* (Grand Rapids: Eerdmans, 2002), esp. 57–62.

10. Francis J. Moloney, *Love in the Gospel of John: An Exegetical, Theological, and Literary Study* (Grand Rapids: Baker Academic, 2013).

(3:16) has no limits. Moloney also rejects the sectarian reading of John's love ethic that has been debated since its forceful articulation by Ernst Käsemann and Wayne Meeks.[11] On the contrary, "Jesus's prayer that disciples be swept into the love that exists between the Father and the Son (17:26) is a prayer for the world that God loved so much that he sent his only Son (3:16–17)."[12]

Parenthetically, we may note that as this survey of recent scholarship indicates, it appears that we have come to a point that Dietrich Bonhoeffer anticipated in his Christology and ethics. He insisted:

> Those who wish even to focus on the problem of a Christian ethic are faced with an outrageous demand—from the outset they must give up, as inappropriate to this topic, the very two questions that led them to deal with the ethical problem: "How can I be good?" and "How can I do something good?" Instead they must seek the wholly other, completely different question: "What is the will of God?"[13]

Bonhoeffer's *Ethics* is not just theocentric; it is based on the model of Jesus Christ and requires formation in the church. These aspects of his *Ethics* are of course also serviceable in a study of John's ethics. Like Bonhoeffer we will begin with the affirmation that for religious, and in our context Christian, ethics, the discourse proceeds from an understanding of God's purpose for humanity. In the Gospel of John, the Prologue contains its initial statement on God's initiatives and will for humankind.

THE ROLE OF THE PROLOGUE AS
INTRODUCTORY EXPOSITION

The Gospel of John is distinctive among the Gospels in that it opens with an elaborate, initially poetic Prologue (1:1–18) that introduces the narrative that follows. The Prologue supplies what Meir Sternberg called chronological, preliminary, concentrated exposition.[14] For our present purposes, we may make the following observations

11. Ernst Käsemann, *The Testament of Jesus: A Study of the Gospel of John in the Light of Chapter 17*, trans. Gerhard Krodel (Philadelphia: Fortress Press, 1968); Wayne A. Meeks, "The Man from Heaven in Johannine Sectarianism," *JBL* 91 (1972): 44–72.

12. Moloney, *Love in the Gospel of John*, 208–9.

13. Dietrich Bonhoeffer, *Ethics*, Dietrich Bonhoeffer Works 6 (Minneapolis: Fortress Press, 2008), 47.

14. Meir Sternberg, *Expositional Modes and Temporal Ordering in Fiction* (Baltimore: Johns

about ways in which the Prologue introduces aspects of the Gospel that have implications for its ethics.

A cursory reading of the Prologue reveals that it speaks to six specific moments of divine initiative:

1. The work of creation through the Logos (v. 3)

2. The giving of the law through Moses (v. 17)

3. The sending of John the Baptist (vv. 6–8, 15)

4. The coming of the light (v. 9) / the incarnation of the Logos (v. 14)

5. The birth of the children of God (vv. 12–13)

6. The revelation of the Father (v. 18)

I will focus on the first of these, and specifically the implications of the role of the Logos in creation for Johannine ethics.[15] Four salient observations inform our discussion:

1. Raymond Brown saw that "the fact that the *Word* creates means that creation is an act of revelation."[16]

2. Marianne Meye Thompson makes the astute observation that "although there are no further references in John to God's creation of the world through the Logos, the emphasis on God's gift of life through the agency of Jesus—the Word incarnate, Wisdom incarnate—shows the unity of the life-giving work of God and Jesus."[17]

3. Jonathan Draper has argued that the Prologue images the Logos as the one who came down on Sinai and delivered the law to Moses: "John understands that it was Jesus who is the YHWH

Hopkins University Press, 1978), 1, 98–99. Cf. R. Alan Culpepper, *Anatomy of the Fourth Gospel* (Philadelphia: Fortress Press, 1983), 18–19.

15. See R. Alan Culpepper, "The Prologue as Theological Prolegomenon to the Gospel of John," in *The Prologue of the Gospel of John: Its Literary, Theological, and Philosophical Contexts; Papers Read at the Colloquium Ioanneum 2013*, ed. Jan G. van der Watt, R. Alan Culpepper, and Udo Schnelle, WUNT 359 (Tübingen: Mohr Siebeck, 2016), 3–26, which contains a fuller version of some of the material presented here.

16. Raymond E. Brown, *The Gospel according to John I–XII*, AB 29 (Garden City, NY: Doubleday, 1966), 25.

17. Marianne Meye Thompson, *The God of the Gospel of John* (Grand Rapids: Eerdmans, 2001), 136.

figure who comes down on Sinai. . . . It is Jesus as the pre-exis-
tent creative Word . . . which continues to work sustaining creation even as the Father works. Moses saw Jesus and wrote of
him."[18]

4. Jan van der Watt has observed that "the Jewish law and tradition
    seem to be the moral bedrock of the value system in the Gospel,"
    and that every Decalogue law is referenced in the Gospel of
    John. He summarizes his argument with the claim that "the
    underlying value system in this Gospel could plausibly be linked
    to the Jewish law and tradition that goes back to, or at least is
    based on, the Decalogue."[19]

If this line of interpretation is correct, the Prologue claims that both
creation and the law came through the Logos. So, for John the Logos
is the source of both of the bases of Jewish ethical tradition: creation
and covenant. The two are intertwined both in Jewish tradition and
in Johannine theology, which I will survey briefly in the following
paragraphs.

Daniel Boyarin has advanced the study of the Prologue by arguing
that Logos theology was a common element in first-century Jewish
theology, as is evident not only in Philo but also in the references to
the Memra in the targumim, where the Memra "is not a mere name,
but an actual divine entity, or mediator," whose functions are much
the same as those of the Logos in John.[20] Boyarin takes the Prologue
as a chronological narrative, perhaps drawn from a homily on the
beginning of Genesis.[21] The first five verses are a midrash on Genesis 1:1–5, informed by the Sophia/Wisdom tradition.[22] The following
thirteen verses serve as a bridge between this midrash on the role of

18. Jonathan A. Draper, "'If Those to Whom the W/word of God Came Were Called
Gods'—Logos, Wisdom and Prophecy, and John 10:22–30," *HvTSt* 71, no. 1 (2015):
http://dx.doi.org/10.4102/hts.v71i1.2905.

19. Jan G. van der Watt, "Ethics and Ethos in the Gospel according to John," *ZNW* 97
(2006): 153–55. Cf. Jey J. Kanagaraj, "The Implied Ethics of the Fourth Gospel: A Reinterpretation of the Decalogue," *TynBul* 52 (2001): 33–60; and Ruben Zimmermann, "Is There Ethics
in the Gospel of John? Challenging an Outdated Consensus," in van der Watt and Zimmerman, *Rethinking the Ethics of John*, 55.

20. Daniel Boyarin, "The Gospel of the *Memra*: Jewish Binitarianism and the Prologue to
John," *HTR* 94 (2001): 243–84 (here 255).

21. Ibid., 264, 267.

22. Ibid., 279. See also Peder Borgen, "Observations on the Targumic Character of the Prologue of John," *NTS* 16 (1970): 288–95; and Borgen, "Logos Was the True Light: Contributions to the Interpretation of the Prologue of John," *NovT* 14 (1972): 115–30.

the Logos in creation and the christological story that follows in the rest of the Gospel. The incarnation does not occur in this chronological narrative until verse 14. Accordingly, verses 6–13 describe the rejection of the *Logos Asarkos*, thus providing a rationale for the incarnation in verse 14. A further implication of this line of interpretation is that "'the law given through Moses' represents precisely the earlier attempt of the Logos to enter the world as adumbrated in vv. 12 and 13."[23]

The theme of creation in John has produced a burst of recent literature, with the most significant work perhaps being written by Carlos Raúl Soza Siliezar.[24] The major contribution of this dissertation is its methodological rigor. The author establishes a clear methodology for evaluating proposed creation imagery in the Gospel, applies it to the most significant links that have been proposed between the Gospel and Genesis 1–2, and then offers suggestions regarding the function of creation imagery in its specific contexts in John and in the Gospel as a whole. By "creation imagery" Siliezar designates "direct assertions about the creation of the world that are not dependent upon a particular OT text" and instances where John may have used terms, images, or concepts from biblical traditions about creation.[25] John evokes the Genesis account of creation in John 1:1–5 by means of the phrase *en archē* (in the beginning), the reference to *ho logos* (the Word), which appears elsewhere in creation discourse, and by the combination of *ginomai* (to become) and *pas* (everything/all). Siliezar also finds that in various references to Jesus's works (esp. 4:34—being sent to "finish his work"; 5:36—completing works and the Sabbath; and 10:32—performing "good works"), John makes use of creation

23. Boyarin, "Gospel of the *Memra*," 280. Cf. Draper's argument cited above (n. 17).

24. Carlos Raúl Soza Siliezar, *Creation Imagery in the Gospel of John*, LNTS 546 (London: Bloomsbury, 2015). Cf. my review of Siliezar (abbreviated here) in *RBL*, August 2016, https://www.bookreviews.org/pdf/10550_11722.pdf. See also Anthony M. Moore, *Signs of Salvation: The Theme of Creation in John's Gospel* (Cambridge: James Clarke, 2013); Mary L. Coloe, "The Structure of the Johannine Prologue and Genesis 1," *ABR* 45 (1997): 40–55; Coloe, "Theological Reflections on Creation in the Gospel of John," *Pacifica* 24 (2011): 1–12; Jan A. du Rand, "The Creation Motif in the Fourth Gospel: Perspectives on Its Narratological Function within a Judaistic Background," in *Theology and Christology in the Fourth Gospel*, ed. Gilbert van Belle, Jan G. van der Watt, and P. Maritz, BETL 184 (Leuven: Leuven University Press, 2005), 21–46; Masanobu Endo, *Creation and Christology: A Study on the Johannine Prologue in the Light of Early Jewish Creation Accounts*, WUNT 2/149 (Tübingen: Mohr Siebeck, 2002); and John Painter, "Earth Made Whole: John's Rereading of Genesis," in *Word, Theology, and Community in John*, ed. John Painter, R. Alan Culpepper, and Fernando F. Segovia (St. Louis: Chalice, 2002), 65–84.

25. Siliezar, *Creation Imagery*, 12.

imagery. Two stories in particular employ creation imagery: Jesus's walking on the water and his healing of the man born blind. John 6:19 echoes Job 9:8 LXX, where God alone walks on the sea. Surprisingly, Siliezar does not appeal to Psalm 77:16–19, a hymn praising God for his work in creation:

Your way was through the sea,
your path, through the mighty waters;
yet your footprints were unseen. (Ps 77:19)

In context, Jesus's walking on the water in John 6 elevates him over Moses. Although there is no direct reference to Genesis 2:7 in John 9:6, Jesus's distinctive act in making mud—the only time Jesus does so in the four Gospels—resonates with the broader background in which "mud" (*pēlos*) is used in creation contexts (Isa 64:7 LXX and Job 10:9 LXX). Similarly, John's description of Jesus breathing on the disciples in John 20:22 echoes Genesis 2:7, a verse that was cited widely in Jewish texts. The link between the two further supports the ideas introduced in the Prologue and earlier in the Gospel. As a result, "the mission of the disciples should be regarded as universal in scope."[26] Siliezar concludes from this rigorous analysis of creation elements in John that the Gospel makes limited use of creation imagery at strategic points in the Gospel and that they function to advance the Christology of the Gospel in three ways. (1) John uses the creation imagery to portray Jesus in close relationship to the Father. (2) John uses this imagery to assert the universal significance of Jesus and his message and set him apart from John the Baptist and Moses. And (3) the creation imagery links past, present, and future, suggesting that Jesus is both the agent of creation and the agent of salvation and revelation.

An example of the affinity between John and Jewish tradition can be seen in a profound reflection on God's love attributed to Rabbi Akiba which affirms that God's love for Israel is manifest in that humankind was created in the image of God, Israelites were called "children of God," and Israel was given the Torah, "the precious instrument by which the world was created." Furthermore, God's love is even greater because each of these gifts was revealed to Israel.

He [Akiba] used to say: Beloved is man for he was created in the image [of God]; still greater was the love in that it was made known to him

---

26. Ibid., 173.

that he was created in the image of God, as it is written, *For in the image of God made he man* [Gen 9:6]. Beloved are Israel for they were called children of God; still greater was the love in that it was made known to them that they were called children of God, as it is written, *Ye are the children of the Lord your God* [Deut 14:1]. Beloved are Israel, for to them was given the precious instrument; still greater was the love, in that it was made known to them that to them was given the precious instrument by which the world was created (m. 'Abot 3:15)[27]

Strikingly, the same elements are intertwined in John, where it is the Logos (not the law) through which the world was created. The law was given to Moses, but the Law and the Prophets, and indeed Moses himself, bear witness to Jesus. Moreover, God's love is manifested in the sending of his Son (John 3:16), who confers on those who receive him the status "children of God" (1:12; 11:52). John has therefore interpreted three fundamental principles of Israel's relationship to God and reminted them in a distinctly parallel but thoroughly christological fashion.

Sherri Brown has shown that the theme of God's covenant with creation extends through the entire Gospel.[28] Brown traces the various covenants from the creation through the covenants with Noah, Abraham, Moses, and David, and the calls for covenant renewal in Joshua 24, the Prophets, and Ezra and Nehemiah. From this overview she defines the five characteristics of the Old Testament covenant relationship: (1) chosenness, (2) covenant promises, (3) covenantal obedience in action ("the corollary human response"), (4) the abiding presence of God, and, the ultimate purpose, (5) the knowledge of God—making God known in creation.[29] Seen in this light, the incarnation is an extension of the work of the Logos in both creation and the giving of the Torah: "The giving of the gift of the Law was God's covenantal activity at Sinai. The incarnation of the Word that is full of the gift which is truth is God's covenantal activity in Jesus."[30] The body of the Gospel then narrates "the *how* of the covenantal claim that the prologue introduces."[31]

27. Herbert Danby, trans., *The Mishnah* (London: Oxford University Press, 1933), 452.

28. Sherri Brown, *Gift upon Gift: Covenant through Word in the Gospel of John*, Princeton Theological Monograph Series (Eugene, OR: Pickwick, 2010), 1. See also Rekha Chennattu, *Johannine Discipleship as Covenant Relationship* (Peabody, MA: Hendrickson, 2006).

29. Brown, *Gift upon Gift*, 64–67.

30. Ibid., 94.

31. Ibid., 95.

The relationship between wisdom, creation, covenant, and Torah in Jewish tradition is widely regarded as the most illuminating context for understanding the roots of the Prologue in Judaism, so I will explore it briefly in the next section.[32]

CREATION IN JEWISH TRADITION

Well before the first century, Jewish sages began to explore the theological and ethical significance of creation. Martin Scott, in *Sophia and the Johannine Jesus*, has observed that the theme of life, "very much a creation theme, is also rooted firmly in the Sophia traditions to which John surely alludes at this point."[33] The sages connected creation with wisdom, ethical instruction, and ultimately the law. This is familiar material, so I will be brief. In Proverbs 8 Wisdom is personified and speaks in the first person, describing how she was the first of God's acts before anything else was created, and then how she was beside the Lord "like a master worker" (Prov 8:30). Immediately, Lady Wisdom goes on to say,

Happy are those who keep my ways.
Hear instruction and be wise,
    and do not neglect it. (Prov 8:32–33)

Wisdom connects creation with ethical instruction: both derive from Wisdom.

Similarly, Job 28:25–28 connects creation and wisdom teaching. Sirach, the wisdom teacher of the second century BCE, opens with a line that anticipates the Prologue, "all wisdom is from the Lord, and with him it remains forever" (1:1).[34] Sirach then declares,

Whoever loves her [Wisdom] loves life,
    and those who seek her from early morning are filled with joy.
(Sir 4:12)

32. Earlier and fuller versions of the material in the next section can be found in Culpepper, "Prologue as Theological Prolegomenon"; and Culpepper, "'Children of God': Evolution, Cosmology, and Johannine Thought," in *Creation Stories in Dialogue: The Bible, Science, and Folk Traditions*, ed. R. Alan Culpepper and Jan G. van der Watt, BibInt 139 (Leiden: Brill, 2016), 3–31, esp. 20–24.

33. Martin Scott, *Sophia and the Johannine Jesus*, JSNTSup 71 (Sheffield: Sheffield Academic, 1992), 99.

34. John Ashton, "The Transformation of Wisdom: A Study of the Prologue of John's Gospel," *NTS* 32 (1986): 166.

Sirach 24 describes how Wisdom came forth from the mouth of the Most High and covered the earth (v. 3). Wisdom is to be found in "the law that Moses commanded us" (v. 23). Wisdom therefore plays a central role in both creation and in moral instruction. Shane Berg argues that "Ben Sira insists that God's law is part of the orderly creation of the world and is fully knowable by humans,"[35] citing Sirach 15:14:

> It was he who created humankind in the beginning,
>   and he left them in the power of their own free choice.

Berg concludes that Sirach's creative retelling of the Genesis account is evidence that "the Genesis creation accounts had become contested ground in Jewish wisdom circles in the Hellenistic age."[36]

In the first century BCE the Wisdom of Solomon traced the course of Wisdom "from the beginning of creation" (Wis 6:22), exalting her further. Solomon claims that "wisdom, the fashioner of all things, taught me" (7:22). He continues:

> in every generation she passes into holy souls
> and makes them friends of God, and prophets;
> for God loves nothing so much as the person who lives with wisdom.
> (Wis 7:27–28)

He confesses, "in kinship with wisdom there is immortality" (8:17; see 9:9–10). Throughout these excerpts we see how Wisdom is both God's creative agent and the supreme teacher of God's ways.

By the first century, wisdom speculation had merged with the rising importance of the Torah, so we begin to hear that the Decalogue, the revelation at Sinai, or the Torah preexisted the creation. Baruch 4:1, for example, connects Wisdom with the law: "She is the book of the commandments of God, the law that endures forever." Pseudo-Philo reports that the Lord "brought them to Mount Sinai and brought forth for them the foundation of understanding that he had prepared from the creation of the world" (LAB 32.7).[37]

---

35. Shane Berg, "Ben Sira, the Genesis Creation Accounts, and the Knowledge of God's Will," *JBL* 132 (2013): 157.

36. Ibid.

37. James H. Charlesworth, ed., *The Old Testament Pseudepigrapha* (Garden City, NY: Doubleday, 1983), 2:346.

This rapid survey reminds us that Second Temple Judaism connected the creation traditions with Wisdom, the pursuit of life, ethical instruction, and ultimately the law. When John introduces Jesus as the incarnation of the Logos, and opens with a reference to the role of the Logos in creation, it evokes this deep and rich tradition—one that has clear implications for the understanding of John's ethics. Further, it establishes that the work of the Logos in creation is revelatory. We may therefore turn to the further question of the ethical significance of creation.

CREATION ETHICS AND COVENANT ETHICS
IN JUDAISM

Extending his already definitive work on Philo and the Gospels, Peder Borgen has recently shown that structural parallels to the beginnings of both Mark and John can be found in Philo's writings.[38] *In Flaccum* begins with the person's entry into public life with no prologue, just as does the Gospel of Mark, while *Legatio ad Gaium* begins with a cosmic prologue, as the Gospel of John does. The prologue in *Legatio*, moreover, serves as the basis for Philo's critique of Gaius's claims to divinity. It also illustrates how Philo could mount an ethical argument on the basis of God's act in creation.

Creation not only establishes the divinity of the Creator, the one true God, but also serves as the fundamental pattern of Jewish life: the regular observance of Shabbat. God's people are to follow the pattern for life laid down by the Creator. Humans were created in the image of God. They were placed in a garden and given dominion, and therefore responsibility, for the care of the earth, and they were created male and female. Like the Creator, they were to rest on the seventh day (Exod 16:23–29; 20:8–11; 31:14–16; 35:2-3; Deut 5:12–15). In his classic treatise on the Sabbath, Abraham Heschel explains that "Judaism is a religion of time aiming at the sanctification of time."[39] It is significant, therefore, that the first occurrence of the word "holy" (*qādôš*) in scripture, the word, "representative of the mystery and majesty of the divine," occurs at the end of the story of creation, not in reference to a place, a mountain, or an altar, but

---

38. Peder Borgen, *The Gospel of John: More Light from Philo, Paul and Archaeology; The Scriptures, Tradition, Exposition, Settings, Meaning*, NovTSup 154 (Leiden: Brill, 2014), 241–60.

39. Abraham Joshua Heschel, *The Sabbath* (New York: Farrar, Straus and Giroux, 1951).

in reference to time: "And God blessed the seventh *day* and made it *holy*."[40] The order is significant: "The sanctity of time came first, the sanctity of man came second, and the sanctity of space last."[41] The connection between the ritual and moral is also fundamental in Jewish ethics. As Alan L. Mittleman notes, "Leviticus 19 begins . . . with an injunction to *all* the Israelites to be holy, for God is holy. Immediately, a crucial 'ritual' observance, the Sabbath, is linked to a 'moral' one, revering father and mother (19:3)."[42]

Rabbinic thought examined the bases for Jewish ethics in both the covenant at Sinai and the primordial covenant at creation. Torah was in the mind of the Creator even before the creation (Genesis Rabbah 1:1, 4), and the whole world was created for the sake of Torah (Genesis Rabbah 1:4; b. Shabbat 88a).

Following this tradition but in a contemporary vein, David Hartman, founder of the Shalom Hartman Institute, explored the relationship between creation ethics and covenant ethics, and the profound implications they have for a Jewish understanding of history. Hartman addressed the tension between the sovereignty of divine purpose in creation and the contingencies of history and human free will that challenge the notion of divine sovereignty:

> One can live in an open universe filled with uncertainty and yet retain the depth of commitment for the God Who is mediated by the drama of creation. History need not exhaust the plenitude of the divine reality, nor need the cosmic consciousness neutralize the significance of human history. Creation and the Sinai covenant can live in mutual interaction without either pole neutralizing and absorbing the other. A human being can yearn for the triumph of justice in history and yet know that the human world is shot through with contingency, uncertainty, and possible destruction.[43]

For Hartman, there is not a necessary continuity between God's act in creation and the course of human history. Others have also gravitated toward creation as a foundation for theology. In his recent book, *Adam as Israel*, Seth Postel views Genesis 1–3 as establishing

---

40. Ibid., 9 (emphasis original).
41. Ibid., 10.
42. Alan L. Mittleman, *A Short History of Jewish Ethics: Conduct and Character in the Context of Covenant* (Chichester, UK: Wiley-Blackwell, 2012), 31.
43. David Hartman, *A Living Covenant: The Innovative Spirit in Traditional Judaism* (Woodstock, VT: Jewish Lights, 1997), 275.

a prototypical Sinai covenant between God and Adam (and Eve).[44] Conversely, Terence E. Fretheim understands the exodus as an act of new creation.[45] Yet another way of thinking about the relationship between creation and Sinai is proposed by Walter Vogels, for whom Israel's covenantal history parallels universal history; that is, Israel's exile is similar to the exile of humanity from Eden, and it is God's will to save the nations also.[46] This exploratory probe is sufficient to establish the vital connection between creation and covenant in Jewish tradition and ethics and to suggest the vitality of this line of thought.

THE SACREDNESS OF HUMAN LIFE
IN JEWISH TRADITION

When we turn to creation ethics, we may note first that creation offers a basis for a universal ethic that focuses on the value and dignity of human life, its place in the created order, and the relationship between the image (*ṣelem*) of God and the imitation of God.[47] The sacredness of human life is rooted in the affirmation in Genesis that God created human beings in God's own image and likeness (*baṣalmēnû kidmutēnû*, Gen 1:26–27; see Ps 8:5–8). Genesis 5:1 also reports that "when God created humankind, he made them in the likeness [*bidmût*] of God." The divine image has been interpreted variously as rationality, free will, the mandate to have dominion, or the capacity for creativity.[48] At a minimum, the principal distinction between human beings and other creatures is their capacity for self-reflective thought and therefore their capacity to live in relationship to God, in covenant and obedience, and to worship God.

Human life is therefore sacred, and one may not take the life of another (Gen 9:6). Rather, life is commanded: "be fruitful and multiply" (Gen 1:28; 9:7). Rabbi Akiba noted that it was a sign of God's love for humanity that God not only created human beings in God's image but also made known to them that they bore the image of God

---

44. Seth D. Postell, *Adam as Israel: Genesis 1–3 as the Introduction to the Torah and Tanakh* (Cambridge: James Clarke, 2012), 115.

45. Terence E. Fretheim, "The Reclamation of Creation," *Int* 45 (1991): 354–65.

46. Walter Vogels, *God's Universal Covenant* (Ottawa: University of Ottawa Press, 1979).

47. I am indebted here to Noam Zion.

48. For a survey of interpretations of "image of God," see W. Sibley Towner, "Clones of God: Genesis 1:26–28 and the Image of God in the Hebrew Bible," *Int* 59 (2005): 341–56, esp. 343–44.

(m. 'Abot 3:17–18). The command to love one's neighbor as oneself (Lev 19:17) then flows directly from the recognition of the sacredness of human life; we are to recognize the image of God in one another. The imperative of human dignity goes even further. Because to be treated like a slave is by definition to be shamed, a Jew was forbidden to treat a Jewish slave like a slave—he had to have the rights of a brother or a guest (Lev 25:39–40). So, if the master had only one pillow or one piece of cake, he was obligated to give it to the slave.[49] The requirement of dignity also set limits on the treatment of non-Hebrew slaves (Exod 21:20–21, 26–27). The life and personality of each person must be protected. It is the duty of the community to ensure that each person has what he or she needs. Just as the Lord provided for Adam and Eve, so each person shall "walk after Adonai your God" (Deut 13:5) and provide for the needs of a fellow human being: food, drink, clothing, shelter, adequate wages, consolation, and burial.

The recognition of the imperative of human dignity is reflected, appropriately, in documents of widely divergent traditions. The UN Declaration of Human Rights begins with three "Whereas" statements that establish the imperative of protecting human rights in the common experience of all humanity, and the first of its thirty articles affirms: "All human beings are born free and equal in dignity and rights. They are endowed with reason and conscience and should act towards one another in a spirit of brotherhood."[50] Similarly, the papal encyclical *Pacem in Terris* (*The Gospel of Peace and Justice*) enumerates twenty-seven specific rights, including "the rights of life and bodily integrity; the right to security in sickness, inability to work, widowhood, old age, unemployment; a right to basic education (and, on the basis of merit and talent, a right to advanced studies); a living wage, to form unions; rights to emigrate and immigrate."[51] Martin Luther King Jr. voiced the same convictions when he wrote: "Deeply rooted in our political and religious heritage is the conviction that every man is an heir of dignity and worth. This innate worth referred to in the phrase 'image of God' is universally shared in equal portion

---

49. Maimonides, *Mishne Torah, Book of Acquisitions, Laws of Slaves* 17; Sifra Section 8.

50. "Universal Declaration of Human Rights," United Nations, http://www.un.org/en/documents/udhr/index.shtml.

51. John A. Coleman, "Catholic Human Rights Theory: Four Challenges to an Intellectual Tradition," *Journal of Law and Religion* 2 (1984): 358. Cf. the encyclical from Pope John Paul II, *Sollicitudo Rei Socialis*.

by all men."[52] Such calls for the protection of the rights and dignity of every person flow naturally from the affirmation that all are created in God's image.

Against this rich background of reflection on the implications of creation for Jewish and universal human ethics, we may turn to the Gospel of John and look for ways in which the affirmation that God created the world through the Logos shaped the ethic implicit and in places explicit in the Gospel.

THE THEME OF LIFE IN JOHN AS AN ETHICAL PRINCIPLE

The theme of life is one of the most pervasive themes in the Fourth Gospel. In the first major section, John 2–4, Jesus celebrates life at a wedding, providing a bountiful supply of wine, alludes to his resurrection in the confrontation in the temple, instructs Nicodemus on what it means to be born from above, explains the "lifting up" of the Son of Man by recalling the life-giving power of the serpent Moses raised up on a pole, promises that everyone who believes in him will have everlasting life (3:16), and teaches the Samaritan woman about living water. The last paragraph of John 4 weaves together the themes of believing and living as it narrates the story of the healing of the royal official's son. I could go on to detail the healing of the man at the Pool of Bethsaida in John 5, the feeding of the multitude in John 6 and the discourse on the bread of life, the raising of Lazarus in John 11, the image of the seed falling into the ground (which Jan van der Watt has already treated at length),[53] the lesson of the footwashing as Jesus prepares to lay down his life for the disciples, and the imagery of Jesus's death, the handing over of the Spirit, Jesus's resurrection, and the feeding of the disciples in John 21. Wherever you are in the Gospel, you are never far from the theme of life.[54]

Both Jesus's words and his signs develop this theme. I have already noted that in John Jesus does not give the sorts of ethical teachings we

---

52. Martin Luther King Jr., "The Ethical Demands for Integration," in *A Testament of Hope: The Essential Writings and Speeches of Martin Luther King, Jr.*, ed. James M. Washington (San Francisco: Harper & Row, 1986), 117–25.

53. Jan G. van der Watt, "Ethics Alive in Imagery," in *Imagery in the Gospel of John*, ed. Jörg Frey, Jan G. van der Watt, and Ruben Zimmermann, WUNT 200 (Tübingen: Mohr Siebeck, 2006), 436–45.

54. This paragraph also appears in Culpepper, "Prologue as Theological Prolegomenon," 8.

find in the other Gospels, such as the beatitudes or injunctions against oaths, lust, divorce, anger, or the temptations of wealth. Nevertheless, the Johannine Jesus does provide general ethical precepts, and not surprisingly these are often set in dualistic antitheses, and often offer precepts that point to the nature of the life to which Jesus calls us. We are familiar with the antitheses in the Sermon on the Mount. Consider the following sample of Johannine antitheses:

> Do not work [*ergasethe mē*] for the food that perishes, but [*alla*] for the food that endures for eternal life. (6:27)

> Do not judge [*mē krinete*] by appearances, but [*alla*] judge with right judgment. (7:24)

> Do not doubt [*mē ginou apistos*] but [*alla*] believe. (20:27)

In each of these we find a prohibition ("Do not") followed by a strong adversative ("but") and an imperative or implied imperative. In John 6:27, the "food that endures for eternal life" comes through belief in God, as Jesus makes clear two verses later. The command to judge not by appearances but with right judgment can be found in the Jewish wisdom tradition (see also 1 Sam 16:7; Isa 11:3). The final antithesis returns to the fundamental imperative of belief. The Johannine antitheses, therefore, concern not commands for specific situations, as do the Matthean antitheses, but rather focus on ultimate values (eternal life, right judgment, and belief) that make ethical living possible. Three related sayings reflect the imperative of "walking" (i.e., living) or working in the light.

> Whoever follows me will never walk in darkness but will have the light of life. (8:12)

> We must do the works of him who sent me while it is day. (9:4)

> Those who walk during the day do not stumble, because they see the light of this world. But those who walk at night stumble, because the light is not in them. (11:9–10)

The language is metaphorical but would have been readily understood. The Hebrew term for instruction or law (*hălākâ*) comes from the verb *hālak*, which means to walk (see 1 John 1:6, 7; 2:6, 11; and various references in the Pauline Letters). In John the metaphorical reference to walking is tied to the dualism of light and darkness.

Another set of sayings sets forth the lofty ideal of laying down one's life for others.

> The good shepherd lays down his life for the sheep. (10:11)

> And I lay down my life for the sheep. (10:15)

> No one has greater love than this, to lay down one's life for one's friends. (15:13)

The repetition of the verbs for "laying down" and "taking up" in John's narration of Jesus's washing the disciples' feet ties the footwashing metaphorically to Jesus's death for the disciples. The connection is further strengthened by the use of the Greek term *hypodeigma* (example, John 13:15), which in other contexts is used of a noble death (2 Macc 6:28, 31; 4 Macc 17:22–23; Sir 44:16).[55] When Jesus says, "You also ought to wash one another's feet" (13:14), the sense may well be that his followers should be willing to die for one another if necessary. The parabolic saying in John 12:24 offers the same precept in a softer form, suggesting that while the sayings about laying down one's life may have had a literal sense in the context of persecution (see 16:2), they can have the more general sense that fulfillment and fruitfulness are found in self-denial and selfless pursuit of eternal values and the good for others.[56]

> Very truly [literally, "amen, amen"], I tell you, unless a grain of wheat falls into the ground and dies, it remains just a single grain; but if it dies, it bears much fruit. (12:24)

To his followers Jesus also extends the promise of blessing in the form of a distinctive quality of life, here and now. He says, "I came in order that they may have life and have it abundantly" (10:10), and this life comes through knowing him in all that that connotes (17:3): knowledge, love, obedience, and blessing. Another version of Jesus's assurance to the disciples declares, "I have said these things to you

55. R. Alan Culpepper, "The Johannine *hypodeigma*: A Reading of John 13," *Semeia* 53 (1991): 133–52.

56. See van der Watt, "Ethics Alive in Imagery," 443: "The proverbial truth presented by this imagery is defining and enlightening key moments in the development of the plot. It remains implicitly and actively present in the rest of this Gospel."

so that my joy may be in you, and that your joy may be complete" (15:11). Nevertheless, knowledge must be expressed in obedience: "If you know these things, you are blessed if you do them" (13:17).

For all the emphasis on punishment, hell, and eternal torment in some brands of Christian preaching, it is worth noting that John gives scant attention to the threat of suffering or punishment as an inducement to ethical living.[57] Judas is referred to as the son of perdition (17:12), and Jesus warns the man at the pool of Bethsaida to sin no more "so that nothing worse happens to you" (5:14). Beyond these few references, the rationale Jesus offers for his ethics is positive—that his disciples may have life.

JOHN'S ETHIC OF DIVINE LOVE
AND ITS FULFILLMENT

We may ask first whether the new command should be read in the context of a creation ethics or covenant ethics. Is it rooted ultimately in creation, so that it has implications for all human beings, or does it derive from the Sinai covenant or the incarnation? Is it restricted to one's fellow disciples (i.e., one's "neighbor"), or is it a command to love all people?

The coming of the Logos as true light was first to the world, with the reminder that "the world came into being through him" (1:10), but the world did not know him. Verse 11 of the Prologue moves from the universal to the particular; he came not only to the world but also to "his own." John 3:16 then declares God's love for the world, which presumably includes all human beings. Moloney's comment is both insightful and corrective: "John grounds his theme of love in the fact that the gift of Jesus to human kind flows from God's love for the world: 'God so loved the world that he gave his only Son' (3:16). All discussion of love in the Fourth Gospel begins

---

57. See Jaime Clark-Soles, *Death and Afterlife in the New Testament* (London: T&T Clark, 2006), which points out that the Fourth Gospel says nothing of hell; there is no posthumous punishment. Clark-Soles also suggests that the Fourth Gospel's view of death and afterlife seems to be especially crafted to respond to Epicurean theology, especially in John 14: "John's view diametrically opposes Epicurus's view in holding that God is not remote and disinterested but is fully and intimately related" (ibid., 140). On the other hand, the Fourth Evangelist "approximates Epicurus in his fundamental concern to assuage thanatological anxiety so that one's present life may be characterized by pleasure (*hēdonē*) in Epicurus's scheme or joy (*chara*) in FE's message" (ibid.).

from this Johannine truth."[58] Jesus's washing of the disciples' feet and his command to the disciples to love one another are not antithetical to an affirmation of God's love for all persons—and therefore the ethical imperative of love for all persons. The stated purpose for the command that the community be marked by its love is that "everyone will know that you are my disciples" (13:35). The community ethic of love is a witness to the world of the love of the Creator that is now found in the nascent community of Jesus followers. Their mission is in the world (17:15, 18), and Jesus prays for those who would believe because of their word, "that they may all be one . . . so that the world may believe that you have sent me" (17:21), thereby reversing the world's rejection of the Logos, which was noted in verse 10 of the Prologue. The mission of both Jesus and the disciples grows out of God's love for the world, therefore, and will culminate in that love being recognized and received, as Jesus declares in John 17:23, "so that the world may know that you have sent me and have loved them even as you have loved me."

Because God's love is universal it is inescapably missiological; that is, God's love is always seeking to reach those who do not "know God" as ultimate reality and therefore live in response to God's love. The prophets expressed this hope long before the Gospel was written:

For the earth will be full of the knowledge of the Lord
     as the waters cover the sea" (Isa 11:9; cf. Hab 2:14)

In his earlier work, *Johannine Faith and Liberating Community*, David Rensberger declared that saving the world "meant to recall it from its self-absorption to its stance as creature before its Creator, yielding an obedience to God that could undo the structures that maintained it apart from God in the darkness of its hatred."[59] More recently he has extended his understanding of John's missiological focus by persuasively arguing that 1 John 4:12 and 18 should be understood and translated as referring not to "perfect love" but to God's love as it is "completed" in us: "No one has ever seen God. If we love one another, God abides in us and his love *has been brought to its completion in us*" (Rensberger's translation).[60] In light of this verse, "the

---

58. Moloney, *Love in the Gospel of John*, esp. 56–61 and 203–9.

59. David Rensberger, *Johannine Faith and Liberating Community* (Philadelphia: Westminster, 1988), 142.

60. David Rensberger, "Completed Love: 1 John 4:11–18 and the Mission of the New Tes-

completion of God's love among the believers obviously consists in their love for one another."[61] Rensberger explains:

> The divine love that sent the Son into the world has as its aim not only the creation of individual believers, but the formation of them into a community of mutual love. Only when this community exists and maintains its love in concrete daily practice has the mission of God, and therefore the mission of the church, reached its goal. Because this goal is still seen in eschatological terms, as God's climactic intervention in human history and society ("the world"), the creation and continued existence of this community in its members' love and care for one another represents the culmination of God's designs for the human race. For this community to be on mission means for it to be engaged with God in the creation of yet more communities of belief and mutual love. Divine love achieves its aims when human love is fully and vividly exercised; for this is what God has intended for humanity all along.[62]

Jesus's interactions with those whom he meets in the course of the Gospel illustrate the ways of such inclusive, divine love. The love of the Johannine Jesus knows no rank or status. Jesus treats the sick, women, and others of low social status with dignity and compassion. Jesus initiates a conversation with the Samaritan woman and asks for a drink from her vessel. He treats the royal official, the man at the Pool of Bethesda ill for thirty-eight years, and the man born blind with the same dignity he extends to Nathanael, his disciples, and his friends at Bethany. Fulfilling the mandate to preserve each person's dignity, Jesus turns water to wine at the wedding at Cana, so that the family would not suffer public embarrassment and shame. He feeds the multitude in Galilee, meeting their basic physical needs, and he provides fish for the unsuccessful fishermen in John 21 as a sign of his resurrection.

The universality of God's love demonstrated by Jesus can also be seen in his pronouncement that he has "other sheep that do not belong to this fold" (10:16), which many interpreters have understood as a reference to gentiles. When Jesus enigmatically tells the servants of the chief priests and the Pharisees that where he is going they cannot come, they mockingly ask if he is going to the diaspora

---

tament Church," in *Communities in Dispute: Current Scholarship on the Johannine Epistles*, ed. R. Alan Culpepper and Paul N. Anderson, ECL 13 (Atlanta: SBL Press, 2014), 249.

61. Ibid., 250.

62. Ibid., 254. Cf. the fifth characteristic of OT covenants identified by Sherri Brown, above, n. 25.

of the Greeks (7:35). Then, as the hour of his death approaches, Greeks come and ask to see him (12:20–21). At this point Jesus speaks the metaphor of the seed that bears much fruit if it dies (12:24–25), and a few verses later he declares that when he is "lifted up" he will draw all people to himself (12:32). For a Gospel that was written for a struggling early Christian community recently separated from the synagogue, John proclaims a remarkably expansive Christology.

IMPLICATIONS OF CREATION ETHICS

Let us review the ground we have covered. In light of the recent turn toward a narrative approach to "implied ethics" in John, I started with the observation that John is the only Gospel that begins with a reference to creation. I explored the significance of this opening for John's ethics. This led to the recognition that in Jewish tradition both creation and the Sinai covenant serve as foundations for ethics, and I surveyed ways in which creation ethics led to a strong affirmation of the dignity and rights of every human being, and therefore the community's obligations toward every person. Turning to the Gospel of John, I found ample evidence that Jesus models an ethic, rooted in the work of the Logos in creation, an ethic that extended God's love to every person.

A creation ethic leads naturally to a high view of the sanctity of life, and especially human life, which has far-reaching ethical implications. My colleague David Gushee recently published a definitive work titled *The Sacredness of Human Life: Why an Ancient Biblical Vision Is Key to the World's Future*, which traces the history of this biblical, theological, and ethical principle and explores its mandate broadly.[63] One chapter, for example, offers an agenda for the people of God in the twenty-first century: "rebuilding the moral fiber after World-War II, abortion, biotechnical innovations, the death penalty, human rights, nuclear weapons, women's rights, and other issues." The next chapter engages the sacredness of God's creation in seven points, among them: the sacredness of life and ecological degradation, the care of creation, the development of alternative theological paradigms, and toward a broadened Christian sacredness-of-life ethic. The range of these issues suggests the importance of creation ethics

---

63. David P. Gushee, *The Sacredness of Human Life: Why an Ancient Biblical Vision Is Key to the World's Future* (Grand Rapids: Eerdmans, 2013).

grounded in both Jewish and Christian theological reflection. A creation ethic must speak to one's obligations to every other human being, as we have seen, but also to the creation itself and to future generations, who also have a role in God's purposes for the creation. It is a mandate which, as Gushee's subtitle claims, is "key to the world's future."

5.

Love Embodied in Action: Ethics and Incarnation in the Gospel of John

JAIME CLARK-SOLES

Indubitably, our ethical selves are inextricably intertwined with our embodied selves. I approach the topic of Johannine ethics primarily as a Johannine scholar, but also as a disability studies scholar with an interest in transhumanism and posthumanism conversations.[1] In this essay, I will read Johannine texts from a disability studies angle. First, I will introduce the reader to some definitions and models. Second, I will provide an example of a disability studies approach to a biblical text by analyzing the role of disability in John 9 as well as scholarly interpretations of the text. Third, I will summarize, draw conclusions,

---

1. "Transhumanism, broadly speaking, is the view that the human condition is not unchanging and that it can and should be questioned. . . . Transhumanism includes life philosophies that seek the evolution of intelligent life beyond its current human form and limitations, using science and technology." Calvin Mercer and Tracy J. Trothen, eds., *Religion and Transhumanism: The Unknown Future of Human Enhancement* (Santa Barbara: Praeger, 2015), 3. With respect to posthumanism, Jennifer Koosed writes: "What does it mean to be human? We are poised somewhere in between animals and divinities; aided, enhanced, and altered by technologies; changing and changed by our environments, but natural and cultural. Arguably, the Bible begins as a speciesist manifesto—only humanity is created in the image of the divine, only humanity is given dominion over the rest of creation. However, the Bible also contains multiple moments of disruption, boundary crossing, and category confusion: animals speak, God becomes man, spirits haunt the living, and monsters confound at the end. All of these stories explore the boundaries of the human in ways that destabilize the very category of the human. All of these stories engage thinking that broadly falls under the umbrella term posthumanism—a catchall of disputed definition that points beyond various human-centric ideologies." Jennifer L. Koosed, ed., *The Bible and Posthumanism* (Atlanta: Society of Biblical Literature, 2014), 3.

and raise questions about the promises and pitfalls of the text as it relates to disability concerns.

As defined by Christopher Skinner in the introductory chapter, my essay falls within the "implied ethics" section of this project. Nowhere does the Fourth Gospel overtly or prescriptively provide a program for ethically engaging people with varied bodies, including those with disabilities. It has no single term for our word *disability*. There are no general statements about how to treat the blind and the lame as in Luke 14. In the Fourth Gospel, we do not have Matthew's language of "the least of these" (which is just as well, since Matthew's language does not originally refer to persons with disabilities or even the "generally marginalized" per se). Thus any ethic we deduce or derive in this area will qualify as "implied ethics."

From start to finish, and at all points in between, the Fourth Gospel is concerned with life (*zōē*): how we get it, how we lose it, how we find it again—or better yet, how we get found by it. To wit:

> All things came into being through him, and without him not one thing came into being. What has come into being in him was *life*, and the *life* was the light of the people. (1:3)[2]

> I came that they might have *life*, and have it abundantly. (10:10)

> But these things have been written that you might believe that Jesus is the Christ, the Son of God, and that through believing you might have *life* in his name. (20:31)

Abundant life, embodied life, eternal life, precious life. How does the Fourth Gospel's ethic of life play out for persons with disabilities?

MODELS AND DEFINITIONS

Disability studies is a relatively new discipline in the humanities (and even newer in biblical studies). Interdisciplinary in nature, it critically analyzes the ways that disability is construed, represented, experienced, navigated, and managed by groups and individuals. Simi Linton states in "What is Disability Studies?":

---

2. All biblical translations are my own unless otherwise noted.

Disability studies introduces a disability reading to a range of subject matter. We prod people to examine how disability as a category was created to serve certain ends and how the category has been institutionalized in social practices and intellectual conventions. Disability studies' project is to weave disabled people back into the fabric of society, thread by thread, theory by theory. It aims to expose the ways that disability has been made exceptional and to work to naturalize disabled people—remake us as full citizens whose rights and privileges are intact, whose history and contributions are recorded, and whose often distorted representations in art, literature, film, theater, and other forms of artistic expression are fully analyzed. We have enlisted people from a broad range of disciplines in redefining the "problem" of disability. What is the problem? Where is it located? Who can fix it? What scholarship is needed to prepare people to fix the problem?[3]

Three models have been used as disability studies has advanced: the medical model, the social model, and, more recently, the cultural model. Robert McCruer evinces the interdisciplinary nature of the cultural model in the introduction of his book:

> Crip Theory: Cultural Signs of Queerness and Disability emerges from cultural studies traditions that question the order of things, considering how and why it is constructed and naturalized; how it is embedded in complex economic, social, and cultural relations; and how it might be changed. In this book. . . . I thus theorize the construction of able-bodiedness and heterosexuality, as well as the connections between them. . . . I put forward here a theory of what I call "compulsory able-bodiedness" and argue that the system of compulsory able-bodiedness, which in a sense produces disability, is thoroughly interwoven with the system of compulsory heterosexuality that produces queerness: that, in fact, compulsory heterosexuality is contingent on compulsory able-bodiedness, and vice versa.[4]

To enable critical inquiry, scholars have developed useful language. Often a heuristic distinction is made between *impairment* and *disability*, noting inevitable overlap. Impairment refers to a physiological, medical phenomenon, while disability is a social phenomenon. A society disables people with impairments by obstructing (whether intentionally or unintentionally) equal access to all the benefits that

---

3. Simi Linton, "What Is Disability Studies," *PMLA* 120, no. 2 (March 2005): 518.
4. Robert McRuer, *Crip Theory: Cultural Signs of Queerness and Disability* (New York: New York University Press, 2006), 2.

nondisabled people with normate (see definition below) bodies enjoy, including transportation, employment, education, political power, and even architecture that can be navigated. For example, if all of us were in wheelchairs, I imagine we would have no curbs, and we would automatically include an elevator in a building with more than one story, and accessing a pulpit in a church would not require navigating steps. None of those architectural choices is inevitable, just typical.

We use the word *normate* instead of *normal* because the word *normal* is, in fact, meaningless in this context. What constitutes a normal body? Is it male, female, intersex? Black, white, brown? Tall or short? How much does it weigh? At which stage in the life cycle? Instead, we use the term *normate* body, which is, of course, itself a construct. Rosemarie Garland-Thomson conceived the neologism *normate* in her book *Extraordinary Bodies*.

> As I examine the disabled figure, I will also trouble the mutually constituting figure this study coins: the normate. This neologism names the veiled subject position of cultural self, the figure outlined by the array of deviant others whose marked bodies shore up the normate's boundaries. The term *normate* usefully designates the social figure through which people can represent themselves as definitive human beings. Normate, then, is the constructed identity of those who, by way of the bodily configurations and cultural capital they assume, can step into a position of authority and wield the power it grants them. If one attempts to define the normate position by peeling away all the marked traits within the social order at this historical moment, what emerges is a very narrowly defined profile that describes only a minority of actual people. Erving Goffman, whose work I discuss in greater detail later, observes the logical conclusion of this phenomenon by noting wryly that there is "only one complete unblushing male in America: a young, married, white, urban, northern, heterosexual, Protestant father of college education, fully employed, of good complexion, weight and height, and a recent record in sports." Interestingly, Goffman takes for granted that femaleness has no part in his sketch of a normative human being. Yet this image's ubiquity, power, and value resonate clearly. One testimony to the power of the normate subject position is that people often try to fit its description in the same way that Cinderella's stepsisters attempted to squeeze their feet into her glass slipper. Naming the figure of the normate is one conceptual strategy that will allow us to press our analyses beyond the simple dichotomies of male/female, white/black, straight/

gay, or able-bodied/disabled so that we can examine the subtle interrelations among social identities that are anchored to physical differences.[5]

While there is some debate about designations, in this essay I will distinguish between nondisabled people[6] and persons with disabilities. There is another important (again, heuristic) distinction to be made: that between *cure* and *healing*. Cure refers to the elimination of a medical impairment and occurs at the individual level. *Healing* may be better understood as a relational, social term to refer to a person's experience of integration and reconciliation to self, or God, or the community (or some combination thereof). Healing may or may not involve a cure. Just as impairment is experienced on an individual basis, so is a cure. Just as a disability is in some ways a communally imposed limitation, so also healing may be tied to communally based liberation.

A final useful preliminary distinction concerns the way in which a person with an impairment views that impairment. While some do, not all impairments cause pain and suffering that require healing. While some do, not all people with impairments consider their disabilities as problems to overcome or tragic losses. As the often-quoted Nancy Mairs states: "I'd take a cure; I just don't need one."[7]

From the outset, one might wonder whether it is anachronistic to employ notions of *disability* when studying ancient texts. How do ancient and modern notions of *disability* compare? This question has been addressed by Nyasha Junior and Jeremy Schipper, upon whose work I partly depend.[8] While the ancients may not have a single word for *disability* as we do to cover a host of conditions, the idea is not foreign to them and disability actually appears often in the Bible. The task is to discern how disability functions in the literature they produced. Junior and Schipper briefly rehearse the medical model and the social model before arguing that the cultural model best suits biblical studies. "The cultural model of disability analyzes how a culture's representations and discussions of disability and nondisability help to

---

5. Rosemarie Garland-Thomson, *Extraordinary Bodies: Figuring Physical Disability in American Culture and Literature* (New York: Columbia University Press, 1997), 8.

6. Some scholars use the term "able-bodied" and still others use "temporarily able-bodied."

7. In Nancy L. Eiesland, *The Disabled God: Toward a Liberatory Theology of Disability* (Nashville: Abingdon, 1994), 46.

8. Nyasha Junior and Jeremy Schipper, "Disability Studies and the Bible," in *New Meanings for Ancient Texts: Recent Approaches to Biblical Criticisms*, ed. Steven L. McKenzie and John Kaltner (Louisville: Westminster John Knox, 2013), 21–37.

articulate a range of values, ideals, or expectations that are important to that culture's organization and identity."[9] As such they warn us against too easily moving from the text's portrayal of disability to the actual lived lives of people with disabilities in that text's culture. Thus, when we study John 9, we are not pretending that we are getting at what quotidian life was like for someone who was blind in antiquity (and that would anyway, of course, depend on many other factors apart from the person's disability, including age, gender, and social class); neither are we aiming at historical reconstructions that catalog medical approaches and diagnoses regarding blindness in the first century. Rather, we are analyzing what values are conveyed by the author in narrating the story in the way that she or he does. Junior and Schipper contend:

> When a literary or artistic work from a given culture includes an image of disability, the image usually represents more than just an objective description of diagnosis of a biological condition. For example, in the United States, many of our books, films, or other forms of artistic expression include representations of disability, such as disability imagery or characters with disabilities. Often, these literary or artistic representations of disability do not seek to provide an accurate portrayal of the everyday experiences of persons with disabilities. Instead, they serve an instrumental role in conveying particular ideals or values that shape our culture such as hope, sin, inspiration or courage.[10]

While their work focuses solely on the Hebrew Bible, their insights apply to the New Testament texts, mutatis mutandis:

> The cultural model is also a good fit for biblical scholars. Instead of assuming a universal meaning behind disability or nondisability across all cultures, a cultural model may help biblical scholars to: (1) focus on the cultural values associated with disability and nondisability in the Hebrew Bible and the ancient Israelite societies that produced this literature; (2) become more aware of the contemporary cultural values that a scholar assumes in his or her interpretation of these biblical representations of disability; and (3) determine whether scholarly interpretations of how disability operates in a given passage find sufficient support in the biblical text.[11]

---

9. Junior and Schipper, "Disability Studies," 23.
10. Ibid.
11. Ibid., 25.

In what follows, I will attend to the ways disability operates in the plot of John 9 and in representative scholarly interpretations of it.

THE FOURTH GOSPEL

"And the Word became flesh and tabernacled among us" (John 1:14). In a Gospel committed to incarnation (and its ethical implications), it makes sense to address bodies, both idealized and actual. Feminist scholars of John have done this, as have African American and queer interpreters.[12] How a text construes or constructs bodies and how interpreters consequently interpret that text reveals particular cultural assumptions and even aspirations.

The Fourth Gospel is a literary text, a narrative.[13] Its rhetoric depends, therefore, on literary techniques including time, plot, characters, setting, and point of view (omniscient narration in this case). To interpret the entire Fourth Gospel from a disability perspective, one would need to treat not only the obvious texts, such as the healing/cure narratives, but also the Gospel's emphasis on creation, incarnation, the peace (*eirēnē*, used six times in John 14–20) offered by Christ (as opposed to that offered by Caesar or any other empire), the passion, and the nature of Jesus's resurrected, holey/holy body that retains its "imperfections." Due to the brief scope of this paper, I cannot address all of those elements, though I have treated many of them elsewhere.[14]

The Fourth Gospel contains only three cure stories. The healing of

12. See Amy-Jill Levine with Marianne Blickenstaff, eds., *Feminist Companion to John*, 2 vols. (Cleveland: Pilgrim, 2003); Gail O'Day, "Gospel of John," in *Women's Bible Commentary*, ed. Carol A. Newsom, Sharon H. Ringe, and Jacqueline E. Lapsley, 3rd ed. (Louisville: Westminster John Knox, 2012), 517–30; Allen Dwight Callahan, "John," in *True to Our Native Land: An African American New Testament Commentary*, ed. Brian K. Blount (Minneapolis: Fortress Press, 2007), 186–212; and Robert E. Goss, "John," in *The Queer Bible Commentary*, ed. Deryn Guest et al. (London: SCM, 2006) 548–65.

13. It is the case that movies have been made from the text, such as *The Visual Bible: Gospel of John*, directed by Philip Saville (Toronto: Think Film, 2003), DVD. One could write a useful, different essay on the way the movie interprets the disability aspects of the Johannine text. In noting that the Fourth Gospel is a narrative, I sympathize with van der Watt's sentiment presented in Skinner's introductory chapter to this volume: "'By means of narration, there is a coherent reflection on values and behavior' embedded within the Johannine literature" (p. xxvi). For my treatment of disability in the Johannine epistolary corpus, see Jaime Clark-Soles, "Disability in the Johannine Literature (Gospel of John, 1–3 John, Apocalypse)," in *The Bible and Disability: A Commentary*, ed. Sarah J. Melcher, Mikeal C. Parsons, and Amos Yong (Waco, TX: Baylor University Press, forthcoming).

14. See Clark-Soles, "Disability in the Johannine Literature."

the royal official's son at Cana (4:46–54) and the man who had been ill for thirty-eight years at Bethsaida (5:1–15) are presented back to back. The man who was born with a visual impairment is found in chapter 9. Only those in chapters 5 and 9 involve a disability rather than an acute illness. Space only allows treatment of one, so which to choose? It is important to note that John employs intercharacterization often; that is, the reader understands a particular character best when that character is also viewed in light of other characters in the Gospel. Thus the evangelist assumes that by the time readers have arrived in chapter 9, they have already read the cure story in chapter 5. As such, they (like the disciples in the narrative) may bring with them various assumptions related to the cultural values about disability expressed in chapter 5, which may include the idea that sin and disability are inherently connected. Chapters 5 and 9 must be viewed together to see that, in fact, the Fourth Gospel does *not* present a uniform or simplistic approach to cure and healing. Neither man asks Jesus to cure him. In neither case is faith a prerequisite for a cure. Both men are cured; one follows, one does not. Jesus patently confronts one of them as a sinner and defends the other as patently not a sinner. Both raise the question of what constitutes the "work of God" in each story. We know that Jesus works the works of him who sent him (5:36); God is still working and so is Jesus (5:17). In each story, what is the work of God and who effects it? Jesus? The disciples? The person with the disability? A combination? The topic is dense and layered in the Fourth Gospel.

While the reader should peruse chapter 5, I have chosen to treat chapter 9 here at length, because it reflects a microcosm of concerns, assumptions, and patterns in the Fourth Gospel (such as those raised in the Prologue). It also exhibits a number of different issues that I want to note, if not fully explore, including but not limited to the use of disability as a metaphor, the question of a disabled person's agency, the social aspect of disability, normate assumptions about persons with disabilities longing for a normate body, narrative prosthesis, and "inspiration porn."

CLUES FROM THE PROLOGUE

John 9 must be interpreted in light of the material that precedes it, including the Prologue. From the Prologue, there are three points worth highlighting with respect to disability before turning to chapter 9.

DIVERSITY/IMPAIRMENT BY DESIGN?

In both Genesis and the Fourth Gospel, embodied diversity appears to be an intentional, positive aspect of the created order. Borrowing the initial words of Genesis, "In the beginning," the Gospel announces that the Word was God and that "everything came into being through [the Word] and without [the Word] not even a single thing came into being" (1:3). Does this imply, then, that "good" bodies come in a variety of forms? If so, then rather than "fixing" bodies that deviate from the "norm," perhaps the concern should be fixing communities to make them inclusive of all bodies. Rather than eradicating difference, perhaps communities should not only accommodate, but even celebrate it? To denigrate differently abled bodies is to denigrate creation and, by extension, its Creator.

From another angle, though, the idea that "impaired" bodies are a part of God's creative design can (and has) itself been used to oppressive rather than liberating effect. Furthermore, there is a vigorous debate in the disability literature about whether those with impairments should seek a cure if possible or whether to do so is to acquiesce to rather than resist the confining, narrow values of normate society. For some, it depends on the very specific nature of the impairment.

FAITH AND CURE

Does the Fourth Gospel depict persons with disabilities as farther away from God, closer to God, or neither? John 1:11–13 adumbrates the plot of the Gospel; namely, Jesus will be rejected by some and accepted by others. All who receive him become children of God, born "not of blood or of the will of the flesh or of the will of a husband, but of God." People with disabilities sometimes find themselves cast as "children of a lesser God," so to speak.[15] Do people with disabilities have to be cured or healed to fully be considered children of God? Many people with disabilities have heard nondisabled people emote: "There but for the grace of God go I"; such a statement

15. A reference to a 1986 movie: Hesper Anderson and Mark Medoff, *Children of a Lesser God*, directed by Randa Haines (Hollywood, CA: Paramount Pictures, 1986), DVD.

is deeply problematic in its implications. Are people with disabilities further from the grace of God, even outside of it? Are nondisabled people especially favored or blessed by God?

In the Fourth Gospel, faith is never a prerequisite for cure. In chapters 5 and 9, Jesus takes the initiative to cure two men; one becomes a follower, the other does not. In the story in chapter 4, faith is inspired as a *result* of the cure. Throughout the Fourth Gospel, Jesus expresses impatience with "signs faith": "Unless you see signs and wonders you will not believe" (4:48). A mature faith requires no magic tricks. Thus, when someone advises a person today with a disability simply to "pray harder" or "have more faith" in order to be cured, the advisor operates against the grain of the Fourth Gospel.

INCARNATION

John 1:14 is central for the consideration of the intersection of disability studies and the Bible, the intersection of bodies and theology: "And the Word became flesh [*sarx*] and tabernacled [*skēnoō*] among us, and we have seen his glory, the glory as of a father's only son, full of grace and truth." Numerous implications derive from this statement.

First, the embodiment of the divine undergirds the whole Gospel. Plato emphasized the distance between the material order and the higher realm, which is summarized by his memorable phrase *soma sēma* (the body is a tomb). In contrast, John depicts the body as a locus and instrument of the divine (hence the use of the word *skēnoō* [tabernacle] and the reference to Jesus's body as a temple [*naos*] in 2:21).[16] In fact, the whole created order reflects and symbolizes God's nature and activity (1:3). Bread is no longer just bread (6:35); water is no longer just water (4:14); flesh is no longer just flesh (6:51).

Second, the Fourth Gospel glories in physical and emotional intimacy. Bodies touch. Jesus is in God's bosom (*kolpos*, 1:18) just as the Beloved Disciple reclines on Jesus's bosom (*kolpos*, 13:23). Jesus rubs mud on the eyes of the man who is blind in chapter 9. Mary the sister of Martha wipes (*ekmassō*) Jesus's feet with her hair (11:2). Jesus washes the disciples' feet and wipes them (*ekmassō*, 13:5). Joseph and

---

16. To explore this further, see Mary Coloe, *God Dwells with Us: Temple Symbolism in the Fourth Gospel* (Collegeville, MN: Liturgical Press, 2001).

Nicodemus wrap and bury Jesus's dead body (19:39–42). Mary Magdalene holds on to Jesus (20:17). Thomas is invited to touch Jesus's wounded hands and side (20:27).

Third, the Gospel is highly sensory and sensual. Seeing, hearing, smelling (11:39), touching, and tasting (2:9) all figure into the narrative significantly.

Fourth, one might argue that in the Fourth Gospel, bodies do not need to be "overcome." They are sites of vulnerability, connection, shame, and glory. Jesus's body experiences a range of states and experiences, and God is in them all. (Note that this Gospel never finds Jesus feeling forsaken by God as he does in Mark 15:34 and Matt 27:46.) He does not try to escape his ordeal and does not feel abandoned. He knows that it is not God, but society, that attempts to disable or erase him. Notably, when he appears in his resurrection, his body is not repaired but continues to bear the wounds in his hands and side.

How do these considerations relate to the specific story found in chapter 9?

JOHN 9: IS SEEING BELIEVING?

The Fourth Gospel uses dramatic techniques in its storytelling. For purposes of analysis, I will structure chapter 9 by its six scenes.

SCENE 1: VERSES 1–7

The chapter opens with Jesus sighting a man born blind. "As he walked along, he saw a man blind from birth." Immediately, the disciples convey the cultural assumption that the man who is blind is "deviant" (does not have the desired normate body that is sighted like theirs) and that blindness is a "problem" that needs at least to be explained if not cured. They facilely connect impairment with moral failure; they assume that the blindness is a punishment for sin, either the man's or his parents. Jesus, on the other hand, intervenes promptly to contest their poor, if popular, theodicy[17] and defend the attack on the man's moral condition (or his parents').

17. The word comes from Greek *theos*, "god" and *dikē*, "justice" and refers to a defense of God's justice. Theodicy puzzles over the question: If God is omnipotent (all-powerful), omniscient (all-knowing), and benevolent (wills the good), then why does God permit evil?

Jesus's next words though, if read in an English translation such as the NRSV, raise serious moral questions about his own theodicy: "Neither this man nor his parents sinned; he was born blind so that God's works might be revealed in him. We must work the works of him who sent me while it is day; night is coming when no one can work" (vv. 3–4). Did God patently cause the man to be born with an impairment in order to use him as a prop in a divine magic show? Does God simply impair the man to use him as the means to an end? What kind of God shows off by curing the very problem that God caused in the first place? And if God does behave this way, why does God choose to cure some congenital impairments and not others? There is certainly never an indication in this story (nor the one in chapter 5) that faith is a prerequisite for a cure.

Given the ethical gravity of this instance, two points concerning the Greek text need to be made. First, the ancient Greek manuscripts with which translators work are composed in *scriptio continua*, continuous script. There are no spaces between words, no punctuation marks, no distinctions between capital and lowercase letters, and no chapter or verse numbers. All of those features are judgments made by modern translators of different English versions.

Second, the phrase the NRSV translates as "he was born blind" does not actually appear in the Greek text. Omitting the capitals and punctuation to be true to the Greek text, we have: "neither this one sinned nor his parents but in order that the works of God might be revealed in him we must work the works of the one who sent me while it is day night is coming when no one can work." Notice the difference in the following two translations of verses 3–4, first the NRSV and then my own.

Translation 1: NRSV	Translation 2: Clark-Soles
Jesus answered, "Neither this man nor his parents sinned; he was born blind so that God's works might be revealed in him. We must work the works of him who sent me while it is day; night is coming when no one can work."	Jesus answered, "Neither this man nor his parents sinned.[18] In order that God's works might be revealed in him, we must work the works of him who sent me while it is day. Night is coming when no one can work."

18. [He was born blind]. The brackets indicate that this sentence is not in the Greek text. If you choose to include it, you should do so only as a matter of fact statement: He was born

These are two very different ways of construing the text. Reading the text according to my translation, we see Jesus moving away from an obsession with determining whose fault the man's impairment was, whether the man's, the parents', or God's. It is simply a fact: the man was born blind. The reality is: he continues to be blind at that moment. While the disciples busy themselves with an academic exercise in theological hairsplitting, here sits a person (a person, not a "case") with an impairment. Even if they could determine fault, the man's situation would not change thereby. Jesus turns their attention away from speculating about the past and toward the person in front of them and asks them to consider whether they are going to work for and with God or, as we see later in the story in the case of the Pharisees, they are going to work for themselves and against God. Jesus definitively declares and demonstrates that, for his part, he sides with God.

Once again (see 1:1), the author alludes to the creation accounts of Genesis by showing Jesus's salutary, salivary creative act using the earth ('ădāmâ) for the sake of the earth creature ('ādām). As in chapter 5, the man does not ask for a cure; rather, the nondisabled Jesus acts on him. The author, through Jesus, upholds the cultural assumption that the man's impairment is a problem that needs to be "fixed" (so that nondisabled people in the narrative as well as the nondisabled reader can feel more comfortable?). Junior and Schipper say, "Disability does not always create a crisis,"[19] but such a sentiment is lost on most nondisabled people. Does this make the person who is blind a pawn without agency? The man does, as in chapter 5, obey Jesus's command and, thus, receives sight. The reference to washing in the pool of Siloam raises baptismal echoes for many. Whereas the man in chapter 5 never enters the waters, this man does. This counts in his favor as a character who conveys the author's values. If the rhetoric of the text succeeds, the reader will imitate his behavior and avoid behaving like the man in chapter 5.

---

blind. Better yet, just leave it out since it does not appear in the Greek text at all.

19. Junior and Schipper, "Disability Studies," 31.

SCENE 2: VERSES 8–12

The rest of chapter 9 narrates various reactions to the cure: the man's, the neighbors', the parents', and the religious authorities'. So completely has his community identified the man with his impairment that now they are befuddled, trying to decide whether he is the same man. The man refuses their binary categories and claims an integrated identity with his response: "I am" (*egō eimi*; note that the word "the man" does not appear in the Greek text but has been inserted by the translators). That is, he is both the very man who used to sit and beg, and he is something more than that, all at once. Moving into one's future story with God, for the Fourth Gospel, does not mean denying one's former life (see John 4; 21). Like most normate gazers,[20] the neighbors identify him with his disability; he does not. He is the same person, blind or sighted. The "I Am" (*egō eimi*) statements constitute one of the most famous and celebrated features of the Gospel's conveyance of its christological claims. Use of the *egō eimi* on his part associates him with Jesus and is a bold expression of identity. The fact that he had to *keep* saying it (the force of the Greek imperfect tense, *elegen*) implies an ongoing interaction and interrogation.

Not surprisingly, perhaps, the neighbors repeatedly (imperfect: *elegon*) demand an explanation; healing usually has social ramifications. When one person receives healing, others want to know whether it will disturb their own equilibrium. We will see the same fear and lack of support from the parents and the religious leaders. The man recounts the experience, using Jesus's name (which implies some knowledge of Jesus) and the same words the narrator used, which certifies the man as a reliable character.

Verse 13 again raises the question of the man's agency. Why would the neighbors "bring" the man to the Pharisees when he can see? If the language is merely figurative, by what authority do they act on the man? The (nondisabled) neighbors continue to treat the man as "lesser than" (perhaps implied already by their naming him a beggar) and assume that they have the right to drag him to the authorities.

20. Read Rosemarie Garland-Thomson, "The Politics of Staring: Visual Rhetorics of Disability in Popular Photography," in *Disability Studies: Enabling the Humanities*, ed. Sharon L. Snyder, Brenda Jo Brueggemann, and Rosemarie Garland-Thomson (New York: Modern Language Association of America, 2002), 56–75.

Those who are in wheelchairs will recognize the experience in which someone approaches them and grabs the handles of the wheelchair and moves them "out of the way" without ever asking permission. People do not seize nondisabled people without permission and move them.

SCENE 3: VERSES 13–17

The reader now learns that, as in chapter 5, Jesus performed the cure/miracle on the Sabbath. On the surface, the conversation appears to be about the miraculous cure, as verse 14 repeats that he "opened his eyes" and verse 15 has the Pharisees continually ask him "how he had received his sight." Once again, the verb is in the imperfect tense (*ērōtōn*), stressing the ongoing ordeal to which the man is being subjected. He stands firmly confident and unabashed as he epitomizes his experience, testifies, and evangelizes. Like the neighbors, instead of celebrating with the man and giving glory to God, the Pharisees bicker among themselves, but this time about the identity of Jesus rather than the man born blind, so that the story transitions to the question of whether Jesus himself is a sinner. The identity of Jesus is this author's main concern; like so many other stories in the Fourth Gospel, this man and his disability are a plot device, a foil even, to get the focus back on Jesus. The man is then called to testify. Whereas he first identified Jesus merely as a person (*anthrōpos*), he now reveals a deeper understanding of who Jesus is: a prophet.[21] To call Jesus a prophet is to ascribe him religious authority; recall that Moses, Elijah, and Elisha all performed cure miracles.

SCENE 4: VERSES 18–23

The Pharisees next interrogate the man's parents to build a case against Jesus. To say that the parents fail to support their son in any way as he attempts to negotiate the power structures of his society is an understatement. They cower, fearing the cost of defending their son, while the man who had been blind speaks truth to power. No matter—like many people with disabilities today, he is probably used

---

21. The same pattern of burgeoning comprehension regarding Jesus's identity appears in the Samaritan woman story in John 4.

to standing (or sitting) *alone* and *against*. But who is more disabled here, the man or his parents?[22]

SCENE 5: VERSES 24–34

Irony based on the verb "to know" (*ginōskō*) abounds in this scene. The leaders claim to know that Jesus is a sinner, and they attempt to bully the man into siding with them and against Jesus. He is caught in the middle of the tension between his healer and the system that would prefer to keep him impaired rather than attempt an overhaul of the system, which might displace their own power. The man pleads ignorance concerning their academic debate but insists on what he does know—Jesus did, in fact, open his eyes (literally and metaphorically). They continue to badger him, but he knows that they are impervious to the gospel so he has a bit of fun at their expense. He *acts up.*[23]

As usual, acting up to the powers that be brings swift castigation, threat, and rejection. They attempt to dissociate Jesus from Moses in order to make the man choose Moses. They base this on their so-called knowledge. The irony remains thick about who knows what. They declare that they do not know where Jesus is from and base their rejection of him on that fact. The experienced reader of John knows that the question of where Jesus is from (above), by whom he has been sent (God),[24] and where he is going (to God) is paramount and that the leaders condemn themselves by accidentally speaking the truth, because, in fact, they do *not* know where Jesus is from and they do not care to learn the truth about him. Both what they know and what they do not know indicts them.

The man commandeers the floor and presents a logical, theological argument. They try to subordinate the man with the statement: "*We* . . . but *you.* . . ." He dismisses their move and in verse 31 declares, "*We* know that God does not listen to sinners, but he does listen to one who worships him and obeys his will [which the leaders are patently failing to do]. . . . If this man were not *from God*, he could

---

22. Note my own use of disability as a "metaphor" here. Is it legitimate?
23. If you are unfamiliar with ACT UP, see www.actupny.org.
24. The author plays on this theme by telling the reader that Jesus sends (9:7) the man to the pool of Siloam (which means "Sent") to wash (which amounts to doing the works of God).

do nothing" (let alone miraculously provide sight).[25] They immediately dissociate themselves once again, using categories of "you" and
"us." The plot of the entire narrative (beginning with 1:11) involves
the quest of the religious leaders to disable Jesus because of his refusal
to accept the unjust, death-dealing, violent terms of normate society.
When this formerly blind man chooses to side with Jesus, they move
to ad hominem attack that focuses on the man's sin, just as the disciples had done at the beginning of this passage. The verb used in
verse 34, *ekballō*, is quite violent; it is the word used for driving out
demons. Demonizing those who refuse to cooperate with hegemonic
systems is common, of course (recall that Jesus is accused of having
a demon in the very next chapter), and is a strategy still deployed
against people with disabilities.

SCENE 6: VERSES 35–41

In the final scene, Jesus once again initiates the interaction and provokes the man's revelation of Jesus as the Son of Man: "You have
seen him." Note the use of the perfect tense here, whose force is to
highlight that the completed action has ongoing effect in the present. So complete is the man's understanding and commitment that
he now calls Jesus not "person" or even "prophet," but "Lord" (*kyrie*)
and declares his belief. The author clearly states that the purpose of
the Gospel is to engender belief (20:31); thus the man perfectly exem-
plifies the call to discipleship. His willingness to engage Jesus and ask
questions about his identity (reminiscent of the Samaritan woman in
John 4) leads him, finally, to worship Jesus (v. 38).

Jesus then speaks to (or for the benefit of) the Pharisees when
he says: "I came into this world for judgment so that those who
do not see may see, and those who do see may become blind"; the
reader recalls Jesus's earlier statements about seeing, light, and darkness: "Very truly, I tell you, no one can see the kingdom of God

25. "The most stringent power we have over another is not physical coercion but the ability
to have the other accept our definition of them" in Stanley Hauerwas, "Community and Diversity: The Tyranny of Normality," in *Critical Reflections on Stanley Hauerwas' Theology of Disability: Disabling Society, Enabling Theology*, ed. John Swinton (Binghamton, NY: Haworth Pastoral
Press, 2004), 40. "Bodies show up in stories as dynamic entities that resist or refuse the cultural
scripts assigned to them" in David T. Mitchell and Sharon L. Snyder, *Narrative Prosthesis: Disability and the Dependencies of Discourse* (Ann Arbor, MI: University of Michigan Press, 2000),
49.

without being born from above" (3:3). Clearly the man born blind sees the kingdom of God. Further, Jesus says:

> And this is the judgment, that the light has come into the world, and people loved darkness rather than light because their deeds were evil. For all who do evil hate the light and do not come to the light, so that their deeds may not be exposed. But those who do what is true come to the light, so that it may be clearly seen that their deeds have been done in God. (3:19–21)

Jesus, the light of the world, has come into the world and is shining in the faces of the Pharisees. They hate the light and want to do the evil deed of disabling Jesus through death. The man born blind sees the light and does the work of God by believing in Jesus. The Pharisees intuit that Jesus refers to them, and they find it incredible that they, given all their knowledge, status, and power, should be considered blind (which is a code word for "ignorant" here). Jesus disrupts the analogy by indicating that those born blind (as was the man they have just accused of being a sinner) are not sinners. Those who stand judged are the nondisabled, physically sighted who claim too much for themselves with respect to insight, and commit the sin of willful ignorance, not to mention abuse of power (see 15:22) and the demeaning of those who are visually impaired.[26]

TWO SCHOLARLY TRAJECTORIES: WARREN CARTER AND KERRY WYNN

I noted earlier Junior and Schipper's suggestion that we should review not only the ways that the texts construe disability but also the ways that interpreters of the texts construe it. I also observed that disability studies is interdisciplinary, so scholars use a variety of methodologies to analyze texts.

Warren Carter performs a disability studies reading of John 5 and 9 through a postcolonial lens and suggests that impaired characters in the Fourth Gospel may be interpreted as having been disabled by

26. I would be remiss here if I did not warn the reader about the legacy of anti-Judaism and anti-Semitism that has resulted from the author's caricatured, vitriolic presentation of the Pharisees and "the Jews." In this interpretation, I am reading compliantly with the author. As an interpreter, I take issue with some of the author's depictions. See Jaime Clark-Soles, "'The Jews' in the Fourth Gospel," in *John*, vol. 1, *Chapters 1–9*, ed. Cynthia A. Jarvis and E. Elizabeth Johnson, Feasting on the Word Commentary (Louisville: Westminster John Knox, 2015), xi–xiv.

the Roman Empire and their own society, a territory occupied inten-
sively by Rome. Imperial powers, both ancient and modern, posture
as providers of health and peace, whose leaders are often referred to as
saviors. In truth, imperial powers disable people in multifarious ways
from very basic needs such as access to nutritious food, clean water,
medicine, and sanitary living conditions to education, employment,
and social mobility. Empires send their own people to war, where
they sustain disabilities and invade other groups where they inflict
disabilities.

As feminists and womanists know deeply, the politics of a society
get mapped onto real bodies, particularly bodies considered deviant
from the normate body of a given society. "These bodies [disabled
bodies in John's Gospel] reveal the lie of imperial claims to be a force
for wholeness and healing even while they compete with and imitate
this imperial vision. John constructs an alternative world that participates in, imitates, and contests Roman power."[27]

The disciples may be right to ask who sinned that this man was
born blind, even if their repertoire of possible answers is too small.
While most commentators worry about the link between individual
sin and disability, Carter asks the important, larger question of the
role of social systems in disabling people: "Who sinned? At least in
part, the empire and every politico-economic-cultural societal system
that deprives people of adequate food resources and creates unjust living conditions that damage and disable people. Imperializing power
and practices—whether ancient or modern, governments or multina-
tionals—should come with a warning: they can be bad for people's
health."[28] The fact that the man was born blind may have to do with
economic and social realities such as lack of access to food and nutri-
tion and medicine. His disability may have made him a mendicant
(beggar), as his career options would have been limited. When Jesus
cures the impairment caused by poverty, he "repair[s] imperial damage" by raising his social class.[29]

Kerry Wynn finds a vigorous, heroic figure in the man born blind,
especially in contrast to the man in chapter 5. Unlike Carter, he has
a rather optimistic view of the man's begging activity, claiming that

27. Warren Carter, "'The Blind, Lame, and Paralyzed' (John 5:3): John's Gospel, Disability
Studies, and Postcolonial Perspectives," in *Disability Studies and Biblical Literature*, ed. Candida
R. Moss and Jeremy Schipper (New York: Palgrave Macmillan, 2011), 129–30.

28. Ibid., 145.

29. Ibid., 144.

it was a legitimate job that made him a part of the religious system of his day (since giving to a beggar was a good deed). "It is more blessed to give than to receive," as the saying goes. The man is living a meaningful life and seems to have dealt with his impairment in a way that he did not feel a severe lack:

> He has rejected the normate stereotype of one disabled as "victim" but has not substituted a need to "overcome" his disability or "pass" as "normal." He is comfortable in his identity as "other" than the normate social stereotypes. . . . It is in his ability to reject the normate perspective and to embrace Jesus in their mutual "otherness," not in the act of healing, that "God's work might be revealed in him" (9:3).[30]

Clearly, John 9 provokes numerous productive avenues of consideration and varied interpretations. I doubt its potential for such will ever be exhausted by a single reader or reading community.

PROMISES AND PITFALLS

Having studied the passage in some detail, let us now consider the promises and pitfalls of John 9 with respect to disability and ethics.

PROMISES

John 9 houses liberative potential for persons with disabilities. First, Jesus corrects the assumptions about impairment and sin. Second, he calls his disciples to work on behalf of those pushed to the margins socially, religiously, and economically by impairment. He calls them to *action*, not mere *contemplation*. Third, this nameless man born blind is a hero of faith in the Fourth Gospel—he gets the spotlight as one of the exemplars of the narrative whom all readers should imitate. He achieves this role not by showing that if one has great faith, one can be cured of a physical impairment. He is not a hero because he was cured (after all, the man in chapter 5 was also cured) or because he "overcame" his disability through pluck and determination. He was not even seeking a cure, as far as we know. He is a paragon because when he has a transformative encounter with Jesus, he responds by

---

30. Kerry H. Wynn, "Johannine Healings and the Otherness of Disability," *PRSt* 34 (2007): 68.

giving glory to God, becoming a disciple of Jesus, and evangelizing those around him. He himself, then, shows the fulfillment of Jesus's promise that his disciples would do greater works than Jesus himself did (John 14:12). That is, this man works the works of God by testifying openly without counting the cost and worshiping Jesus with a proper understanding of the Gospel's Christology. Like Jesus, after publicly declaring his identity with the statement "I am" (*egō eimi*), this man gets to work for the sake of God. Fourth, also like Jesus, the man claims his voice and insists on the truth as he knows it, even though those with more education, power, and status try to induce doubt and "keep him in his place." The text supports acting up on behalf of justice.

The text overtly challenges any nondisabled reader who views persons with disabilities according to physiognomy,[31] assuming to know something about the person's character or life by a mere gaze according to Colleen Grant.[32] Furthermore, able-bodied people who paternalistically think they know what is best for those with disabilities should feel addressed by the text. The voices of those actually experiencing the disability should be heard and heeded. That is, the voices of the "invalids" are *valid* beyond all telling of it. At first, the narrative displays able-bodied people who objectify the man. The more the man himself speaks, the more the categories of center and margins are redefined. In Grant's view, "the typical sin/sickness metaphor is reversed so that blindness is no longer a symbol for humanity's sinfulness, but instead representative of a state of innocence and openness to revelation."[33]

Finally, the text provokes questions about how and why some people have impairments (recall Carter's commentary) and how the community should respond.

---

31. The dictionary.com definition of "physiognomy" is "the art of determining character or personal characteristics from the form or features of the body, especially of the face."

32. Grant indicates that the punch line might be that nondisabled people, in their hubris and pride about their able-bodiedness compared to the "poor disabled in need of healing," may not realize that they are more in need of healing because their sin of stereotyping and excluding remains; see Colleen Grant, "Reinterpreting the Healing Narratives," in *Human Disability and the Service of God: Reassessing Religious Practice*, ed. Nancy L. Eiesland and Don E. Saliers (Nashville: Abingdon, 1998), 85. Referring to the diagnostic gaze of Ezra and Nehemiah, Kerry Wynn writes: "The 'gaze' in Ez./Neh. creates a narrative based on the presuppositions of the observer which shapes the image of the object observed"; see Kerry H. Wynn, "Second Temple Literature: I & II Chronicles, Ezra, Nehemiah, Esther," in Melcher, Parsons, and Yong, *The Bible and Disability*.

33. Grant, "Reinterpreting the Healing Narratives," 85.

PITFALLS

While the text clearly stands as one of the most liberative in the Bible with respect to disability, a few concerns should be noted. First is the use of blindness as a metaphor for sin and ignorance. On the positive side, the person who is literally blind in the story is good and those who are only metaphorically blind are bad. On the negative side, the association between sin and ignorance, even if "only" metaphorical, remains unhelpful to actual blind persons trying to function in nor-mate society (see 12:40 especially). In his treatment of John 9 in *In the Beginning There Was Darkness: A Blind Person's Conversation with the Bible*, John M. Hull explains how the Gospel of John may be problematic:

> Although blindness is symbolic of sin and unbelief in the three earlier Gospels, it is in the Fourth Gospel that this connection reaches its cli-max. John's Gospel was the first book in Braille that I read after I had become blind in my adult life. As I read it, rather laboriously, I was delighted to have access once again to so many familiar and greatly loved passages. However, the symbolism made me feel uneasy and I soon came to realize that this book was not written for people like me, but for sighted people. No other book of the Bible is so dominated by the contrast between light and darkness, and blindness is the symbol of darkness.[34]

Grant's admirable liberative reading of the narrative finds her putting a positive spin on blindness as a metaphor. Instead of sin and igno-rance, blindness now represents "innocence" and "openness to reve-lation." Even if one could be convinced of this flip, however, it may lead to the opposite problem—the idealizing of blindness (and blind people), which can be patronizing and infantilizing. Just as people with disabilities tire of being considered especially sinful, neither are they especially saintly. In addition, it is a short step from idealizing blindness to "inspiration porn," a phrase coined in 2012 by writer and disability activist Stella Young. "And I use the term porn

---

34. John M. Hull, *In the Beginning There Was Darkness: A Blind Person's Conversations with the Bible* (Harrisburg, PA: Trinity Press International, 2002), 49–50. African American interpreters also routinely draw attention to the association of darkness with negative characteristics; for further detailed discussion about this as it relates to the Fourth Gospel, see Jaime Clark-Soles, *Reading John for Dear Life: A Spiritual Walk with the Fourth Gospel* (Louisville: Westminster John Knox, 2016), 29–33.

deliberately, because they [certain images of disabled people] objectify one group of people for the benefit of another group of people. So in this case, we're objectifying disabled people for the benefit of nondisabled people."[35] Thus readers should be careful about the tendency to erase disability by interpreting the narrative only metaphorically, as the text pushes the reader to do. It lulls the reader away from "the real world" and interrogating hegemonic systems that disable real, embodied people. It also reduces persons with disabilities to a mere "moral lesson" of one sort or another for nondisabled people.

Another issue concerns the application of disability metaphors to nondisabled people. Junior and Schipper note: "Frequently, the Hebrew Bible uses language and imagery of disability to describe the experiences and struggles of the presumably nondisabled" (in our case in John 9, the Pharisees).[36] "Quite a lot of Isaiah's blind and deaf people have normal eyes and ears."[37] Isaiah 56:10, a text that sounds like one John might have had in mind when critiquing the Pharisees in John 9, declares: "Israel's lookouts are blind, All of them do not know; All of them are mute dogs that are not able to bark" (Junior and Schipper's translation). "This text does not focus on people with disabilities themselves. Instead, it uses the words 'blind' and 'mute' to criticize certain parties within Israel's leadership."[38] The same dynamic is in effect in John 9 (see 12:40).

Second, cure stories give the impression that everyone with an impairment wants a cure or at least should want a cure so that their body can come to resemble the normate body more closely. Such an assumption is problematic on multiple levels.

Third, Sharon Snyder and David Mitchell raise important concerns about what they term "the limits of redemption narratives."[39] Miraculous healings and resurrections are problematic insofar as they rely on the eradication of disability as a resolution to human-made exclusion. The social constructions that propagate the exclusion and oppression of people with disabilities remain intact. With this in mind, it would

35. Stella Young, "I'm Not Your Inspiration, Thank You Very Much," TED video, 3:10, filmed April 2014, http://www.ted.com/talks/stella_young_i_m_not_your_inspiration_thank _you_very _much?language=en.
36. Junior and Schipper, "Disability Studies," 27.
37. Ibid.
38. Ibid.
39. David Mitchell and Sharon Snyder, "'Jesus Thrown Everything Off Balance': Disability and Redemption in Biblical Literature," in *This Abled Body: Rethinking Disabilities in Biblical Studies*, ed. Hector Avalos, Sarah J. Melcher, and Jeremy Schipper (Atlanta: Society of Biblical Literature, 2007), 178.

be more impressive and hope-inducing in some ways, if, instead of curing the disabled body to fit normate society, normate society were healed so that the society would accommodate all types of bodies. As noted, "The acceptance of disabled people can no longer be predicated on the perverse interests that underwrite fantasies of erasure, cure, or elimination of bodily difference. Such longings for human similitude ultimately avoid rather than engage the necessity of providing provisions for our meaningful inclusion in social life."[40]

Thus, on the plus side, the author makes the man a hero of the faith, a paradigmatic disciple. But (unfortunately?) he only becomes the hero after he becomes sighted. The author uses him as an ironic tool to make a point about (1) proper christological knowledge; (2) how an engaged encounter with Jesus leads to faith; and (3) manifesting a bold, public witness to Jesus. One wonders if the irony would have been more powerful had the man remained physically blind. In either case, the man's disability is a prop for the plot. His disability has been erased—he has been made acceptable, more like the normate. It is noteworthy that while in the Gospels people who are presented with disabilities are usually cured, "characters in the Hebrew Bible tend to live with their disabilities."[41] What is it about Jesus that makes them get cured? Presumably the cures, in part, convey the Christology of the author. The apostle Paul, however, is never cured of his thorn in the flesh, and that experience affects and conveys Paul's own Christology (among other things).

SUMMARY AND CONCLUSION

With respect to persons with disabilities, the Fourth Gospel has both liberative and problematic potential in terms of implied ethics. The emphasis on diversity in creation; the incarnation; a person who is blind as a hero; the role of the community in healing; and the ability to seize life, joy, and peace in the present even in the midst of difficulty are a welcome balm. But the texts also sound warnings. Empires and societies tend to disable some people. Nondisabled people assume a normate view that disables people with certain impairments. This happens both in the way that nondisabled people *narrate* stories and *interpret* stories. In the process, people with disabilities are often

40. Ibid., 183.
41. Junior and Schipper, "Disability Studies," 27.

presented as a mere morality lesson and remain objects rather than agents in the plot. Erasure occurs.

In the end, by insisting on material creation as the locus of God's attention and activity, the Fourth Evangelist emboldens the reader to interpret in ways that promote the flourishing of all, even when the ethic of life entails resisting some of the evangelist's own moves.[42]

42. For an exemplary model of performing such a reading, I highly recommend Adele Rein- hartz's exercise in ethical criticism in *Befriending the Beloved Disciple: A Jewish Reading of the Gospel of John* (New York: Continuum, 2001), in which she models four different ways to read the Fourth Gospel: compliant, resistant, sympathetic, and engaged.

6.

The Lyin' King? Deception and Christology in the Gospel of John

ADELE REINHARTZ

The introduction to this volume traces the changing views about ethics in the Gospel of John. It then situates this collection of essays within the current reclamation of John for ethical purposes, arguing that the earlier consensus—that the Gospel was unconcerned with ethics—was based on a narrow definition of ethics and therefore faulty. A better—broader and deeper—definition of ethics, the editors suggest, offers the grounds for critiquing this earlier consensus and thereby understanding the Gospel as a rich resource for ethical reflection. Recent work by Ruben Zimmerman and Jan van der Watt demonstrates that it is indeed possible to use the Gospel as a foundation for such ethical reflection, and many of the essays in this book certainly do the same.[1]

My rather contrarian contribution to the conversation does not concern the question of whether ethics can be inferred from the Gospel or whether the Gospel sets out a broad and deep ethical

---

1. Ruben Zimmermann, "Is There Ethics in the Gospel of John? Challenging an Outdated Consensus," in *Rethinking the Ethics of John: "Implicit Ethics" in the Johannine Writings*, ed. Jan G. van der Watt and Ruben Zimmermann, Kontexte und Normen neutestamentliche Ethik/Contexts and Norms of New Testament Ethics 3, WUNT 291 (Tübingen: Mohr Siebeck, 2012), 44–80; Ruben Zimmermann, "The 'Implicit Ethics' of New Testament Writings: A Draft on a New Methodology For Analysing New Testament Ethics," *Neot* 43, no. 2 (2009): 399–423; Jan G. van der Watt, "Ethics of/and the Opponents of Jesus in John's Gospel," in van der Watt and Zimmerman, *Rethinking the Ethics of John*, 175–91.

agenda. Rather, it addresses the more specific question of whether the Gospel proposes Jesus as a model for positive interpersonal relationships—what in lay terms may be termed ethical behavior toward others.[2] As will soon become clear, my answer is an unequivocal no.

By defining the question in terms of Jesus's actions, my argument remains within the narrow, behavioral definition of ethics. This definition does not contradict the broader and deeper definition that the introduction to this volume is promoting. Rather, it constitutes a subcategory of this larger definition. Indeed, Ruben Zimmermann includes the behavioral element in his view of ethics, as indicated in his conviction that "the Gospel of John wants to reveal that the person of the Johannine Jesus (through his life and deeds) is also the basis of actions between people."[3] It is this interpersonal dimension that I will explore here.

Elsewhere, I have argued that by responding curtly to his mother in John 2:4, and by delaying his visit to the dying Lazarus (11:4–6), John's Jesus violates the norms for ethical behavior as they would have been understood by ancient Jewish and gentile audiences alike.[4] In these cases, the Gospel subordinates ethical behavior to christological demonstration, and as a consequence provides a glimpse of what it means for the divine Word to become flesh, warts and all. In the present essay, I will examine yet another Johannine example of the same dynamic: Jesus's deception of his brothers prior to the Feast of Tabernacles. I will do so primarily from a literary-critical perspective that will consider the Gospel as a unified, deliberately crafted narrative and focus primarily on characterization.[5] I will bracket historical questions, such as whether and how John's portrayal may relate to the historical Jesus, as well theological concerns, such as whether and

2. Although the Gospel likely underwent a lengthy and complex process of composition, my focus is on the final form, excluding 7:53–8:11.

3. Zimmermann, "Is There Ethics in the Gospel of John?"; Zimmermann, "The 'Implicit Ethics' of New Testament Writings"; van der Watt, "Ethics of/and the Opponents of Jesus in John's Gospel."

4. Adele Reinhartz, "A Rebellious Son? Jesus and His Mother in John 2:4," in *The Opening of John's Narrative*, ed. R. Alan Culpepper and Jörg Frey (Tübingen: Mohr-Siebeck, 2017), 235–49; Reinhartz, "Reproach and Revelation: Ethics in John 11:1–44," in *Torah Ethics and Early Christian Identity*, ed. Susan J. Wendel and David Miller (Grand Rapids: Eerdmans, 2016), 92–106.

5. Recent works on characterization, such as Christopher W. Skinner, ed., *Characters and Characterization in the Gospel of John* (London: Bloomsbury T&T Clark, 2013); Cornelis Bennema, *Encountering Jesus: Character Studies in the Gospel of John*, 2nd ed. (Minneapolis: Fortress Press, 2014), do not treat this topic in any detail.

how John's depiction can be useful for the modern Christian ethical reflection.

LITERARY ANALYSIS: JESUS AND HIS BROTHERS PRIOR TO TABERNACLES

The narrative in John 7 is set just prior to and during Tabernacles (*Sukkoth*), one of three annual Jewish pilgrimage festivals. As the chapter opens, Jesus is going about in Galilee, avoiding Judea, because, as the narrator explains, "the Jews were looking for an opportunity to kill him" (7:2).[6] Jesus's brothers then urge him to go to Judea to show himself to the world (7:3). Jesus responds, "Go to the festival yourselves. I am not going to this festival, for my time has not yet fully come." Yet after his brothers depart for Jerusalem, Jesus does the same, "not publicly but as it were in secret" (7:8). Jesus's wish to avoid Judea is understandable; although the narrative is not explicit on this point, it implies that Jesus is concerned about his safety should he show up in Jerusalem for the festival. Yet the brothers have a valid point: it behooves Jesus to go to Judea "so that your disciples also may see the works you are doing; for no one who wants to be widely known acts in secret" (7:3–4). The narrator attempts to shape our interpretation of the exchange by explaining that "not even his brothers believed in him" (7:5). This comment provides a context for Jesus's otherwise unexpected outburst: "My time has not yet come, but your time is always here. The world cannot hate you, but it hates me because I testify against it that its works are evil" (7:6–7). It is at this point that he declares that he will not go to the festival (7:8–9).

The ethical problem in this passage is not Jesus's (reasonable) refusal to go with his brothers. The narrator explains that a return to Judea would put Jesus's life at risk. Furthermore, their request is premature; a return to Jerusalem could trigger his crucifixion and glorification before their appropriate time.[7] Rather, the ethical problem lies in the abrupt reversal in 7:10: "But after his brothers had gone to the

6. Unless otherwise indicated, English translations are drawn from the NRSV.

7. The "hour" in John refers primarily to the hour when the Son of Man is to be glorified (12:13), the hour at which he will "depart from this world and go to the Father" (13:1). John 7:30 and 8:20 depict Jesus speaking openly and even being threatened, but not being harmed, "because his hour had not yet come." The topic is treated in the major commentaries; see also Michael A. Daise, *Feasts in John: Jewish Festivals and Jesus' "Hour" in the Fourth Gospel*, WUNT 2/229 (Tübingen: Mohr Siebeck, 2007).

festival, then he also went, not publicly but as it were in secret." Jesus has lied to his brothers.

COPING WITH CONTRADICTION

The contradiction between Jesus's words to his brothers and his behavior is apparent not only to later readers but to the Gospel's narrator as well. The Greek, in contrast to the NRSV, does not begin with the adversative conjunction "but" (but after his brothers had gone). Later on in the verse, however, it uses *alla* to contrast his secret travel to Jerusalem with the open appearance that his brothers had urged: "At the same time as his brothers went . . . Jesus also went up but in secret" (*hōs de anebēsan hoi adelphoi autou eis tēn heortēn, tote kai autos anebē ou phanerōs alla [hōs] en kryptō*). This verse explains why Jesus lied: he did not wish to go up to Jerusalem openly with them, but secretly on his own. This point follows as a natural consequence of the points made earlier in the passage, including the reference to Jewish hostility, to the prematurity of the hour, and to the brothers' lack of belief.

The narrator, then, seems untroubled by the fact of Jesus's deception of his brothers. He does not deny the lie but rather justifies it by providing a rationale that makes sense on both narrative grounds (the Jews were trying to kill him) and christological grounds (his hour had not yet come). In contrast to the narrator, scribes and commentators from the ancient period to the present have bent over backward to avoid the obvious literal meaning of Jesus's behavior with regard to his brothers, that is, to deny that he was lying.

The manuscript tradition presents two different versions of 7:8. Important manuscripts such as Codex Sinaiticus, Codex Bezae, the Latin, and the Old Syriac read: "I am *not* going up [*egō ouk anabainō*]." Porphyry, who drew attention to this contradiction, also appeared to have a text that read *ouk* (not).[8] Some of the earliest manuscripts, however, such as P66 and P75, read: "I am *not yet* going up [*egō oupō anabainō*]."[9] According to the text-critical criterion of *lectio difficilior*

8. Wayne Campbell Kannaday, *Apologetic Discourse and the Scribal Tradition: Evidence of the Influence of Apologetic Interests on the Text of the Canonical Gospels* (Atlanta: Society of Biblical Literature, 2004), 97.

9. Raymond E. Brown, *The Gospel according to John I–XII*, AB 29 (Garden City, NY: Doubleday, 1966), 307; Chrys C. Caragounis, "Jesus, His Brothers and the Journey to the Feast (John 7:8–10)," *SEÅ* 63 (1998): 177–87.

probabilior (the more difficult reading is likely to be the more authentic), most scholars consider *ouk* to be the likely reading; it is easier to understand why a scribe would change "not" to "not yet" than it is to understand why a scribe would change "not yet" to "not."[10]

There are dissenting voices, to be sure. Among them is Chrys C. Caragounis, who attempts to provide exegetical justification for favoring *oupō*. In line with his argument that the "not yet" reading is better than the "not" reading, Caragounis suggests that none of the interpretations offered by the commentators can be correct because they have applied the criterion of *lectio difficilior probabilior* too rigidly and therefore misunderstood the textual history of the passage.[11] He argues, "In adhering to the currently accepted reading, we have an unsolvable problem in our hands."[12] His arguments for the *oupō* reading, however, are no more convincing than the arguments that he dismisses. He suggests, for example, that scribes may have been trying to avoid the repetition of *oupō*, which had already appeared in 7:6, without noticing the contradiction that the *ouk* reading introduces. Most scholars have not been persuaded.

Caragounis is unquestionably correct on one point, however. At the same time as most commentators accept the *lectio difficilior*, they also are at pains to explain away the contradiction exegetically.[13] D. Moody Smith simply states that "in the Gospel of John, Jesus acts at the behest of no one," perhaps implicitly acknowledging and justifying the lie.[14] C. K. Barrett suggests that Jesus's negative response did not refer to his intention, but constituted a rejection of the brothers' request.[15] Rudolf Schnackenburg argues that Jesus's refusal stems from his knowledge that this is not the feast at which his hour (the appointed time for his crucifixion, ascension, and glorification)

---

10. Schnackenburg notes that the *ouk* reading "qualifies as a *lectio difficilior*, since it seems probable that the other was introduced to harmonize with v. 10 or by contamination from the *hupo* in v. 6." He further notes that this example shows that the "early Egyptian text [p66, p75] is not necessarily always the original." Rudolf Schnackenburg, *The Gospel according to St. John* (New York: Seabury, 1980), 1:141. See also C. K Barrett, *The Gospel according to St. John: An Introduction with Commentary and Notes on the Greek Text*, 2nd ed. (Philadelphia: Westminster, 1978), 311.

11. Caragounis, "Jesus, His Brothers and the Journey to the Feast," 181.

12. Ibid., 178.

13. Ibid., 177. Among those who do not accept *ouk* as the earliest reading is Ernst Haenchen, *John 2: A Commentary on the Gospel of John*, trans. Robert W. Funk, ed. Robert W. Funk and Ulrich Busse, Hermeneia (Philadelphia: Fortress Press, 1984), 7.

14. D. Moody Smith, *John*, ANTC (Nashville: Abingdon, 1999), 169.

15. Barrett, *Gospel according to St. John*, 313.

will come, and not from a desire to deceive his brothers.[16] Craig Keener compares Jesus's response to his brothers to his gruff words to his mother in 2:4: "As with his mother, so here Jesus does what is requested, after he has established that he acts for different reasons from those for which the request was originally made."[17] Raymond Brown argues that Jesus's words to his brothers are an example of the two-level meaning that is characteristic of Johannine narrative technique:

> The answer that Jesus gives his brothers in vss. 6–10 is a classic instance of the two levels of meaning found in John. On the purely natural level it appears to the brothers that Jesus does not find this an opportune time to go up to the festival at Jerusalem. Jesus' subsequent behavior in going up to the festival shows us, however, that this was not really what he meant. John has prepared the reader to understand Jesus' real meaning by the reference to death at the hand of "the Jews" in vs. 1. When Jesus speaks of his "time," he is speaking on the level of the divine plan. . . . At this festival he will not *go up* (vs. 8), that is, go up to the Father.[18]

These proposals do not address the problem of Jesus's deception head on; rather, they explain it away by offering interpretations that contradict the commonsense meaning of the passage. This amounts to an implicit acknowledgment that Jesus has misled his brothers without labeling the behavior, and therefore without addressing the ethical question.

What commentators seem not to have noticed—or are unwilling to notice—is that the contradiction disappears if we are able to accept that the Johannine Jesus lied to his brothers. As noted above, this point seems not to have bothered the evangelist. While it is possible that the Gospel writer did not recognize that he had placed Jesus in an ethically compromising situation, the nature of his explanation suggests that he recognized the lie but was not troubled by it. In other

16. Caragounis, "Jesus, His Brothers and the Journey to the Feast," 180; Schnackenburg, *Gospel according to St. John*, 1:141.

17. Craig S. Keener, *The Gospel of John: A Commentary* (Peabody, MA: Hendrickson, 2003), 1:704.

18. Brown, *Gospel according to John I–XII*, 308. Brown argues that John is playing on the verb *anabainein*, which can mean to go up in pilgrimage to Mount Zion and Jerusalem, and can also mean "to ascend.". . . The two levels of meaning were recognized by early commentators. Epiphanius (*Pan.* 6.25; GCS 31:295) says: "He speaks to his brothers spiritually and in a mystery, and they did not understand what he said. For he told them that he would not ascend at that feast, neither into heaven nor on the cross to fulfill the plan of his suffering and the mystery of salvation."

words, the evangelist did not find it necessary to portray Jesus as "turning the other cheek" or otherwise behaving "well" and courteously with regard to his unbelieving brothers.

JESUS AS BIBLICAL HERO

In this regard, the Johannine narrator resembles his counterparts in the Jewish Scriptures. The Tanak recounts several incidents in which lying played a central and, in some cases, positive role for the fate of Israel. Abram, later Abraham, lied twice when he claimed that Sarah was his sister and not his wife (Genesis 12 and 20). Isaac similarly lied about Rebecca (Gen 26:6–11); and he in turn was deceived in his old age when his younger son Jacob claimed to be his older twin, Esau (Gen 27:1–38). In the Exodus narrative, Moses lied to Pharaoh about the true purpose of their exodus (Exod 10:7–11). In Joshua 2, the prostitute Rahab lied to the messengers of the king of Jericho in order to protect the two Israelites whom she was hiding (2:1–5).

These biblical stories have two points in common: The person being deceived is labeled "bad" within the narrative; and the deceit is necessary for the survival of an important character or to move a divinely approved project forward. These same points are true in John 7. The brothers are on the side of Jesus's enemies; the deceit allows Jesus to make his way to Jerusalem in secret. This may have had the advantage of avoiding detection by the Jews who were aiming to kill him, but it also—contradictorily—provided an opportunity for Jesus to speak to the crowds at the temple, at least some of whom were receptive to the message.

In portraying Jesus as deceiving his brothers, the Gospel of John therefore places him in the category of some of the great figures of the Torah. There is no hint within the passage that these parallels are intended. Neither do they cohere with the Gospel's direct references to Abraham, Jacob, and Moses. Jacob is mentioned in conjunction with the well at which Jesus meets the Samaritan woman (4:5). Abraham is prominent in Jesus's discourse in John 8:33–59, in which Jesus contradicts the Jews' claim that Abraham is their father and insists that "before Abraham was, I am" (8:58). The comparison with Moses extends throughout the Gospel; in 1:17, the narrator states that "the law indeed was given through Moses; grace and truth came through Jesus Christ." Nevertheless, the Gospel, like the Torah, does not make anything of the ethical breaches of its main character. Indeed, it implicitly justifies them, or at least this one, on christological grounds.

"YOU SHALL NOT BEAR FALSE WITNESS AGAINST YOUR NEIGHBOR" (EXODUS 20:16)

Jerome Neyrey reminds us not to presume that our twenty-first-century values were also held by those who lived two millennia ago. Rather, "the ancient world most definitely held different views of deception and lying than we do, and it would be ethnocentric and anachronistic to expect them to conform to our changing and perhaps relative standards of morality in this area."[19]

This may be true; nevertheless, it is hard to imagine that the Gospel writer was unaware of the ethical difficulty inherent in this narrative. He would surely have known that lying is explicitly forbidden in the Decalogue: "You shall not bear false witness against your neighbor" (Exod 20:16). He may also have known that "a lying tongue" was among the "six things that the Lord hates," according to Proverbs 6:16–19.

Lying was also frowned on in the broader Greco-Roman society. To be sure, Socrates, in book 3 of Plato's *Republic*, proposes that rulers present a "noble lie" to their subjects. This noble lie is in the form of a myth of origins. The myth has two parts: it asserts, first, that everyone was created under the earth and then brought forth by the earth, which is their mother (*Republic* 3.414de); and, second, that everyone has metal—gold, silver, iron, or brass—running in their veins, which in turn determines their social roles: rulers, helpers, and so on (*Republic* 3.415a–d).[20] But people other than rulers "must surely prize truth most highly" (*Republic* 3.389b).

In his *Nicomachean Ethics*, Aristotle describes falsehood as culpable, whereas truth is "noble and worthy of praise. Thus, the truthful man

---

19. Jerome H. Neyrey, *The Gospel of John in Cultural and Rhetorical Perspective* (Grand Rapids: Eerdmans, 2009), 280.

20. The noble lie has been the subject of numerous studies. For example, see David Lay Williams, "Plato's Noble Lie: From Kallipolis to Magnesia," *History of Political Thought* 34, no. 3 (2013): 363–92; Daniel Dombrowski, "Plato's 'Noble' Lie," *History of Political Thought* 17, no. 4 (1997): 565–78.

is another case of a man who, being in the mean, is worthy of praise, and [the] untruthful man [is] culpable." By contrast, he continues:

> The man who in the matters in which nothing of this sort [justice] is at stake is true both in word and in life because his character is such. But such a man would seem to be as a matter of fact equitable. For the man who loves truth, and is truthful where nothing is at stake, will still more be truthful where something is at stake; he will avoid falsehood as something base, seeing that he avoided it even for its own sake; and such a man is worthy of praise. He inclines rather to understate the truth; for this seems in better taste because exaggerations are wearisome. (Aristotle, *Nicomachean Ethics* 4.7)[21]

For Aristotle, then, even minor falsehoods make a person culpable. That lying is "not right" is presumed by Epictetus, who uses lying to explain philosophical thinking in the *Enchiridion* (ca. 135 CE).

> The first and most necessary topic in philosophy is that of the use of moral theorems, such as, "We ought not to lie"; the second is that of demonstrations, such as, "What is the origin of our obligation not to lie"; the third gives strength and articulation to the other two, such as, "What is the origin of this is a demonstration." For what is demonstration? What is consequence? What contradiction? What truth? What falsehood? The third topic, then, is necessary on the account of the second, and the second on the account of the first. But the most necessary, and that whereon we ought to rest, is the first. But we act just on the contrary. For we spend all our time on the third topic, and employ all our diligence about that, and entirely neglect the first. Therefore, at the same time that we lie, we are immediately prepared to show how it is demonstrated that lying is not right. (Epictetus, *Enchiridion* 52)[22]

Whether John was directly aware of the works of Plato and Aristotle, or of the Stoic thought world of his near-contemporary Epictetus, cannot be determined. Nevertheless, the discussions in these widely read works may well have reflected ideas with which he would have been familiar.

Several New Testament texts also proscribe lying. Colossians 3:9–10 grounds its opposition to lying in the "new self" that believers

---

21. Aristotle, *The Nicomachean Ethics*, ed. W. D. Ross and J. O. Urmson (Oxford: Oxford University Press, 1980), 101.

22. Epictetus, *The Works of Epictetus, His Discourses, in Four Books, the Enchiridion, and Fragments*, ed. Thomas Wentworth Higginson (New York: Thomas Nelson & Sons, 1890), 400.

have acquired: "Do not lie to one another, seeing that you have stripped off the old self with its practices and have clothed yourselves with the new self, which is being renewed in knowledge according to the image of its creator." First Timothy 1:9–11 includes liars in its lengthy list of the guilty, comprising "the lawless and disobedient, for the godless and sinful, for the unholy and profane, for those who kill their father or mother, for murderers, fornicators, sodomites, slave traders, liars, perjurers, and whatever else is contrary to the sound teaching that conforms to the glorious gospel of the blessed God." The same is true of Revelation 21:8, which promises that for "the cowardly, the faithless, the polluted, the murderers, the fornicators, the sorcerers, the idolaters, and all liars, their place will be in the lake that burns with fire and sulfur, which is the second death." It is clear, then, that lying was frowned on in Jewish, Greco-Roman, and New Testament sources.

Furthermore, Torah and New Testament alike view truth-telling as a characteristic of the divine. Balaam informs Balak that

> God is not a human being, that he should lie,
> or a mortal, that he should change his mind.
> Has he promised, and will he not do it?
> Has he spoken, and will he not fulfill it?" (Num 23:19)

This same point is emphasized in New Testament texts. Titus 1:2 refers to "the hope of eternal life that God, who never lies, promised before the ages began." Hebrews 6:17–18 explains that "when God desired to show even more clearly to the heirs of the promise the unchangeable character of his purpose, he guaranteed it by an oath, so that through two unchangeable things, in which it is impossible that God would prove false, we who have taken refuge might be strongly encouraged to seize the hope set before us." Acts even provides a paradigmatic episode in which lying was punished by death, when Ananias and Sapphira lied about the property that they were bringing into the community upon joining.

> But a man named Ananias, with the consent of his wife Sapphira, sold a piece of property; with his wife's knowledge, he kept back some of the proceeds, and brought only a part and laid it at the apostles' feet. "Ananias," Peter asked, "why has Satan filled your heart to lie to the Holy Spirit and to keep back part of the proceeds of the land? While it remained unsold, did it not remain your own? And after it was sold,

were not the proceeds at your disposal? How is it that you have contrived this deed in your heart? You did not lie to us but to God!" Now when Ananias heard these words, he fell down and died. And great fear seized all who heard of it. (Acts 5:1–5)

LIES AND TRUTH IN THE GOSPEL OF JOHN

Although Jesus does not speak the truth to his brothers, the Fourth Gospel, like other scriptural texts, does place a high value on truth. John 19:35 and 21:24 emphasize that the testimony of the beloved disciple is true. In 8:45–46, Jesus himself claims to tell the truth: "But because I tell the truth, you do not believe me. Which of you convicts me of sin? If I tell the truth, why do you not believe me?" In 5:31–32, Jesus discusses truth in a forensic context: "If I testify about myself, my testimony is not true. There is another who testifies on my behalf, and I know that his testimony to me is true."

While this passage discounts the forensic truth value of Jesus's words, elsewhere his words are described as "true," as in John 16:7, in which Jesus tells the disciples: "I tell you the truth: it is to your advantage that I go away, for if I do not go away, the Advocate will not come to you; but if I go, I will send him to you." In John 8, Jesus asserts his own truthful nature while condemning the Jews as murderers: "Now you are trying to kill me, a man who has told you the truth that I heard from God. This is not what Abraham did" (8:40). John's Jews are not only murderers but also liars: "You are from your father the devil, and you choose to do your father's desires. He was a murderer from the beginning and does not stand in the truth, because there is no truth in him. When he lies, he speaks according to his own nature, for he is a liar and the father of lies" (8:44). The charge of being liars is made more directly in 8:55, in which Jesus says, "You do not know him. But I know him; if I would say that I do not know him, I would be a liar like you. But I do know him and I keep his word."[23]

---

23. The interpretation and English translation of the Greek *Iudaios/Ioudaioi* remain highly contentious issues in Johannine studies. For detailed discussion of my own position, including my advocacy for the translation of *Ioudaioi* as "Jews" throughout the Gospel, see Adele Reinhartz, "'Jews' and Jews in the Fourth Gospel," in *Anti-Judaism and the Fourth Gospel: Papers of the Leuven Colloquium, 2000*, ed. Reimund Bieringer, Didier Pollefeyt, and Frederique Vandecasteele-Vanneuville (Assen: Royal Van Gorcum, 2001), 341–56; Reinhartz, "The Vanishing Jews of Antiquity," *Marginalia Review of Books*, June 24, 2014, http://marginalia.lareviewofbooks.org/vanishing-jews-antiquity-adele-reinhartz/.

The Gospel of John associates Jesus closely with truth, through the words of the narrator as well as Jesus himself. The Prologue describes Jesus as "the true light, which enlightens everyone" (1:9) and asserts that "those who do what is true come to the light, so that it may be clearly seen that their deeds have been done in God" (3:21).

Indeed, truth is an important characteristic of the divine that is shared by God and by Jesus. God is true (17:3) and his word is truth (17:17). The narrator states that "whoever has accepted his testimony has certified this, that God is true" (John 3:33). Jesus cries out in the temple during the Feast of Tabernacles: "You know me, and you know where I am from. I have not come on my own. But the one who sent me is true, and you do not know him" (7:28) and later on to the Jews: "I have much to say about you and much to condemn; but the one who sent me is true, and I declare to the world what I have heard from him" (8:26). Jesus is the true bread from heaven (6:32); his flesh and blood are true food and drink (6:55); he is the true vine (15:1), full of grace and truth (1:14, 17); he is the "way, and the truth, and the life" (14:6), and the truth that sets "you" free (8:32). After his departure, the Father will send an Advocate, the spirit of truth (14:17; 15:26; 16:13).

Truth is also a characteristic of those who believe in Jesus and come to him. Jesus tells the Samaritan woman that "the hour is coming, and is now here, when the true worshipers will worship the Father in spirit and truth, for the Father seeks such as these to worship him" (4:23). In his final prayer, Jesus asserts that the disciples have received the words from Jesus that God has given him, "for the words that you gave to me I have given to them, and they have received them and know in truth that I came from you; and they have believed that you sent me" (17:8). He calls on God to "sanctify them in the truth" (17:17; see 17:19). Finally, he informs Pilate about the nature of his mission: "For this I was born, and for this I came into the world, to testify to the truth. Everyone who belongs to the truth listens to my voice" (18:37).

Despite this emphasis on the truth, and on Jesus's role as truth, the Gospel writer is not concerned with whether Jesus was truthful in his every interaction. Rather, its main, indeed its only, interest is in Christology. Jesus may have lied to his brothers, but on the theological and cosmological planes Jesus is committed to the fundamental truth. This fundamental truth is christological and self-referential:

God is true; as his son, Jesus, is also true; the truth to which Jesus points is the truth that he is his God's Son and has come to the world to bring people to faith in himself as God's Son and thereby sanctify them in God's truth. In this broad context, Jesus's deception of his brothers is not even a blip on the radar screen.

SECRETS AND LIES: THE CHRISTOLOGICAL CONTEXT

Jesus's deception of his brothers serves a number of rhetorical and christological aims. John 7:1–10 and other passages—including those that express ambiguity, evasion, riddles, parables, and double entendres—conform to a cross-cultural and transhistorical model that Jerome Neyrey refers to as the sociology of secrets.[24] In this model, secrecy is a system "that determines who can or should be entrusted with what secret."[25] This perspective would suggest that the brothers are urging Jesus to go to Jerusalem in order to reveal secrets to his as-yet-uninformed disciples in Jerusalem. Jesus, and the narrator, in turn, are countering that it is the brothers who are and will remain outside the web of secrets, on account of their unbelief. This exchange reinforces the binary distinctions that are made throughout the Gospel between believers and unbelievers, such as the vine branches that will bear fruit and those that will be tossed aside and burned (15:2–6). These binary distinctions are one way in which the Gospel's rhetoric identifies the beliefs that it wishes to reinforce in its audiences.

The theme of deception introduced in 7:8–10 is continued throughout the chapter, but to a degree it undermines the theme of secrecy that I have traced above. In 7:11–12, the crowds at the temple themselves wonder about him: "The Jews were looking for him at the festival and saying, 'Where is he?' And there was considerable complaining about him among the crowd. While some were saying, 'He is a good man,' others were saying, 'No, he is deceiving the crowd.'" In 7:47, after the police return without having arrested him, the Pharisees say, "Surely you have not been deceived too, have you?" The idea that Jesus could be a deceiver, however, is voiced only by those who do not understand (some of the crowd) or who refuse to believe (the Pharisees). The ones whom Jesus is deceiving (the brothers) do

---

24. Neyrey, *Gospel of John in Cultural and Rhetorical Perspective*, 252–81, esp. 260–61.
25. Ibid., 255.

not recognize that they have been deceived, whereas the ones who fear they are being deceived have actually been in the presence of the truth without recognizing it.

This matter of deception, however, has a force far greater than the lie that Jesus has told his brothers. The biblical background of the verb *planaō* (to deceive, to lead astray) pertains to idol worship, specifically to leading the people astray to the worship of idols or other gods. In Deuteronomy 4:19, Moses warns the people: "And when you look up to the heavens and see the sun, the moon, and the stars, all the host of heaven, do not be led astray and bow down to them and serve them." Deuteronomy 13:13 refers to "scoundrels from among you [that] have gone out and led the inhabitants of the town astray, saying, 'Let us go and worship other gods,' whom you have not known." Psalm 40:4 praises

> those who make
>   the LORD their trust,
> who do not turn to the proud,
>   to those who go astray after false gods.

This same usage is evident in the "little apocalypse" in Mark 13 and parallels, in which Jesus warns his audience that "any will come in my name and say, 'I am he!' and they will lead many astray" (Mark 13:6; Matt 24:5). In John, the accusation that Jesus is deceiving or leading the people astray is therefore not merely that he is withholding information from them, as per the secrecy model described by Neyrey, but that he is violating the norms of monotheism that the God of Israel requires. The vigorous assertions that Jesus not only speaks the truth but also *is* the truth refute such charges.

The secrecy motif serves not only to set up the issue of monotheism but also to demonstrate that, in addition to being the King of Israel (John 1:49), the prophet (9:17), the Messiah and Son of God (20:31), the Son of Man (13:31), and of the house of David (7:42), Jesus is the hidden messiah described in apocalyptic literature. This motif comes to the fore in John 7 after Jesus arrives in Jerusalem and reveals himself in the middle of the festival: "Now some of the people of Jerusalem were saying, 'Is not this the man whom they are trying to kill? And here he is, speaking openly, but they say nothing to him! Can it be that the authorities really know that this is the Messiah? Yet we know where this man is from; but when the Messiah comes, no one will know where he is from" (7:25–27). The theme also appears during the high priest's interrogation: "Then the high priest questioned Jesus about his disciples and about his teaching. Jesus answered, 'I have spoken openly to the world; I have always taught in synagogues and in the temple, where all the Jews come together. I have said nothing in secret'" (18:19–20). This may in fact be another lie, for according to 12:36, Jesus hid himself from the people, and after that point in the narrative he does indeed speak privately, to the disciples alone.

The belief in the hidden messiah can be documented from Second Temple Jewish sources, as one of many strands of Jewish messianism from this period. Steven Weitzman notes that, like the canonical gospels, "Jewish tradition . . . holds the expectation that the Messiah will go unrecognized, revealing himself only to a few select initiates, before revealing himself to all."[26] The most developed examples of this motif are found in rabbinic literature, such as b. Sanhedrin 98a, but it is possible that this tradition predates the rabbinic period by some centuries.[27] In Justin's *Dialogue with Trypho* 8.4, Trypho turns this tradition against Christian claims about Jesus: "Christ—if He has indeed been born, and exists anywhere—is unknown, and does not even know him Himself, and has no power until Elias come to anoint Him, and make Him manifest to all. And you, having accepted a groundless report, invent a Christ for yourselves, and for his sake are inconsiderately perishing."[28]

The motif also appears in apocalyptic texts such as 1 Enoch 62:7: "For the Son of Man was concealed from the beginning, and the Most High One preserved him in the presence of his power; then he revealed him to the holy and the elect ones."[29] Fourth Ezra 7:28–29 has God explain that "my son the Messiah shall be revealed with those who are with him, and those who remain shall rejoice four hundred years. After those years my son the Messiah shall die, and all who

---

26. Steven Weitzman, "He That Cometh Out: On How to Disclose a Messianic Secret," in *Rethinking the Messianic Idea in Judaism*, ed. Michael L. Morgan and Steven Weitzman (Bloomington: Indiana University Press, 2015), 66.

27. Ibid.

28. *ANF* 1:1199.

29. Adela Yarbro Collins, "The Secret Son of Man in the Parables of Enoch and the Gospel of Mark: A Response to Leslie Walck," in *Enoch and the Messiah Son of Man: Revisiting the Book of Parables*, ed. Gabriele Boccaccini (Grand Rapids: Eerdmans, 2007), 338–42.See also Weitzman, "He That Cometh Out"; Markus Bockmuehl, *Revelation and Mystery in Ancient Judaism and Pauline Christianity* (Tübingen: J. C. B. Mohr, 1990), 38. Other relevant sources can be found in 1 Enoch 38:2; 69:26–29, 62:6; 48:27. Rabbinic sources can be found in b. Sukkah 62a; b. Pesaḥ 54a.

draw human breath." Fourth Ezra 7:31–32 states: "And as for the lion whom you saw rousing up out of the forest and roaring and speaking to the eagle and reproving him for his unrighteousness, and as for all his words that you have heard, this is the Messiah whom the Most High has kept until the end of days, who will arise from the offspring of David, and will come and speak with them."[30]

CONCLUSION

No complicated exegetical gymnastics are required to explain the contradiction between Jesus's words to his brothers in 7:8 and his subsequent behavior in 7:10 if we accept the commonsense conclusion that Jesus lied to his brothers because he did not want them to know that he was going up to Jerusalem for Tabernacles. The references to the Jews' murderous intentions toward Jesus, and to the brother's lack of belief, as well as to the "hour" that has not yet come, justify the deception (the brothers deserved it) but they do not deny it. The whole problem could have been avoided had Jesus been evasive rather than lying outright. For example, he could have promised to catch up with them later, or pleaded workload (as in, "I have to finish this rush carpentry order").

From a literary perspective, Jesus's lie throws the main themes of John 7 into relief. As Neyrey has discussed, the discourse as a whole revolves around matters of secrecy and openness, deception and truth-telling.[31] In the end, however, the deception extends only to his brothers. Although Jesus goes up to the festival secretly, he speaks openly to the crowds after he arrives. By deceiving his brothers, John's Jesus draws attention to the christological controversy that took place at the feast, and underscores the truth: that he fulfills all Jewish messianic criteria, including that of the hidden messiah. In doing so, he not only conveys but also constitutes the most important truth of all: that he is the divine Word sent into the world to save the world (3:16) from the "ruler of this world" (12:31; 14:30; 16:11).

30. Harry Attridge points out that John does not merely adopt the "hidden messiah" tradition but adapts it for his own purposes "by focusing on a point that the 'hidden Messiah' motif does not highlight: the point of origins." In rabbinic and Second Temple Jewish sources, as well as the *Dialogue with Trypho*, the focus is rather on the point that the messiah's location immediately prior to his revelation as messiah is unknown, not his point of origin. Harold Attridge, "Some Methodological Considerations Regarding John, Jesus, and History" (paper delivered at Princeton Theological Seminary, March 2016), cited with permission of the author.

31. Neyrey, *Gospel of John in Cultural and Rhetorical Perspective*, 260.

Far from leading the people astray, he is leading them to God, as "the way, and the truth, and the life" (14:6).

If we allow ourselves to get distracted by the ethical question, that is, if we focus on explaining away the lie, we risk missing the main point: that the Gospel of John is entirely, and exclusively, interested in Christology. Jesus's actions, whether "good" (as in the healing stories) or "bad" (rudeness in 2:4, lying in 7:8, failing his friend in 11:5–6), are not intended to model behavior for others to follow.[32] Rather, for John, everything he does is meant to demonstrate his glory and draw attention to his christological identity. By healing the lame man, Jesus demonstrates that he is the Son of God: he works on the Sabbath just like his father does (5:17). By healing the man born blind, Jesus allows the works of God to be "revealed in him" (9:3). For this author, Christology is primary, all other considerations, including ethics, are secondary, or rather, they are important only insofar as they contribute to the main hcristological claim: that Jesus is the Messiah, the Son of God. By having Jesus violate the norms of ethical behavior—not only our norms but also ancient norms—the Gospel makes this point crystal clear.

32. Commentators who excuse Jesus's behavior to his mother on various grounds include Brown, *Gospel according to John I–XII*, 99; Schnackenburg, *Gospel according to St. John*, 1:329; Keener, *Gospel of John*, 1:506; Judith M. Lieu, "The Mother of the Son in the Fourth Gospel," *JBL* 117, no. 1 (1998): 65–66. For an alternate view, see Turid Karlsen Seim, "Descent and Divine Paternity in the Gospel of John: Does the Mother Matter?," *NTS* 51, no. 3 (2005): 361–75.

7.

John's Implicit Ethic of Enemy-Love

MICHAEL J. GORMAN

It is commonly stated that the Fourth Gospel has little in the way of explicit ethics. Some interpreters find this lacuna rather troubling,[1] while others remind us that commandments and other forms of explicit ethical teaching are not the only way to convey moral concerns.[2] The "ethos" of a biblical writing (i.e., the attitudes and corollary practices it reflects), its narrative world, its portrayal of characters, its central metaphors and images, its allusions to scripture and to oral tradition, and its theology—claims about God and all things in relation to God—are all possible vehicles of ethical teaching. Such vehicles advocate moral values and practices in more *implicit* than *explicit* ways.[3]

Furthermore, what the Gospel of John actually says *explicitly* on the subject of human love seems restricted to love within the community of disciples: "love one another" (13:34–35; 15:12, 17; cf. 13:14). There is no obvious commandment to love outsiders, much less enemies. This apparent omission has given rise to some stark claims about John

---

1. E.g., Wayne A. Meeks, "The Ethics of the Fourth Evangelist," in *Exploring the Gospel of John: In Honor of D. Moody Smith*, ed. R. Alan Culpepper and C. Clifton Black (Louisville: Westminster John Knox, 1996), 317–26.

2. E.g., Jan G. van der Watt, "Ethics and Ethos in the Gospel according to John," *ZNW* 97 (2006): 147–75.

3. See van der Watt, "Ethics and Ethos"; Jan G. van der Watt and Ruben Zimmerman, eds., *Rethinking the Ethics of John: "Implicit Ethics" in the Johannine Writings*, Kontexte und Normen neutestamentliche Ethik/Contexts and Norms of New Testament Ethics 3, WUNT 291 (Tübingen: Mohr Siebeck, 2012); Ruben Zimmermann, "The 'Implicit Ethics' of New Testament Writings: A Draft of a New Methodology for Analysing New Testament Ethics," *Neot* 43, no. 2 (2009): 399–423; and additional publications noted in this volume's introduction.

by scholars both "conservative" and "liberal." The evangelical Robert Gundry has written, "Just as Jesus the Word spoke God's word to the world . . . so Jesus' disciples are to do. But they are not to love the unbelieving world any more than Jesus did. . . . It is enough to love one another and dangerous to love worldlings."[4] Even more scathing are the often-quoted words of the critical scholar Jack Sanders. He complains about the alleged "weakness and moral bankruptcy" of Johannine ethics. Unlike the good Samaritan in Luke 10, contends Sanders, the Johannine Christian asks the man left half dead, "Do you believe that Jesus is the one who came down from God?" The Johannine Christian then tells him, "'If you believe, you will have eternal life,' . . . while the dying man's blood stains the ground."[5]

The claim of this chapter is that, in spite of these apparent gaps and these sorts of criticism, the Gospel of John possesses an implicit love ethic, not merely of love toward outsiders generally, but of *enemy*-love.[6] This ethic is grounded in the divine act of sending the Son into a hostile world to save it, drawing people into the sphere of the love that exists between the Father and the Son. It is further grounded in the acts of Jesus narrated in the Gospel that embody such love of enemy.[7] Moreover, this ethic of enemy-love is implied in the Son's similar sending of the disciples into the same hostile world with him as their example of love, and with the gift of God's shalom and God's Spirit to empower them.

READING A GOSPEL, READING JOHN

This chapter's overall claim is dependent in part on understanding what we are reading when we read a New Testament Gospel, and particularly the Fourth Gospel. Although a Gospel is certainly *more* than an ancient biography, it is not *less* than one. The main purpose of an ancient biography was to remember a person by telling the story of the person from the perspective of the biographer. The

4. Robert H. Gundry, *Jesus the Word according to John the Sectarian: A Paleofundamentalist Manifesto for Contemporary Evangelicalism, Especially Its Elites, in North America* (Grand Rapids: Eerdmans, 2002), 61.

5. Jack T. Sanders, *Ethics in the New Testament* (Philadelphia: Fortress Press, 1975), 99–100.

6. I assume a common definition of "enemy": someone who opposes, strongly dislikes, or hates someone or something and may seek to harm that person or thing.

7. For a similar approach to love in John, though without specifically speaking of enemy-love, see Francis J. Moloney, *Love in the Gospel of John: An Exegetical, Theological, and Literary Study* (Grand Rapids: Baker Academic, 2013).

individual's ethical concerns were conveyed not only by reporting words but also by narrating deeds, in part so that those deeds might be imitated (or, if bad, avoided).[8] Thus a major purpose of ancient biography was imitation, or *mimēsis*. A common ancient cultural belief was that good teachers and deities should be imitated; Jews connected these two, believing that imitating holy teachers was imitating the holy God.[9]

One insightful way of describing John is as "a biography about the love of God breaking into our world in the person of Jesus the Jew."[10] John's apparent lack of ethical material, therefore, need not dismay us, for Jesus's activity expresses the divine love and life that he offers. Thus we need to link the activity of Jesus, as God the Father's agent, with claims the Gospel makes about God—especially God's love—and with the overall implicit, and sometimes explicit, exhortation for the disciples to imitate Jesus's practices of divine love.

The Gospel of John, then, is not just a story of a good, heroic figure; it is a narrative about God: the Word that became human (1:14) *was* God (1:1), and *explained* God (1:18). This incarnate Word is "one" with his Father (10:30; 17:11, 22; cf. 5:17–27, 30). Recognizing John as a narrative about God, while thinking about ancient ethics as imitation of the divine, correlates well with a common early Christian conviction: that God (or Christ) became what we are so that we might become what God (or Christ) is. Affirming this "marvelous exchange" led certain church fathers, and others since their era, to speak of the purpose of the incarnation as deification, or theosis—becoming like God by participating in the life of God. This purpose is expressed in the Prologue's language about the Son of God becoming flesh (1:14, 18) so that we might become children of God (1:12).[11] Similarly, Jesus the light of the world (8:12; 9:5; 12:46) has as

---

8. See especially Richard Burridge, *Imitating Jesus: An Inclusive Approach to New Testament Ethics* (Grand Rapids: Eerdmans, 2007), 19–32.

9. See ibid., 77–78.

10. Ibid., 322.

11. For a succinct statement of this claim, see Marianne Meye Thompson, *John: A Commentary*, NTL (Louisville: Westminster John Knox, 2015), 32. For an extended exposition of the topic, see Andrew Byers, *Ecclesiology and Theosis in the Gospel of John*, SNTSMS 167 (Cambridge: Cambridge University Press, 2017), esp. 49–71. On the centrality of becoming God's children, see also Sherri Brown's essay in this volume. Note: the "Prologue" (1:1–18) is more than an introduction or overview, but I retain that common designation for simplicity's sake.

his mission that people might believe in the light and become children of [the] light (12:36).[12] Theosis is also Christosis.[13]

Although theosis means more than becoming like God ethically, for it includes, by divine grace, sharing in God's immortality and eternal glory, it most definitely encompasses a robust moral dimension. Accordingly, reading John in light of the Prologue (1:1–18)—the Gospel's own "reading guide"—means taking the transformation of humans into Godlike, Christlike persons as one of the Gospel's chief purposes, and the mission of its divine protagonists.[14] We might say this goal is for people to share in the divine "DNA."

The approach taken to John in this chapter is to look at the final form of the text as a literary whole, from the Prologue to chapter 21. We will not consider the (largely older) approach to John that looks at its alleged compositional, or redactional, history. Nor will we consider the purported phases of the Johannine community that various stages of composition might have reflected. It is tempting, however, to pursue such approaches, as they might explain the centrality of "love one another" and the absence of "love your enemies" in John (specifically in the Farewell Discourse, or perhaps Mission Discourse:[15] chaps. 13–17) as the product of a beleaguered community in need of internal harmony and mutual care. But such an approach is ultimately unsatisfying historically, literarily, and theologically. Accordingly, our goal will be to focus "not on the community that *produced* John's Gospel, but on the sort of community John's Gospel *seeks to produce*."[16]

With these principles of reading John in hand, we will look at what John *states* about God's enemy-love, *narrates* about Jesus's enemy-love, and *infers* about the disciples' enemy-love. Only a very few interpreters have suggested that the Gospel implicitly enjoins love of

---

12. For Jesus and/as light, see also 1:4–9; 3:19–21; 11:9–10; 12:35.

13. See further Michael J. Gorman, *Abide and Go: Missional Theosis in the Gospel of John* (Eugene, OR: Cascade, forthcoming 2018). The term "Christosis" has recently been used especially by Ben C. Blackwell. See, e.g., his *Christosis: Engaging Paul's Soteriology with His Patristic Interpreters* (Grand Rapids: Eerdmans, 2016).

14. For a similar approach to John, see Byers, *Ecclesiology and Theosis*.

15. In *Abide and Go*, I argue for "Mission Discourse" as preferable to "Farewell Discourse" to characterize John 13–17.

16. Byers, *Ecclesiology and Theosis*, 3 (emphasis added).

enemies.[17] The goal of this essay is to strengthen their case, and perhaps to increase their number.

"FOR GOD SO LOVED THE WORLD"

"For God so loved the world that he gave his only Son, so that everyone who believes in him may not perish but may have eternal life" (John 3:16).[18] If, as 1 John says (see 4:8–10, 16), God *is* love, then this well-known Gospel text claims that God *does* love, *practices* love; divine being and action are inseparable.

For John, the demonstration of divine love is the gift of the Son, sent by the Father to bring the divine love, light, and life to humanity. This divine mission is displayed in various "signs" and culminates in the Son's healing, saving death, as the immediate context of 3:16 makes clear: "And just as Moses lifted up the serpent in the wilderness, so must the Son of Man be lifted up, that whoever believes in him may have eternal life" (3:14–15). Jesus reaffirms this mission of giving life through death in several places, but perhaps no more dramatically than in 12:32 ("And I, when I am lifted up from the earth, will draw all people to myself "): that people may be "swept" into the eternal relationship of love shared by the Father and the Son.[19]

"The world" (Greek: *kosmos*) in 3:16 refers to humanity: humanity as a whole, and each individual—the "whoever" of 3:15, the "all people" of 12:32. But the world that God loves is hostile toward God the Father and his primary agent, or emissary, the Son, as well as toward his secondary agents, namely, Jesus's disciples, who are sent out by the Son as the Father had sent him (17:18; 20:21).[20]

The word "world" (*kosmos*) appears seventy-eight times in John. Sometimes "the world" means "the created order" (1:10; 12:25; 16:21, 28; 17:24); and occasionally it refers especially to Jesus's own people (e.g., 7:4; 18:20) who, by and large in John, reject Jesus. But on the whole, even in the latter sorts of instances, the world for John is

17. A brief but significant example is D. Moody Smith, "Ethics and the Interpretation of the Fourth Gospel," in *Word, Theology, and Community in John*, ed. John Painter, R. Alan Culpepper, and Fernando F. Segovia (St. Louis: Chalice, 2002), 109–22: the command to love one another is "capacious, capable of infinite expansion" (111; cf. 116).

18. Scripture quotations are from the NRSV.

19. See Moloney, *Love in the Gospel of John*, 61, 62–64, et passim.

20. See Stanley B. Marrow, "*Kosmos* in John," *CBQ* 64, no. 1 (2002): 90–102; The *kosmos*, argues Marrow, "comes to embody . . . the rejection of the revelation, the opposition to the Revealer [Jesus], and the resolute hatred" of all who do receive the Revealer.

humanity, and the treatment of Jesus by his own people, especially their leaders, is representative of the world's treatment of God—its hatred (e.g., 15:18–25).[21]

Several texts illustrate this situation of divine loving activity in the face of human ignorance, hostility, and hatred toward the Father and the Son. John 1:10 says, "He [the Logos/Word] was in the world, and the world came into being through him; yet the world did not know him," while in 12:47 Jesus declares, "I do not judge anyone who hears my words and does not keep them, for I came not to judge the world, but to save the world"—an echo of 3:16–19. In John, the world is ruled by an anti-God figure (Satan) and is itself in a profound state of anti-Godness.[22] Yet God the Father and the Son still love the world (humanity), for Jesus was both sent by the Father (3:16) and willingly came (12:47) to save the very world that hates them. *This is nothing other than divine love for enemies.* As Craig Koester puts it:

> John's ominous portrayal of "the world" gives depth to his understanding of the love of God and the work of Jesus. . . . In John's Gospel God loves the world that hates him; he gives his Son for the world that rejects him. He offers his love to a world estranged from him in order to overcome its hostility and bring the world back into relationship with its creator (3:16).[23]

In Pauline language, we could say that "in Christ God was reconciling the world to himself" (2 Cor 5:19); that "God proves [manifests] his love for us in that while we still were sinners Christ died for us," for "while we were enemies, we were reconciled to God through the death of his Son" (Rom 5:8, 10). For John, as for Paul, the gift of the Son is a gift for enemies.

If the "mission" of the Fourth Gospel, and of the God to whom it bears witness, is to engender children of God who resemble their Father (1:12), sharing the divine DNA, then it would seem inevitable that such children will share the fundamental divine character trait of love for the world, which means also love for enemies.

We turn next to the Son, and particularly to the narrative theme of his love for enemies—God's enemy-love in the flesh.

---

21. See ibid., 100–101.

22. Satan is three times called "the ruler of this world" (12:31; 14:30; 16:11).

23. Craig R. Koester, *The Word of Life: A Theology of John's Gospel* (Grand Rapids: Eerdmans, 2008), 81.

"THE LOGOS TAKES THE SIDE OF HIS ADVERSARIES"

This quotation about the Logos from the great theologian Karl Barth[24] sums up one key claim of the Gospel's Prologue noted above.

> He was in the world, and the world came into being through him; yet the world did not know him. He came to what was his own, and his own people did not accept him. But to all who received him, who believed in his name, he gave power to become children of God. (1:10–12)

Although the word "love" does not appear in this passage, it is clearly about Christ's love for the world. This is a text about grace—a word that will occur four times just after these lines (1:14–17). It is difficult to call this anything other than enemy-love. How does this love play itself out in the Gospel narrative itself?

JESUS BRINGS LIFE TO ENEMIES

John 3:1—4:54 portrays three individuals who encounter Jesus, illustrating the Son's offer of life to all and various responses to him. The three include a Jew, the Pharisee Nicodemus (3:1–21); an unnamed Samaritan woman (4:1–42); and an unnamed "royal official" (*basilikos*, 4:46, 49), who is probably to be understood as a gentile, or at least a gentile sympathizer (4:46–54). These three figures—a Jew, a "half-Jew," and a non-Jew—together symbolize and emphasize the universality of Jesus's mission mentioned in 1:10–12 and the universal scope of God's love noted in 3:16. Together they illustrate that Jesus is "the Savior of the world" (4:42). Moreover, the two unnamed figures also represent Israel's enemies: the Samaritans and the Romans.

John 4:1–42 narrates Jesus encountering the Samaritan woman at the well and offering her "living water" (4:10), even though "Jews do not share things in common with Samaritans" (4:9b). The no-contact policy existed because the two groups were religious enemies; "the

---

24. Karl Barth, *Erklärung des Johannes-Evangeliums (Kapitel 1–8)*, ed. Walter Fürst, Gesamtausgabe 2 (Zurich: TVZ, 1976), 110, quoted in Martin Hengel, "The Prologue of the Gospel of John as the Gateway to Christological Truth," in *The Gospel of John and Christian Theology*, ed. Richard Bauckham and Carl Mosser (Grand Rapids: Eerdmans, 2008), 284.

opposition between the two peoples was proverbial."[25] Indeed, the book of Sirach claims that the Samaritans were even *God's* enemies:

> Two nations my soul detests,
>   and the third is not even a people:
> Those who live in Seir, and the Philistines,
>   and the foolish people that live in Shechem [in Samaria].
> (Sir 50:25–26).[26]

Moreover, in John 8:48 Jesus is accused of being a Samaritan and being demon-possessed—evidence of the strongly negative view of Samaritans assumed by the gospel to be "normal." Thus the typical interpretations of Jesus interacting with the Samaritan woman as boundary breaking—ethnic, cultural, religious, gender, and perhaps even ethical (given the woman's "history")—is not wrong, but it is inadequate.[27] Jesus is transgressing the boundary between friend and enemy in a profound act of loving the despised. This Savior of the world, representing the God of Israel, does not hate the enemy but loves the enemy.

The claim that Jesus "had to go through Samaria" (4:4) on his way back to Galilee from Judea would be incorrect with respect to itinerary, for there were other possible routes.[28] The claim is a theological one; the necessity is related to God's plan and Jesus's mission.[29] Jesus has to travel into Samaria, not merely because his mission is to the world but also because God loves the world that opposes God, and this divine enemy-love is incarnate in Jesus. Furthermore, implicitly, God in Jesus is also reconciling human enemies to one another, represented by Jews and Samaritans and by their coming together to

---

25. Craig R. Keener, *The Gospel of John: A Commentary* (Grand Rapids: Baker Academic, 2003), 1:599.

26. For more on Jewish-Samaritan relations, see ibid., 1:599–601; Gary N. Knoppers, *Jews and Samaritans: The Origins and History of Their Early Relations* (New York: Oxford University Press, 2013). Relations ebbed and flowed with various degrees of animosity, and the "no-contact" policy was not always strictly observed. Nonetheless, characterizing Samaritans as the Jews' "enemies" is on the whole accurate for the first century and, for John (as for Luke), theologically significant.

27. On breaking boundaries, see, e.g., Keener, *John,* 1:591–98.

28. See, e.g., Raymond E. Brown, *The Gospel according to John I–XII*, AB 29 (Garden City, NY: Doubleday, 1966), 169.

29. Ibid.; see also, e.g., Keener (*John,* 1:590), who notes other references to divine "necessity."

worship the one Father in (the) Spirit and the Truth, Jesus (4:23; cf. 14:6).[30]

The following short episode (4:46–54) involves someone "who to some [in the first century] will appear as suspicious as the Samaritan woman."[31] A "royal official" is clearly a member of the powerful elite. In light of the apparent narrative progression of characters Jesus engages in John 3–4 (Jew, half-Jew, non-Jew), he is likely a gentile. But whether a gentile Roman official, a member of the Herodian family, or a Jew in the service of Herod Antipas (tetrarch of Galilee and Perea), this man would have been viewed by the people of Jesus's (and John's) day as a member of, or collaborator with, the Roman oppressors—the enemies.

From the "human" side of John's narrative, in view of the various persons who encounter Jesus in John, the point of this story is that even unexpected characters (as with the Samaritan woman) can have faith in Jesus and receive the life he came to bring: the man's son, the man himself, and his "whole household" (4:53). This sign of life has occurred once again at Cana (4:46), the site of the wedding episode (2:1–11), symbolizing the eschatological gift of abundant life.

From the "divine" side of John's narrative, with a focus on Jesus as God's agent and God's self-revelation, the point of this story (once again in parallel with the story of the Samaritan woman) is God's love for enemies. The Roman official could not be more a part of "the world"—the world in opposition to God, the world of oppressors and even killers. After all, it will be Roman soldiers, under the direction of a Roman official of the highest order—Pontius Pilate, procurator (governor) of Judea—who will execute Jesus as an act of loyalty to royalty itself: the emperor (19:12–16). For Jesus, according to the Jewish authorities, had made himself royalty—Greek *basilea*—in direct competition with the emperor (19:12, 15), who was the true *basilea* of the empire, and the one whom the *basilikos* ultimately served.[32]

---

30. See also Willard M. Swartley, *Covenant of Peace: The Missing Peace in New Testament Theology and Ethics* (Grand Rapids: Eerdmans, 2006), 277, 304–23. Some scholars believe John 4 represents a "Samaritan mission" phase in the Johannine community's history. It is at least an impetus for both cross-cultural mission and reconciliation with enemies.

31. Keener, *John*, 1:630.

32. On this and similar themes in John, see Warren Carter, *John and Empire: Initial Explorations* (New York: T&T Clark, 2008).

JESUS WASHES THE FEET OF ENEMIES

The story of Jesus washing his disciples' feet in John 13 symbolizes both the unique salvific (cleansing, forgiving) effect of his upcoming death and its paradigmatic character as an act of self-giving love. The footwashing is an act of "socially deviant behavior" (not normally performed by hosts, or masters) that "defines the focal point" of John 13.[33] Some would contend, however, that even if there is a narrative of love for others and perhaps even enemies early in John, when we arrive at the narrative of Jesus's death (his consummate act of love), beginning with the footwashing scene, Jesus restricts his love to his disciples and teaches his disciples to act similarly—to love one another. Period.

More specifically, the phrase "Having loved his own who were in the world, he loved them to the end [and/or "to the uttermost"]" in 13:1 has sometimes been interpreted in an exclusive way as a reference to Jesus's disciples who are "in the world" (17:11). After all, Jesus washes the feet of his gathered disciples, whom he will soon call his "friends" (15:13–15); he does not go out into the streets and invite others in to have their feet washed as a symbol of his undying (and dying) love for them. As noted above, some have even suggested that God loved the world, but *Jesus* only loved his own disciples.[34] This Jesus would be the founder of an isolationist, "sectarian" group.

Yet—apart from the utter incomprehensibility in John's Gospel of the Son not loving and dying for the whole world, as the agent of the Father's universal love—the verbal echo of 1:10–11 in 13:1 should at least give us pause about an exclusivist interpretation:

He was in the world [*en tō kosmō*], and the world [*ho kosmos*] came into being through him; yet the world [*ho kosmos*] did not know him. (1:10)

He came to what was his own [*ta idia*], and his own people [*hoi idioi*] did not accept him. (1:11)

Having loved his own who were in the world [*tous idious tous en tō kosmō*], he loved them to the end. (13:1)

---

33. Van der Watt, "Ethos and Ethics," 169.
34. E.g., Gundry, *Jesus the Word*, 58–59.

The occurrence of language in 13:1 that is so similar to that of 1:10–11 could well imply that Jesus's love of "his own" in 13:1 is not restricted to the circle of disciples but is inclusive of all his own people and, by extension, the rest of the world.[35] This sort of interpretation is quite ancient. For instance, in his *Commentary of the Gospel of John 9*, Cyril of Alexandria (d. 444) interprets Jesus's love for "his own" as his love for humanity ("us who are in the world") rather than for angels.[36]

The indiscriminate love implied in 13:1 receives confirmation by the mention of Judas in the very next verse, 13:2. Why is Judas mentioned here? And why does Jesus not speak to his traitor or reveal his identity until *after* the footwashing (13:21–30)? Since the narrator tells us both in 6:70–71 and here in 13:2 (cf. 13:27) that Judas will be inhabited by Satan—"the ruler of this world" (12:31; 14:30; 16:11)—and is going to betray Jesus, his presence during the meal has powerful symbolic value. Judas represents the hostile world that is ruled by Satan and does not accept Jesus. In fact, this Judas-world persecutes Jesus, handing him over to death. The verb *paradidōmi*, which means "betray" or "hand over," occurs three times in chapter 13—in verses 2, 11, and 21. John will use the same verb in the passion narrative (chapters 18–19) to tell us not only that Judas hands Jesus over to death (18:2, 5; 19:11) but also that the Jewish leaders (18:30, 35–36) and the Roman Pilate (19:16)—representing the Jewish and gentile halves of the world—do the same. Jesus washes the feet even of his betrayer; his death is meant to benefit the entire world (12:32), the world that participates in Judas's handing over of Jesus.

Also present at the meal, of course, is Peter, who wholeheartedly embraces Jesus's mission (6:68) and wants to share fully in it, even if he does not really understand it or its possible implications for him (13:6–10, 36–38). But Peter the Jesus-enthusiast will soon become Peter the Jesus-denier (13:38; 18:15–18, 25–27).

Here, then, once again, is enemy-love. Jesus washes the feet of his

---

35. "In context 'his own' (*tous idious*) refers to Jesus' disciples but does not deny that the people of Israel are 'his own'" (Thompson, *John*, 284, referring to her comments on 1:11). It is also possible that "his own" and "his own people" in 1:11 refer to all of humanity ("the world," as in 1:10), which would make the phrase in 13:1 even more certainly inclusive. See Christopher W. Skinner, "The World: Promise and Unfulfilled Hope," in *Character Studies in the Fourth Gospel: Literary Approaches to Seventy Figures in John*, ed. Steven Hunt, D. François Tolmie, and Ruben Zimmermann, WUNT 314 (Tübingen: Mohr Siebeck, 2013), 61–70 (here 63–64).

36. Citation in Joel C. Elowsky, ed., *John 11–21*, ACCS NT 4b (Downers Grove, IL: InterVarsity Press, 2007), 84. Cyril is connecting this text to Heb 2:16.

betrayer, the "archetype of the evil disciple."[37] He washes the feet of his enthusiastic friend turned friend-renouncing enemy, representative of all of Jesus's faithless friends. The footwashing is a countercultural and counterintuitive act of grace, of enemy-love. And because Jesus is the "unique self-exegesis" of God (Udo Schnelle's term in light of 1:18[38]), then *Jesus's* love in motion, as he stoops to wash feet, is *God's* love in motion. The footwashing tells us something profound, not only about the self-emptying, self-giving love of *Jesus*, but also about the gratuitous, hospitable, self-emptying love of *God*—a love that reaches out in love to save even enemies, as we saw above. In John 13 we enter "'the heart'" of this Gospel, where we find "the extraordinary revelation of God—'God at our feet.'"[39] This is the God of whom Jesus's disciples are to become children, sharing in such divine DNA.

In John, then, Jesus is not only a "friend of sinners";[40] he is a "lover of enemies." He willingly gives life *to* the world (6:33), and he does so by giving his flesh *for* the world (6:51, 57) despite its hostility toward him, his Father, and his disciples. As Jan van der Watt rightly contends, "Sharing meals has definite ethical implications."[41] Accordingly, Jesus's decision to share this last meal with sinners and enemies like Judas and Peter, and to wash their feet, is an implicit example and exhortation for Jesus's followers to act in analogous ways toward their own enemies.

JESUS REJECTS VIOLENCE TOWARD ENEMIES AS HE PREPARES TO DIE FOR THEM

Judas and Peter reappear in the dramatic scene of Jesus's arrest, in which Peter commits an act of violence just after Jesus twice identifies himself as the divine "I am."[42]

---

37. Moloney, *Love in the Gospel of John*, 112.

38. Udo Schnelle, *Theology of the New Testament*, trans. M. Eugene Boring (Grand Rapids: Baker Academic, 2009), 674.

39. Brendan Byrne, *Life Abounding: A Reading of John's Gospel* (Collegeville, MN: Liturgical Press, 2014), 228. Similarly, Moloney, *Love in the Gospel of John*, 108.

40. Burridge, *Imitating Jesus*, 334–44.

41. See Van der Watt, "Ethics and Ethos," 166, though he does not make the connection to enemy-love.

42. See 18:5, 8 (cf. 18:6), and Exod 3:11–15; Isa 43:10–13. The "I am" is often mistranslated as "I am he."

Then Simon Peter, who had a sword, drew it, struck the high priest's slave, and cut off his right ear. The slave's name was Malchus. Jesus said to Peter, "Put your sword back into its sheath. Am I not to drink the cup that the Father has given me?" (John 18:10–11)

This incident is also narrated in the other Gospels (Matt 26:51–54; Mark 14:47; Luke 22:49–51). In Matthew (26:52) and Luke (22:51), as in John, Jesus rejects violence on his behalf against his enemies. In all three Synoptics, the incident itself and/or its immediate aftermath is interpreted either as the fulfillment of Scripture (Matthew, Mark) or as the dramatic climax of the power of Satan (Luke); that is, the event itself is bigger than the actions of the human characters. So too in John. Immediately before Peter's attack on the slave, Jesus's request to let his disciples go is interpreted as the fulfillment of Scripture (18:9). Moreover, in his response to Peter, Jesus reaffirms his need to "drink the cup that the Father has given me"—that is, to fulfill his Father's will by going to the cross.

The irony in the Johannine narrative is palpable. Only in John is Peter—as well as the slave Malchus—named. The man who would "lay down my life for you" (13:37) may now be dangerously close to taking someone else's life for Jesus's sake. Peter thinks he is *defending* Jesus, but his violent deed is an act of *denying* Jesus, a preamble to his flat-out denial to come. His violence is a repudiation of Jesus's example of loving enemies (chap. 13), of his gift of peace in the midst of hostility from the world (14:27; 16:33), and of his guarantee that what he is doing and how he is doing it is a victory over the hostile world (16:33)—though not by means of worldly ways (cf. 18:36, discussed below). Furthermore, this victorious Jesus is not merely able to call for his Father's angels; he is the very presence of God, as his double "I am" statement implies just before the sword incident (18:5, 8). The Son who is one with the Father, the agent of creation, hardly needs a disciple, a sword, or even a multitude of the heavenly host for protection or battle. Yet the powerful Word, who can knock soldiers to their knees with a word, "does not destroy his captors; instead, he gives himself to them."[43]

Jesus's penetrating rhetorical question to Peter, "Am I not to drink the cup that the Father has given me?" (18:11b), is much more than acceptance of his fate. Jesus is stating that he is going to fulfill his saving mission that gives ultimate expression to God's love for the world

43. Thompson, *John*, 364.

and draws people to himself—even people like the high priest and his slave. (Malchus's name is known because he likely became a follower of Jesus.) The image of "drinking the cup" is found only here in John, but it appears also in the Synoptic tradition as a reference to Jesus's suffering and death and to the meal that both precedes and commemorates that death (Matt 20:22–23; 26:27–29, 39; Mark 10:38–39; 14:23–25, 36; Luke 22:17–20, 42). In Mark and Matthew, the cup imagery is first used as an image, not only for Jesus's death, but also for his disciples' "drinking the same cup," that is, sharing in Jesus's fate (Matt 20:22–23; Mark 10:38–39[44])—which means taking up their own cross, even to the point of suffering and death (Matt 10:37–38; Mark 8:34—9:1 par.; 9:33–37 par.; 10:35–45 par.). Even if John does not know one or more of the actual Synoptic Gospels, John 18:11 is a clear echo of the Synoptic Jesus tradition, oral or otherwise. Thus Peter is implicitly being invited not only to accept Jesus's death, and Jesus's non-violent response to his persecutors, but also to accept his own participation in that dying and nonviolence—that is, receiving rather than inflicting violence. In 21:18–19, this implicit invitation will become an explicit call to discipleship for Peter, and a prophecy concerning him.

The Christology of this narrative in its context is critically important. Eleven times in chapters 18 and 19 Jesus is referred to as a "king."[45] The question at the heart of the passion narrative in John is, what kind of king is Jesus? The answer? He is an otherworldly king, meaning not that his reign is invisible and spiritual, but that it is defined by its source: heaven, the abode of God the Father, who *is* love and *does* love—even toward enemies. "My kingdom is not from [or "of"] this world," says Jesus. "If my kingdom were from this world, my followers would be fighting to keep me from being handed over to the Jews. But as it is, my kingdom is not from here" (18:36). His is a kingdom that is not shaped, propagated, or defended by the violence of human kingdoms.[46]

The incident in the garden, then, is at once revelatory of God (it is a theophany of sorts, as all fall down); of Jesus the godly king, the

44. Luke lacks the explicit text (i.e., "You will drink my cup"), but implies the idea in several ways, not least in the narrative of the Last Supper.

45. See Swartley, *Covenant of Peace*, 284. The references are 18:33, 37 (2×), 39; 19:3, 12, 14, 15, 19, 21 (2×).

46. See also ibid., 299–300. On the whole passage and its implications, see Eben Scheffler, "Jesus' Non-violence at His Arrest: The Synoptics and John's Gospel Compared," *Acta Patristica et Byzantina* 17 (2006): 312–26.

nature of his mission, and his commitment to that mission; and of the *inappropriate* way to participate in that mission (with violence), which also means, implicitly, the *appropriate* way: by forsaking violence and taking up the cross that draws all kinds of people, even enemies, to the Crucified One.

JESUS OFFERS HIS DISCIPLES SHALOM AND THE SPIRIT, AND REHABILITATES THE VIOLENT PETER

John 20 and 21 narrate the resurrection appearances of Jesus. Each chapter contains numerous connections to earlier parts of the Gospel.

At the supper, Jesus had promised the Spirit, or Paraclete/Advocate (14:15–17, 25–27; 15:26–27; 16:7–15), to his disciples, together with his gift of peace, or shalom (14:27; 16:33) as the disciples were about to be sent into a hostile world to bear witness and fruit. When Jesus appears to his disciples after the resurrection, he reaffirms the gift of peace (20:19, 21, 26) and breathes the Spirit into them so they can continue the "chain" of mission: Father → Son → disciples.

> Jesus said to them again, "Peace be with you. As the Father has sent me, so I send you." When he had said this, he breathed on them and said to them, "Receive the Holy Spirit. If you forgive the sins of any, they are forgiven them; if you retain the sins of any, they are retained." (20:21–23)

As in the Farewell (or Mission) Discourse, the gifts of the Spirit and shalom are for the work of mission, specifically mission that is continuous in character with the mission of Jesus, which can only mean embodying the love of God for the hostile world. In that mission, the disciples are to practice peace by offering not condemnation, but forgiveness—just like their heavenly Father—though there is no guarantee that their mission as Spirit-empowered agents of the Father and the Son will always be accepted and forgiveness thereby granted (cf. 3:18). The gift of shalom should therefore not be construed narrowly as "inner tranquility." It is a missional peace, a gift that implicitly continues the message to Peter in the garden: the kingdom of Jesus does not come through or give rise to violence.[47]

Peter is explicitly the main subject of chapter 21, and many inter-

---

47. See also Swartley, *Covenant of Peace*, 288.

preters have noted the connections between it and earlier chapters. Two matters are of interest.

First, the Greek verb *helkō*, "draw, haul," occurs five times in John. It is used to signify the activity of the Father and the Son in drawing people to themselves (6:44; 12:32), the hauling in of fishing nets (21:6, 11—the latter referring to Peter), and Peter's drawing his sword to cut off the ear of Malchus (18:10). Apart from this last occurrence, the verb is employed in John to express mission, whether the outreach of the Father and the Son or, symbolically, the disciples' mission of fishing for people. It is not accidental that it is *Peter* who hauled out a sword (18:10) in *disobedience* to the way of Jesus, and *Peter* who hauled the net of fish ashore (21:11) in *obedience* to Jesus. Peter is being portrayed as one whose task is to draw people to Jesus, as a participant in Jesus's shalom-filled mission, rather than one whose mission is to draw the sword in violent acts against enemies to protect or promote Jesus.

Second, the charcoal fire (21:9—*anthrakian*) that is associated with the presence of the risen Jesus in chapter 21 is a clear echo of the scene of Peter's threefold denial around the same kind of fire (18:18—*anthrakian*). The charcoal fire anticipates the upcoming moment of restoration for Peter the denier, through an appropriate threefold question-and-affirmation session with Jesus (21:15–17). This is a time of renewal not only for Peter but also for all the disciples, whom he represents. That renewal implicitly includes especially leaving behind "worldly" ways of establishing the kingdom of the Father and the Son, particularly by means of violence, and embracing the worldwide mission of "fishing" for people (suggested by the 153 fish, 21:11), feeding the resulting "sheep" (21:15–17), and—like the Good Shepherd himself (10:11–18)—being willing to sacrifice one's own life in the service of that divine, life-giving mission (21:18–19).[48]

Our examination of aspects of the Johannine narrative has strongly suggested that Jesus both practiced enemy-love and implicitly taught it to his disciples. The question before us now is how this *implicit* ethic relates to the *explicit* ethic simply to "love one another."

---

48. Similarly, Byers (*Ecclesiology and Theosis*, 222–23) finds in Peter an example of a "divinized," or Christlike, character who, as an "under-shepherd," shares in the suffering of Jesus the Good Shepherd.

"I HAVE SET YOU AN EXAMPLE"

A basic text from the Dead Sea Scrolls, Rule of the Community (1QS), begins with a requirement to love God wholeheartedly by loving whatever God has chosen and hating whatever God has rejected (I, 1–4). Specifically, this obligation means to "love all the sons of light" and "hate all the sons of darkness" (I, 9–10). Moreover, at some future date, according to the War Scroll (1QM, 4QM), the sons of light will destroy the chief sons of darkness, the gentile rulers (*Kittim*).[49] Is this possibly what "love one another" implies in John?

One often hears that, unlike the Synoptics, John contains no general exhortation to love one's neighbor or the particular command to love one's enemies (so Matt 5:44; Luke 6:27, 35). It is also normally said, however, that at least John, unlike the Dead Sea Scrolls, neither describes nor prescribes reciprocal hatred of enemies.[50] While true, the latter observation does not really get to the heart of the matter, or of the fundamental difference between John and such texts from the scrolls. For in each case, the root question is this: What does it mean to be children of the light, children of God, and thus to become like God? As John Meier explains, the rationale for the scrolls' promoting hatred of the children of darkness is that "only in that way can one align oneself with God, who likewise hates them and dooms them to eternal destruction."[51]

Since the purpose of a gospel as an ancient biography is, in part, to narrate its audience into the story and way of life of its protagonist, and since for John Jesus in motion is in fact God in motion, then the ethics implied by Jesus's activity—including his enemy-love—is, in part, what it means implicitly in John to become like God (theosis). But does the *explicit* ethic of "love one another" in chapters 13 and 15 contradict this compelling, but only *implicit*, ethic of imitating God?

49. See the helpful summary in John P. Meier, *A Marginal Jew: Rethinking the Historical Jesus*, vol. 4, *Law and Love*, AYBRL (New Haven: Yale University Press, 2009), 537–39.

50. E.g., Burridge, *Imitating Jesus*, 334; Swartley, *Covenant of Peace*, 277, adapting an earlier work.

51. Meier, *Law and Love*, 539.

NO GREATER LOVE

In John 15:13, Jesus famously declares, "No one has greater love than this, to lay down one's life for one's friends," describing his friends as those who obey him (15:14). Does this automatically limit Jesus's love and its corollary ethic to one's friends? Two points need to be made. First, the maxim in verse 13 is one of *definition* rather than *exclusion*. Jesus is not *limiting* his own love or that of his disciples to friends. Rather, he says that self-giving love, even to the point of giving up one's life, as he himself is about to do, is the essence of friendship. Second, ever since the patristic period, some commentators have interpreted this text in connection with Jesus's example of enemy-love and his injunction to his disciples to love their enemies. For example, Augustine calls to mind Paul's words about God's enemy-love in Romans 5, noted earlier.

> So there you are. In Christ we do find greater love, seeing that he gave up his life not for his friends but for his enemies. How great must be God's love for humanity and what extraordinary affection, so to love even sinners that he would die for love of them! (Augustine, *Sermon* 215.5)[52]

Does Augustine mute the distinctive voice of John? The narrative of John's Gospel suggests not. As we have seen, Peter will soon disobey and thereby "unfriend" Jesus, yet there is every evidence that Jesus dies for, forgives, and rehabilitates Peter. That is, Jesus loved and died for Peter in spite of Peter's betrayal; he loved and died for the friend-turned-enemy so that that the enemy could once again become a friend. Peter, in this narrative capacity, is both an individual and a representative of all disciples.

Gregory the Great reads 15:13 similarly, connecting it to Luke 23:34 ("Father, forgive them; for they do not know what they are doing") and focusing on its ethical implications:

> The Lord had come to die even for his enemies, and yet he said he would lay down his life for his friends to show us that when we are able to win over our enemies by loving them, even our persecutors are our friends. (Gregory the Great, *Forty Gospel Homilies* 27)[53]

52. Quoted in Elowsky, *John 11–21*, 174.
53. Quoted in ibid., 173–74.

EMISSARIES OF ENEMY-LOVE

There will be no ears lopped off slaves—or anyone else—by the new Peter, the disciple refriended by Jesus, and all he represents. Instead, they will be emissaries of enemy-love. The context of the love command supports this claim.

Earlier we argued that if the activity of Jesus is also the activity of God, then when Jesus tells the disciples that he has given them an "example" (13:15), he is telling them not only that such footwashing imitates him but also that it imitates the Father. Moreover, if God has washed not only the feet of friends but also the feet of enemies, then the action to which the footwashing points is not merely servant-love for friends (so 15:13–15) but also servant-love for enemies. The narrative context, therefore, of "love one another" when Jesus first pronounces the words (13:14, implicitly; 13:34–35) is itself the example of enemy-love.

The context of "love one another" is also mission. The (so-called) Farewell Discourse consists of a cluster of interrelated themes, but all are connected to the overarching theme of mission, culminating in the long missional prayer and commissioning in chapter 17. The exhortation to "love one another," and to the unity such love produces, is never far from words about the disciples' being sent and bearing witness:

"One another"	*Missional context*
So if I, your Lord and Teacher, have washed your feet, you also ought to wash one another's feet. (13:14)	a servant is not greater than the master, nor is a messenger [*apostolos*] greater than the sender. (13:16; NRSV alt.)
	Whoever receives one whom I send receives me; and whoever receives me receives him who sent me. (13:20)
. . . love one another. Just as I have loved you, you also should love one another. (13:34)	
	By this everyone will know that you are my disciples . . . (13:35a)
. . . if you have love for one another. (13:35b)	
. . . love one another as I have loved you	. . . I chose you. And I appointed you

. . . love one another (15:12b, 17b)	to go and bear fruit, fruit that will last (15:16)
As you, Father, are in me and I am in you, may they also be in us . . . (17:21a)	. . . so that the world may believe that you have sent me. (17:21b)
. . . that they may be one, as we are one, I in them and you in me, that they may become completely one . . . (17:22b-23a)	. . . so that the world may know that you have sent me and have loved them even as you have loved me. (17:23b)

Loving one another does not require disciples to go anywhere, but loving a hostile world certainly does (15:16, "go"). Thus Jesus's love command and example do not end with love among the disciples, nor do they have internal unity as their ultimate goal. Such love and unity are meant to bring others into the divine love and life.[54] "As you have sent me into the world, so I have sent them [his disciples] into the world," prays Jesus (17:18). That is, the disciples are sent out of divine love, shared among themselves, to bring others, even haters and persecutors, into the love of the Father, Son, and community. A Brian Wren hymn summarizes the Johannine sentiment: "We'll go with joy, to give the world, the love that makes us one."[55]

These two essential contexts of the love command—enemy-love and mission—come together in the warnings Jesus issues about hostility. The disciples' witness will also have negative consequences (15:18–25; cf. 13:16) simply because Jesus's own love for the world—for enemies—had such results. Parallel to the chain of mission, there is a chain of hatred and hostility similarly focused on Jesus as the center link, flanked by the sending Father and the sent disciples (15:18, 20–21, 23–24; cf. 16:33; 17:14–16; 1 John 3:13).[56]

In context, then, "love one another" includes love for the world and for enemies. Ultimately this is because "God so loved the world," and because Jesus "shows us what the divine love is like, so that we can imitate him and so participate in the divine life."[57] This is clearly a spirituality of participation, even of theosis, that is inherently missional in character. To participate in the life of God, according to John, is to love others, including enemies.

John's *explicit* ethic, then, does not contradict its *implicit* ethic. But does Jesus's own behavior contradict it?

---

54. See also Moloney, *Love in the Gospel of John*, 129–32.
55. The last lines of "I Come with Joy" (1971).
56. See also Thompson, *John*, 355.
57. Burridge, *Imitating Jesus*, 345.

"YOU ARE FROM YOUR FATHER THE DEVIL" (JOHN 8:44)—COUNTERFACTUAL EVIDENCE?

If the Fourth Gospel implicitly advocates enemy-love, is not the hate speech we find in it, even on the lips of Jesus (especially in chap. 8), a telling counterfactual proof of just the opposite? If an ancient biography was supposed to encourage imitation of the subject, then what do we do with John when the behavior of the divine subject(s)—the Son and the Father—looks unworthy of imitation?

One answer would be to take such behaviors as negative examples, which would be appropriate for a standard ancient biography, but hardly so—at least for most Christians in either the first or the twenty-first century—for a biography of Jesus the Son of God. Another answer, commonly offered by commentators on John, is to interpret the strong critique of "the Jews" in light of the alleged historical situation of a community under fire from the synagogue, together with the purported normalcy of invective speech in ancient rhetoric. In that social and rhetorical context, it has been argued, such strong language placed on the lips of Jesus is at least somewhat understandable, even if it is ultimately deemed inappropriate or worse. In this scenario, the "historical" Jesus is exonerated and the community or social world blamed.

But this explanation does not satisfy, either historically or theologically. Historically, there is significant doubt about what we can know about the Johannine community and its situation.[58] And theologically, we are still left wondering, "How can Jesus, remembered by the Johannine Christians as representing the God who loves the world, even the hostile world, spew such venom?" Furthermore, we must wonder, "How can Jesus's disciples then or now be expected to imitate Jesus if the Jesus they imitate does such things?"

The answer to how we can explain Jesus's strong language literarily and theologically lies in at least two dimensions of the phenomenon of "enemies" in Johannine perspective.

First of all, in the poetic and prophetic traditions of Israel, enemies are regularly identified by name and/or activity (e.g., Psalms 9–10, 14, 35–36, 74, 83; Isaiah 13–24; Amos 1–2).[59] Enemies must first

58. See especially David A. Lamb, *Text, Context and the Johannine Community: A Sociolinguistic Analysis of the Johannine Writings*, LNTS (London: Bloomsbury T&T Clark, 2014).

59. See Stephen Motyer, *Your Father the Devil? A New Approach to John and "the Jews"* (Carlisle, UK: Paternoster, 1997), 134–40.

be identified before there can be an appropriate response to them. Throughout the Fourth Gospel, Jesus identifies those who reject him and thereby reject God—what the Scriptures of Israel refer to as the enemies of God. And yet, even as those enemies are *identified* by Jesus in John, they are not ultimately *rejected*. Despite all the rejection of Jesus (and thus of God the Father) by "the world," and most especially by his own people (1:11), Jesus dies for all. In addition to the manifestation of this universal love in the footwashing as an icon of the cross, this universal love for the hostile world is displayed—literally—on the cross itself. The inscription on the cross, "in Hebrew, in Latin, and in Greek" (19:20), not only announces Jesus as King, but also indicates the *kind* of king he is—the king of suffering love, in radical contrast to the king of oppressive power (the emperor and his representative Pilate) and in radical continuity with the God revealed in the footwashing. "In this is love, not that we loved God but that he loved us and sent his Son to be the atoning sacrifice for our sins" (1 John 4:10). In other words, the naming of Jesus's enemies does not negate the fact that he loves them on behalf of the Father; the inscription on the cross is in "Hebrew" (possibly Aramaic) because "the Jews"—whatever the precise referent (the Jewish people, the Judeans, Jewish leaders, Jewish opponents of Jesus, synagogue members)—are still the object of God's love, of Jesus's love. Perhaps the Pharisee Nicodemus, the seeker turned defender turned friend (3:1–10; 7:50–52; 19:38–42), is a narrative sign of that reality.

Second, the Gospel of John depicts an apocalyptic conflict between two fathers and their children: God, the Son of God, and the children of God versus Satan and his children. As in the Synoptics and Paul, and as already noted, the ultimate enemy of God and Jesus (and therefore of humanity) is Satan, the ruler of this world, "the evil one" (17:15).[60] For John, calling those who oppose the Father and the Son children of "your father the devil" (8:44) is not hate speech. It is, within the Johannine perspective, naming the enemies, a statement of fact: "an essentially neutral" observation "about the natural course of affairs, not . . . hateful or unloving accusations."[61] For "the Johannine

---

60. Jesus of course defeats Satan in the cross and resurrection, an act of "cosmic exorcism" (Swartley, *Covenant of Peace*, 280).

61. Tom Thatcher, "Cain the Jew the AntiChrist: Collective Memory and the Johannine Ethics of Loving and Hating," in van der Watt and Zimmerman, *Rethinking the Ethics of John*, 350–73 (here 372).

premise" is that "actions reveal ancestry."[62] Indeed, what is remarkable, in contrast to the Dead Sea Scrolls that also depict a conflict between the children of God/light and the children of darkness, is that neither Jesus himself nor the narrator calls on the children of light to hate—much less exterminate—the children of darkness. The implicit theology in the Dead Sea Scrolls, as we saw earlier, is essentially one of deification, or theosis—sharing in the divine character: if you hate your enemies, you will be like God! The implicit theology and ethic of John is also one of theosis, but a theosis that is antithetical to that of the Scrolls: although you have enemies, do not hate them but love them, because you are disciples of God's Son and children of God the Father.[63] This participatory love, this sharing in the divine DNA, is at the heart of John's apocalyptic spirituality and ethic of theosis.

CONCLUSION

Not all that is important in a text is explicit. As Jan van der Watt points out, in John believers are never called to love God, yet everything about the Gospel indicates the presumption that believers will live in loving obedience to their Father.[64] Similarly, although the Fourth Gospel never declares "Love your enemies," it implies precisely that in its presentation of God, the activity of Jesus, the love command, and the Spirit-empowered mission of the disciples.

In the Dead Sea Scrolls, we find an explicit exhortation to hate enemies. Its theological grammar is "Hate your enemies, and you will be like God." The well-known theological grammar of Matthew and Luke is "If you love your enemies, you will become like your (perfect/merciful) heavenly Father" (see Matt 5:43–48; Luke 6:27–36). We have discovered that the theological grammar of John is, "If you are children of God, enlivened with his Spirit, you will love as your heavenly Father does and as Jesus the Son did, which means loving enemies." The fundamental issue in all of these cases is becoming like God, or deification (theosis). For Matthew and Luke, on the one hand, and John, on the other, the theological grammar is slightly different, but the net result is the same: Godlike love of enemies. And

---

62. Ibid., 354.
63. Ibid., 356.
64. Van der Watt, "Ethics and Ethos," 160.

throughout John, Jesus is the one who incarnates, models, and enjoins this sort of divine love for his disciples then and now.[65]

65. I am grateful to Gary Staszak and Michelle Rader for their research and proofreading assistance with this chapter. I am also grateful to my colleagues at St. Mary's Seminary and University and to the members of the Ehrhardt Seminar in biblical studies at the University of Manchester for their feedback on drafts of this chapter. And I am especially grateful to the Henry Luce Foundation and the Association of Theological Schools for the gift of a sabbatical grant as a Henry Luce III Fellow in Theology in 2015–16, during which this research and writing took place.

8.

Just Opponents? Ambiguity, Empathy, and the Jews in the Gospel of John

ALICIA D. MYERS

Of all the ethical categories at play in John's Gospel, the presentation of the Jews (*hoi Ioudaioi*) ranks among the most fraught and contentious.[1] Given the horrifically negative ethics that this Gospel has been used to justify against Jewish people, John's often negative portrayal of the Jews in his narrative requires continued study and reflection. Perhaps the most enduring suggestion has been the argument of a two-level drama by J. Louis Martyn, which argues for a historical conflict prompting the separation of Johannine Christians from

---

1. The translation of *hoi Ioudaioi* is a matter of some debate among Johannine interpreters, including whether one should use quotation marks around a translation to denote the literary and constructed nature of the characters of "the Jews" within John. Tina Pippin offers an especially fervent argument concerning translation in "'For Fear of the Jews': Lying and Truth-Telling in Translating the Fourth Gospel," *Semeia* 76 (1996): 81–97. She writes, "There is ultimately no clearly good translation option" since all do some injustice to the text and threaten violence in contemporary contexts (93). Adele Reinhartz argues against the use of quotation marks that can "whitewash" the historical realities of the characterization not only for the Johannine believers but throughout history as well ("'Jews' and Jews in the Fourth Gospel," in *Anti-Judaism and the Fourth Gospel*, ed. Reimund Bieringer, Didier Pollefeyt, and Frederique Vandecasteele-Vanneuville [Louisville: Westminster John Knox, 2001], 225–27). Ruben Zimmermann, however, prefers using quotation marks "in order to make the hermeneutical problem [of the literary nature of John's "Jews"] at least visible" ("'The Jews': Unreliable Figures or Unreliable Narration?" in *Character Studies in the Fourth Gospel*, ed. Steven A. Hunt, D. Francois Tolmie, and Ruben Zimmermann, WUNT 314 [Tübingen: Mohr Siebeck, 2013], 74n19). In this essay, I have followed Reinhartz's lead although I also acknowledge the logic of those who, like Zimmermann, prefer to use quotation marks.

Judaism.[2] The significant work of Adele Reinhartz and others, how-ever, problematizes the ease of this reading on the basis of additional textual evidence, the potential justification of anti-Jewish elements that it may provide, as well as a greater awareness of ambiguity in Johannine characters.[3] As a way to continue this conversation, this chapter will offer an overview of past perspectives on John's presen-tation of the Jews before turning to some insights that ancient prac-tices of characterization can provide. As an ancient biography, the Gospel of John shapes a number of characters within its narrative with the express intent of shaping the characters of its audiences as well. Exploring ancient characterization practices, therefore, provides an inroad to understanding the ethics endorsed by the Gospel of John, even though it includes few explicit ethical demands.

Using contemporary literary methods for observing the Gospel's characters, recent scholars have noted the ways in which the Fourth Gospel crafts ambiguous characters. These observations push back against past interpretations that emphasized typological, flat, and rep-resentational readings. In these past readings, the Jews were often considered opponents, consistent enemies of Jesus. In more recent appraisals, however, the Jews are shown to have greater depth in their ambiguous stances toward Jesus. This chapter will argue that exploring the Gospel's characters through the lens of ancient rhetor-ical practices of characterization supports the conclusions of these recent studies. The commonplaces and techniques used to character-ize the Jews render an ambiguous portrait; they are neither simply nor always Jesus's opponents. The Gospel of John's creation of the Jews as an ambiguous character reinforces its own, more stable

2. J. Louis Martyn, *History and Theology in the Fourth Gospel*, 3rd ed., NTL (Louisville: West-minster John Knox, 2003). See also Raymond E. Brown, *The Community of the Beloved Disciple: The Life, Loves, and Hates of an Individual Church in New Testament Times* (New York: Paulist Press, 1979).

3. Adele Reinhartz, *Befriending the Beloved Disciple: A Jewish Reading of the Gospel of John* (New York: Continuum, 2001). Some additional scholars who offer alternatives to Martyn's theory include Udo Schnelle, *Antidocetic Christology in the Gospel of John: An Investigation of the Place of the Fourth Gospel in the Johannine School*, trans. Linda M. Maloney (Minneapolis: Fortress Press, 1992); Stephen Motyer, "The Fourth Gospel and the Salvation of Israel: An Appeal for a New Start," in Bieringer, Pollefeyt, and Vandecasteele-Vanneuville, *Anti-Judaism and the Fourth Gospel*, 84–87; Brian D. Johnson, "'Salvation Is from the Jews': Judaism in the Gospel of John," in *New Currents Through John: A Global Perspective*, ed. Francisco Lozada Jr. and Tom Thatcher, RBS 54 (Atlanta: Society of Biblical Literature, 2006), 83–99; Edward W. Klink III, *The Sheep of the Fold: The Audience and Origin of the Gospel of John*, SNTSMS 141 (Cambridge: Cambridge University Press, 2007).

characterization of Jesus. The result of such rhetoric is to shape the characters (*ēthoi*) of its own audience to believe in and imitate Jesus, while encouraging their reliance on the Gospel as the hermeneutical key for such belief. The Jews' ambiguous characterization, therefore, can create an ethic of empathy with the Jews instead of antipathy against them, since the audience discerns Jesus as God's Son only by virtue of the Gospel's guidance.

INTERPRETING THE JEWS IN JOHN: AN OVERVIEW OF PERSPECTIVES

In a 2008 publication, Judith Lieu opens her essay on the topic of Jews and Judaism in John with the following words: "No defense is needed for identifying 'anti-Judaism' as a *necessary*, and not merely a possible, topic to be addressed in any exploration of the Gospel of John and Christian theology."[4] Although this present volume focuses specifically on Johannine ethics, Lieu's point remains intact. Regardless of one's appreciation of (or distaste for) the Gospel of John, its presentation of Jews has long been a troubling feature of the text. The Jews frequently debate with Jesus, express disbelief, attempt to kill Jesus twice before his crucifixion (8:59; 10:31), and are even called the children of the devil by Jesus himself (8:44). It is not surprising, therefore, to discover a history of interpretation that has utilized John's Gospel as justification for anti-Semitism not only in the Nazi movement but in contemporary neo-Nazi groups as well. Even apart from groups expressing straightforward anti-Semitic views and actions, the Gospel of John can fuel undercurrents of anti-Jewish theologies alive and well among Christians. When John's unbelieving Jews act as foils to John's believing disciples, despite the fact that both Jesus and his disciples are also Jewish, it is all too easy for contemporary readers to paint all Jews (past, present, and future) with the same, antagonistic brush.

Wrestling with this Gospel and its history of interpretation, scholars have devoted significant attention to the issue of John's characterization of the Jews.[5] Of particular importance in this regard is

4. Judith Lieu, "Anti-Judaism, the Jews, and the Worlds of the Fourth Gospel," in *The Gospel of John and Christian Theology*, ed. Richard Bauckham and Carl Mosser (Grand Rapids: Eerdmans, 2008), 168 (emphasis added).

5. The extensive writing on this topic prevents a full overview of research here. Ruth Sheri-

the work of J. Louis Martyn. Reaching near-consensus level among Johannine scholars, Martyn theorized that the Gospel of John polemicizes the Jews as Jesus's quintessential opponents because it reflects a division of the Johannine believers from local, Jewish synagogues. Martyn finds support for this reading primarily from the three *aposynagōgoi* (out of the synagogue) passages in John 9:22, 12:42–43, and 16:2. In these scenes, those who confess Jesus as the Christ either are, or fear being, expelled from the synagogue by the Jews. As a result, Martyn argued that although Jews themselves, the Johannine believers were forced out of synagogues as a result of their confession of Jesus as God's Christ, a belief the larger community of Jews did not accept. As a result of their expulsion, the Johannine believers cast the general community of Jews as enemies in their Gospel; they are unbelievers and hostile to Christ along with the world and the Romans. The Johannine believers, however, are encouraged to persist in their faith in Christ and to proclaim that faith publicly, even at the cost of excommunication from synagogues. With such confidence and confession, the Johannine believers align themselves squarely with Jesus and squarely against the Jews. According to this reading, the Jews emerge as Jesus's most ardent opponents. They are, as Cornelis Bennema writes, "the quintessence of hostility, rejection and unbelief towards Jesus."[6]

Yet, for all its potential and popularity, Martyn's theory is not without problems, including in its understanding of the Johannine Jews.[7] Reinhartz, for example, has noted that it is possible to interpret

dan (*Retelling Scripture: "The Jews" and the Scriptural Citations in John 1:19–12:15*, BIS 110 [Leiden: Brill, 2012], 37–46) and Ruben Zimmermann ("The Jews," 71–81) offer recent, more comprehensive, histories of research.

6. Cornelis Bennema, "The Identity and Composition of OI IOYΔAIOI in the Gospel of John," *TynBul* 60 (2009): 261; see also Bennema, *Encountering Jesus: Character Studies in the Gospel of John*, 2nd ed. (Minneapolis: Fortress Press, 2014), 87–100; Tom Thatcher, "Cain the Jew the AntiChrist: Collective Memory and the Johannine Ethic of Loving and Hating," in *Rethinking the Ethics of John: "Implicit Ethics" in the Johannine Writings*, ed. Jan G. van der Watt and Ruben Zimmermann, Kontexte und Normen neutestamentliche Ethik/Contexts and Norms of New Testament Ethics 3, WUNT 291 (Tübingen: Mohr Siebeck, 2012), 350–73; Jan G. van der Watt, "Ethics of/and the Opponents of Jesus in John's Gospel," in van der Watt and Zimmermann, *Rethinking the Ethics of John*, 176–77.

7. Martyn's main piece of external evidence for the expulsion of Johannine Christians from synagogues is the *Birkath Ha-Minim* (Blessing/cursing of the heretics) from the end of the first century. Yet there is no evidence that these "blessings" were in widespread use by late first-century Jews. Reinhartz, *Befriending the Beloved Disciple*, 39–40; R. Alan Culpepper, "Anti-Judaism in the Fourth Gospel as a Theological Problem for Christian Interpreters," in Bieringer, Pollefeyt, and Vandecasteele-Vanneuville, *Anti-Judaism and the Fourth Gospel*, 61–82 (here 61–62). See also the recent response to such critiques by Joel Marcus, "*Birkat Ha-Minim* Revisited," *NTS*

the Gospel's depiction of events in an alternative way. While the Gospel *could* reflect a definitive separation between Johannine Christians and Jews, it could also indicate a period of "self-definition" during which the Johannine believers left the synagogues on their own due to their divergent beliefs concerning Jesus, or it could be offering a "warning" to Johannine believers not to "return, or turn, to Judaism" in a manner similar to Pauline admonitions.[8] In a 2015 article, Reinhartz adds the suggestion that the Gospel could be relating the "trauma" experienced by the community as a result of Jesus's incarnation, rather than his crucifixion, since this event radically reshaped God's interaction with humanity. "It is the incarnation," she writes, "that breaks open the boundaries between the divine and human realms."[9] None of these options requires the forceful expulsion of the Johannine Christians from the synagogues that Martyn's theorizes, but they do still interpret a hostile relationship between the Jews and the Johannine Christians.

In addition to challenging the consensus of Martyn's theory, Reinhartz's work also makes clear that interpreters should be aware of the range of possible understandings of the Jews in the Gospel of John. One's interpretation depends greatly on whose perspective is prioritized. While one can choose to agree with the Gospel narrator that Jesus is God's Word made flesh, one can also choose to resist, instead prioritizing the perspective of the Jews over and against that of Jesus and his followers. According to their perspective, it is Jesus who is a threat to authentic faith and life. To ignore this range of perspectives, she explains, runs the risk of justifying and promulgating John's anti-Jewish stance since the polemics in the Gospel are presented as an appropriate response to negative behavior of the Jews both in the Gospel narrative (against Jesus) and in subsequent periods (against Johannine believers).

Recognizing the importance of perspective when interpreting John has encouraged some recent scholars to notice and explore the ambiguity of some of John's characters, including the Jews. Exploring the Gospel from the perspective of the Jews within the story makes

55 (2009): 523–51; Ruth Sheridan, "Identity, Alterity, and the Gospel of John," *BibInt* 22 (2014): 202–3.

8. Adele Reinhartz, "Judaism in the Gospel of John," *Int* 63 (2009): 391; Reinhartz, *Befriending the Beloved Disciple*, 40–53.

9. Adele Reinhartz, "Incarnation and Covenant: The Fourth Gospel through the Lens of Trauma Theory," *Int* 69 (2015): 40.

clear the gaps of knowledge they have for Jesus. As a result, the Jews express unbelief *and* belief in Jesus throughout the Gospel sometimes in the form of ambiguous, individual Jewish characters (e.g., Nicodemus), as groups of confessing crowds (2:23–25; 8:30–31), or as a divided cohort seeking to decipher Jesus's unusual words or behavior (7:35–36; 8:31–59; 10:21–42; 11:45–53).[10] Far from having a complete understanding of Jesus, the Jews are repeatedly left trying to reconcile Jesus's appearance with his unusual words and behaviors. Thus they are left believing and disbelieving in him. Indeed, Colleen Conway argues that "minor characters," such as the Jews, often "do more to complicate the clear choice between belief and unbelief than to illustrate it."[11] Rather than straightforwardly negative characters, the Jews highlight the difficulty of recognizing Jesus as God's Son without explicit divine involvement, or the entirety of the Gospel story. Privileged with previous revelations recorded in scripture, even the Jews need help to discern the Word that now stands enfleshed before them. Instead of antipathy, their confusion can spark empathy.

Although rooted in modern literary critical methods, the increased awareness of ambiguity in John's characters, including in his presentation of the Jews, also resonates with ancient rhetorical practices of characterization. When cited, ancient rhetoric has often been used alongside Martyn's hypothesis to justify uniformly negative readings of the Johannine Jews. In the second half of this essay, however, I will show that a closer examination of these practices reveals ways in which ancients, too, had the capacity for ambiguity. Rather than necessitating a negative rendering of the Jews, ancient rhetoric again exposes the mixed presentation of the Jews in John. In fact, the Jews' ambiguity contrasts sharply with the Gospel's much more straightforward characterization of Jesus and, in this way, reinforces the rhetorical aims of the Gospel.

---

10. Susan Hylen, *Imperfect Believers: Ambiguous Characters in the Gospel of John* (Louisville: Westminster John Knox, 2009), 23–40, 113–34; Zimmermann, "The Jews," 107–9; Craig R. Koester, "Theological Complexity and the Characterization of Nicodemus in John's Gospel," in *Characters and Characterization in the Gospel of John*, ed. Christopher W. Skinner, LNTS 461 (London: Bloomsbury T&T Clark, 2013), 169; R. Alan Culpepper, "Nicodemus: The Travail of New Birth," in Hunt, Tolmie, and Zimmermann, *Character Studies in the Fourth Gospel*, 253.

11. Colleen M. Conway, "Speaking through Ambiguity: Minor Characters in the Fourth Gospel," *BibInt* 10 (2002): 325. See also Hylen, *Imperfect Believers*, 6–7.

THE JEWS IN JOHN: APPLYING AN ANCIENT RHETORICAL PERSPECTIVE

While recent scholars have noted the importance of perspectives for interpretation, as well as the increasing awareness of ambiguity in Johannine characters, relatively little sustained work has been done on how ancient perspectives on creating and interpreting characters might affect our understanding of the Jews in John.[12] In the past, New Testament scholars have focused on Aristotle's often-quoted subversion of characters beneath plot in his discussion of tragedies (*Poetics* 6). As a result, Aristotle is cited as proof that ancients did not focus on a character's internal development over the course of a work; instead, ancients expected characters to remain "static" throughout a narrative.[13] A character was revealed rather than developed. For the Jews in John, therefore, Aristotle becomes a means to support interpreting their role as opponents only.

Aspects of this reading of Aristotle's *Poetics* resonate with ancient expectations, but it is, nevertheless, short-sighted, not least because it does not take into account the variety of ancient sources on the topic of characters. Although Greco-Roman authors do show less attention to the internal development of individual characters than contemporary writers, they do depict characters with depth, even if a personality is more revealed than shaped over the course of a narrative.[14] Moreover, Aristotle's subordination of character to plot in tragedies ignores the variety of genres present in the ancient world, some of which focus on characters almost entirely, such as eulogies and biographies. Biographical writings were meant to praise (as encomia) or shame (as invective) a subject of some historical or legendary significance, thereby encouraging its audiences either

---

12. More attention is being given to ancient rhetorical practices of characterization, including in the Gospel of John. However, most of this work focuses on the protagonist, Jesus, rather than minor characters. Jerome H. Neyrey, "Encomium versus Vituperation: Contrasting Portraits of Jesus in the Fourth Gospel," *JBL* 126 (2007): 529–52; Alicia D. Myers, *Characterizing Jesus: A Rhetorical Analysis on the Fourth Gospel's Use of Scripture in Its Presentation of Jesus*, LNTS 458 (London: Bloomsbury T&T Clark, 2012); see also Lindsey Trozzo's contribution to this volume.

13. R. Alan Culpepper, *Anatomy of the Fourth Gospel* (Philadelphia: Fortress Press, 1983), 101; Craig R. Koester, *Symbolism in the Fourth Gospel: Meaning, Mystery, Community*, 2nd ed. (Minneapolis: Fortress Press, 2003), 36–39.

14. Christopher R. Pelling, ed., *Characterization and Individuality in Greek Literature* (Oxford: Clarendon, 1990); Tim Duff, *Plutarch's "Lives": Exploring Virtue and Vice* (Oxford: Clarendon, 1999); Sheridan, *Retelling Scripture*, 68–70; Myers, *Characterizing Jesus*, 55–61.

to imitate the subject's virtue or to avoid their shame. Plutarch, the author of numerous biographies comparing the lives of prominent Greeks and Romans, offers this summary of the purpose behind his writing in the introduction of his *Life of Aemilius Paulus*:

> I began the writing of my "Lives" [biographies] for the sake of others, but I find that I am continuing the work and delighting in it now for my own sake also, using history as a mirror and endeavoring in a manner to fashion and adorn my life in conformity with the virtues therein depicted. (1.1 [Perrin, LCL])

With such attention to characterization and ethics, it is not surprising that ancients also had established practices of characterization, commonplaces (*topoi*) and techniques, meant to encapsulate and present the key components of identity. In collections of preliminary rhetorical exercises (*progymnasmata*) and more advanced rhetorical handbooks, commonplaces can be arranged topically or chronologically, but are meant to summarize the major topics ("places") of a person's character. In his discussion of writing narratives (*diēgēma*), for example, Aelius Theon lays out his list of various commonplaces needed when constructing a character (literally "person," *prosōpon*), which include origin, nature, training, disposition, age, fortune, morality, actions, speech, manner of death, and what follows death (Theon, *Prog.* 78).[15] Some techniques used for presenting these commonplaces were comparison (*synkrisis*), detailed visual description (*ekphrasis*), and speech (*prosōpopoiia*). The technique of comparison was so important for framing character that it is also listed as a commonplace in some topic lists (Aphthonius the Sophist, *Prog.* 22R; Nicolaus the Sophist, *Prog.* 43; John of Sardis, *Prog.* 180.16–181). Authors could also employ a number of rhetorical figures within a character's speech

---

15. This is but one of many lists of commonplaces found in ancient sources. Theon himself has another list arranged topically in his instructions for encomia and invectives. He breaks this second list into three categories: (1) external goods, including birth, education, friendship, reputation, official position, wealth, children, and good death; (2) goods of the body, including health, strength, beauty, acuteness of sense; and (3) goods of the mind or soul (*psychē*), which focuses on virtues of "character" (*ēthos*) such as prudence, temperance, courage, justice, piety, generosity, magnanimity, and the actions and speeches that stemmed from them (*Prog.* 109–10). Other lists in additional books of preliminary and more advanced rhetorical exercises are similar (e.g., Quintilian, *Inst.* 3.7.12–15; 4.2.2). For a more complete overview see Myers, *Characterizing Jesus*, 42–47.

to reveal their level of education and intelligence, as well as employ additional exercises and arrangements of argumentation.[16]

Authors and speakers do not always use every possible commonplace or technique in characterizing a person in their works. The existence of various and remarkably consistent lists of such commonplaces and techniques, as well as their demonstrable use in different literatures, nevertheless shows their popularity and effectiveness. Main characters were described with the most commonplaces and techniques, subordinate characters with fewer. Consistency in various traits heightened the credibility and persuasive power of a character's presentation, but inconsistency and ambiguity could be as much a consistent trait as clear conviction.[17] Thus, while ancients often reveal characters rather than develop them in a contemporary sense, that revelation could as often show a character to be ambiguous as it could show another to be reliably virtuous or even villainous.

Turning to the Gospel of John, we find a number of these commonplaces and techniques in the narrative's characterization practices. Most of them, again, emerge in the Gospel's characterization of Jesus, who features as its main character. They are, however, also decipherable in its presentation of subordinate characters, including the Jews. Although fewer, these commonplaces and techniques are no less significant. In what follows, I will argue that the relative sparseness of commonplaces and techniques used in their characterization in comparison with Jesus's heightens the persistent ambiguity of the Jews in John. As a result of this rhetorical move, the Jews' character is never clarified as much as that of Jesus. The Jews' confusion over Jesus's behavior within the Gospel is thus mirrored in the confusion left concerning their own identity, and positions of faith, for the Gospel audience. While such ambiguity encourages the audience to come to a clearer faith, it also enables the audience to identify with the Jews who struggle to understand Jesus, and who often simultaneously straddle the stances of belief *and* unbelief.

16. Jo-Ann A. Brant notes various rhetorical figures used in Jesus's and other characters' speeches in the Gospel of John (*John*, Paideia Commentaries on the New Testament [Grand Rapids: Baker Academic, 2011]), while Keith A. Reich has recently examined the extensive use of rhetorical figures in Jesus's speech in Luke (*Figuring Jesus: The Power of Rhetorical Figures of Speech in the Gospel of Luke*, BIS 107 [Leiden: Brill, 2011]).

17. Tim Duff demonstrates this aspect in his analysis of the characterization of the Athenian general Alcibiades by Plutarch (*Plutarch's "Lives,"* 237). Constantly shifting like a "chameleon," Alcibiades features as a consistently inconsistent character whose wavering nature discourages imitation even as his virtues encourage it (Plutarch, *Alc.* 23.4).

AN INDISTINCT IDENTITY: THE JEWS IN JOHN

When the Jews are introduced in John 1:19–28 the audience is given critical information concerning their origins, actions, indirect speech, and comparisons that shape their initial characterization. These commonplaces lay the foundation for the characterization of the Jews that follows in the remainder of the Gospel. In verse 19 "the Jews" reportedly "sent priests and Levites from Jerusalem" to question John (the Baptist) concerning his identity.[18] Peppering him with questions, this representative group wants answers to take back to the Jews who sent them. In verse 24, this sending group is now not identified as "the Jews," but as "the Pharisees."[19] From the outset of the Gospel, then, several features about the Jews emerge.

Starting with origins, the Gospel locates the Jews in Jerusalem, the Judean capital and home of the temple, the residence of God's glory on earth. Their association with the temple is further emphasized by their actions. They send "priests and Levites" to the "wilderness," on the other side of the Jordan River, to question John (1:23–28). This group is powerful enough to send others, and seemingly, to expect answers. The language of sending also creates a comparison with the introduction of John (the Baptist) and Jesus in the Gospel's Prologue. In 1:6–9 John is introduced as "a man sent from God" in order to "testify to the light," namely, Jesus. John's origins "from God" mean that he acts as God's representative to identify the Messiah. In contrast, "the priests and Levites" are the representatives for the Jews in 1:19–28, speaking on their behalf. Unlike John (the Baptist), however, these representatives are *not* testifying, but questioning, even though they come from the place where God's glory is supposed to be. The audience might be surprised by this twist of events. The priests and Levites must *leave* the holy capital of Jerusalem in order to learn about God's activity from an outsider, from someone

---

18. In John's Gospel, the baptizing prophet, John, is never given the moniker "the Baptist" as he is in the Synoptics. I will, however, refer to him as John (the Baptist) so as to avoid confusion with the discussion of the Gospel itself as "John."

19. Urban C. von Wahlde interprets this change of language as an indication of a new stage in the composition of the Gospel ("The Terms for Religious Authorities in the Fourth Gospel: A Key to Literary-Strata?" *JBL* 98 [1979], 243–44; more recently von Wahlde, *The Gospel and Letters of John*, ECC [Grand Rapids: Eerdmans, 2010], 2:44–47). The synchronic approach here, however, focuses on interpretive possibilities of the final form of the Gospel in light of ancient rhetorical practices. Rather than assuming consistency in language is necessary, it is argued here that inconsistency also has rhetorical impacts useful for ancient authors.

"across the Jordan," the very edges of God's promised land (John 1:28; Josh 1:1–15).[20] This comparison reinforces the Gospel's statements in 1:14–16 that God's glory now resides more fully in a new place: Jesus, the Word made flesh.

From their introduction in the Gospel, therefore, the Jews are placed in a seemingly contradictory position. Their origins and prestige in Jerusalem should privilege them to receive knowledge directly from God, yet their need to send representatives outside of Jerusalem to question John creates distance. Those who should be closest to God's glory must now go out to seek it anew; God is changing things and it is difficult to understand, *even* for those "in the know." In this way, the scene in John 1:19–28 sets the stage for the conflicts that develop between Jesus and the Jews in Jerusalem, especially in the temple during festivals that commemorate God's actions on behalf of the Jewish people (John 2–10).

The overt commonplaces in John 1:19–28 also reveal additional, more implicit, commonplaces in the Jews' characterization: their perceptiveness and disposition (Theon, *Prog.* 109–10). The Jews recognize that God is acting through John (the Baptist), and they want to know more. Something about John and his activities sparks their sending of representatives, although it does not prompt a visit from the Jews themselves. The conversation between these representatives and John need not be interpreted as a hostile interrogation. Instead, the confusion the Jewish representatives experience highlights the strangeness of God's actions in and through John, and later, through Jesus. It is not that the Jews do not want to know what God is doing—they do! This is why they send representatives, priests and Levites who had official standing with the temple and knowledge of Jewish Scripture, to ask questions. They will continue to ask questions, debate, and even become divided among themselves throughout the rest of the story (e.g., 6:41–58; 7:10–24; 8:21–30; 11:36–46). The correct identification of God's actions, after all, is not easily attained. In fact, the strangeness of the incarnation was just emphasized for the Gospel audience in John (the Baptist's) words from 1:15–18:

---

20. The phrase "across the Jordan" (*peran tou Iordanou*) is used each time John (the Baptist) is mentioned in the Gospel of John (1:28; 3:26; 10:40); it is also used twenty times throughout Joshua to identify the Israelites' progress into and conquest of the promised land (LXX).

This is the one of whom I said, "The one coming after me has come
to be before me, because he was prior to me, because out of his fullness
we all received grace upon grace, because the law was given through
Moses, the grace and the truth came to be through Jesus Christ. No one
has seen God before; the unique God, who is in the breast of the Father,
that one showed the way." (author's translation)[21]

The difficulty of these verses reinforces the difficulty of discerning
Jesus's true identity in John's Gospel for the characters who encounter
him. If no one has ever seen God before, how are they to recognize
the incarnate agent, Jesus, at first sight? Even John (the Baptist)
describes his need for help in 1:29–34, reporting twice that he did
not recognize (*ēdein*) Jesus until God provided help in the form of a
descending and remaining spirit. The confusion experienced by the
Jews' proxies in 1:19–28, and later by the Jews themselves, reinforces
this theme.

Reading through the rest of the Gospel, such confusion remains
a consistent component of the Jews' overall characterization, and of
their own identity. They are repeatedly a difficult group to discern,
even as they struggle among themselves to discern Jesus. For example, although the audience is given an origin for the Jews with
Jerusalem in 1:19, they are not entirely decipherable from other Jewish contingents here or in the remainder of the narrative. In John
1:19–28, the Jews enter the narrative indirectly, represented by others rather than taking the stage themselves. Their implicit identification as temple authorities who have power over "priests and Levites"
in 1:19–23 sits awkwardly next to verses 24–28 when they are either
called or conflated with "the Pharisees," a group whose power base
lay outside the temple and who traditionally competed with temple
authorities for influence.[22] In 2:13–22, however, the Jews again seem
to be temple authorities, able to question Jesus as they seek justification for his expulsion of merchants who enabled the purchasing
of sacrifices for Passover. They have this same role in John 5:10–47,
where they not only question Jesus but also appear to have enough
power to be a threat to the man he healed by the pool of Bethsaida, pressuring him to reveal the identity of his healer and opening
Jesus up to their "pursuit" (*diōkō*) in 5:10–18. The repeated refrain

21. Brant notes that John 1:15–18 was considered part of John (the Baptist's) testimony
throughout early church tradition (*John*, 26–27, 35–36).

22. Shaye J. D. Cohen, *From the Maccabees to the Mishnah*, LEC 7 (Louisville: Westminster
John Knox, 1987), 143–64.

that people experience "fear of the Jews" also seems to emphasize such a characterization (7:13; 9:22; 19:38; 20:19). As a result, some interpreters and translations understand the Jews to be Jewish religious leaders such as temple authorities, Pharisees, or some mixture of both.[23]

In other contexts, however, such an interpretation makes less sense. In John 6, the Jews are indistinguishable from the crowd who follows Jesus after receiving his miraculous provision of bread in the Galilean wilderness (6:22–59). In John 7–10, they pop in and out of scenes alongside various other cohorts—"the people of Jerusalem" (7:25), the crowds (7:12, 20, 31–32, 40, 43, 49), the Pharisees and Nicodemus (7:32, 45–48; 8:13–59; 9:13–41), as well as the temple police and chief priests (7:32–52)—before taking center stage at 8:31–59 and again at 10:21–39. In these scenes, Jesus's debates with the Jews reflect concerns from all these Jewish groups, rather than the cares of the religious elite alone.

The Gospel even casts the Jews' origins into doubt in John 8:31–59 when they engage Jesus in a debate over paternity. Jesus's argument emphasizes actions as the key identifier of origins rather than physical descent; if the Jews accept him, they are Abraham's "seed" and "children of God." If the Jews reject them, however, they are "murderers" and children of the devil (8:34–44). Their attempts to stone Jesus at 8:58–59 and again at 10:31–39 would seem to place the Jews on the diabolical side according to Jesus, but again, the Gospel is not content to leave their place resolved.

In 11:45–53 some Jews believe, while, in a reversal of their position of power in 1:19–23, other Jews *report back* to the Pharisees and chief priests, who decide to kill Jesus. John 12:9–11 retains this divided and subordinate position for the Jews when the chief priests worry because "many of the Jews were deserting and were believing in Jesus" (12:11). The Jews even blend with Jesus himself, who has access to the temple while participating in Jewish festivals, exhibits knowledge of scripture throughout the Gospel, and is called a "Jew" (*Ioudaios*) by the Samaritan woman in 4:9 (see also 4:22, 42). In the end, then, the Jews blend in with all of these people *and* with none of them completely. There is no single identity for them. The

23. E.g., CEB; NET; Martinus C. de Boer, "The Depiction of 'the Jews' in John's Gospel: Matters of Behavior and Identity," in Bieringer, Pollefeyt, and Vandecasteele-Vanneuville, *Anti-Judaism and the Fourth Gospel*, 141–42; Bennema, *Encountering Jesus*, 88–89.

Jews, even with their sixty-seven appearances in the Gospel, remain indistinct.

Even though this blurred rendering of the Jews has often left scholars puzzled, it contributes significantly to the Jews' characterization. Rather than seeking to tidy up their identity by aligning the Jews with the religious leadership alone, it is better to let the ambiguity created by the narrative stand. In so doing, readers are swept up in the conflation of the Jews with the crowds, who also question and debate Jesus's identity. In these scenes, the potential official position for the Jews slips from the foreground and they blend in with all those seeking to understand Jesus and his often confounding words. Like all the other characters in the Gospel, the Jews need help to decipher Jesus's identity correctly in order to receive eternal life.

AMBIGUITY AND EMPATHY: THE JEWS
AND JOHANNINE RHETORIC

The consistent ambiguity of the Jews, and the sparse commonplaces used to describe them, contrasts with Jesus's characterization for the Gospel audience. In this way, the Gospel persists in its well-known use of irony to reinforce the superior perspective of the Gospel audience, who alone has access to the entirety of the Gospel story. Like the Jews, minor characters within the Gospel often struggle to identify Jesus rightly. For them, Jesus appears to be a Galilean Jewish man, under the age of fifty, uneducated and of no special position of power (6:41; 7:15; 8:57). When he arrives in Jerusalem or holds court in Galilee, he shocks the crowds who surround him with his claims. They simply do not match up with his appearance, and he is rightly questioned and, for some, rejected. For the Gospel audience, however, Jesus's words and actions make sense because they have heard the Prologue, which establishes Jesus's identity as God's Word made flesh. As Jesus says in 8:51, for him to speak or act in any way differently than he does might make him more palatable to the characters in the Gospel, but it would also make him a liar. The rhetorical ploy of the Gospel, then, is that the more Jesus does to divide, and even alienate, other characters in the Gospel, the more he affirms the initial and robust characterization of him from the Gospel Prologue. In this way, the identity of Jesus that the Gospel purports becomes more persuasive for those listening to the story than to those within it.

The Gospel, therefore, twists the perspective of the Jews and other characters in the story in an attempt to make its argument more effective for those on the outside listening to it in its entirety. For these listeners, Jesus's character is clear; there are numerous commonplaces and techniques to identify him, and he behaves in ways that are consistent with his initial characterization as God's Word, regardless of the consequences. At the same time, it is exactly this identity for Jesus that remains so obscure for the characters in the story, such as the Jews, who never know the Prologue or hear the entire story. What the Jews in the Gospel do assert, however, is knowledge of their own identity: they are the children of Abraham, they have never been slaves to anyone, and God is their Father (8:33–41). They know scripture, follow the law of Moses, and faithfully observe festivals marking God's faithfulness to them (5:39). Yet, for the Gospel audience, the Jews are always something of a mystery. Even in their first appearance they are hidden behind representatives. As the narrative progresses, their character becomes even more unstable as Jesus's actions and words cause confusion, anger, and belief. This group that would seem to be united and to be able to discern God's activity turns out to be a diverse and ambiguous mix of people. Their struggles to understand Jesus—and even to understand themselves—again highlights the strangeness of the Word's incarnation and revelation.

Although various scholars have attempted to resolve the Jews' presentation with a negative evaluation of their character, to do so overlooks the ethical implications of their ambiguous characterization. As mentioned above, ancients found consistent characters to be especially persuasive, but such consistency does not necessitate flatness or homogeneity. Instead, ambiguity or even inconsistency *can* be a consistent character trait. Moreover, such ambiguity contributes greatly to the rhetoric of a narrative when it appears. In John, the Jews' sparse characterization and fluctuating responses to Jesus contrasts sharply with Jesus' own characterization for the Gospel audience. Jesus's consistency reinforces his, rather improbable, identity: he is God's Word made flesh. The Jews' difficulty in determining this identity, on the other hand, reinforces the unique nature of the incarnation. God is doing something new, even if it is rooted in the Gospel's interpretation of scripture. Jesus's identity and claims are not easy to discern; they necessitate divine involvement for comprehension. The Jews' consistent ambiguity serves to reinforce this theme.

Such rhetoric can create an ethic of connection and empathy with the Jews, even while it reasserts the authority of Johannine traditions. In its characterization of the Jews, the Gospel offers a message of caution to its audiences; no matter how sure one is of identity and divine access, God is able to surprise and confound. The Gospel of John emphasizes that claiming to see can be very different from actual sight (9:40–41).

Furthermore, if we remove the assumption that John's Gospel is written to explain a separation of Jews from Christians that Martyn's theory asserts, we remove the assumption that John's audiences were antagonistic toward the Jews from the start. Instead, the Gospel's Jewish worldview can reassert an empathetic disposition toward, and response to, the Jews. Not only does the Gospel infer a Jewish audience who was already convinced of the authority of Jewish traditions, but also, in affirming Israel's Scripture, the Gospel agrees that the Jews are right to claim a special relationship with God. Israel's story emphasizes God's self-disclosure to them repeatedly, and Jesus's incarnation is no different (1:29–51). In this, Jesus affirms their understanding by agreeing that the Jews *are* Abraham's descendants. Like Abraham, God has sent them a divine visitor (Genesis 18). Moreover, just as the story of the Jews throughout scripture demonstrates, this group can be divided when God acts in their midst; some comprehend God's work, while others do not; some may think they understand, and some may make no claim at all. It is not surprising, then, that when Jesus appears—the one whom the Gospel presents as God's most profound revelation of his glory—the Jews would be divided once again. It is in this vein that Jesus can also simultaneously say that they are *not* Abraham's "descendants." Unlike Abraham, they do not display faith in John 8 when they reject the visitor sent to them. Even in this rejection, however, the Jews in John *are* consistent with the characterization of Israel throughout scripture. Abraham's descendants are never a homogenous group.

In this way, the characterization of the Jews in the Gospel reinforces the character-shaping of the audiences outside of it. Rather than experiencing straightforward antipathy, the Gospel audience can identify with the Jews since they, too, have the challenge of deciphering Jesus's identity and their response to him. In these tasks, the Gospel argues that its audience has a clear advantage: namely, itself (20:30–31). The Gospel shapes the characters of its listening audience to rely on it as the hermeneutical key for Jesus. Only with the additional information it provides can one have the full picture it asserts. Without it, the audience is just like the Jews. They may desire to discern God, but they are locked in a world that does not make such discernment easy, especially when God acts in such a unique way by means of Jesus. When this audience relies on the Gospel, however, they become more like individuals within the narrative, most of them also Jewish, who receive special revelation: the audience's revelation is the Gospel itself. From this perspective, the Jews are not always or only opponents of Jesus, they are the Gospel audience but without their advantage. They must answer the same questions without the revelation that is the Gospel to guide them. The resulting ethic is not to treat the Jews in John (and elsewhere) as enemies, but as fellow travelers struggling to discern God's work in the world.

CONCLUSION

The questions and perspectives concerning John's characterization of the Jews in this Gospel have long been debated and will no doubt continue. This chapter has sought to offer an overview of proposals on the topic, as well as provide another avenue for reflection. The growing tendency of scholars to move away from Martyn's theory as an explanation for the polemical episodes toward the Jews in John has allowed for an increased awareness of the importance of perspective and ambiguity in Johannine characterizations, including that of the Jews. There are, indeed, multiple ways to hear and to read a text. Such ambiguity is particularly poignant in the case of John's characterization of Jews due to the troubled history of this Gospel. As Ruth Sheridan writes, one does not "draw a straight line through history from the Gospel of John to the Shoah (the 'Holocaust')," but one can nevertheless see the connection between simple, antagonistic readings of the Jews in John and anti-Judaism that reverberates throughout history.[24] Not only do such interpretations reinforce explicit and implicit anti-Jewish stances, but they also ignore the ambiguity inherent in John's characterization of the Jews. Questioning more deeply the ethics promoted by John's presentation of the Jews, as well as the ethics of our own interpretations of them, is not only a warranted aspect of interpreting this text but also a crucial one.

24. Sheridan, "Identity," 208.

Paying attention to ancient rhetorical practices of characterization can aid in these ethical reflections. Ancient authors actively sought to portray characters in ways that were meant to shape the characters of their audiences. This is as much the case with John's characterization of the Jews as it is with his characterization of Jesus. Employing commonplaces and techniques known in the ancient Mediterranean world, the Gospel casts a pervasive yet indistinct portrait of the Jews who, like their ancestors, struggle to decipher God's revelation in their midst. Playing on the contrast between their own expressed certitude of identity and their confusion over Jesus's, the Gospel's rhetoric elevates its own audience with privileged information that clarifies Jesus's character while obfuscating that of the Jews. For this reason, the Jews both express belief and disbelief in Jesus throughout the Gospel—sometimes praising him, and sometimes seeking his death. Rather than forcing a negative evaluation, however, the ambiguity of the Jews' characterization enables empathy, as the Johannine audience likewise struggles to identify and express faith in a man named Jesus, whom they have neither seen nor heard (20:29).

Acknowledging the ambiguity of the Johannine Jews should also encourage contemporary readers to be shaped to experience empathy with them as well. Such empathy, however, should be honest; there is always the risk that empathy can shift into pity and condescension when the Gospel's rhetorical perspective is unreflectively enshrined. Without reflection, even empathetic readings easily deteriorate into a flat, negative rendering of the Jews who are left struggling, rather than comprehending. Instead, all readers of the Gospel should keep in mind that the Gospel *does* employ rhetoric. It is a story meant to persuade and affirm an audience already on its side, and it makes use of ancient techniques to do so. This rhetoric, however, will not be compelling to all who hear the story. For some, the Jews in John are just opponents—that is, righteous opponents—who rightly debate Jesus and his claims. For others, the Jews are simply opponents—who wrongly reject Jesus as God's revelation to them. Yet, all perspectives benefit from deeper reflection on the persistent ambiguity of the Johannine Jews, who both believe and disbelieve Jesus's claims simultaneously. In this way, the Jews serve as a model for, and of, all who seek to discover God's actions in this world and, as a result of such seeking, struggle, question, debate, accept, reject, and rejoice along the way.

9.

The Johannine Request to "Come and See" and an Ethic of Love

TOAN DO

John's account of the first days of Jesus's appearance and public ministry has been the focus of much christological discussion.[1] Jesus's invitation to the two disciples of John the Baptist (henceforth the Baptist) to "come and see" (1:39, 46) has been closely linked with this discussion.[2] For example, commenting on the unusual titles attributed to Jesus in John 1:35–51 (Messiah, Son of God, King of Israel, and Son of Man), Peter J. Judge draws this conclusion: "At the beginning of the Gospel, to be sure, the first disciples and readers will need to flesh out their understanding of these titles. . . . What follows in the Gospel, beginning with chapter 2, are the means of that fleshing-out:

---

1. Beginning with Marie-Emile Boismard, *Du Baptême à Cana (Jean 1:19–2:11)* (Paris: Cerf, 1956). See C. K. Barrett, "The Lamb of God," *NTS* 1 (1954–1955): 210–18; Wilhelm Michaelis, "Joh 1:5, Gen 28:12 und das Menschensohn-Problem," *TLZ* 85 (1960): 561–78; S. Virgulin, "Recent Discussion of the Title, 'Lamb of God,'" *Scripture* 13 (1961): 74–80; Raymond E. Brown, *The Gospel according to John I–XII*, AB 29 (Garden City, NY: Doubleday, 1966), 73–92; Brown, *An Introduction to the Gospel of John*, ed. Francis J. Moloney, ABRL (New York: Doubleday, 2003), 252–59.

2. See Rudolf Bultmann, *The Gospel of John: A Commentary*, trans. G. R. Beasley-Murray, R. W. N. Hoare, and J. K. Riches (Philadelphia: Westminster, 1975), 97–108; Brown, *Gospel according to John I–XII*, 78–79; and C. K. Barrett, *The Gospel according to John: An Introduction with Commentary and Notes on the Greek Text*, 2nd ed. (London: SPCK, 1978), 180. Unless otherwise noted, all translations from the Greek text come from the NRSV. Translations from German are mine.

Jesus' signs, which point beyond themselves to himself, his discourses for all and for 'his own,' and finally his death and resurrection."[3]

With slight variations, the "come and see" imperative occurs several times in John from various inviter(s) to invitees: first from Jesus to the Baptist's two disciples (1:39), second from Philip to Nathanael (1:46), third from the Samaritan woman to her villagers (4:29), and finally from the villagers of Bethany to Jesus (11:34). While each occurs at a different place and on a different occasion, they are all related to Jesus, being the implicit inspiration behind the request: they come to Jesus, remain with him, see what he does, and *allegedly* believe in him. Accordingly, Johannine scholarship often revolves around questions about what initiates the inviters' invitation and whether such an imperative leads to the invitees' initial and, then, lifelong acceptance of Jesus? Suggested answers to these questions imply that Christology is key to the invitees' motivation for remaining faithful to Jesus.[4]

In response to the never-ceasing interest in Johannine Christology, this essay poses a question to the current Johannine christological debate:[5] Is Christology a sufficient response to the come-and-see invitation, especially in the case of Philip's invitation to Nathanael? This question points *beyond* any christological exclamations *to the way in which* the proclaimers achieve their faith in Jesus. When this invitation is actually enfleshed and realized in actions, the claim of christological confessions becomes the most challenging aspect of Jesus's

3. Peter J. Judge, "Come and See: The First Disciples and Christology in the Fourth Gospel," in *Studies in the Gospel of John and Its Christology: Festschrift Gilbert Van Belle*, ed. Joseph Verheyden et al., BETL 265 (Leuven: Peeters, 2014), 69.

4. Ibid., 61–69. Similarly, in Steven A. Hunt, D. Francois Tolmie, and Ruben Zimmermann, eds., *Character Studies in the Fourth Gospel: Narrative Approaches to Seventy Figures in John*, WUNT 314 (Tübingen: Mohr Siebeck, 2013), scholarly descriptions run as follows: "ideal disciples" (Garry Manning, 128), "magnificent confessions" (Martinus de Boer, 145), and "profound confessions of faith" (Steven Hunt, 192).

5. Frank J. Matera, *New Testament Ethics: The Legacies of Jesus and Paul* (Louisville: Westminster John Knox, 1996), 92, notes: "For anyone interested in the study of the New Testament ethics, the Gospel according to John is a major challenge." In contrast, Jan G. van der Watt and Ruben Zimmermann, introduction to *Rethinking the Ethics of John: "Implicit Ethics" in the Johannine Writings*, ed. Jan G. van der Watt and Ruben Zimmermann, Kontexte und Normen neutestamentliche Ethik/Contexts and Norms of New Testament Ethics 3, WUNT 291 (Tübingen: Mohr Siebeck, 2012), ix–x, contend Matera's point: "Recently, the climate has changed. . . . A few key publications (throughout this volume) not only challenged the methodological approach to the ethics of John, but also indicated that there is much more in John [and 1–3 John] than meets the eye, when it comes to ethics. . . . The dynamics of Johannine ethics became alive."

disciples and subsequent followers. Several passages in the Gospel and Epistles pose a clear inadequacy of the christological emphases in this Johannine invitation. For example, the dialogue between Jesus and his disciples Thomas and Philip in John 14:5–15 questions the disciples' *alleged* confession, and insists instead on a gradual growth in love for Jesus. This love-for-Jesus command ought to play the fundamental role in each invitee's faithfulness to Jesus; and it has everything to do *with the way in which* Jesus's followers live out their discipleship.[6] Replying to the questions raised by Thomas and then Philip, Jesus says: "If you [plural] love me, you will keep my commandments" (14:15). This command is expressed even more clearly in the Johannine communities that bore the Christian image in the post-Jesus and Gospel eras. The ethical reality of this command is not simply based on verbal confessions, but manifested in the actions of each member's love for one another (1 John 2:3–6). Admonishing his community members, for instance, the author of 1 John writes: "Whoever says, 'I have come to know him [Jesus],' but does not obey his commandments, is a liar" (1 John 2:4).[7]

In the course of the invitees' response to the come-and-see invitation (i.e., coming to, seeing, knowing, remaining with, and believing in Jesus), Christology is downplayed not only by John but also by the subsequent Johannine authors, who experienced the challenge of *living* their christological *confessions*. Aided by a narrative-critical reading of the relevant texts, therefore, the argument of this essay progresses in three steps. First, it presents that John pervasively alludes to Christology in John 1:19–51, and that such an allusion has unfortunately influenced scholars to interpret Jesus's invitation in 1:39 as a messianic expectation.[8] Next, it shows that the four occasions where

6. Possibility remains. Francis J. Moloney, *Love in the Gospel of John: An Exegetical, Theological, and Literary Study* (Grand Rapids: Baker Academic, 2013), 198, comments: "Reading 1 John's statement on love in a setting of the rejection of 'the other' within contexts that reflect conflict indicates that *living* the perfect law of love in the community that produced and then inherited the Gospel of John was more difficult than *proclaiming* it." Yet, while the enactment of Jesus's love command may not always be easily manifested, its ethical aspects are real and appealing.

7. I hold that the Gospel's author is not the same authors who wrote 1–3 John. The Johannine Letters were written as epistolary formats of communication among early Christian communities. For discussion on this topic, see Toan Do, *Rethinking the Death of Jesus: An Exegetical and Theological Study of Hilasmos and Agapē in 1 John 2:1–2 and 4:7–10*, CBET 73 (Leuven: Peeters, 2014), 3–26. See Urban C. von Wahlde, *The Gospel and Letters of John*, ECC (Grand Rapids: Eerdmans, 2010), 1:6–7.

8. Construing this invitation as a model of Johannine expression of Christology and faith in

this invitation occurs (1:39, 46; 4:29; 11:34) point to John's well-known stylistic practice of repetition and variation. Finally, it argues that the invitation would only be fulfilled by an ethic of love in keeping Jesus's command (John 14:15; 1 John 3:11, 23; 4:11).

JOHN'S ALLUSION TO CHRISTOLOGY

An appealing way to explain John's Christology in 1:19–51—or any part of the Gospel, for that matter—starts with critical readings of the relevant narrative. The reader should be aware that the entire Gospel was written *about*, not *for*, individual characters within the narrative.[9] But when this awareness concerns a particular character, the reader faces some discrepancies. With regard to John 1:1–51, for example, this concern comes to the fore: should the reader start with 1:6, where the Baptist is introduced for the first time, or at 1:19, where he appears as the one being asked about his identity by the Jerusalem delegates? Johannine scholars seem to have faced a dilemma between characters and characterization in the Gospel.[10] Jesus is surely witnessed and proclaimed as the principal figure in John's narrative, but allusion to Jesus's christological designations from the Baptist's viewpoint does not begin until 1:20. There the Baptist disclaims himself as the Messiah.

On the very first day in the narrative,[11] John introduces the reader to three titles: Messiah, Elijah, and prophet. Each occurs twice within 1:19–28.[12] Yet the reader begins to see that these titles are not given to the Baptist, since in fact he flatly denied them.[13] Rather, they are

---

Jesus, Judge, "Come and See," 68, argues: "In a very proleptic way, the disciples' question and Jesus' invitation anticipates in a nutshell what the disciples discover as the Gospel unfolds."

9. In John 20:31, the second-person plural (*pisteu[s]ēte* "you may believe or continue to believe" and *echēte* "you may have life") is clearly not meant for the characters in the Gospel, but for the subsequent Johannine Christians. See Christopher W. Skinner, "Characters and Characterization in the Gospel of John: Reflections on the *Status Quaestionis*," in *Characters and Characterization in the Gospel of John*, ed. Christopher W. Skinner, LNTS 548 (London: Bloomsbury T&T Clark, 2013), xvii–xxvii.

10. See Bultmann, *Gospel of John*, 13; Herman N. Ridderbos, *The Gospel according to John: A Theological Commentary* (Grand Rapids: Eerdmans, 1992), 17; and Martinus C. de Boer, "The Original Prologue to the Gospel of John," *NTS* 61 (2015): 453.

11. This presumes *tē epaurion*, "on the next day," in 1:29 to be the second day, making 1:19–28 the first day.

12. Early Christians would have understood either of these three titles to be the proper designation for Jesus. See Brown, *Gospel according to John I–XII*, 45–54.

13. Marianne Meye Thompson, *John: A Commentary*, NTL (Louisville: Westminster John Knox, 2015), 43.

introduced for a single purpose, namely, making the reader aware of christological allusions to the coming Jesus—the one who comes after the Baptist but ranks ahead of him (1:30). As Jesus appeared for the first time, the Baptist was able to give Jesus the proper title. The Baptist's testimony points to the preeminence of Jesus, who is mightier and first in every respect (1:26–27).[14]

Familiar with the three roles that the Baptist disclaimed for himself, the reader begins to see how John introduces the title: the Lamb of God.[15] This designation occurs twice and is directly attributed to Jesus. John starts with the Baptist's proclamation (1:29), then introduces the two disciples who heard their master's verbatim proclamation (1:35–36). One wonders about the logical significance of the Baptist's proclamations of Jesus.[16] In introducing the Baptist's disciples into the scene, however, John expands his narrative by putting

14. The Baptist later elevates Jesus: "He must increase, and I must decrease" (3:30).

15. Much christological speculation has been devoted to this designation. See Reimund Bieringer, "Das Lamm Gottes, Das die Sünde der Welt hinwegnimmt (1,29)," in *The Death of Jesus in the Fourth Gospel*, ed. Gilbert Van Belle, BETL 200 (Leuven: Leuven University Press, 2007), 230–31, concludes: "In 1,29-34 (35–42) ist *ho amnos tou theou* eine Parallele von *ho huios tou theou*. Der Ausdruck *ho amnos tou theou* beschreibt die Beziehung zwischen Gott und Jesus mittels der Hirte-Schaf Terminologie. Als Beziehungsterminologie verweist sowohl *amnos* als auch *huios* auf eine vertraute Liebesbeziehung." My transliteration and translation: "The title 'the Lamb of God' in 1:29–34 (35–42) is in parallel with 'the Son of God.' The expression 'the Lamb of God' describes the relationship between God and Jesus by means of the shepherd-sheep terminology."

16. To make a point in Christology regarding this proclamation, Boismard, *Du Baptême*, 93, invokes the theory of the "hidden Messiah," which Justin Martyr debated with the Jew Trypho in the second century (*Dialogue with Trypho* 110). However, would the Baptist's proclamation of Jesus being the Lamb of God be enough for the two disciples to understand Jesus's identity as the *hidden* Messiah and subsequently to attribute christological titles to him? The oddity of the Baptist's dual proclamation of the Lamb of God lies in the audience of the first instance: to whom did the Baptist declare the title "the Lamb of God"? To Jesus alone, which might be true, but rather strange and irrelevant, or to the two disciples who were not yet present? Certainly, *tē epaurion*, "on the next day," implies that the Jerusalem delegates were no longer present. When the Baptist appears for the first time in 1:19, the narrative shifts back and forth between him and the delegates (1:19–28). Besides the delegates, there is no clear indication of the Baptist's adherents who might be present in this narrative (i.e., neither his disciples nor those whom he would baptize). This observation is supported by the Baptist's reply to the delegates' question: "I baptize with water" (1:26a). The Baptist's answer, *egō baptize en hydati*, has no direct objects regarding the baptized, except the prepositional phrase "by means of water." The absence of direct objects also occurs in the delegates' question: *ti oun baptizeis*, "why are you [singular] baptizing?" (1:25). While it is evident that the Baptist was baptizing "adherents" (1:25), John gives no indication that he was baptizing the delegates (see Matt 3:1–10; Mark 1:4–6; Luke 3:7–9). In fact, their series of questions to the Baptist betrays any possibility that he would baptize any of them. In 1:29, John reports that when the Baptist saw Jesus coming toward him, he declared: "Here is the Lamb of God who takes away the sin of the world." From 1:19 to 1:34, there is no suggestion that any of his disciples was present. The two disciples appear for the first time on the next day (1:35), which is followed by the Baptist's second Lamb of God proclamation

on Andrew's lips two more titles for Jesus: Rabbi (1:38) and Messiah (1:41). As Jesus found Philip (1:43), and then Philip found Nathanael (1:45), John introduces three more titles coming from Nathanael's proclamation: Rabbi, the Son of God, and the King of Israel (1:49). The narrative concludes with Jesus implicitly calling himself the Son of Man (1:51).[17]

By the end of chapter 1 (four days), John has already introduced no fewer than seven titles. Some of them are intentionally repeated for purpose of narrative emphasis.[18] Each of these is replete with allusive christological significance: Messiah, Elijah, prophet, Lamb of God, Rabbi, King of Israel, and Son of Man. The following summarizes the narrative development surrounding John's exalted Christology (bold type added):[19]

Verse	Narrative	Speaker
1:20	*egō ouk eimi **ho christos***	John the Baptist
	I am not **the Messiah**	
1:21a	*ouk eimi [**Ēlias**]*[20]	the Baptist
	I am not [**Elijah**]	
1:21b	*ouk eimi **ho prophētēs***	the Baptist
	[I am not **the prophet**]	
1:29	*ide **ho amnos tou theou** ho airōn tēn hamartian tou kosmou*	the Baptist
	Here is **the Lamb of God** who takes away the sin of the world	
1:36	*ide **ho amnos tou theou***	the Baptist
	Look, here is **the Lamb of God**	

(1:36). Having heard the Baptist, they followed Jesus (1:38). A clear incident where the Baptist actually baptizes "adherents" occurs in 3:23.

17. Caution goes with the implication that Jesus speaks about himself. This verse has been long considered a later insertion into the Gospel by the redactors. See Brown, *Gospel according to John I–XII*, 88–91.

18. John repeats "Rabbi" and "Messiah" several times (see 1:38, 41).

19. See note 1.

20. In 1:21a, Elijah in brackets [*Ēlias*] is my reconstruction of John's narrative. The prose is literally rendered: "What then? Are you Elijah? And he says: 'I am not.' Are you a prophet? And he answered: 'No.'" Similar is my reconstruction of the Greek prose of 1:21b.

1:38	*rabbi ho legetai methermnēneuomenon didaskale*	the Baptist's two disciples
	Rabbi (which translated means **Teacher**)	
1:41	*heurēkamen ton Messian, ho estin methermnēneuomenon christos*	Andrew (one of these two)
	We have found **the Messiah** (which is translated **Anointed**)	
1:49	*rabbi, su ei ho huios tou theou, su basileus ei tou Israēl*	Nathanael
	Rabbi, you are the **Son of God**! You are the **King of Israel**!	
1:51	*amēn amen legō hymin opsesthe . . . ton huion tou anthrōpou*	Jesus
	Very truly, I tell you, you will see . . . **the Son of Man**	

Jesus is unapologetically witnessed to and proclaimed as the Son of God. Yet there remains unresolved answers among scholars. Can each character understand what these titles mean without short-sighted failure? Why does John fill this narrative of John 1:19–51 with repeated titles attributed to Jesus, had these indeed not presented major challenges to the proclaimers? On the one hand, the author of the Gospel aims to show in these titles that proclamation of faith in Jesus as the Christ is most significant for a disciple. On the other hand, the authors of the Epistles demonstrate that what one believes directly affects how one acts. For the subsequent Johannine community members, the Christian's articulation of faith must accompany their right actions. In this regard, Christology alone proves to become the *forefront* issue that eventually divided the Johannine communities.

COME-AND-SEE AS STYLISTIC REPETITION AND VARIATION

John 1:19–51 leaves a strong christological impression on the reader. The evangelist twice employs the come-and-see invitation: from Jesus to the Baptist's two disciples (1:39) and from Philip to Nathanael (1:46). Because Jesus personally invites these two, answers to the above questions have surrounded *only* the first come-and-see invitation. This is often construed as the connection between the Baptist's announcement (1:29, 36) and the various proclaimed titles by Jesus's disciples (1:38, 41, 49; see 1:51). Scholars have argued that Jesus's invitation serves as the christologically based model of John's expressions of faith.

Yet the reader notices that John employs this invitation on four occasions. The following displays the narrative development surrounding the four invitations.

Verse	Narrative	Syntax	Speaker of Invitation
1:39	*erchesthe kai opsesthe //* *idete*	2nd per. pl.	Jesus to the Baptist's two disciples
	Come and see		
1:46	*erchou kai ide*	2nd per. sg.	Philip to Nathanael
	Come and see		
4:29	*deute idete*	2nd per. pl.	Samaritan woman to her villagers
	Come [and] see		
11:34	*erchou kai ide*	2nd per. sg.	Bethany villagers to Jesus
	Come and see		

These four invitations expect a similar outcome, namely, the narrative figures (the disciples and respective villagers) in the stories eventually come to Jesus and *allegedly* believe in him. A closer look at these narratives, however, indicates that the four imperatives are typical Johannine expressions without much Christology. These texts can simply be read as John's stylistic repetition and variation.

Recent studies have shown that John tends to repeat himself, and that in many instances different vocabularies carry *little to no* difference in meaning.[21] Repetitions and variations are typical Johannine

---

21. Famous is John's uses of *agapaō* and *phileō* across 21:15–17. Scholars had hitherto argued in theological favor for *agapaō* over against *phileō*. Such a position has been disputed by David Shepherd, "'Do You Love Me?' A Narrative-Critical Reappraisal of ἀγαπάω and φιλέω in John 21:15–17," *JBL* 129 (2010): 777–92; and Do, *Rethinking the Death of Jesus*, 215–75, esp. 264–69. Francis T. Gignac, "The Use of Verbal Variety in the Fourth Gospel," in *Transcending*

style.[22] These observations suggest that scholarly emphasis on Christology in John's narrative of Jesus's invitation to the Baptist's two disciples may be untenable. The narratives surrounding these invitations raise critical questions to a possible exaggeration of christological emphasis.

The Baptist twice proclaims Jesus as the Lamb of God (1:29, 36). Between these two statements, however, the reader is to notice that in 1:29 John does not point out whether there is any audience who might have heard the Baptist's announcement.[23] In addition, John 1:29–34 shows no evidence that any other person, besides the Baptist, who speaks and Jesus who might hear him speaking, would have heard this announcement. John is obviously not writing *for* the Baptist or Jesus, but *for* the reader. The scene in the second announcement is public (1:35–37): the Baptist was surrounded by two of his disciples.[24] As the two disciples were standing nearby, the reader can expect that the Baptist was teaching his disciples, and that they might hear him speaking.

Although the two disciples are nearby (1:35) and hear the Baptist's saying (1:37), it is unclear nevertheless that his proclamation is necessarily directed at the disciples. One might wish to stress that the disciples are there and witness the Baptist's proclamation. Yet a question remains, namely, how one reconciles the idea that such a statement was meant to encourage them to abandon their own teacher in order to follow Jesus *simply* because he is the Lamb of God. At this point in the narrative, John has not yet given any indication whether these two disciples understood the meaning of "the Lamb of God."[25] John

Boundaries: Contemporary Readings of the New Testament. Essays in Honor of Francis J. Moloney, ed. Rekka M. Chennattu and Mary L. Coloe (Rome: Las, 2005), 191–200, shows that John employs a number of verbal parities interchangeably or synonymously.

22. See Gilbert van Belle, Michael Labahn, and P. Martiz, eds., *Repetitions and Variations in the Fourth Gospel: Styles, Text, Interpretation*, BETL 223 (Leuven: Peeters, 2009).

23. See n. 17. The Baptist's disciples do not appear until v. 35.

24. In 1:35, *ek tōn mathētōn autou duo* (literally "two of his disciples") may be construed that the Baptist had more disciples than these two (See 3:23–30). But the scene does not imply more than two disciples.

25. The Baptist's statement in 1:29 provides more information: "Here is the Lamb of God who takes the sin of the world." If the disciples were absent in 1:29–34, would they comprehend the Baptist's saying in 1:36, "Behold the Lamb of God," without the qualifying explanation "who takes away the sin of the world"? The narrative gives no hint at their understanding. Thus, 66* C* Ws 892* 1241 *rell* indicate their suspicion of the disciples' comprehension by inserting: "who takes away the sin(s) of the world." Obviously, this redaction was added to ease the respective scribes' doubt that the two disciples would have comprehended what "the Lamb of God" meant to them.

makes a simple statement that these two disciples left their teacher and followed Jesus (see 2:22).

The announcement by the Baptist in 1:36 anticipates subsequent actions; and the response to this can be either positive or negative.[26] The two disciples who hear the Baptist's saying decide to follow Jesus. Their following behind Jesus results in his questioning them: "what are you looking for?" (1:38a). Thompson interprets Jesus's question as a means "to challenge these fledgling disciples, and the reader through them, to deeper insight."[27] Yet *ti zēteite* literally means: "what are you [plural] seeking?" (translation mine). Here *ti*, "what," is a nominative neuter singular. Although the majority of manuscripts cite *ti*, "what," Jesus's question may be understood in terms of a person, namely, "whom are you seeking?" (translation mine). In their response-question, they ask Jesus, "Rabbi, where are you staying" (1:38). John's use of "Rabbi" may suggest that these two disciples are looking for a true teacher—the one who "ranks ahead of" the Baptist.[28]

JOHN 1:19–51

Instead of answering Jesus, the disciples address him as "Rabbi," which John translates as "Teacher" (1:38b). They were unable to answer Jesus's question. Their inability to answer the question also recalls the Baptist's earlier and incomplete statement that Jesus was the Lamb of God (cf. 1:36 with 1:29). This observation is supported by the fact that Jesus's question was directed at these disciples (*autois*), but they did not answer his question. They continue to engage Jesus by asking: "Where are you staying?" (1:38c). Even though they may

---

26. There is no practicality for the Baptist to have his "own" disciples leave him and follow Jesus. The narrative of 1:19–34 does not favor the idea that the two disciples might have participated in the dialogue between the Baptist and the Jerusalem delegates. Difficulty remains, even if we may resort to what the Baptist says in 1:23, 27, 34, that he is the voice, the inferior, and the witness to the coming Jesus. How does one explain the reason for the Baptist to make such an announcement, so as for his disciples to abandon him and follow Jesus? On the other hand, what is the rationale for Jesus to welcome these disciples who have abandoned their teacher? In 3:23–30, moreover, the Baptist does not recommend that his disciples leave him and follow Jesus.

27. Thompson, *John*, 49.

28. Judge, "Come and See," 63, notes: "By asking *what* they seek here in 1,38, however, the Johannine Jesus provides an opening to the surface-level meaning of their question-in-reply but, more importantly on a deeper level, he probes the existential and ultimate meaning of their quest and that of the reader as well."

not entirely understand Jesus's question, nonetheless this dialogue can be interpreted as the disciples' initial faith in Jesus.

Jesus addresses the two disciples directly with an invitation: "Come and see" (1:39a). This leads to them staying with Jesus that day (1:39b), and Andrew—one of these two disciples—later finding his brother Simon (1:40–41a). It is Andrew who declared to his brother: "'We have found the Messiah' (which is translated Anointed)" (1:41b).[29] As expected from this chain of actions, Andrew brought his brother to Jesus, who in turn gave Simon the Aramaic sobriquet "Cephas." John provides a Greek equivalent "Peter" (1:42).

Scholars have interpreted this invitation as the key to John's exalted Christology. Raymond E. Brown notes: "Jesus answers with the all-embracing challenge to faith: 'come and see.' Throughout John the theme of 'coming' to Jesus will be used to describe faith (3:21; 5:40; 6:35, 37, 45; 7:35; etc.). Similarly, 'seeing' Jesus with perception is another Johannine description of faith."[30] Further, Raymond F. Collins suggests that "they [the disciples] should come to perceive that Jesus abides with the Father and the Father with him . . . [and] that they should come to experience the mutual indwelling with Jesus which is the essence of the Christian life."[31] These observations, however, will face difficulty when one reads the dialogue in John 14:5–15, in which Jesus rebukes the disciples that they have misunderstood him and his role. This dialogue presents a major christological challenge to Andrew, his fellow disciples, and the subsequent Johannine Christians.

John employs profound irony when he describes how the disciples misunderstood Jesus. The irony begins with Andrew's statement to his brother Simon by saying, "We have found the Messiah" (1:41). The narrative of 1:35–42 shows little indication that, together with the unnamed disciple, Andrew has found Jesus. In 1:36, the Baptist announces Jesus to be the Lamb of God when he sees Jesus passing by. The result of the disciples' hearing this statement is that they leave the Baptist and follow Jesus. Andrew seems to be exaggerating in

29. John's presentation of Jesus's first disciples is sharply different from the Synoptics (see Mark 1:16–20).

30. Brown, *Gospel according to John I–XII*, 79.

31. Raymond F. Collins, *John and His Witness*, Zacchaeus Studies: New Testament (Collegeville, MN: Liturgical Press, 1991), 44. See Judge, "Come and See," 68, who notes: "As the disciples respond to Jesus' invitation and remain with him it is intimated that they are invited into a similar relationship with Jesus as he has with the Father in the Spirit."

his statement to Simon.[32] Francis J. Moloney has commented on this proclamation by Andrew. "However wonderful the claim to have found the Messiah might appear to be, it falls short of a correct recognition of Jesus as he has been described in the Prologue (vv. 1–18). . . . A lie has been told."[33] Neither Andrew nor his companion has found the Messiah; rather they have followed Jesus, and the initiative lies entirely with Jesus, who invites them to come and see. As a result, this first exaggeration will make its way into the second exaggeration.

On the next day, Jesus finds Philip in Galilee (1:43b).[34] When Philip finds Nathanael, he tells a lie in 1:45: "We have found him [Jesus]." Several elements are crucial here. First, Philip is the object of the verb "to find" in 1:43b, so neither has he found nor does he find Jesus. Second, verse 44 is John's annotation of Philip's origin in Bethsaida, the same city of Andrew and Peter. This verse should not be construed inclusively as the subject of the first-person plural "we" in 1:45. Third, that verses 43–45 narrate only Jesus and Philip in the scene indicates that Philip's use of the first-person plural "we" is untrue. This untruth in turn takes effect in his invitation to Nathanael to come and see in 1:46. Nathanael's confessions of Jesus as Rabbi, the Son of God, and the King of Israel in 1:49 take root in the lie from Philip.[35] These affirmations, which are characterized by John's profound sense of irony, reflect much of Jesus's reservation from his question-in-reply to Nathanael's confessions: "Do you believe because I said to you that I saw you under the fig tree? You will see greater things than these" (1:50).[36] This question is best construed as

32. I do not claim that the author is exaggerating Andrew's confession. It is rather that without the Prologue (1:1–18), John's narrative of 1:19–51 does not say enough about this confession.

33. Francis J. Moloney, *The Gospel of John*, SP 4 (Collegeville, MN: Liturgical Press, 1998), 54–55.

34. That "Jesus found Philip" is my reading (see NRSV). The Greek text is ambiguous regarding the subject of *ēthelēsen* (aorist indicative third-person singular) and *heuriskei* (present indicative third-person singular). Literally, 1:43 reads: "On the next day he wanted to go to Galilee and he finds Philip and Jesus says to him: 'Follow me.'" Following others, von Wahlde, *Gospel and Letters*, 2:60, speculates that it is Andrew, rather than Jesus, who finds Philip. Much of this debate relies on where one places punctuations and how one construes the conjunction *kai* "and, then." Yet both *heuriskei* and *legei* are employed in parallel and in the present indicative with Jesus as the nominative of the subject. This parallel supports the reading that Jesus is the subject of these two verbs (See Moloney, *Gospel of John*, 61).

35. Moloney, *Gospel of John*, 56, notes: "These words climax a series of confessions of Jesus from the first disciples (See vv. 41, 45) but, like the earlier confessions, it falls short of the mark. The terms Nathanael uses to address Jesus can be understood as the expressions of first-century messianic hope."

36. This question anticipates Jesus's similar question-in-reply to Thomas in 20:29.

John's attempt in correcting not only the disciples' misunderstanding of Jesus' identity but also the insufficiency of their christological confessions.

JOHN 4:1–42

Toward the end of Jesus's dialogue with the Samaritan woman (4:7–29), the woman leaves the site of their conversation when the disciples return from their excursion (4:8, 27–28a). Upon her return to the village, she invites the people to come and see the man (implying Jesus) who told her everything she had done (4:29a). Scholars have seen in the woman's invitation (4:29) not only a testimony of her acceptance of and faith in Jesus but also a means to bring others to faith.[37] In the narrative, however, John gives little indication whether the woman has come to faith in Jesus or the townspeople will have come to faith *on account of* her testimony. In fact, there is much doubt in the woman's invitation. Most questionable in this dialogue is the woman's follow-up question to the townspeople: *mēti houtos estin ho christos* (4:29b)—for which the NRSV renders: "He cannot be the Messiah, can he?"[38] The fact that John employs the particle *mēti* indicates that the question expects a negative answer (see 4:33; 8:22; 18:35).[39] By using *mēti*, instead of *ouk*, the woman raises doubt about her knowledge of Jesus and expects that the townspeople would agree with her suspicion that Jesus was not the Messiah. Though she invites the townspeople to come and see Jesus (4:29), it is not this invitation per se that brings them to faith. John places a full stop on Christology in the woman's invitation when he reports on their final words to her: "They said to the woman, 'It is no longer because of what you

---

37. Thompson, *John*, 106–7, argues: "The Samaritan people come to Jesus *because of* the woman's testimony to him as Messiah, inviting them to come and see a man with amazing knowledge . . . ; yet on another level it [her departure] hints that she has accepted Jesus' promise to give her living water that surpasses anything she can draw from Jacob's well" (emphasis added). See von Wahlde, *Gospel and Letters*, 2:190; and Moloney, *Gospel of John*, 146.

38. Literally, however, the question is tagged: "He is not the Messiah, is he?" In this tag question, the expected answer is generally negative, though such a question can be used to communicate reticence or hesitancy. See Henri van den Bussche, *Jean: Commentaire de l'Évangile Spirituel* (Bruges: Desclée de Brouwer, 1976), 195; and Elizabeth Danna, "A Note on John 4:29," *RB* 106 (1999): 219–23.

39. Herbert W. Smyth, *Greek Grammar* (Oxford: Benediction Classics, 2014), §1772. BDAG, 649, notes: "*mēti* [is] a marker that invites a negative response to the question that it introduces."

said that we believe, for we have [known and] heard for ourselves,[40] and we know that this is truly the Savior of the world'" (4:42). The townspeople's belief in Jesus occurs mutually *because of* their invitation to Jesus and *as a result* of Jesus's staying with them.

Critical elements can be drawn from this invitation in 4:29. The end of this dialogue suggests that the woman's invitation is far from being the basis for the townspeople's coming to faith, and that growth in belief essentially and gradually occurs through their indwelling with Jesus by hearing and knowing him. The townspeople's belief in Jesus is hardly related to any of the christological confessions; and stress should be placed on the fact that belief occurs as a result of personally hearing and knowing Jesus. The townspeople have come to belief (*pisteuomen*) *before* they commit themselves to calling Jesus the savior of the world, whereas, as narrated in 1:19–51, Andrew, Philip, and Nathanael inadequately proclaim christological titles to Jesus *even before* coming to belief. From the townspeople's perspective, therefore, the woman's invitation does not yield faith in Jesus.[41]

JOHN 11:11–44

On his way to the tomb in Bethany to raise the dead man Lazarus (11:11–44), Jesus meets several characters. He meets Martha (11:20); Martha leaves Jesus to tell her sister Mary (11:28). He meets Mary accompanied by some villagers from Bethany (11:31–33). This phenomenon gives rise to another occasion where the last Johannine invitation occurs (11:34); and these encounters happen prior to their arrival at the tomb (11:38). Interestingly, the townspeople invite Jesus to come and see the tomb where Lazarus is laid. Verses 38–44 report the miracle in which Jesus raised Lazarus. The townspeople's invitation has a split result. On the one hand, having seen the miracle that Jesus raised Lazarus (11:38–44), many of the bystanders come to belief (11:45). On the other hand, some others report to the Pharisees what Jesus has done (11:46). One may argue from silence that this group of

---

40. NRSV leaves untranslated *kai oidamen*, "and we have known."

41. John does not use the verb *pisteuō*, "to believe," on the woman, but only on the lips of the townspeople *pisteuomen*, "we believe" (1:42). For a full discussion on this point, see Toan Do, "Revisiting the Woman of Samaria and the Ambiguity of Faith in John 4:4–42," *CBQ*, forthcoming.

the townspeople did not come to belief. Because of their report to the Pharisees, the Sanhedrin plans to put Jesus to death (11:47–53). This last invitation differs significantly from the previous ones, in that it is directed at Jesus and not at the recipients who would eventually come and believe in him.

Despite the trend of scholars focusing on Jesus's come-and-see invitation as the fundamental and principal key to Johannine Christology, the overall narrative scheme demonstrates that such an invitation is more likely a Johannine stylistic repetition. The four occasions where the invitation occurs (1:39, 46; 4:29; 11:34) show either the characters' misunderstanding or their inadequate faith in Jesus. What follows attempts to explain this typical Johannine invitation in terms of *keeping* and *doing* Jesus's command.

COME AND SEE AND AN ETHIC OF LOVE

A narrative-critical appraisal of John's narrative suggests that Christology is an insufficient answer to the Johannine invitation (1:39, 46; 4:29; 11:34). The christological confessions surrounding these narratives demonstrate how Andrew, Philip, Nathanael, the Samaritan woman, and some Bethany villagers have misunderstood Jesus and his role. In the attempt to explain this Johannine invitation more effectively, however, what follows appeals to Jesus's own command—one that is based on an ethic of love (John 14:15; see 13:34–35; 15:12–17).[42] This latter point is felt in the Johannine communities when the authors remind the members of the ethical dimensions of Jesus's love-command (1 John 2:3–6, 7–11; 3:11–12, 23–24; 4:7–10, 20–21; 2 John 5–6).

Having foretold Peter's triple denial (13:36–38), Jesus addresses the rest of the disciples on the eve of his departure (14:1–4).[43] Jesus is going away to prepare a place for the disciples. At the end of this speech, Jesus states that the disciples know the place where he is going

---

42. Jesus's love command appears several times in John, but only in 14:1–31 does this specifically involve some disciples by name: Thomas (v. 5), Philip twice (vv. 8–9), and Judas not Iscariot (v. 22). The command in 14:15 is my focus in this section. Here Jesus addresses his disciples because of Philip's request that he show them the Father (14:8). In retrospect, Philip is the one who invites Nathanael to come and see (1:46), which results in the latter's inadequate confessions of Jesus.

43. "The rest of the disciples" here includes those at the foot-washing, minus Judas Iscariot (13:30–31). Yet one should not presume this group to be the eleven traditional disciples.

(14:4).[44] This statement implies that Jesus expects the disciples to have known him, despite repeated evidence to the contrary. Repeating Jesus's verb twice in 14:5, Thomas's question negates the disciples' knowledge of Jesus: "Lord, we do not know where you are going. How can we know the way?" Replying to Thomas's denial, Jesus explains that he is the way, the truth, and the life, and that his way is the way to the Father (14:6).

At this point, John shifts to another verb of knowing; and the change of verbs adds further emphasis to the disciples' ignorance. Verse 7a continues Jesus's previous statement in verse 6, "If you [plural] know me, you will know my Father also." The disciples' knowledge of Jesus in verse 7a is conditioned by *ei*, "if." One can easily read Jesus's reply as a statement that the disciples have not known him because in verse 7b he says: "From now on you do know him and have seen him." The implication here is clear that the disciples have not previously known or seen God, but now they *do* because they have known and seen Jesus.

Showing his ignorance of Jesus, Philip then asks, "Lord, show us the Father, and we will be satisfied" (14:8). Frustrated with their ignorance, Jesus singles out Philip by name (14:9): "Have I been with you all this time, Philip, and you still do not know me?[45] Whoever has seen me has seen the Father. How can you say, 'Show us the Father'?" For the next several verses (14:10–14), Jesus continues his speech on the oneness between him and God. More relevant is Jesus's petition that they believe in him and in God; and this petition is directed at the disciples, not just Philip alone.[46]

The irony in this narrative lies in the disciples' ignorance of Jesus. More poignant is Philip's request that Jesus show "them" the Father

44. While textual tradition divides between longer and short readings of 14:4, the manuscripts agree on Jesus's use of the verb *oidate*, "you [plural] know." See Bruce M. Metzger, *A Textual Commentary on the Greek New Testament*, 2nd ed. (Stuttgart: Deutsche Bibelgesellschaft, 1994), 207. For the verbal forms of this Ionic-Hellenistic *oida*, see Smyth, *Greek Grammar*, §§794–99; BDF, §99; and Robert W. Funk, *A Beginning-Intermediate Grammar of Hellenistic Greek*, 3rd ed. (Salem, OR: Polebridge, 2013), §487.5.

45. If this question is tagged, the Greek is more forceful in 14:9a: *ouk egnōkas me, Philippe*, "you have known me, haven't you, Philip?" With *ouk*, Jesus's question affirms that Philip has indeed known him. However, John's irony runs deep in this dialogue. In 14:7, Jesus says that the disciples now know the Father because they know Jesus. Like Thomas in 14:5, Philip's request in 14:8 that Jesus show them the Father negates what Jesus has just reassured them in 14:7. Thus the ironic meaning of Jesus's question in 14:9 is that Philip has *not* really known either Jesus or the Father.

46. From 14:10b to 14:14, the subjects, verbs, and pronouns are all in the second-person plural.

(14:8). This request betrays any possibility that they might have known or believed in Jesus. Such a portrayal of ignorance echoes John's deep sense of irony in 1:35–51, in which he describes how the disciples (Andrew, Philip, and Nathanael) have inadequately confessed Jesus with various titles. Any argument in favor of the disciples' christological confessions of Jesus in 1:35–51 is therefore challenged by this dialogue in 14:1–14 between Jesus and Thomas and Philip.

John has downplayed Christology with regard to the come-and-see invitation (1:39, 46; 4:29; 11:34). Christology is not the first or prerequisite of faith in Jesus, but is indeed the most confronting reality in the Johannine communities. For this reason, when John reports the scene at the foot of the cross, he suggests that even Jesus's prominent disciple Peter has deserted him, and that the scene is portrayed with only four figures: Jesus's mother, her sister Mary the wife of Clopas, Mary Magdalene, and the disciple whom Jesus loved (19:25–27). For John, the climax of faith in Jesus is clearly not christological confessions, but rather the action that the disciple/follower takes, namely, does one love Jesus? This question brings us back to Jesus's command in John 14:15 and forward to its reminiscence in 1 John 2:4.

At the end of Jesus's petition that the disciples believe in the oneness between him and the Father (14:1–14), he tells them: "If you [plural] love me, you will keep my commandments" (14:15). The mood in Jesus's statement is significant, namely, a future more vivid conditional statement.[47] Jesus's command is simple, but direct, and consists of two parts. First, in the apodosis (or "then" clause), Jesus says that the disciples *will* keep his commandments (*tērēsete*, "you will keep").[48] Second, in the protasis (or "if" clause), Jesus raises a condition (*ean*, "if") that the disciples "love" him.[49] The protasis complements the apodosis, which also sets a "real" condition for it. Put

---

47. The mood of this future more vivid condition has the following formula: *ean* with subjunctive (protasis), and future indicative or equivalent (apodosis). This condition ought to be carefully compared with the "less real" or "unreal" condition in 14:7, which has the following formula: *ei* with perfect or imperfect indicative (protasis), and imperfect indicative with *an* (apodosis). On these conditional types, see Toan Do, "Εἰδῆτε, ἴδητε, οἴδατε, and Scribal Activities in 1 John 2:29a," *Babelao* 5 (2016): 90–91, esp. n52; and Smyth, *Greek Grammar*, §§2297, 2323–28.

48. Smyth, *Greek Grammar*, §2323, notes that "in the apodosis, the future indicative or any other form [is] referring to future time." Thus the fact that some manuscripts (e.g., A D K *rell*) cite an aorist imperative *tērēsate* still carries the same force of a future action.

49. Smyth, *Greek Grammar*, §2325, explains that the present subjunctive (*agapate*, "you love") followed by (*ean*, "if") "views an act as continuing (not completed)."

differently, the disciples will *not* be able to keep Jesus's love command if they *do not* love him. Compared to the statement in verse 7, which is *less* real regarding the disciples' knowledge of him, Jesus's love command here in verse 15 carries the full force of their having future love for him. The enactment of this ethical love echoes what Jesus has told them in 13:34–35 and will remind them again in 15:12–17 that all *other* people will recognize them as his disciples *if* they love one another.[50] The action of doing "any" thing for "any" others reaches its climax when one shows love by dying for the others (15:13). For John, the only person who has ever performed this real act of love for others is Jesus (19:25–27). In Jesus's command, the enactment of love for Jesus and for one another is *all* that the disciples ought to have. This is virtually the only command that Jesus has for his disciples—one that is full of hope and expectation, namely, they will do what he has asked of them. On more than one occasion, therefore, John reminds his audience that only after the Jesus event would the disciples remember what he has said and done, and they would come to believe in Jesus (2:22; 12:16; 17:7, 19, 36; 16:4) or, at least, promise (represented by Peter) to have love for Jesus by loving others (21:15–17). For John, the love command is the prerequisite to knowledge and true faith in Jesus and God (see 1 John 2:3–6).

Many christological elements that scholars have detected in John's invitations (1:39, 46; 4:29; 11:34) have in reality been replaced by Jesus's love command. This replacement is felt most clearly in the post-Jesus-event and Gospel era, when the subsequent Johannine Christians had to live through their faith and confessions in Jesus and God, whom they had never seen or known (1 John 4:12). In fact, christological confessions have come to a head in 1–3 John, when the authors variously address controversial positions in Christology. These epistles bear witness to a significant group of members whose Christology contrasts with that of the authors; these dissidents are first called *pseustēs*, "liar," or "pseudo-Christian" (1 John 2:3–6) and then named *ho antichristos*, "the antichrist" (1 John 2:18–27; 4:1–6; 5:6–12; 2 John 7–11; 3 John 10). The authors describe the dissidents' view that Jesus is not the Christ. Although the Johannine Epistles nowhere provide a clear description of how the Johannine communi-

---

50. The plural of "my commandments" in 14:15 may be explained as a single command of love—one that has a twofold ethical, relational enactment: love for Jesus and love for one another (Jesus ← love → one another). The love command is for one another (13:34–35), for Jesus (14:15), and for one another (15:12).

ties and the dissidents came to distance themselves from one another, the phrase "they have gone out into the world" (1 John 2:19; 4:1, 5; 2 John 7) likely indicates that Christology was a determining factor for some separation among members who formerly belonged to the same group of communities (3 John 10). Because they have left, the authors deny that these dissidents have ever had any true association with the communities. This breakdown in christological agreement is clearly embedded in the literary genre of the subsequent Johannine communities.

Once again, the remedy for this breakdown in christological positions lies in the authors' repeated appeal to the love command. Using the same verb of knowing (*ginōskō* as referred to the ignorance of Thomas and Philip in 14:7, 9), the author of 1 John states: "Now by this we may be sure that we know him, if we obey his commandments" (1 John 2:3). If placed parallel to each other, 1 John 2:3 can be construed as a paraphrase of Jesus's love command in John 14:15. Although the author does not mention Jesus by name in "his" commandments, he implies so in the preceding verses (1 John 2:1–2). Then he explains how this love command is to be enacted and executed; namely, one does not hate one's siblings or another Christian, but loves one's brothers and sisters (1 John 2:9–11). Later, he repeats this explanation several times: "For this is the message you have heard from the beginning, that we should love one another" (1 John 3:11, 14–15, 18, 22–23; 4:7, 21; 5:2). Finally, if christological confessions have been the cause of fracture for some members who formerly belonged to the Johannine communities, then the love command is the author's only and single appeal to the remaining members. "For the love of God is this, that we obey his commandments. And his commandments are not burdensome" (1 John 5:3).

CONCLUSION

"With justice," says Brown, Johannine "christology can be called the highest in the NT."[51] When coupled with the come-and-see invitation (1:39, 46; 4:29; 11:34), Brown's observation may sound relevant *only* with regard to John's pervasive allusions to Christology.[52] The actual situation of each character in the Gospel and members of

---

51. Brown, *Community of the Beloved Disciple*, 45.
52. On this point, see John Painter, "The 'Opponents' in 1 John," *NTS* 32 (1986): 48–71,

the communities represented by the Epistles has proved that Christology is indeed the most confronting factor that a Johannine Christian faces; this calls for an ethical response. The authors of both the Gospel and Epistles must have experienced this failure of each character and member in living up to Johannine Christology. As seen in the narratives, each author appeals to the love command in their own ways: John narrates Jesus's command while the author of 1 John recalls this same instruction. Yet their appeals to this command result from suggestions that Christology was no longer a determining principle of a Christian life, or that Christology may not be as serious a problem as is sometimes suggested, but that ethical behavior was. "No one has ever seen God; if we love one another, God lives in us, and his love is perfected in us" (1 John 4:12). Whether each Johannine Christian can live the law of love is a matter beyond the authors' control. The different Johannine "parties" may not, in fact, have differed radically in their Christology. But their lives, their relationships with one another, and their "ethics" did not reflect their christological beliefs. The love command appeals to every ethical and relational, rather than christological, aspect of all Christian lives, namely, *doing* love for one another would complete the joy (*hē chara*) of Johannine Christianity and manifest the oneness between Jesus and God, his disciples, and the Johannine Christians (John 15:11; 1 John 2:5; 4:11–12). Seen from this perspective, the come-and-see invitation is best explained in terms of an ethic of love—one that is exemplified by Jesus (*hypodeigma* in John 13:15; 15:12, 17) and serves as an exhortation to subsequent Johannine Christians (1 John 2:10; 3:11, 23; 4:7).

which he later develops more fully in *The Quest for the Messiah: The History, Literature and Theology of the Johannine Community* (Nashville: Abingdon, 1993), 427–64.

10.

God, Eschatology, and "This World": Ethics in the Gospel of John

FRANCIS J. MOLONEY, SDB

Definitive for Christian narrative ethics is its specific imprinting within a particular story, namely the story of God in Jesus Christ.[1]

A number of essays in this volume survey the "change in direction" that has gone on in discussions of ethics in the Gospel of John. The brilliant existentialist interpretation of Rudolf Bultmann, an essential element of his project of demythologizing the New Testament, especially its narratives, opened an era of extreme skepticism about the relevance of a discussion of Johannine "ethics."[2] Emblematic, in a choir of harmonious voices, have been Ernst Käsemann, Jack T. Sanders, and Wayne Meeks.[3] They articulate a widespread opinion

---

1. Ruben Zimmermann, "Is there Ethics in the Gospel of John? Challenging an Outdated Consensus," in *Rethinking the Ethics of John: "Implicit Ethics" in the Johannine Writings*, ed. Jan G. van der Watt and Ruben Zimmermann, Kontexte und Normen neutestamentlicher Ethik/ Contexts and Norms of New Testament Ethics 3, WUNT 291 (Tübingen: Mohr Siebeck, 2012), 66.

2. See especially Rudolf Bultmann, *Theology of the New Testament*, trans Kendrick Grobel (London: SCM, 1955), 2:3–92; Bultmann, "New Testament and Mythology," in *Kerygma and Myth by Rudolf Bultmann and Five Critics*, ed. Hans Werner Bartsch, trans. Reginald H. Fuller (New York: Harper & Row, 1961), 1–44.

3. Ernst Käsemann, *The Testament of Jesus: A Study of the Gospel of John in the light of Chapter 17*, trans. Gerhard Krodel (London: SCM, 1968); Jack T. Sanders, *Ethics in the New Testament: Change and Development* (London: SCM, 1985), 91–100; Wayne Meeks, "The Ethics of the Fourth Evangelist," in *Exploring the Gospel of John. In Honor of D, Moody Smith*, ed. R. Alan Culpepper and C. Clifton Black (Louisville: Westminster John Knox, 1996), 317-26.

that the world behind the Fourth Gospel, the world in the text, and the world receiving the text was essentially self-focused.

Even "middle of the road" interpreters have found it challenging to trace a clear picture of an "ethic" in the Fourth Gospel,[4] but the past decade of Johannine research has reversed this tendency. Excellent summaries are available in the recent studies of Michael Labahn, Ruben Zimmermann, and Fredrik Wagener.[5] These reviews highlight a number of alternative approaches to the Johannine narrative that open the question of the behavior required of the Johannine Christian and, perhaps more importantly in the light of the above perception of the self-referential ethic, an insistence that the Fourth Gospel looks beyond the community itself to "the world."[6] Zimmermann rightly points out that the search for a Johannine ethic often asks a modern question of an early Christian text. Set within a discussion of a more ancient understanding of friendship, the Johannine insistence on mutual love and support "possesses a degree of effectiveness that extends beyond the narrow scope of individual relationships."[7]

Labahn, Zimmermann, and Wagener draw attention to the contribution of narrative approaches to the Gospel, featuring the ethical challenge to persevere in the face of hatred, to accept the narrative's point of view as a way to understand oneself, and the behavior and action of characters that act as "explicit commandments." This is exemplified in the use of characterization as an attempt to influence the behavior of the audience. This "narratological" approach has been

---

4. See, for example, Frank J. Matera, *New Testament Ethics: The legacies of Jesus and Paul* (Louisville: Westminster John Knox, 1996); Richard B. Hays, *The Moral Vision of the New Testament: A Contemporary Introduction to New Testament ethics* (San Francisco: HarperSanFrancisco, 1996); Richard A. Burridge, *Imitating Jesus. An Inclusive Approach to New Testament Ethics* (Grand Rapids: Eerdmans, 2007).

5. See Michael Labahn, "'It's Only Love'—Is That All? Limits and Potentials of Johannine 'Ethic'—Critical Evaluation of Research," in van der Watt and Zimmerman, *Rethinking the Ethics of John*, 3–43; Zimmermann, "Is There Ethics in the Gospel of John?" 44–88; Fredrik Wagener, *Figuren als Handlungsmodelle: Simon Petrus, die Samaritische Frau, Judas und Thomas als zugänge zu einer narrativer Ethik des Johannesevangeliums*, Kontexte und Normen neutestamentlicher Ethik/Contexts and Norms of New Testament Ethics, WUNT 2/408 (Tübingen: Mohr Siebeck, 2016), 47–66. See also Francis J. Moloney, *Love in the Gospel of John: An Exegetical, Theological, and Literary Study* (Grand Rapids: Baker Academic, 2013), 203–9.

6. On the universal appeal of the Johannine rhetoric, directed to the original receivers, and even more so to its reception within the Christian tradition, see Labahn, "'It's Only Love'," 20–28.

7. Zimmermann, "Is There Ethics?," 74–79 (here 78).

exquisitely developed by Wagener. His lengthy study is a model for all such subsequent work.[8] Johannes Nissen has drawn attention to the call to care for others in a hostile social environment (John 9:22–35, 15:1–17). It is also present in the evangelist's use of a "role model Christology," the summons to follow Jesus, as sheep of the Good Shepherd (10:1–21) no matter what the cost (John 13:1–17; 11:43–44; 21:15–24), and the call to holiness (6:69; 10:36; 17:17–19).[9]

Given the high Christology of the Fourth Gospel it would appear obvious that no character in the story, or audience receiving the story, can ever claim *identity* with Jesus. How can one identify with the Word of God who has preexisted all time in an intense union with God (1:1–2)? He has indeed become flesh and dwelled among us, but as the only Son of the Father. We gaze upon his glory, and his name is Jesus Christ (1:14–18). There can only be one such figure. Nevertheless, Jesus asks his followers to follow his "example" (*hypodeigma*, 13:15), and to love one another as he has loved them (13:34; 17:12, 17).[10] Indeed, this will be the clearest indication to "the world" that they are his disciples (13:35; 17:21, 23). It cannot be claimed that Jesus is not presented as a "role model," or that he does not issue commands. They may only be few, focused on loving, believing, and obeying his commands (13:34; 14:11, 15, 21, 23–24; 15:10, 12, 17), but the relationship between disciple and Lord, in which a follower is instructed by the master, is part of the narrative (see 13:12–17, 21–38; 14:1–16:33).

Udo Schnelle suggests that the entire text of the Fourth Gospel is a "master story" that provides a sense of orientation for its audience, thus becoming an element in the audience's "formation of meaning" (*Sinnbildung*). Such "formation" is received "from the literary form of the Gospel of John itself from which one must expect ethical directions."[11] The Fourth Gospel, as gospel, necessarily involves ethics,

8. Wagener, *Figuren als Handlungsmodellen*, describes the development of a narrative ethic (6–47), and develops an exacting methodology (83–217) for his intense reading of the "figures" of Simon Peter (chap. 3: "The Shepherd Learns to Be Shepherd"), the Samaritan woman (chap 4: "Faith Overcomes Boundaries"), Judas (chap. 4: "Judged"), and Thomas (chap. 5: "The Way into a Believing Community"). This 620-page study will serve as a model for all subsequent use of Johannine characters to trace an ethic of characters ("figures") *in the narrative* that addresses the audience *of the narrative*.

9. For the cited expression, see Labahn, "'It's Only Love,'" 38.

10. On the close relationship between the "example" of 13:15 and the new commandment of Jesus's loving self-gift that disciples must imitate in v. 34, see R. Alan Culpepper, "The Johannine *hypodeigma*: A Reading of John 13:1–38," *Semeia* 53 (1981): 133–52.

11. Udo Schnelle, "Theologie als kreative Sinnbildung: Johannes als Weiterbildung von

even though it might lack the explicit ethical teachings of such passages as the Sermon on the Mount and on the Plain (Matt 5:1–7:29; Luke 6:12–49).

> It provides an orientation, developed by and from the narrator and his story for readers in present and future situations. Collecting and re-narrating the cultural memories of the addressees, the Gospel builds meaning from past events and develops a specific value system that aims at behaviour and at reflection and decision in moral terms.[12]

The essay that follows reflects on the possible presence of ethics in John's Gospel, joining those studies that approach the text from a narrative-critical perspective. But it is more text oriented and less philosophical/hermeneutical than some of the scholarship mentioned above. Beginning with the well-established textually based truth that the Gospel of John is primarily about "the story of God in Jesus Christ" (Zimmermann), it will further insist that the narrative and theological dynamic of the story is "glued together" by a number of *relationships* that begin and end in God. None of this is novel. However, more attention needs to be given to an element that is crucial to most religious discussions of ethics and morality: eschatology. It should also be drawn into a discussion of Johannine ethics.

Fascinated by the existentially challenging Johannine "realized eschatology," little attention is devoted to the truth that the Gospel *never abandons* a traditional eschatology (e.g., 5:28–29; 6:39–40, 44, 54; 11:26). Once this is recognized as an element in the Johannine story, then it is legitimate to ask whether the Johannine narrative requires an ethical behavior of its audience, based on the teaching of resurrection unto life and resurrection unto condemnation after death (5:28–29).

THE STORY OF GOD IN JESUS CHRIST

Despite the obvious high Christology that is a feature of the Fourth Gospel, God is the dominant agent throughout the narrative. God

---

Paulus und Markus," in *Das Johannesevangelium—Mitte oder Rand des Kanons? Neue Standortsbestimmungen*, ed. Thomas Söding, QD 203 (Freiburg: Herder, 2003), 119–45 (here 144). My translation.

12. For this summary of Schnelle's narrative ethics and "formation of meaning" (*Sinnbildung*), see Labahn "'It's Only Love,'" 40–41 (here 40).

(1:1), the Father of Jesus (1:14), makes things happen. From the Prologue (1:1–18) to the closing statement (20:30–31), the dependence of Jesus on the Father who sent him as "Son of God," and thus Messiah, is made clear (1:14, 17–18; 20:31).[13] This case has been cogently and convincingly argued, from a variety of different and rich perspectives, for some decades.[14] The incarnation of the preexistent Word (1:1–2, 14) enables a human story that makes God known (v. 18). The truth made known by Jesus Christ perfects the original gift of God through Moses (v. 17). Jesus describes his mission as bringing to completion the task given to him by the one who sent him (4:34; 5:36; 17:4).

Making God known means living a life that tells a story (*exēgēsato*, 1:18) making known a God who so loved the world that he sent his only Son, not to judge the world but to save it (3:16–17). It is God's love that determines the sending of the Son, so that the world might have eternal life. In his final prayer, Jesus explains what is meant by "eternal life": "This is eternal life, that they may know you, the only true God" (17:3a). That knowledge, however, is communicated through the life story of Jesus Christ (v. 3b). This passage of life and love from God through the Son to "the world" is fundamentally *relational*. God has a *relationship* of love with the Son (see 3:35; 15:9; 17:24, 26). God has a *relationship* of love with the world. Because of that relationship, God has sent his Son into the world (3:16–17). An obedient Son does "the work" (*to ergon*) of the Father (see 4:34;

13. Throughout the Gospel Jesus's messianic mission is subordinated to his being the Son and sent one of God. Thus the affirmation that Jesus is the Christ in 20:31 depends on his being the Son of God. The Johannine Jesus is the Christ insofar as he is the Son of God. Among many, see Francis J. Moloney, *The Gospel of John*, SP 4 (Collegeville, MN: Liturgical Press, 1998), 542–45; see also Moloney, "The Fourth Gospel's Presentation of Jesus as 'the Christ' and J. A. T. Robinson's *Redating*," in *Johannine Studies 1975–2017*, WUNT 372 (Tübingen: Mohr Siebeck, 2017), 169–83.

14. See, for a selection, C. K. Barrett, "Christocentric or Theocentric? Observations on the Theological Method of the Fourth Gospel," in *Essays on John* (London: SPCK, 1982), 1–18; Gail O'Day, *Revelation in the Fourth Gospel: Narrative Mode and Theological Claim* (Philadelphia: Fortress Press, 1986); Craig Koester, "Hearing, Seeing, and Believing in the Gospel of John," *Bib* 70 (1989): 327–48; Jean Zumstein, "L'évangile johannique, une stratégie du croire," *RSR* 77 (1989): 217–32; John Painter, "Inclined to God: The Quest for Eternal Life—Bultmannian Hermeneutics in the Theology of the Fourth Gospel," in *Exploring the Gospel of John*; Tord Larsson, *God in the Fourth Gospel: A Hermeneutical Discussion of the History of Interpretation*, ConBNT 35 (Lund: Almqvist, 2001); Marianne Meye Thompson, *The God of the Gospel of John* (Grand Rapids: Eerdmans, 2001); Francis J. Moloney, "Telling God's Story: The Fourth Gospel," in *The Forgotten God: Perspectives in Biblical Theology; Essays in Honor of Paul J. Achtemeier on the Occasion of his Seventy-Fifth Birthday*, ed. A. Andrew Das and Frank J. Matera (Louisville: Westminster John Knox, 2002), 107–22; Moloney, *Love in the Gospel of John*, 37–69.

5:36; 17:4; 19:30) so that others may enter into that *relationship* and thus continue the mission of Jesus (see 13:34–35; 15:12, 17; 17:17–19, 20–23). Jesus prays for an ultimate time and a place where all will be swept into *the relationship of love* that unites the Father and the Son (17:24–26).[15] The Father *acts* in sending his Son; the Son, Jesus Christ, *acts* in making God known, consummately in his death on the cross.[16] The story of the Gospel, from its beginnings in preexistence (1:1–12), to its closure in Jesus's return to the glory that was his before the world was made (17:5; 20:17), depends on *relationships*. Within the intimacy of the gathering for a meal, the footwashing and the gift of the morsel, Jesus instructs his disciples on the need to live lives that reflect their knowledge of this truth. Such "knowledge" is the source of blessing for those who "act" accordingly: "If you *know these things*, blessed are you, if you *do these things*" (13:17, my translation). Blessedness depends on performance.[17]

But that is not the end of relationships. Jewish thought and earlier Christian teaching had already spoken about the Spirit of God (e.g., Hos 4:12; Isa 32:15–20 Ezek 11:19–20; 36:26–27; Joel 28:29; Wis 12:1; Romans 8; Luke 24:44–49; Acts 2:1–13). In the Fourth Gospel, in a way similar to the Gospel of Luke, the Paraclete, the Holy Spirit (14:26), becomes a character whom the Father will send after the departure of Jesus as the presence of Jesus, despite his absence, leading, instructing, comforting believers, and judging the world (see 14:15–17, 25–26; 15:26–27; 16:7–11). The relationship that exists between the Father and the Son extends to the Paraclete, who, in his own turn, relates to the believers. The gift of the Paraclete is intimately linked with the continuation of the ministry of the absent Jesus. As Jesus is the former Paraclete, the Holy Spirit is "another Paraclete."[18] The Paraclete is sent by both the Father and the departed Jesus (14:16; 15:26; 16:7, 15).

Never in the Gospel of John are the disciples exhorted to love God. They are to love Jesus (8:42; 14:15, 21, 23, 24, 28) and love one

15. For a more extensive development of this sketch, see Moloney, *Love in the Gospel of John*, 37–69.

16. Ibid., 135–60.

17. For a helpful essay on the establishment of "relationships" as part of Johannine ethics for the postresurrection church, focusing on John 15, see Chrys Caragounis, "'Abide in Me': The New Mode of Relationship between Jesus and His Followers as a Basis for Christian Ethics," in van der Watt and Zimmerman, *Rethinking the Ethics of John*, 250–63.

18. Francis J. Moloney, "The Fourth Gospel: A Tale of Two Paracletes," in *The Gospel of John: Text and Context*, BIS 72 (Leiden: Brill, 2005), 241–59.

another (13:34–35; 15:12, 17; 17:21, 23). Behind this insistence is a belief and a trust in God as the one who sends his Son (3:34; 4:34; 5:23, 30; 6:38-39; 7:16; 8:16, 18, 26, 29; 9:4; 13:16; 16:32), and who will love them if they love the Son (see 14:23–24). But *never* is the expected behavior of the disciple described as transcending their relationships with one another and with Jesus, into some form of "otherworldly" belief in Jesus. Only in Jesus's final prayer, as is fitting for the literary form of a prayer, does Jesus pray that the disciples be taken to "another place": into the oneness of love that exists between the Father and the Son (17:25–26). The narrative raises "this-worldly" questions: *where, when, and how* does the disciple make love known? This is a critical question, as interpreters tend to short-circuit an investigation into Johannine ethics by identifying it with an impossible command to mutual love (13:34–35; 14:15; 15:12, 17) and belief in and love of Jesus (14:1, 11, 21, 23–24, 28; 15:9; 16:27). They conclude that such an ethic is sectarian, and ultimately a counterproductive mode of self-absorbed interest.[19]

Ruben Zimmermann has reacted against this by focusing on the Johannine interest in the verb *poiein* (to do, to make). He limits his interest to the obvious relationship of *doing* God's will that exists in the Son's relationship to the Father, and a brief indication that the audience is also invited to associate itself with *doing* God's works (6:68), and the possibility that they might *do* right or wrong (5:29). The association between doing the right thing and living a good life "can be regarded as a central subject of ancient philosophy and ethics."[20] This is important and helpful, but further dimensions can be added by focusing on the temporal constraints the message of the Fourth Gospel places on potential disciples.[21]

---

19. For centuries interpreters have debated whether it is possible for Christians to live Matthew's beatitudes. However, no one questions the existence of a Matthean ethic, on the basis of its impossible demands. For the discussion, see Jan Lambrecht, *The Sermon on the Mount: Proclamation and Exhortation*, GNS 14 (Wilmington, DE: Michael Glazier, 1985), 20–24. For a recent insistence that they apply to everyday Christian life, see Frank J. Matera, *The Sermon on the Mount: The Perfect Measure of the Christian Life* (Collegeville, MN: Liturgical Press, 2013).

20. Zimmermann, "Is there Ethics?," 8–9 (here 9).

21. Ruben Zimmermann's important focus on the importance of deeds (*erga*) and doing (*poieō*) as an entrance into a Johannine ethic has been developed in a 2014 doctoral dissertation at the Johannes Gutenberg University, Mainz, by Karl Weyer-Menkhoff, *Die Ethik des Johannesevangeliums in sprachlichen Feld des Handelns*, Kontexte und Normen neutestamentlicher Ethik 5, WUNT 2/359 (Tübingen: Mohr Siebeck, 2014). For a summary of his work, see Weyer-Menkhoff, "The Response of Jesus: Ethics in John by Considering Scripture as Word of God," in van der Watt and Zimmermann, *Rethinking the Ethics of John*, 159–74.

Is there anything in the Gospel of John that indicates *when and where* the disciple of Jesus must *do something* in order to manifest obedience to Jesus's commands to love and believe? The later Letters of John were written to insist that the community never forget that "from the beginning" they have been called to life-giving relationship with the Father and his Son Jesus Christ (see 1 John 1:1–4). In order to do this, they must keep the commandments of Jesus that have been with them from the beginning of their entering the Christian community (2:3–11). The act of loving as Jesus loved (see 2:8–11; 3:11–24) faced many challenges. The anxiety of the author concerning the unity of the community (see 2:18–19), and the preservation of the "old commandment," which is ever new (2:7-8), along with the indications of the eventual collapse of oneness across the community indicated in 2 and 3 John (2 John 7–11; 3 John 8–11), are evidence of the tensions that existed among the Johannine communities. This is not the place to enter into that debate.[22] I raise it merely to indicate that the Johannine communities reflected in the Letters were built on an ethic that was "this-worldly," and had to be lived within the constraints of a given time and place.[23]

LIVING THE IN-BETWEEN-TIME

A feature of the temporal aspect of the Fourth Gospel is no doubt what has come to be known as its "realized eschatology." The Jewish notion of a final judgment that will take place at the end of time has less importance. Life and judgment flow from acceptance or refusal of the revelation of God *now*. There is no need to wait till the end of time. Many significant Johannine passages could be cited, but a sample selection of passages from early in the Gospel makes the point clearly.[24] Particularly striking are those passages that claim: "The hour has come, and now is" (e.g., 4:23; 5:25).

---

22. For a more complete discussion, see Moloney, *Love in the Gospel of John*, 191–214.

23. Jörg Frey, *Die johannische Eschatologie*, vol. 2, *Das johanneische Zeitversändnis*, WUNT 110 (Tübingen: Mohr Siebeck, 1998) provides an excellent and detailed study of the use of "time" across the Fourth Gospel.

24. I will generally (but not always) cite the NRSV text, even though there are many places where it betrays the original Greek. In the texts that follow, the NRSV regularly changes a singular subject into a generic plural, to avoid a male pronoun. I have accepted that oddity for the sake of inclusivity.

To all who received him, to all who believed in his name, he gave power to become children of God. (1:12)

Just as Moses lifted up the serpent in the wilderness, so must the Son of Man be lifted up, that whoever believes in him may have eternal life. (3:14–15)

For God so loved the world that he gave his only Son, that whoever believes in him should not perish but have eternal life. . . . Those who believe in him are not condemned; those who do not believe are condemned already. (3:16, 18a)

Whoever believes in the Son has eternal life; whoever disobeys the Son shall not see life, but must endure God's wrath. (3:36)

The hour is coming, and now is, when the true worshipers will worship the Father in spirit and in truth. (4:23)

As the Father raises the dead and gives them life, so also the Son gives life to whom he will. The Father judges no one but has given all judgment to the Son, that all may honor the Son, even as they honor the Father. He who does not honor the Son does not honor the Father who sent him. Truly, truly, I say to you, he who hears my voice and believes him who sent me has eternal life; he does not come into judgment but has passed from death to life. *Truly, truly, I say to you, the hour is coming, and now is,* when the dead will hear the voice of the Son of God, and those who hear will live. For as the Father has life in himself, so he has granted the Son also to have life in himself; and he has given him authority to execute judgment because he is the Son of Man. (5:21–27)

John makes it clear that divine filiation (1:12), eternal life (3:15; 5:21, 24, 25, 26), judgment (3:16–18, 36; 5:22, 24, 27), and union with the Father (4:23) are available *now* to the one who believes in Jesus. The hour is coming, *and now is* (4:23; 5:25). There can be no gainsaying John's conviction that the believer enjoys favorable judgment, eternal life, and an intense belonging to God through faith and love of Jesus *on this side of death.*[25]

But that is not John's only conviction about sonship, eternal life, judgment, and oneness with the Father, even though it may be the dominant one. Perennially puzzling for interpreters has been his

25. On the eschatology of John 3, see Jörg Frey, *Die johanneische Eschatologie*, vol. 3, *Die eschatologische Verkündigung in den johanneischen Texten*, WUNT 117 (Tübingen: Mohr Siebeck, 2000), 242–321.

juxtaposing the so-called realized eschatology, indicated by the passages selected from John 1–5 above, with clear statements of a traditional eschatology. A traditional eschatology, as found for example in the Letters of Paul and the Synoptic tradition, looks to God's final judgment that will take place, through Jesus as judge (often as Son of Man in the gospels), *on the other side of death*. The long passage cited from 5:24–27, with its heavy stress on "the hour is coming and now is" (v. 25), draws on traditional language about Jesus's judging role as Son of Man in verse 27. No doubt that judgment is the *krisis* (crisis) that is brought about in the "here and now,"[26] but reference to the Son of Man as judge in verse 27, looking back to Daniel 7:13, leads directly into a statement concerning judgment *on the other side of death* in verses 28–29.

> Do not be astonished at this, for the hour is coming when all who are in the graves will hear his voice and will come out—those who have done good to the resurrection of life, and those who have done evil, to the resurrection of condemnation. (5:28–29)

What puzzles is the proximity of these sharply different eschatological views: life and judgment *now*, depending on belief in Jesus, and life or condemnation *on the other side of death*, depending on good or bad deeds.[27]

Equally puzzling is the repetition of the same juxtaposing of realized and traditional eschatology in Jesus's discourse on the bread from heaven in 6:25–59. As in 5:19–30, the discourse is dominated by a realized eschatology. But it is regularly moderated by reference to the end time.[28] The bulk of the discourse is a presentation of Jesus as the true bread from heaven that brings to perfection the original bread from heaven, associated with the gift of the law, once the manna ceased as Israel entered the land (see Josh 5:12). The Father of Jesus gave the bread through Moses, but now gives the true bread, Jesus Christ (6:32). This bread "gives [*didous*] life to the world" (v. 33), and Jesus promises that "whoever comes [*ho erchomenos*] to me will never

---

26. On 5:27, see Francis J. Moloney, *The Johannine Son of Man*, 2nd ed. (Eugene, OR: Wipf & Stock, 2007), 68–86. On its use of Dan 7:13, see 80–82.

27. On the eschatology of John 5, see Frey, *Die eschatologische Verkündigung*, 322–401.

28. I use the expression "moderated" to distance myself from those who insist that any elements of traditional eschatology present in the Gospel have been added to an original story entirely written from a "realized" eschatological perspective (see above, n15). See ibid., 391–400.

be hungry, and whoever believes [*ho pisteuōn*] in me will never be thirsty" (v. 35). All the verbs (gives, comes, believes) are in the present tense. A satisfied life is available *now* through belief in Jesus. But without explanation this eschatological view is rendered traditional.

> I have come down from heaven, not to do my own will, but the will of him who sent me. And this is the will of him who sent me, that I should lose nothing of all that he has given me, but raise it up on the last day. This is indeed the will of my Father, that all who see the Son and believe in him may have eternal life; and I will raise them up on the last day. (vv. 38–40)

This juxtaposing of realized and traditional eschatology persists in verses 43–44 and verse 54. The regularity and consistency of this juxtaposing of realized and traditional views of "when" judgment, life, salvation, or condemnation takes place indicates that John wished to communicate that belief in Jesus give life *here* and *hereafter*.

That such is the case is made clear in John 11, a narrative that, among other issues, deals with the question of death in the community, and an adequate Johannine response to the reality of death.[29] In her dialogue with Jesus, Martha articulates the recent Jewish understanding of life after death that was shared by the Pharisees and Jesus: "I know that he will rise again in the resurrection on the last day" (11:24). Jesus responds to her with his famous self-revelation as the resurrection and the life (v. 25a). Belief in Jesus, the resurrection and the life, transcends normal expectations of Jewish beliefs and traditions. Jesus explains: "Those who believe in me, even though they die, will live, and everyone who lives and believes in me will never die" (vv. 25b–26a). Because Jesus is the resurrection and the life, all assumptions about life and death have been transformed for those who believe in him. John's narrative addresses a community, wondering about the destiny of those who have died, with a characterization carried by Lazarus: "Lazarus is dead" (v. 14). The deceased

---

29. See ibid., 403–62. I regard John 11:1—12:8 as a literary unit (see Mary in v. 2, and the role of Mary in 12:1–8), and especially its function as a Johannine narrative exhortation to a belief that breaks all boundaries, even the boundary of human death. See Francis J. Moloney, "Can Everyone Be Wrong? A Reading of John 11:1—12:8," in *Text and Context*, 214–40. This essay was first published in *NTS* 49 (2003): 505–27. See also Sandra M. Schneiders, "Death in the Community and Eternal Life: History, Theology, and Spirituality in John 11," *Int* 41 (1987): 44–56.

Lazarus is not active in the story until he responds to the call of Jesus (vv. 43–44).

Often missed by interpreters, attracted to Jesus's stunning self-revelation, and their delight over Martha's apparently perfect expression of Johannine faith in verse 27, the narrative as a whole is not about success on the part of those called to faith, but about their failure. The disciples fail to understand that Jesus's delay in going to Lazarus was "so that you may believe" (v. 15), as Thomas suggests that they join Jesus in a journey to martyrdom (v. 16). Martha thinks that the uniqueness of Jesus lies in something that she has "always believed" (*pepisteuka*): Jesus fulfils her messianic expectations (v. 27). Despite an initially hopeful response to Jesus, Mary joins "the Jews" in their "wailing" (*klaiō* is used [vv. 31, 33]), and Jesus sheds tears in his frustration (*dakryō* is used [v. 35]).[30] Not one character in the narrative manifests belief in Jesus as the resurrection and the life (v. 25a).[31] Standing at the tomb, surrounded by Martha, Mary, and the disciples, Jesus in his prayer to the Father explains the significance of the episode: "so that they may believe that you sent me" (v. 42. See v. 15). To this point, he has had little success. The first sign of the emergence of a belief in what God is doing through Jesus appears in the actions of Mary (12:1–8), which reverse the fear of a bad odor expressed by Martha (11:39). "The house was filled with the fragrance of the perfumed oil" (12:3). Criticized by Judas Iscariot, she is defended by Jesus. Only Mary has recognized the uniqueness of the presence of Jesus (vv. 4–8).[32]

30. Throughout this essay, the expression "the Jews" (*hoi Ioudaioi*) will always be in quotation marks. They are one side of a christological debate, and should not be identified with a race. Some attempt to soften this expression (e.g., "the authorities"). This eliminates the fact that for the Johannine community (themselves mainly Jews) their opponents were Jews. See Adele Reinhartz, "Judaism in the Gospel of John," *Int* 63 (2009): 382–93. However, one must "recognise in these hot-tempered exchanges the type of family row in which the participants face one another across the room of a house which all have shared and all call home" (John Ashton, *Understanding the Fourth Gospel* [Oxford: Clarendon, 1991], 151). See also Francis J. Moloney, "'The Jews' in the Fourth Gospel: Another Perspective," in *Text and Context*, 20–44. See especially the important collection of Reimund Bieringer, Didier Pollefeyt, and Frederique Vandecasteele-Vanneuville, eds., *Anti-Judaism and the Fourth Gospel: Papers of the Leuven Colloquium, 2000* (Assen: Van Gorcum, 2001).

31. See Moloney, "Can Everyone Be Wrong," 222–32.

32. See the rich reflections of Dorothy Lee, *Flesh and Glory: Symbolism, Gender and Theology in the Gospel of John* (New York: Crossroad, 2002), 197–211. I proposed that the faith journey of the characters across 11:1–12:8 is not completed until 12:1–8 in my essay "Can Everyone Be Wrong?" in 2003. It has been largely ignored or rejected since then. Scholars refuse to examine the twofold use of *embrimasthai* in vv. 33 and 38, and ignore the narrative significance of Jesus's harsh words to Martha in v. 40. These words presuppose unbelief.

Jesus, the sent one of God, offers resurrection and life to all who believe in him: in this life and in the life to come. As frequently across the Gospel, Jesus states a message to those who believe, and who have not yet died: "everyone who lives and believes in me will never die" (v. 26a). Embracing this message of the fullness of life *now* for those who believe, however, is only part of Jesus's teaching. It is all very well to believe that faith in Jesus produces eternal life *now*. What of those members of the community who have already died? Have they failed in some way? Does Jesus also promise life *on the other side of death* to those who believe in him? In verse 26b Jesus's words add to the promise of life *now* a further promise to those who have already died: "Those who believe in me, even though they die, will live" (v. 26b). Those who believe will have life *on the other side of death*. Theologically and pastorally, a central aspect of the Johannine message is the promise of judgment, life, and oneness with God to those who have believed and have died physically. The question of the destiny of those who have died had to be faced in a community telling its story of Jesus some seventy years after the death and resurrection. Some believers may even have been slain in that "in-between-time" (see 16:3). Is life also available to them?

A narrative that communicated *only* a message of realized eschatology would prove to be unsatisfactory for those living who looked back in wonder about the destiny of those who have preceded them and died. John has not abandoned a traditional eschatology that promised judgment and life *on the other side of death*. Juxtaposing a realized eschatology with a traditional eschatology is the Johannine way to communicate the delight that flows from belief *in this world*, side by side with the promise of the identical experience for those in the community who have died. The Johannine Jesus promises eternal life to all who believe in him, *here and hereafter*.[33]

Finally, John tells not only of the *time* of the gift of life (both here and hereafter) but also of a *place* that transcends the geographical constraints of living "in the world." John 17:1–26 is dedicated to Jesus's prayer to the Father for himself and his mission (vv. 1–8), his immediate disciples and their mission (vv. 9–19), and for all who would come

---

33. See Andrew T. Lincoln, *The Gospel according to Saint John*, BNTC (New York: Crossroad, 2005), 324; and Jean Zumstein, *L'Évangile selon Saint Jean*, CNT 4a, second series (Geneva: Labor et Fides, 2014), 1:374–75. See also Brendan Byrne, *Life Abounding: A Reading of John's Gospel* (Collegeville, MN: Liturgical Press, 2014), 190–92.

to believe in him through the preaching of his disciples (vv. 20–23). Closing the prayer, he asks the Father to gather all for whom he has prayed into a "new place": "Father, I desire that those also, whom you have given me, may be with me *where I am*" (v. 24a: *hopou eimi egō*). Swept up into the love that united the Father and the Son, those who believe in Jesus will no longer be "in the world" (v. 25). They dwell in the glory generated by the loving unity between the Father and the Son that existed between them from all time, before the world was made (v. 26. See 1:1–2; 17:5).

This aspect of the life and teaching of the Johannine Jesus must be given due importance. The disciples of Jesus certainly have life *now* because of their belief in Jesus. But John insists that there will be a *time* (5:28–29; 6:38–40, 43–44, 54; 11:25–26; 12:48) and a *place* (11:24–26) that lie outside the parameters of worldly time and space, when all believers will be one with the Father and the Son. As Gustav Stählin wrote in 1934, "Alongside and interwoven are the 'already now' and the 'not yet.' The life in the 'now' and the life 'looked forward to' in the future belong together. This is the basis not only of Johannine devotion but of the New Testament as a whole."[34] Much of Jesus's "ethical imperative" in the gospels is motivated by the "not yet" (see, e.g., Mark 13:24–37; 15:62; Matt 24:29–51; 25:31–46; 27:63–64; Luke 19:11–27; 20:9–18; 21:25–36). Perhaps the same should be claimed for teaching of the Johannine Jesus.

LIFE "IN THE WORLD"

Already in the Prologue to the Gospel, the audience meets a threefold meaning for the expression *ho kosmos* (the world): "The true light, which enlightens everyone, was coming into world [v. 9: *eis ton kosmon*]. He was in the world [v. 10a: *en tō kosmō ēn*], and the world [v. 10b: *ho kosmos*] came into being through him, yet the world [v. 10c: *ho kosmos*] did not know him." The expression is used to speak of a geographical space, within which people work out their lives. Jesus Christ came into this world, and lived in this world. This use of "the world," which interests me most in this essay, could be regarded as "neutral." It exists, and has its existence because of the creative action of God (v. 10b). Along with everything else in creation, the world

34. Gustav Stählin, "Zum Problem der johanneischen Eschatologie," *ZNW* 33 (1934): 258. My translation.

is "modeled" on the Logos ("Word"; see v. 3).[35] "The world" is not judged; it is the "place" where God's action takes place in and through Jesus. It is in the world that the characters in the narrative are called to decision (see 3:19; 6:14; 7:4; 10:36; 11:9; 12:46; 13:1; 16:20–21, 28, 33, 17:5, 6, 11, 13, 24; 18:20, 36).

But the world is not only "modeled" on the Logos. As "the world" has its very existence through him (v. 10b), the expression is used to describe "a place" that is more than a geographical space. It is the object of God's saving love and saving action (3:16–17). God's revelation of love takes place in the world, because God loves the world, and sends the disciples, after the departure of Jesus, into the world, to continue his mission (see 1:29; 4:42; 6:33, 51; 8:12, 26; 9:5; 9:39; 11:27; 12:19; 12:25; 12:47; 14:31; 17:18–19, 21, 23, 37). Finally, "the world" carries a negative meaning. It is used to indicate those inhabitants of the world who reject Jesus's revealing presence among them, as they reject that he was sent by the Father. Consequently, such people in the world are hostile to all who have accepted Jesus Christ:

> If the world hates you, be aware that it hated me before it hated you.
> If you belonged to the world, the world would love you as its own.
> Because you do not belong to the world, but I have chosen you out of the world—therefore the world hates you. (15:18–19)

This is that part of creation that has fallen under the aegis of "the ruler of this world" (14:30; see 7:7; 8:23; 12:31; 14:17, 19, 22, 27, 30; 15:18–19; 16:8, 11; 17:9, 14, 15, 25). It is the place where "the evil one" reigns among women and men (17:15).[36]

---

35. On the relationship between the Logos and "the world," see Moloney, *Gospel of John*, 35–36.

36. Because the majority use of the expression in 1 John is very negative (see 1 John 2:15–17; 3:1, 17; 4:1–9; 5:4–5, 19, 7), colored by such expressions as "the whole world lies under the power of the evil one" (5:19), it is often taken for granted that the Johannine understanding is negative, and this creates an impression that the Gospel is "otherworldly." This is not the case, as its use is evenly spread across the Gospel. On this, see N. H. Cassem, "A Grammatical and Conceptual Inventory of the use of κόσμος in the Johannine Corpus with some Implications for a Johannine Cosmic Theology," *NTS* 19 (1972–73): 81–91. See further, Craig R. Koester, *Symbolism in the Fourth Gospel: Meaning, Mystery, Community*, 2nd ed. (Minneapolis: Fortress Press, 2003), 277–86, and Christopher W. Skinner, "The World: Promise and Unfulfilled Hope," in *Character Studies in the Fourth Gospel: Narrative Approaches to Seventy Figures in John*, ed. Steven A. Hunt, D. Francois Tolmie, and Ruben Zimmermann, WUNT 314 (Tübingen: Mohr Siebeck, 2013), 61–70. Some of the above allocations of the appearance of *ho kosmos* above could be contested. However, it is important to see that the threefold use of expression is evenly spread, however one might to locate one or other of its occurrences. For a cautionary note on the negative interpretation of the use of "the world" in 1 John, see Toan Do, "Does

The Gospel of John belongs to a world full of human characters, Jews: Pharisees (1:24 etc.) and "the Jews" (1:19; 2:18; etc.), named Jewish characters (John the Baptist, Andrew, Philip, Nathanael, Simon Peter, Judas Iscariot, the other Judas, Jesus's mother, Nicodemus, Mary, Martha, Lazarus, Malchus, Annas, Caiaphas), Jesus's brothers (7:2–9), temple police (7:32 etc.), and unnamed characters (5:5; 9:1; etc.). There are Romans (18:3 etc.), including Pontius Pilate (18:29 etc.), Samaritans (4:1–42), and gentiles (4:46–54; 12:20–22). The narrative is cluttered with disciples, crowds, believers, unbelievers, friends, and enemies.[37] There are also homes (1:38–39; 19:27; 20:10), the city of Jerusalem (2:13 etc.), the temple (2:14 etc.), synagogues (9:22; 12:42; 16:2), mountains (6:3, 15; etc.), a lake (6:1 etc.), the pool of Siloam (9:7, 11), Solomon's porch (10:23). The final days take place at the Kidron valley (18:1), a garden (18:1), the courtyard and the dwelling of the high priest (18:12–27), the Roman praetorium (18:28 etc.), a stone pavement named Gabbatha (19:13), at Golgotha (19:17), in a new tomb, again in a garden (19:41), and many other locations spread across the land of Israel that are not specified by name, including a wedding reception to which Jesus is invited, and a royal official who comes to Jesus, in a Galilean town called Cana (2:1, 11; 4:46, 54). It is a mistake to follow Eusebius's reported assessment of Clement of Alexandria that the Gospel of John is "the spiritual Gospel" (Eusebius, *Ecclesiastical History* 6.14.5–7).

Despite the high Christology, there is a great deal of flesh-and-blood presence of Jesus to a multitude of characters in many locations in "the world" of the Fourth Gospel. The response of the Johannine

περὶ ὅλου τοῦ κόσμου Imply 'the Sins of the Whole World' in 1 John 2:2?," *Bib* 94 (2013): 415–35.

37. See the comprehensive survey of seventy such characters in Hunt, Tolmie, and Zimmermann, ed., *Character Studies*. For a synthetic table listing all characters in the Gospel, see pp. 34–45, compiled by the editors. The recent interest in characters and characterization in the Fourth Gospel, exemplified by this book and others, especially the work of Cornelis Bennema, "A Theory of Character in the Fourth Gospel with Reference to Ancient and Modern Literature," *BibInt* 17 (2009): 375–41, and Bennema, *Encountering Jesus: Character Studies in the Gospel of John*, 2nd ed. (Minneapolis: Fortress Press, 2014), is a step in the right direction in recognizing the "flesh-and-blood" nature of the Johannine story. The same could be said for the renewed interest in the Gospel of John as history. I indicate my concern, however, that these newer directions run the risk of losing touch with the inspired and inspiring theological and christological rhetoric of the Johannine utterance. The most balanced approach to the question remains that of R. Alan Culpepper, *Anatomy of the Fourth Gospel: A Study in Literary Design* (Philadelphia: Fortress Press, 1983), 99–148. See also the valuable collection of Christopher W. Skinner, ed., *Characters and Characterization in the Gospel of John*, LNTS 46 (London: Bloomsbury T&T Clark, 2014).

believer must take place "in this world." The Fourth Gospel directs believers of all ages to an ethic of quality relationships "in this world." It is only there that they can do good deeds (3:19–21), so that they may one day be swept up into the love that exists between the Father and the Son (17:24–26). They will no longer be "in the world," but in the place where Jesus enjoys the glory that was his before the world was made (17:25–26; see also 17:5).[38]

Jesus's word and presence thus challenges an audience living "in the world." It is true that the only explicit command that he directs to the disciples in the story, and the centuries of disciples who have been the audience of this narrative, is that they love one another as he has loved them (13:34–35; 14:15; 15:12, 17). He, their lord and master, has given them an example that they must follow in their *relationships* with one another (13:15). These relationships, however, are not to be pursued simply because Jesus commanded them to behave in a certain way. The believer must *act* as Jesus has acted, *do* what Jesus *did*. And they must do so "in the world."

> Laying down one's life is not about words but about *action*. [I wish to] focus on the *actions* of a God who sends, on the task of the Johannine Jesus to make God known, on the request that disciples and followers of Jesus *love in a certain way*, and on the inevitable fruits of that love.[39]

The Johannine Jesus makes it clear on several occasions that there is a right and a wrong way to *do* things. In his description of the judgment that flows from the presence of the light in the world, Jesus states that some prefer the darkness to the light, "because their deeds were evil" (3:19). Such people hate the light, and do not come into the light because they do evil deeds. They do not wish their evil deeds to be exposed (v. 20). On the other hand, there are those who are happy to dwell in the light, because their deeds have been done (*ergasmena*) in God (v. 21). The same criteria are used in Jesus's words, stressing traditional end-time judgment, in 5:28–29: "The hour is coming when all who are in the graves will hear his voice and will come out—those who have done good [*hoi ta agatha poiēsantes*], to the

---

38. The narrative theory of the relationships that exist between an implied reader in the text, an original audience, and all subsequent readers of the text is presupposed by these few sentences. On this, see Francis J. Moloney, "Who Is 'the Reader' in/of the Fourth Gospel?," in *Johannine Studies 1975–2017*, 77–89.

39. Moloney, *Love in the Gospel of John*, xi (emphasis added).

resurrection of life, and those who have done evil [*hoi de ta phaula praxantes*], to the resurrection of condemnation."

Living in the time between Jesus's departure and his return (see 14:1–4, 20–21, 28; 16:16), the disciples are to do the works (*ta erga*) of Jesus. Indeed, they will do even greater works (14:12). "The Jews" ask the right question when they find Jesus and the disciples at Capernaum after the miraculous feeding by the lake (6:1–15). They ask: "What must we do [*ti poiōmen*] to perform the works [*hina eirgazōmetha ta erga*] of God" (v. 28). For John, these works must be associated with the nurturing and development of quality *relationships* that reflect the *relationship* that exists (1:1–2, 18), has always existed (17:5, 24), and will continue to exist (17:26) between the Father and the Son.[40] The transformation of the disciples from "servants" to "friends" (15:15) because Jesus has chosen them and sent them out (v. 16) reflects the unconditional love that Jesus has for them (13:1: *eis telos*), a love Jesus shares with his Father, and passes on to them (15:9–10).

High sounding as this may be, Johannine Christians are nevertheless challenged to live lives "in this world" of people and places in response to this ethical imperative. God, Jesus, and the believers are caught up in a *relationship* that has its beginnings in the love of God, and its end in the love that believers have for one another, so that the world might come to believe that Jesus is the sent one of God (17:21, 23). Not only are believers challenged to such a response, but also they are to do it "in this world," with the ground under their feet, the skies above them, and their neighbors, good, bad, and indifferent, around them.

But there is more. Not only must they respond by nurturing and developing quality *relationships* as they live concrete lives in a given geographical and temporal setting, but they have also been instructed that the way they live *on this side of death* will determine how they will be judged *on the other side of death*. Jesus commands that they must walk in the light (8:12), but this journey requires lives marked by good deeds (5:29: *hoi ta agatha poiēsantes*). Such an ethical response is the only possible indication that can be seen. Those who do good deeds are happy to dwell in the light, so that they can be seen; those

---

40. For a very good survey of the Johannine use of *ergon*, see Hermut Löhr, "Ἔργον as an Element of Moral Language in John," in van der Watt and Zimmermann, *Rethinking the Ethics of John*, 228–49.

who do evil are ashamed, and prefer to hide in the darkness (see 3:19–21). They respond to the command to love as Jesus loved by leading good lives "in this world," doing good deeds, so that after death they will emerge from their graves, hear the voice of the Son of Man, and enter the resurrection of life (5:27–29; see also 11:25–26).[41] This is the mutuality that Jesus asks of his Father for his disciples, so that "this world" in which they live out their complex of relationships, with Jesus, and with one another, empowered by the Spirit Paraclete, may come to believe that Jesus is the sent one of God (13:34–35; 15:12; 17:21, 23). Jack Sanders's (in)famous caricature of Johannine ethics could not be further from the truth.[42]

CONCLUSION

God's relationship with humankind, humankind's relationship with God, through Jesus Christ, and relationships with one another, in obedience to the commands of Jesus (see 13:34–35; 15:12, 17), are to be acted out *within human history*, in "this world." In the light of Jesus's promise that he will return (e.g. 14:3, 18–21, 28; 16:16, 22, 25–26), the Fourth Gospel speaks to Christians living between the now and the not yet, awaiting the return of Jesus, guided, strengthened, protected, reminded, and instructed by "another Paraclete" (14:15–17, 25–26; 15:26–27; 16:7–11, 12–15). However, blessed by God's gift of life *now* as a consequence of belief in Jesus, all the members of the Johannine community and their Jesus story's subsequent audiences, knew that they would die. They thus looked to the Gospel, seeking guidance on how they should live *now* so that they may never experience condemnation, but enjoy being part of the oneness of love that has always united the Father and the Son (17:24–26).

Christians expect to hear something from their "scripture" about Jesus that provides for them instructions from Jesus on *how* they are to live that Paraclete-filled in-between-time.[43] Asking Christians to love Jesus and be loved by God so that they may eventually be

41. For a brief, but accurate, assessment on the role of a traditional eschatology in assessing Johannine ethics, see Noël Lazure, *Les Valeurs Morales de la Théologie Johannique, Évangile Et Épîtres* (Paris: Gabalda, 1965), 22–24, 268–71. This theme is noticeably lacking in van der Watt and Zimmermann, *Rethinking the Ethics of John*.

42. See Sanders, *Ethics*, 100.

43. On the Gospel of John as Scripture, see Francis J. Moloney, "The Gospel of John as Scrip-

swept into the love that has from all times united the Father and the Son (17:24–26), the Fourth Evangelist also tells them *how* they *do* it: through unconditional commitment to quality relationships, so that others might come to belief (17:21, 23). The Fourth Gospel demands an ethic marked by "good deeds," a life lived in the light, and the avoidance of "shameful deeds" that must hide in the darkness (see 3:20–21; 5:28–29).

There are many subtle and learned discussions of what "ethics" means.[44] For John, it means *what one must do or not do* in order to achieve an eternal oneness with God, the Father of Jesus. Johannine ethics is about *what one does* in the in-between-time. Like most early Christian ethics, the realities of judgment or condemnation after death also plays a critical role in Johannine ethics (see 3:19–21; 5:28–29). However, the message of a mutually loving relationship between a Father and a Son that exists from "before the world was made" (1:1–2; 17:5) dominates the Son's time among us "in the flesh" as Jesus Christ (1:14–18). It generates a unique starting point for a Christian ethic. Subordinated to God and Jesus Christ, but deeply caught up in a relationship with Jesus Christ, the believer reflects that relationship in a life that loves and cares for "the other." The disciples in the narrative and the audience of the narrative are to "do these things." A lifestyle marked by generous and loving *actions* for the other is a necessary consequence of an audience's exposure to this narrative. Such a lifestyle is *never* self-absorbed. It is so that the "everyone [*pantes*] may know" (13:35), and so that "the world" (*ho kosmos*) may come to believe that Jesus is the sent one of the God (17:21, 23).[45]

Jesus knew that the hour had come for one of his disciples to betray him. Another would deny him, and all the disciples were "confused," unable to understand what footwashing and the gift of the morsel to even the most negative character in the story might mean

---

ture," in *Text and Context*, 333–47, and Moloney, "'For as Yet They Did Not Know the Scripture' (John 20:9): A Study in Narrative Time," in *Johannine Studies 1975–2017*, 505–9.

44. For a summary, see Zimmermann, "Is There Ethics," 11–15.

45. In making this affirmation, I endorse Udo Schnelle's claim ("Theologie als kreative Sinnbildung," 119–45) that a literary form of a gospel necessarily generates an ethic. Jörg Frey's important study rightly links the Johannine eschatology with its Christology. However, it appears to me that this important work fails to see the link between eschatology and ethics. He focuses on the intimate bond between eschatology and Christology. See his summary in *Die eschatologische Verkündigung*, 464–88, especially 469–70. No doubt John's ethics do not determine his eschatology, but his eschatology does lead to important ethical consequences.

(see 13:22: *aporeumenoi*). Knowing these things, however, he moved into action, disrobing himself and serving them as the lowest slave (13:1–5). *Knowing* everything, he *did* something unimaginable for a lord and master. The blessedness of the disciple in the story and the audience of the story results from a way of life made up of *deeds* that flow from the *knowing* imitation of a relationship of such quality: "*If you know these things*, blessed are you, *if you do these things*" (13:17).[46] In the Gospel of John, disciples are never told to love God. They are to love Jesus, be loved by Jesus, and to love one another in *actions* that reflect their trust in the ultimate victory of God in and through the death and resurrection of Jesus. "In the world you face persecution. But take courage; I have overcome the world" (see 16:33).

---

46. For an interpretation of John 13 in support of these closing sentences, see Moloney, *Love in the Gospel of John*, 99–117; Moloney, "Εἰς τέλος as the Hermeneutical Key to John 13:1–38," *Salesianum* 86 (2014): 27–46.

PART III

Moving Forward

11.

Genre, Rhetoric, and Moral Efficacy: Approaching Johannine Ethics in Light of Plutarch's *Lives* and the *Progymnasmata*

LINDSEY TROZZO

Genre analysis is often seen as a foundational "first step" on which every other aspect of interpretation depends.[1] Generic categories imply certain purposes, and thus a text's participation in a genre shapes audience expectations and frames interpretation.[2] If participation in generic categories is one means by which an author can communicate meaning to his or her audience, then an analysis of the Fourth Gospel's participation in one or more generic categories should influence interpretation of the text.[3] This essay explores genre as a means to discover what expectations would have guided the audience of the Fourth Gospel and thus what implicit ethics they might have recognized in their experience of the narrative. As we will see, the Fourth Gospel's participation in the *bios* genre opens

---

1. E. H. Gombrich, *Symbolic Images*, Studies in the Art of the Renaissance 2 (London: Phaidon, 1972), 121.

2. Heta Pyrhönen, "Genre," in *The Cambridge Companion to Narrative*, ed. David Herman, Cambridge Companions to Literature and Classics (Cambridge: Cambridge University Press, 2007), 109. See Margaret Davies, *Rhetoric and Reference in the Fourth Gospel*, JSNTSup 69 (Sheffield: JSNT Press, 1992), 67.

3. For a discussion of genre in terms of "use value," see Thomas O. Beebee, *The Ideology of Genre: A Comparative Study of Generic Instability* (University Park: Pennsylvania State University Press, 1994), 1–24. See Carolyn R. Miller, "Genre as Social Action," *Quarterly Journal of Speech* 70 (1984): 163.

the possibility for ethical interests despite the lack of explicit ethical material. After a brief survey of my approach to genre analysis, I will explore how implicit ethics functioned in a group of biographical texts that included an explicitly moral purpose—the *Lives* of Plutarch. To conclude, I will examine the Fourth Gospel's incorporation of ancient rhetorical topics for speeches of praise (encomiastic topics[4]) and consider how the Johannine rhetoric engages the audience in its implicit ethics.

GENRE AND RHETORIC IN THE FOURTH GOSPEL

Genre is conceived in various ways, but most conceptions include groups of texts divided into categories based on recognizable shared features of style, form, or content.[5] In some respects, audiences create these groups, and classification is a heuristic or investigative device externally applied to a text. In other respects, genre is intrinsic to a text—whether it be a generic convention adopted intentionally by an author or features within the text itself that "place it" among similar writings and therefore within a certain genre.[6]

Aristotle strongly emphasized aspects of structure and imitation in his discussion of genre, seeing genre in terms of a fixed and exhaustive classification system.[7] He lists distinguishing features of a genre to

4. See Michael W. Martin ("Progymnastic Topic Lists: A Compositional Template for Luke and Other Bioi?," *NTS* 54 (2008): 18–41) and Alicia Myers's helpful discussion in *Characterizing Jesus: A Rhetorical Analysis on the Fourth Gospel's Use of Scripture in Its Presentation of Jesus*, LNTS 458 (London: T&T Clark, 2012), 46. The encomiastic topics can also be seen to some extent in the Synoptic Gospels, at least Matthew and Luke. See, for example, Philip L. Shuler, *A Genre for the Gospels: The Biographical Character of Matthew* (Philadelphia: Fortress Press, 1982); Philip L. Shuler, "The Rhetorical Character of Luke 1–2," in *Literary Studies in Luke-Acts: Essays in Honor of Joseph B. Tyson*, ed. Richard P. Thompson and Thomas E. Phillips (Macon, GA: Mercer University Press, 1998), 173–90; Charles H. Talbert, *Matthew*, Paideia Commentaries on the New Testament (Grand Rapids: Baker Academic, 2010).

5. Pyrhönen, "Genre," 109.

6. See, for example, Gian Biagio Conte, *The Rhetoric of Imitation: Genre and Poetic Memory in Virgil and Other Latin Poets*, trans. Charles Segal, Cornell Studies in Classical Philology 44 (Ithaca, NY: Cornell University Press, 1986); Hans Robert Jauss, *Toward an Aesthetic of Reception*, trans. Timothy Bahti, Theory and History of Literature 2 (Minneapolis: University of Minnesota Press, 1982).

7. See Aristotle, *Poet.* 6–10; and Horace, *Ars poetica* 73–98. Aristotle includes at least three generic categories: tragedy (superior-dramatic), epic (superior-narrative), and comedy (inferior-dramatic). His extended discussion on the latter is missing and may have included a fourth category, parody (inferior-narrative). See, M. Cavitch, "Genre," in *The Princeton Encyclopedia of Poetry and Poetics*, ed. Stephen Cushman et al., 4th ed. (Princeton: Princeton University Press,

which a text should correspond, and he issues a qualitative judgment based on the extent to which they do so. His system is flexible, however, allowing that no piece of literature adheres perfectly to the constraints of a particular genre (Aristotle, *Poet.* 9). Nevertheless, the view of a static literary system prevailed in the neoclassical literary criticism of the seventeenth and eighteenth centuries.[8] This rigid and formalist system met resistance with certain thinkers among the Romantics, who began to reject the notion of genre altogether,[9] because it shifts attention away from a text's singularity.[10] Emphasis on the freedom and original creating power of the artist (as opposed to imitation) began to expand the limited mechanical approach to genre.[11]

Modern genre theory continued to push against Aristotelian and neoclassical concepts of genre but maintained that genre was an invaluable concept for literary analysis.[12] This way of thinking conceived of a system that was open and flexible (not fixed) and descriptive (not prescriptive or evaluative), bringing a reconfiguration of categories in which a text could exhibit shifting combinations of

2012), 551–54. Tom Thatcher ("The Gospel Genre: What Are We After?," *ResQ* 36 [1994]: 135) helpfully describes how Aristotle is operating at a higher conceptual level than biblical scholars since biblical scholars work within the one medium of literature and look at genre within this context.

8. For more on literary criticism in this period, see French writers René Le Bossu, *Traité du poème épique* (Paris: Chez Michel Le Petit, 1675); Nicolas Boileau Despréaux, *L'art Poétique* (Paris: Hachette, 1922); François Hédelin Aubignac, *La pratique du théâtre* (Paris: Chez Antoine de Sommaville, 1657). Pierre Corneille, *Trois discours sur le poème dramatique: (texte de 1660)*, ed. Louis Forestier (Paris: Société d'Édition d'Enseignement Supérieur, 1982) paved the way for more flexibility. English critics like Alexander Pope, *Essay on Criticism* (London, 1711) and Samuel Johnson extended this way of thinking. Though Johnson's theory fit within neoclassicism, his bent for practicality made him less dogmatic than his predecessors, and so he acts as a transitional figure pointing to the age of the Romantics.

9. Harold Bloom and Janyce Marson, eds., *William Wordsworth* (New York: Bloom's Literary Criticism, 2009); Victor Hugo, *Cromwell* (Paris: Garnier-Flammarion, 1968), esp. 107; William Wordsworth, *William Wordsworth*, ed. Stephen Gill (Oxford: Oxford University Press, 2010), esp. 182; Madame de Staël, *De l'Allemagne*, ed. Simone Balayé (Paris: Garnier-Flammarion, 1968); Friedrich von Schlegel, *Literary Notebooks, 1797–1801*, ed. Hans Eichner (Toronto: University of Toronto Press, 1957); Schlegel, *Philosophical Fragments* (Minneapolis: University of Minnesota Press, 1991). See the discussion of these figures in Alastair Fowler, *Kinds of Literature: An Introduction to the Theory of Genres and Modes* (Cambridge, MA: Harvard University Press, 1982), 17; Cyrus Hamlin, "The Origins of a Philosophical Genre Theory in German Romanticism," *European Romantic Review* 5 (1994): 9–11; Tilottama Rajan, "Theories of Genre," in *The Cambridge History of Literary Criticism*, ed. Marshall Brown (Cambridge: Cambridge University Press, 2000), 226–49.

10. Famously, Benedetto Croce, *Estetica come scienza dell'espressione e linguistica generale: Teoria e storia* (Paris: Ulan, 2012).

11. See further discussion in Rajan, "Theories"; Hamlin, "Origins."

12. See Cavitch ("Genre") for a brief survey of the various modern conceptions of genre.

features (formal, thematic, stylistic, or mimetic). Genre theory today notices that texts (or their authors) have the ability to deviate self-consciously from a generic form. This fact does not argue against generic classification per se; rather, it perceives that generic features form the stable norms by which a single text's uniqueness can be measured.[13] David Aune, for example, suggests that while a "hard core" of prototypical members exhibiting a high degree of "family resemblance" to one another make up the heart of a genre, genre also includes other, less typical members (we might say texts that participate in the genre rather than being categorized as prototypes of that genre).[14] So, without abandoning genre systems altogether, I join modern genre critics who speak—with Derrida—of a text "participating in" a genre rather than "belonging to" a generic category.[15] Further, a text's participation within a certain genre (or genres) can direct audience interpretation since generic norms build expectations that guide encounters with the text.[16]

Johannine scholars have recently taken up this approach to genre criticism in the impressive volume *The Gospel of John as Genre Mosaic*,

---

13. Pyrhönen, "Genre," 112. See, Tzvetan Todorov, *Genres in Discourse* (Cambridge: Cambridge University Press, 1990), 14.

14. David Edward Aune, ed., *Jesus, Gospel Tradition and Paul in the Context of Jewish and Greco-Roman Antiquity: Collected Essays II*, WUNT 303 (Tübingen: Mohr Siebeck, 2013), 25–56.

15. Carol Newsom, "Spying Out the Land: A Report from Genology," in *Bakhtin and Genre Theory in Biblical Studies*, ed. Roland Boer, SemeiaSt 63 (Leiden: Brill, 2008), 21. First printed in Newsom, *Seeking Out the Wisdom of the Ancients: Essays Offered to Honor Michael V. Fox on the Occasion of His Sixty-Fifth Birthday*, ed. Ronald L. Troxel, Kelvin G. Friebel, and Dennis Robert Magary (Winona Lake, IN: Eisenbrauns, 2005), 437–50. See Colleen M. Conway, "John, Gender, and Genre: Revisiting the Woman Question after Masculinity Studies," in *Gospel of John as Genre Mosaic*, ed. Kasper Bro Larsen (Göttingen: Vandenhoeck & Ruprecht, 2015), 69–70. See also Jacques Derrida, "The Law of Genre," in *Signature Derrida*, ed. Jay Williams (Chicago: University of Chicago Press, 2013), 7. Participation in multiple genres is not only a modern concept. As Alexander mentions, a "new biographical mood" was emerging near the time of the Fourth Gospel, where biographies like Tacitus's *Agricola* and Lucian's *Demonax* blended generic forms. Loveday Alexander, "What Is a Gospel?," in *The Cambridge Companion to the Gospels*, ed. Stephen C. Barton (Cambridge: Cambridge University Press, 2007), 27. See Simon Swain, "Biography and Biographic in the Literature of the Roman Empire," in *Portraits: Biographical Representation in the Greek and Latin Literature of the Roman Empire*, ed. M. J. Edwards and Simon Swain (Oxford: Clarendon, 1997), 1–37; Arnaldo Momigliano, *The Development of Greek Biography* (Cambridge, MA: Harvard University Press, 1993).

16. David Duff, *Modern Genre Theory* (Harlow, UK: Longman, 2000), 1–24; David E. Aune, "The Gospels as Hellenistic Biography," *Mosaic* 20 (1987): 2. See also John Fitzgerald, "The Ancient Lives of Aristotle and the Modern Debate about the Genre of the Gospels," *ResQ* 36 (1994): 210; Thatcher, "The Gospel Genre," 132–35.

edited by Kasper Bro Larsen.[17] In his contribution to this volume, Harold Attridge develops his notion of genre bending and tasks interpreters to "trace the arc of the bending," a suggestion that he and other contributors (George Parsenios and Jo-Ann Brant) take up in their essays. Other contributors (Colleen Conway and Ole Davidsen) suggest that the Gospel participates in multiple genres including *bios*, romance, and prototypical tragicomedy.[18]

So what does it mean for a text to participate in a genre? Within biblical studies, David Hellholm's threefold paradigm set a standard for genre studies, suggesting that texts sharing similarities in content, form, and function were considered ripe for comparison.[19] Improving on Hellholm's model, Tom Thatcher suggested that form and function are the most significant aspects for generic classification. In his explanation, genre becomes a functional category when the interpreter acknowledges the relevance of the intended purpose of the text for its audience and how significantly the worldview of the author and audience shapes the composition.[20] Aune suggests that individual texts signal affiliation with a genre through textual clues (like corresponding to a known narrative mode or an expected list of topics).[21] These clues set audience expectation, influencing them to experience the text within a certain interpretive schema. Generic categories imply certain purposes based on generic correspondences and generic tensions (places where the text resists conformity, strays from convention, or uniquely applies conventional features).[22] Thus

17. Kasper Bro Larsen, ed., *Gospel of John as Genre Mosaic* (Göttingen: Vandenhoeck & Ruprecht, 2015).

18. Several of the volume's essays also treat micro/simple genres within the Gospel including the Prologue (Sheridan, Estes), miracle stories (Frey), the Farewell Discourse (Engberg-Pedersen), recognition scenes (Larsen), type scenes (Smith and Svärd), historiography (Becker), and parables (Zimmermann). For more on ancient and modern genre theory, see the essays by Attridge and Auken. See also Harold W. Attridge, *Essays on John and Hebrews*, WUNT 264 (Tübingen: Mohr Siebeck, 2010), 61–78.

19. David Hellholm, "The Problem of Apocalyptic Genre and the Apocalypse of John," *Semeia* 36 (1986): 13–64.

20. Thatcher, "The Gospel Genre," 137. His definition builds on the outer form/inner form paradigm presented by René Wellek and Austin Warren, *Theory of Literature*, 3rd ed. (Harmondsworth, UK: Penguin, 1963). For more on the relationship between genre and the rhetorical effects of a text, see Robert Hurley, "Le genre 'évangile' en fonction des effets produits par la mise en intrigue de Jésus," *LTP* 58 (2002): 243–57.

21. Aune, *Jesus, Gospel Tradition and Paul*, 33.

22. For an extended discussion of genre criticism within the context of rhetorical criticism, see Karlyn Kohrs Campbell and Kathleen Hall Jamieson, "Form and Genre in Rhetorical Criticism: An Introduction," in *Form and Genre: Shaping Rhetorical Action* (Falls Church, VA: The Speech Communication Association, 1978).

participation in a genre (whether straightforward correspondence, genre-bending, or playful affiliation) presents a set of "rules" that affects the relationship between the author and the audience member by establishing expectations or boundaries for meaning.[23]

Attention to the Fourth Gospel's participation in any number of genres can be fruitful for the pursuit of particular interpretive questions.[24] Although genre questions continue to circulate in New Testament scholarship,[25] most agree that the Fourth Gospel corresponds significantly to works categorized within the *bios* (ancient biography) genre in narrative shape and style. Like other ancient biographies, the Fourth Gospel includes a formal preface (though a unique one). Like the encomiastic narrative practice often used in ancient biographies, the Fourth Gospel presents Jesus's "great deeds" to authenticate his status. Like other ancient biographies (especially Philostratus's *Apollonius of Tyana* and Satyrus's *Euripides*), the Fourth Gospel varies continuous prose with extended dialogues and discourses. Also (like *Cato Minor* and *Apollonius of Tyana*), the Fourth Gospel devotes approximately one-third of the space to the last week of the hero's life. Though none of these features proves that the Fourth Gospel should be *categorized* within the *bios* genre, they suggest significant *participation* within this genre. In what follows, I will explore the implications of this overlap particularly for the question of Johannine ethics. Might

23. Jauss, *Toward an Aesthetic of Reception*, 76–109, discusses this in terms of "the horizon of expectations of a genre system that pre-constituted the intention of the works as well as the understanding of the audience" (108). See also Pyrhönen, "Genre"; Sean Freyne, "Mark's Gospel and Ancient Biography," in *The Limits of Ancient Biography*, ed. Brian C. McGing and Judith Mossman (Swansea: Classical Press of Wales, 2006), 72.

24. Whether or not we agree that the Fourth Gospel belongs exclusively to the *bios* genre (see Charles H. Talbert, *What Is a Gospel? The Genre of the Canonical Gospels* [Macon, GA: Mercer University Press, 1985], 134–35, and Richard A. Burridge, *What Are the Gospels? A Comparison with Graeco-Roman Biography*, 2nd ed. [Grand Rapids: Eerdmans, 2004]), the correspondences between ancient biographies and the Fourth Gospel argue strongly that the Fourth Gospel participates in the *bios* genre. See, Richard A. Burridge, "Biography," in *Handbook of Classical Rhetoric in the Hellenistic Period, 330 B.C.—A.D. 400*, ed. Stanley E. Porter (Leiden: Brill, 1997), 373–74. Momigliano, *Development of Greek Biography*, 114–15.

25. Limited space here precludes a survey of the state of the question on gospel genre and the genre of the Fourth Gospel. For a more thorough treatment, see chapter two in Lindsey M. Trozzo, *Exploring Johannine Ethics: A Rhetorical Approach to Moral Efficacy in the Fourth Gospel Narrative*, WUNT series 2 (Tübingen: Mohr Siebeck, forthcoming). See also D. Moody Smith, *The Fourth Gospel in Four Dimensions: Judaism and Jesus, the Gospels and Scripture* (Columbia: University of South Carolina Press, 2008), 144–55; Andreas J. Köstenberger, "The Genre of the Fourth Gospel and Greco-Roman Literary Conventions," in *Christian Origins and Greco-Roman Culture: Social and Literary Contexts for the New Testament*, ed. Stanley E. Porter and Andrew W. Pitts, TENTS 9 (Leiden: Brill, 2013), 435–62.

participation in the *bios* genre reveal something about the Gospel's rhetorical purpose?

To approach this question, I will consider a literary comparison that exhibits similar participation in the *bios* genre and implicit ethical presentation. As the history of research on this topic has shown, comparisons that feature explicitly ethical non-narrative texts or that focus on explicit ethical material within narrative contexts have proved less helpful for the pursuit of Johannine ethics, since the Fourth Gospel contains little to no *explicit* ethical material.[26] Therefore, a comparison with a group of texts that matches the Fourth Gospel's form of chronological narrative, focuses on one main character, and exhibits evidence of *implicit* ethics will be more helpful for the particular aims of this project. Plutarch's *Parallel Lives* stand in close chronological proximity to the Fourth Gospel and resemble its chronological narrative form.[27] Plutarch's other writings attest to his interest in ethics, and the explicit statements in the front matter and summaries of his *Lives* disclose that these biographical narratives include a moral purpose.

RHETORIC AND ETHICS IN PLUTARCH'S *LIVES*

Plutarch presents his *Lives* so that the reader will draw moral conclusions from those examples. This purpose can be found in Plutarch's own hand in the introduction to *Timoleon*, where he describes the narrative as a "mirror" for assimilating virtues and an "effective means of moral improvement" (*Timol.* 1. [Perrin, LCL]).[28] Plutarch presents the *Lives* of his subjects as paradigms for virtue and vice that one can either appropriate or avoid for moral growth.[29] Although the

26. See Michael Labahn, "'It's Only Love'—Is That All? Limits and Potentials of Johannine 'Ethic'—Critical Evaluation of Research," in *Rethinking the Ethics of John: "Implicit Ethics" in the Johannine Writings*, ed. Jan G. van der Watt and Ruben Zimmermann, Kontexte und Normen neutestamentliche Ethik/Contexts and Norms of New Testament Ethics 3, WUNT 291 (Tübingen: Mohr Siebeck, 2012), 3–43; Ruben Zimmermann, "Is There Ethics in the Gospel of John? Challenging an Outdated Consensus," in van der Watt and Zimmerman, *Rethinking the Ethics of John*, 44–80; See also the introductory chapter in Trozzo, *Exploring Johannine Ethics* and Christopher Skinner's essay at the beginning of this volume.

27. C. J. Gianakaris, *Plutarch* (New York: Twayne, 1970), 18.

28. Myers, *Characterizing Jesus*, 45.

29. Timothy E. Duff, *Plutarch's "Lives": Exploring Virtue and Vice* (Oxford: Clarendon, 1999), 50. For mimesis in the Fourth Gospel, see Cornelis Bennema, "Mimesis in John 13: Cloning or Creative Articulation?," *NovT* 56 (2014): 261–74. See also Bennema, "Mimetic Ethics in the

Lives were often presented in pairs followed by a formal comparison (*synkrisis*) that clarified the ethical import of the pair, Plutarch also included implicit features to engage the reader in ethical discourse. Thus Plutarch's presentation is more complex than it might first appear.[30]

At the most basic level, the differences between the hero and the audience members demanded that Plutarch's audience interpret the virtues and vices presented and translate them into their own context. Since the majority of Plutarch's readers were not statesmen or generals, literal imitation of the hero's specific actions was not intended. As A. J. Gossage explains, however, imitation was possible without exact replication of actions, since a reader could use the general virtues of the character "as a pattern for building up his own moral principles."[31] Because the historical setting of the *Lives* was not immediately relevant for the contemporary situation, Plutarch's readers would have to identify the moral principles demonstrated in one context and translate them into their own contemporary situation.

Furthermore, at times, the ethics arising from the presentation of an individual *Life* was less than straightforward. Even the formal *synkrisis* that often followed a pair of *Lives* was not a straightforward ethical presentation but a challenge provoking the reader to explore the issues raised by the *Lives*, pointing the reader back to the narrative. The "closural dissonance," or tension between the content of the *Lives* themselves and that of the formal comparison, invited the reader to reconsider judgment on the *Lives* in question.[32] Compare, for example, the description of Antony's death within the narrative and the description of his death in the closing *synkrisis*. Plutarch closes his narrative presentation saying that Antony died "not ignobly" (*ouk agennōs*, *Antony* 77.7). The concluding comparison, however, describes it in almost opposite terms: "Antony took himself off,—in

Gospel of John," in *Metapher-Narratio-Mimesis-Doxologie: Begründungsformen Frühchristlicher Und Antiker Ethik*, ed. Friedrich W. Horn, Ulrich Volp, and Ruben Zimmermann, WUNT 1/356 (Tübingen: Mohr Siebeck, 2016), 205–17, and his forthcoming monograph, *Mimesis in the Johannine Literature*, LNTS (London: Bloomsbury T&T Clark, forthcoming).

30. Plutarch presents the "signs of the (hero's) soul" (Plutarch, *Alex.* 1.3). The Fourth Gospel uses the same word—*sēmeion*—throughout its narrative to describe the miraculous works that reveal the identity of Jesus (2:11, 18, 23; 3:2; 4:48, 54; 6:2, 14, 26, 30; 7:31; 9:16; 10:41; 11:47; 12:18, 37; 20:30).

31. A. J. Gossage, "Plutarch," in *Latin Biography*, ed. T. A. Dorey (New York: Basic Books, 1967), 49.

32. Duff, *Plutarch's "Lives,"* 265–86.

a cowardly, pitiful, and dishonorable [*atimōs*] way" (*Demetrios and Antony* 6). The presented comparison, where it stands in tension with the narrative content, has a destabilizing effect, which encourages the audience to reevaluate simple, moral assumptions about noble death.

Discussing several examples of this dissonance within the *Lives*, Duff concludes that it has an important function in the moral *programme*, forcing the audience member to reassess the implicit moral principles and paradigms in the text.[33] "Where questions of ethics are concerned," he writes, "Plutarch is more ready to ask questions than to provide simple answers."[34] Duff continues,

> A number of factors stand in the way of an approach to the *Parallel Lives* which looks for the kind of easily extractable moral lessons that Plutarch seems to promise. First, most *Lives* provide very little explicit guidance as to how to understand the moral position of their subjects or of the actions narrated. Plutarch rarely intervenes into the narrative to point out where right and wrong lie. . . . On the whole moral judgments are left implicit.[35]

The fact that the *Lives* are complex narratives rather than straightforward ethical commentaries like moral treatises does not mean they have nothing to offer in terms of ethics. Rather, their challenging complexity invites the audience to engage in ethical discourse.[36] Such an ethical presentation fits what Christopher Pelling calls descriptive or exploratory moralism. While protreptic or expository moralism carries an explicit injunction for the reader to put into effect, descriptive or exploratory moralism raises moral issues without attempting to guide conduct directly.[37] This second category opens up possibilities to explore a text for forms of ethics that might be missed if expository moralism alone is pursued. Though Plutarch at times presents explicit moralism in the introductory prologue or the concluding *synkrisis*, he only rarely breaks into the narrative to make an

33. Examples from *Philopoimen* and *Flamininus, Nikias* and *Crassus, Agesilaos* and *Pompey, Demetrios* and *Antony*, and *Coriolanus* and *Alkibiades* are also included. See Duff, *Plutarch's "Lives,"* 265–86.

34. Ibid., 286.

35. Ibid., 54–55.

36. Ibid., 309.

37. Christopher B. R. Pelling, "The Moralism of Plutarch's Lives," in *Ethics and Rhetoric: Classical Essays for Donald Russell on His Seventy-Fifth Birthday*, ed. Dorren Innes, Harry Hine, and Christopher Pelling (Oxford: Oxford University Press, 1995), 343–61. See Duff, *Plutarch's "Lives,"* 68–69.

explicit moral comment (e.g., *Arist.* 6.1–5; *Dem.* 42.8–11; *Lys.* 23.3; *Aem.* 5.10). This implicit approach fits with the compositional and rhetorical pedagogy of the day, which suggested that the addition of explicit ethical material (such as moralizing maxims) would mar the quality of the narrative.[38]

Plutarch's descriptive or exploratory moralism relies on the reader to negotiate the ethics embedded within the story. In Duff's words, "Plutarch expects his reader to recognize, and to question, where an action is to be commended, and where blamed."[39] Further, as Alicia Myers points out, Plutarch utilizes the first-person plural to build a connection to his readers.[40] Such metaleptic boundary breaking invites the audience to engage the narrative. Plutarch thus involves his readers in the deliberative ethical process rather than presenting an ethical system wholesale. The onus is on the reader to identify the moral categories being employed, to discern the degree to which those categories should extend into his or her situation, and to put the principles into practice appropriately.[41]

Delivering complex and implicit moralism, Plutarch's *Lives* engage the reader in ethical discourse,[42] providing an interesting corollary

38. See Theon, *Prog.* 91.25–27, as cited in Craig A. Gibson, "Better Living through Prose Composition? Moral and Compositional Pedagogy in Ancient Greek and Roman Progymnasmata," *Rhetorica* 32 (2014): 18.

39. Duff, *Plutarch's "Lives,"* 55.

40. Myers, *Characterizing Jesus,* 32. See Pelling, "Plutarch," in *Narrators, Narratees, and Narratives in Ancient Greek Literature,* ed. I. F. de Jong, René Nünlist, and Angus Bowie, Studies in Ancient Greek Narrative 1 (Leiden: Brill, 2004), 405–6; 412. As we will see below, the Fourth Gospel's self-aware first-person narrator has a similar metaleptic effect on the audience.

41. Duff, *Plutarch's "Lives,"* 55. Plutarch likely intended his readers to engage in this deliberation within the boundaries of his own philosophical system. Plutarch's reading of Plato understood reason as a guide to which the nonrational aspects of the soul responds. His complex presentations in the *Lives* demonstrate the value of education or training, which can help the soul respond to reason and produce virtue. His paradigm presented a middle way between the ethical ideals of Stoicism (focus on reason alone) and Epicureanism (pleasure as the ultimate goal), which he saw as misguided. His interpretation of Plato included open dialectical inquiry but also maintained the possibility of reaching firm conclusions. Such an emphasis on dialectic in the process is evident in the complex ethical presentation within his *Lives.* See, for example, George Karamanolis, "Plutarch," in *The Stanford Encyclopedia of Philosophy,* ed. Edward N. Zalta, fall 2014 ed., https://plato.stanford.edu/archives/fall2014/entries/plutarch/; Timothy E. Duff, "Models of Education in Plutarch," *JHS* 128 (2008): 1–26.

42. The idea that the past offered moral knowledge that was applicable to contemporary life was central for Plutarch. Specifically, his heroes illustrated the virtue of political cooperation that his readers would need to thrive in the Roman Empire. See more on how Plutarch's narratives resisted escapism and moved readers to bridge the gap between the heroes of the past and the contemporary situation in Alan Wardman, *Plutarch's Lives* (Berkeley: University of California Press, 1974), 100–104.

for some of the difficulties related to the pursuit of Johannine ethics. Like the ethics in the *Lives*, a number of factors stand in the way of an approach to the Fourth Gospel that looks for the kind of easily extractable moral lessons offered in the ethical discourses of the other Gospels or elsewhere within the canon.[43] The Fourth Gospel reveals an interest in ethics, yet it contains limited explicit ethical material.[44] The way Plutarch includes implicit ethics and engages the audience in ethical discourse, however, opens up new possibilities and facilitates questions that may prove helpful for the pursuit of Johannine ethics. By participating in the *bios* genre, the Fourth Gospel guides its audience to look expectantly for implicit ethics in the story. Thus, in light of our literary comparison with Plutarch's *Lives*, we are encouraged to press on in our rhetorical investigation of implicit ethics in the Fourth Gospel.[45]

The exploration of the rhetoric employed in Plutarch's *Lives* leads us to ask what elements in the Fourth Gospel engage the audience in ethical discourse. As we have seen, the Fourth Gospel's participation in the *bios* genre opens the possibility for ethical interests, despite the lack of explicit ethical material. As the *Lives* of Plutarch illustrated, a narrative biography, influenced by rhetoric, can engage the audience and challenge them to consider how the hero ordered his life and how that orientation might translate to their own context. With these things in mind, it is plausible that the early audience of the Fourth Gospel expected the narrative to include a moral/ethical purpose. As with Plutarch's *Lives*, we will miss the full ethical dynamic of the text if we overlook the implicit ethics that can be discovered in the rhetorical exchange between author and reader.[46]

---

43. See the comments above on Duff, *Plutarch's "Lives,"* 54–55. Explicit forms of moral instruction found elsewhere in the canon include maxims, paraenetic sections, sermons, letters with practical instructions, etc.

44. Noteworthy exceptions include the love commandment and the call to imitate Jesus's actions in the footwashing episode. For more on the complexities of Johannine ethics, see Zimmermann, "Is There Ethics"; Labahn, "'It's Only Love.'" See also Trozzo, *Exploring Johannine Ethics*.

45. Duff, *Plutarch's "Lives,"* 54–55.

46. See also Davies, *Rhetoric and Reference in the Fourth Gospel*, 367.

EXTENSION OF THE ENCOMIASTIC TOPICS

This section extends beyond broad genre considerations to focus more particularly on how the Fourth Gospel facilitates the communication of its ethical dimension to its audience. Such a question, concerning the communicative exchange at the intersection of author, text, and audience, calls for a rhetorical examination. Because biography was not discussed in rhetorical handbooks or in the treatment of genres according to Aristotle or Quintilian, it developed by drawing on other genres and utilizing rhetorical topics toward a specific end.[47] Rhetorical topics were especially important for the *bios* genre, since, as Burridge points out, it was influenced by a number of other genres.[48] This influence is precisely the case with the Fourth Gospel, which incorporates the encomiastic topics for a formal speech of praise. The incorporation of these topics has resulted in one of the most apparent features of the Fourth Gospel, its elevated presentation of Jesus. This explicitly high Christology complicates some approaches to imitation ethics, but it also brings attention to Jesus's unity with the Father as an indispensable concept for understanding Jesus's life orientation.[49] The theme of unity with the Father, which grounds Jesus's exalted status, is also explicitly linked to Jesus's actions in the Fourth Gospel. Further, the encomiastic topics (topics for a formal speech of praise) are extended to include Jesus's followers in the narrative as well as his followers among the audience of the Fourth Gospel.

In the Fourth Gospel, Jesus repeatedly refers to his connection with the Father when he is asked about what he does or why he does it.[50] Thus, in addition to forming the basis of Jesus's exalted status in

47. Burridge, "Biography," 373–74.

48. Ibid., 374. See also Momigliano, *Development of Greek Biography*, 17, 114–15; David E. Aune, ed., *Greco-Roman Literature and the New Testament: Selected Forms and Genres*, SBLSBS 21 (Atlanta: Scholars Press, 1988), 109–10; Christopher B. R. Pelling, *Characterization and Individuality in Greek Literature* (Oxford: Clarendon, 1990); Jerome H. Neyrey, "Encomium versus Vituperation: Contrasting Portraits of Jesus in the Fourth Gospel," *JBL* 126 (2007): 530n5.

49. Lindsey Trozzo, "Elevated Christology and Elusive Ethics in the Fourth Gospel," in *Johannine Christology*, ed. Stanley E. Porter and Andrew W. Pitts, Johannine Studies 3 (Leiden: Brill, forthcoming).

50. See, for example, John 5:19, 36; see 3:35; 4:34; 10:18, 32, 37–38; 14:10–11; 17:4. Karl Weyer-Menkhoff, "The Response of Jesus: Ethics in John by Considering Scripture as Work of God," in van der Watt and Zimmerman, *Rethinking the Ethics of John*, 159–74. See Jan G. van der Watt, "Ethics of/and the Opponents of Jesus in John's Gospel," in van der Watt and Zimmerman, *Rethinking the Ethics of John*, 175–91.

the Fourth Gospel, unity with God is also determinative for Jesus's actions and his mission. Having used the encomiastic topics to present unity with God as the basis for Jesus's status and for his actions, the Fourth Gospel extends these encomiastic topics to include Jesus's followers. The extension of these topics to believers establishes that unity with God can be the determinative factor for their identity and actions as well.[51] Not only do the topics extend to Jesus's followers in the narrative world, these topics extend beyond the narrative into the sphere of the audience. Thus the topics reach into the arena within which Johannine ethics can be found—the rhetorical exchange that takes place between the story and the audience member.

First, the narrative extends the topic of *origin*. The Word who was with God in the beginning gives those who believe in him the power "to become children of God" (1:12). Though these believers come from different earthly and physical family lines, the Fourth Gospel introduces a new family "not of blood or the will of the flesh or of the will of a man, but of God" (1:13, my translation), a new birth, from above (3:3, 7), or "of the Spirit" (3:6). Like Jesus is the "Son of God" (1:34, 49; 3:18; 11:4, 27; 19:7; 20:31), those who believe become children of God (1:12; see 14:1–2; 20:17). While his earthly brothers did not believe in him (7:5), the risen Jesus calls his disciples "my brothers" (20:17). In a moving scene at the cross (19:26–27), the narrative introduces a new family in bringing together Jesus's mother and his Beloved Disciple.[52]

The gospel audience, identifying with the Beloved Disciple, would resonate with this image, especially if the audience is experiencing isolation from their current religious community.[53] Jesus's words, "I

51. Zimmermann ("Is There Ethics," 70–74) discusses numerous places where christological titles and images used to describe Jesus are extended to include his followers, many of which are referenced below. See also Zimmermann, "Metaphoric Networks as Hermeneutic Keys in the Gospel of John," in *Repetitions and Variations in the Fourth Gospel: Style, Text, Interpretation*, ed. Gilbert van Belle, Michael Labahn, and P. Maritz, BETL 223 (Leuven: Peeters, 2009), 381–402. See Mary L. Coloe, *God Dwells with Us: Temple Symbolism in the Fourth Gospel* (Collegeville, MN: Liturgical Press, 2001), 3, 220–21; Klaus Scholtissek, *In ihm sein und bleiben: die Sprache der Immanenz in den Johanneischen Schriften*, Herders biblische Studien (Freiburg: Herder, 2000), 372.

52. Raymond E. Brown, *The Death of the Messiah: From Gethsemane to the Grave, a Commentary on the Passion Narratives in the Four Gospels*, 2 vols. (New York: Doubleday, 1994), 1023–25; Veronica Koperski, "The Mother of Jesus and Mary Magdalene: Looking Back and Forward from the Foot of the Cross in John 19, 25–27," in *The Death of Jesus in the Fourth Gospel*, ed. Gilbert van Belle, BETL 200 (Leuven: Leuven University Press, 2007), 858; Coloe, *God Dwells with Us*, 185–90.

53. Ute E. Eisen, "Metalepsis in the Gospel of John: Narration Situation and 'Beloved Disci-

will not leave you orphaned" (14:18), which make use of this family theme, would be poignant for a group who feels ostracized from its religious and cultural community.[54] Spoken in the context of an extended first-person discourse, the audience would experience these words spoken directly to them as if from Jesus himself.[55] Just as the characters in the story are offered a new family, the audience is assured that they too are a part of this family—the same family to which Jesus himself belongs.

Second, the narrative extends the topic of *nurture and training.* The Prologue describes Jesus as "the one who is in the bosom of the Father" (*eis ton kolpon* in 1:18, my translation). As Alicia Myers discusses, this same imagery is used (only one other time in the Gospel) to describe the Beloved Disciple, who is "in the bosom of Jesus" (*en tō kolpō* in 13:23, my translation). The imagery demonstrates the unity between Jesus and the Beloved Disciple and invites the audience into this unity.[56] The Fourth Gospel also presents Jesus as a teacher with credentialed authority, whose words came from the knowledge received from the Father (3:31–35; 5:19–24; 6:45–46; 7:16–18;

ple' in New Perspective," in *Über Die Grenze, Metalepse in Text—und Bildmedien Des Altertums,* ed. Ute E. Eisen and Peter von Möllendorff (Berlin: de Gruyter, 2013), 333–34.

54. The idea that separation from the synagogue stands in the background to John's Gospel began with a theory proposed by J. Louis Martyn in *History and Theology in the Fourth Gospel,* 3rd ed., NTL (Louisville: Westminster John Knox, 2003). Martyn's theory has been much discussed, and many alternative suggestions for the background of the Gospel have been presented. See, for example, Adele Reinhartz's important work *Befriending the Beloved Disciple: A Jewish Reading of the Gospel of John* (New York: Continuum, 2001) as well as Udo Schnelle's *Antidocetic Christology in the Gospel of John: An Investigation of the Place of the Fourth Gospel in the Johannine School,* trans. Linda M. Maloney (Minneapolis: Fortress Press, 1992) and Edward W. Klink III's *The Sheep of the Fold: The Audience and Origin of the Gospel of John,* SNTSMS 141 (Cambridge: Cambridge University Press, 2007). See also Alicia Myers's contribution to this volume. On the acceptance of the basic outline of the two-level drama and more on the history of the Johannine community from this perspective, see D. Moody Smith, "The Contribution of J. Louis Martyn to the Understanding of the Gospel of John," in *History and Theology in the Fourth Gospel,* 3rd ed., NTL (Louisville: Westminster John Knox, 2003), 1–18; Wayne A. Meeks, "Breaking Away: Three New Testament Pictures of Christianity's Separation from the Jewish Communities," in *"To See Ourselves as Others See Us": Christians, Jews, "Others" in Late Antiquity,* ed. Jacob Neusner, Ernest S. Frerichs, and Caroline McCracken-Flesher, Studies in the Humanities 9 (Chico, CA: Scholars Press, 1985), 95; John Ashton, *Understanding the Fourth Gospel,* 2nd ed. (Oxford: Clarendon, 2007); Ashton, *The Gospel of John and Christian Origins* (Minneapolis: Fortress Press, 2014); Trozzo, *Exploring Johannine Ethics.*

55. Eisen, "Metalepsis in the Gospel of John"; Trozzo, "Elevated Christology."

56. Myers, *Characterizing Jesus,* 66–67. See Eisen, "Metalepsis in the Gospel of John," 331–33. See also Alicia D. Myers, "'In the Father's Bosom': Breastfeeding and Identity Formation in John's Gospel," *CBQ* 76 (2014): 481–97, which further considers the ancient Mediterranean milieu of the breastfeeding imagery and its role in forming the identity of the Johannine community.

8:26–28; 12:47–50). In the narrative, Jesus extends these credentials to his followers, saying that those who have come to him have learned from the Father (6:45) and will continue to learn from the Spirit in Jesus's absence (14:25–26; 16:13–15). Through this discourse (again part of an extended first-person address, which would have been performed directly to the audience), the Fourth Gospel assures its audience, who had lost their own community leader, of sustained connection to Jesus and to the authority of his Father.[57]

Third, the narrative extends the topic of *noble deeds*. While the Fourth Gospel focuses on the "fine actions" of Jesus, it also predicts that his followers will perform even greater deeds than he performed (14:12). Only once does the Fourth Gospel speak directly in terms of imitating a specific action. After Jesus washes his disciples' feet, he says, "You also ought to wash one another's feet. . . . You also should do as I have done to you" (13:14–15). However, the symbolic act does more than set an example of a particular act of service.[58] This episode depicts the trajectory of Jesus's disciples being brought into the unity that Jesus shares with the Father ("unless I wash you, you have no share with me," 13:8).[59] The act of footwashing, seen in its ancient context, symbolized not only humility but also hospitality.[60] In this way, the narrative nods to the practical result of the internal unity—that it is opened to the world at large inviting them to share in the unity.[61] Further, the sent language at the conclusion of the episode (13:16, 20) shows that the footwashing also brings the disciples into Jesus's mission. Jesus's deeds always flow out of his understanding of his mission as the "sent one" of the Father. Later in the narrative, Jesus tells his followers directly, "As the Father has sent me, so I send you" (20:21; see 17:18). In this way, Jesus's mission to the

57. Ashton, *Understanding the Fourth Gospel*, 418–53.

58. See also Bennema ("Mimesis in John 13"), who suggests that mimesis primarily involves "the creative truthful, bodily articulation of the idea and attitude that lie behind the original act" rather than exact replication. We see here how the idea behind the act of footwashing includes the theme of unity, which is meant to empower acts of service.

59. On footwashing as a welcome into God's household see Mary L. Coloe, "Welcome into the Household of God: The Footwashing in John 13," *CBQ* 66 (2004): 414. As Jesus welcomed in his followers, his followers are to welcome in others.

60. Jo-Ann A. Brant, *John*, Paideia Commentaries on the New Testament (Grand Rapids: Baker Academic, 2011), 205–6.

61. As R. Alan Culpepper and others have pointed out, the episode also directs the audience's attention forward to Jesus's death, another example of service to the point of extreme sacrifice. R. Alan Culpepper, "The Johannine *hypodeigma*: A Reading of John 13," *Semeia* 53 (1991): 133–52; Raymond E. Brown, *The Gospel according to John XIII–XXI*, Anchor Bible 29a (Garden City, NY: Doubleday, 1970), 551.

world becomes the mission of his followers.[62] Just as Jesus's deeds flowed from his connection with the one who sent him, so his followers' deeds should flow from their shared unity with God.

John defines the "work of God" as believing in Jesus whom God has sent (6:28–29).[63] We see here that the Johannine conception of ethics includes belief as an ethical action. The Prologue revealed that Jesus's work in the world was to lead the way to God, to show the world the God they had not been able to see—a mission that was only possible because of Jesus's complex and mystical unity with God (1:18).[64] Since belief is the means by which Jesus's followers are brought into unity with God, belief is the first essential ethical action.[65] Karl Weyer-Menkhoff's discussion of this dynamic is helpful: "Believing could be defined as a mode that enables humans to act in such a way that God becomes co-actor."[66] Thus the Fourth Gospel focuses not on the specific ethical actions that will result from this proper relationship, but on the *necessary first action* of believing. Only those who believe in Jesus take part in the unity with God that enables them to act in accordance with their new identity and mission.[67]

In Jesus's final prayer, the narrative again acknowledges the audience (those who "will believe") and emphasizes the unity with God brought about by belief (17:20; 20:29). The audience is challenged to believe in Jesus and, experiencing the unity brought about by belief, to join God's mission for the world. It is this unity and mission that should drive the audience members' actions in the world. The act of

---

62. Zimmermann, "Metaphoric Networks," 70–74; Kobus Kok, "As the Father Has Sent Me, I Send You: Towards a Missional-Incarnational Ethos in John 4," in *Moral Language in the New Testament: The Interrelatedness of Language and Ethics in Early Christian Writings*, ed. Ruben Zimmermann and Jan G. van der Watt, WUNT 296 (Tübingen: Mohr Siebeck, 2010), 168–93.

63. On the importance of believing in John, see Brian K. Blount, *Then the Whisper Put on Flesh: New Testament Ethics in an African American Context* (Nashville: Abingdon, 2001), 98–99.

64. Definitions of *exēgeomai* in LSJ include "to lead," "to show the way to," "to expound," "to tell at length, relate in full." Various interpretations have been suggested for the complex phrase *monogenēs theos*. However it is interpreted (even readings that take *huios*), this description emphasizes Jesus's unity with God as the reason he could be the revealer of God. See also Rudolf Bultmann, *The Gospel of John: A Commentary*, trans. G. R. Beasley-Murray, R. W. N. Hoare, and J. K. Riches (Philadelphia: Westminster, 1971), 81–83; Frederick Dale Bruner, *The Gospel of John: A Commentary* (Grand Rapids: Eerdmans, 2012), 40–41.

65. Peder Borgen, "God's Agent in the Fourth Gospel," in *The Interpretation of John*, ed. John Ashton (London: SPCK, 1986), 67–78.

66. Weyer-Menkhoff, "Response of Jesus," 164.

67. Volker Rabens, "Johannine Perspectives on Ethical Enabling in the Context of Stoic and Philonic Ethics," in van der Watt and Zimmerman, *Rethinking the Ethics of John*, 122.

believing then establishes the community's identity and verifies the community's authority (the first two encomiastic topics). The support of a new family and the confidence inspired by confirmation of their proper training will result in noble deeds (the third encomiastic topic).

Finally, the narrative extends the topic of *death*. While the Fourth Gospel vividly depicts Jesus's noble death, the suffering and death of his followers is not recounted. However, the Fourth Gospel does address this topic in reference to those who follow Jesus. Using the image of wheat, which must die in order to bear fruit, the Fourth Gospel puts the suffering of Jesus's followers in the same sphere of Jesus's "noble death"—which would benefit others and would have lasting value over and above the cost (12:24–26).[68] Jesus's death functions to open the community to include the world at large, as his earlier words remind us: "I, when I am lifted up . . . will draw all people to myself" (12:32). Through his death, Jesus reveals the extreme sacrificial service to be practiced outside of the community in order to fulfill the mission of bringing the world into unity with God.[69]

The narrative presents the expectation that Jesus's followers will also suffer, and like Jesus's death, their suffering will benefit the world: "You will weep and mourn, but the world will rejoice" (16:20). Jesus specifically links the suffering of his followers to their connection with him: "If the world hates you, be aware that it hated me before it hated you. . . . If they persecuted me, they will persecute you" (15:18–20).[70] The emphasis on Jesus's noble suffering would have been significant to the community, who felt ostracized. The Gospel narrative ascribes meaning to their suffering, showing how the persecution of Jesus brought about God's mission for the world.

---

68. Zimmermann, "Is There Ethics," 70–74. On "noble death" see Jerome H. Neyrey, *The Gospel of John in Cultural and Rhetorical Perspective* (Grand Rapids: Eerdmans, 2009), 282–312. See also Demosthenes (*Epitaph.*), Thucydides (*History* 2.42–44), Plato (*Menex.* 237, 240e–249c), the *Progymnasmata* attributed to Hermogenes (16) and Theon (*Prog.* 110), and Aristotle (*Rhet.* 1.9.16–25). Neyrey (*Gospel of John*, 295–300) also locates these themes in 1 Macc 4 and 9; 2 Macc 6–7; 4 Macc 5–11; and Josephus, *Ant.* 17.152–154.

69. For more on whether the Johannine community was an exclusive, sectarian group, see R. Alan Culpepper, "Inclusivism and Exclusivism in the Fourth Gospel," in *Word, Theology, and Community in John*, ed. John Painter, R. Alan Culpepper, and Fernando F. Segovia (St. Louis: Chalice, 2002), 85–108; Carsten Claussen, "John, Qumran, and the Question of Sectarianism," *PRSt* 37 (2010): 421–40.

70. It is likely that the prediction "they will put you out of the synagogues" (16:2) would have had significance for the situation of the early audience. See the comments on the situation of the Johannine community above.

The extension of this topic challenges the Johannine community to resist capitulating or otherwise avoiding suffering. Rather, if they endure as Jesus did, they will fulfill their role in continuing God's mission for the world. At this juncture the relationship among the encomiastic topics becomes clearer. Given such a challenge, a foundation of identity and community belonging would be essential, lest the community falter in order to regain the comfort from their previous group. Affirmation that they had the proper teaching would give the Johannine Christians confidence in their testimony. The vision of sharing with Jesus in God's mission would motivate bold and compassionate behavior even in the face of suffering.

The Fourth Gospel's use of the encomiastic topics demonstrates that those who believe in Jesus (both within the narrative and among the audience) are brought into the unity with God that formed the basis for Jesus's identity and his actions. A new family with a new credential for authoritative training, a new mission to determine deeds and pursuits, and a shared suffering for the benefit of the world—the particular Johannine use of these topics reveals a rhetorical trajectory that demonstrates unity with God through belief in Jesus as the key to the implicit ethics in the Fourth Gospel.[71]

CONCLUSION

Although Johannine ethics can be elusive, the Fourth Gospel's participation in the *bios* genre invites us to explore its implicit ethics by attending to the rhetorical exchange between the author and audience. Like the *Lives* of Plutarch, the Fourth Gospel engages its audience in ethical discourse. The rhetoric of the Johannine narrative, carried out by the incorporation of encomiastic topics, suggests an ethic based on participation in the relational unity shared between the Father and the Son, rather than imitation of specific actions or obedience to explicit commands or rules. Because belief in Jesus brings the disciples (and audience members) into God's mission for the world and empowers them to act in such a way as to fulfill that mission, the Fourth Gospel presents belief as an essential ethical action from which other proper actions will flow. Although the Fourth Gospel does not address many topics that we might expect to be treated in an ethical text, the story sets the stage for ethical deliberation and establishes the

71. Zimmermann ("Is There Ethics," 80) calls it "responsive, reactive ethics."

necessary understanding of identity so that the community can live in line with their new mission. In so doing, the Fourth Gospel offers a flexible approach to ethics for a struggling community.[72]

To articulate Johannine ethics, we must move beyond the narrative world of the Fourth Gospel to explore how the audience might have appropriated the ethical presentation within the story. The narrative shows that unity with Jesus and mutual love within the community empowers the audience to join Jesus in fulfilling God's mission for the world.[73] It is plausible, then, that the rhetorical trajectory of the Gospel would move the audience to continue believing, to embrace their identity in unity with Jesus, to act in ways that build a mutually supportive community, and finally to extend that inner-community love to the world outside in pursuit of God's mission to reconcile the world to Godself.[74] Such an approach would have been especially powerful for a group struggling to find its identity in the escalating conflict with their Jewish community. The Fourth Gospel empowers its audience by demonstrating their inclusion in the unity that Jesus shares with the Father and engages them by inviting their participation in God's mission for the world.[75]

72. For more on how ethical decision-making worked within the community, see Glen Lund ("The Joys and Dangers of Ethics in John's Gospel," in van der Watt and Zimmerman, *Rethinking the Ethics of John*, 264–89), who helpfully suggests that a number of moral imperatives in the Fourth Gospel itself, paired with corporate memory of Jesus, values from the Torah, community deliberation, and guidance from the Holy Spirit would mitigate the risks of this unconventional ethic.

73. Marianne Meye Thompson, *The Incarnate Word: Perspectives on Jesus in the Fourth Gospel* (Peabody, MA: Hendrickson, 1993), 103; Richard B. Hays, *The Moral Vision of the New Testament: A Contemporary Introduction to New Testament Ethics* (San Francisco: HarperSanFrancisco, 1996), 150–51.

74. Practically, this could mean that the community would collectively engage in discerning ethical parameters guided by this identity and mission. Paul N. Anderson, "Discernment-Oriented Leadership in the Johannine Situation," in van der Watt and Zimmerman, *Rethinking the Ethics of John*, 307.

75. See also Demetrius, *Eloc.* 222 on the rhetorical strategy of leaving things unmentioned. For more on "gap theory," see Kathy Reiko Maxwell, *Hearing between the Lines: The Audience as Fellow-Workers in Luke-Acts and Its Literary Milieu*, LNTS 425 (London: Bloomsbury T&T Clark, 2010); Michael R. Whitenton, *Hearing Kyriotic Sonship: A Cognitive and Rhetorical Approach to the Characterization of Mark's Jesus*, BIS (Leiden: Brill, 2016).

12.

Creation, Ethics, and the Gospel of John

DOROTHY A. LEE

Is it possible to discern a distinctive and plentiful store of ethics within the Gospel of John? If so, how do we recognize and articulate the contours of such a Johannine moral theology in a text that lacks the explicit ethical material we find in the other Gospels, such as Matthew's Sermon on the Mount (Matt 5:1–7:29) or Luke's Sermon on the Plain (Luke 6:17–49)? To push the question even further: Is it conceivable that such a perspective might be enlarged to include creation within the ethical bounds of the Fourth Gospel, turning its moral compass towards the nonhuman world, beyond the faith community and indeed the human realm? To answer these questions means addressing a text where both themes—that of ethics and that of creation—are often regarded as opaque.

The hermeneutical issue lying behind these questions is whether the Gospel of John can be interpreted in such a way as to raise an ethical voice in the ecological crisis of the contemporary world or whether such interpretation is anachronistic: that is, asking a question of an ancient text that it cannot fairly be expected to answer. Biblical interpretation inevitably involves the risk of reading and construing the text with unexamined assumptions about its scope and meaning. One of these assumptions is that salvation in the Fourth Gospel (and elsewhere in the New Testament) is concerned only with human beings and has little or no concern for other living creatures. Such an outlook is characteristic, in many respects, of the Western style of interpreting scripture, which is heir to an Enlightenment tradition with its individualism and concern only with human welfare.[1]

This chapter seeks to challenge both assumptions: first, the presupposition that creation is effectively invisible in the Johannine text and, second, the conviction that ethical principles are absent from within the purview of the Fourth Gospel. Beginning with the argument that the Gospel of John does indeed set forth and confirm a distinctive ethical framework within its narrative bounds, the chapter moves to contest the other presupposition that creation has negligible status in Johannine cosmology and anthropology. Disputing these two presumptions frees us to turn our attention to the theological issue of how this Gospel might reflect a broader and more inclusive outlook: an outlook that extends its ethical principles to all creation and implies a moral responsibility on the part of the community of faith for all living creatures.

ETHICS AND THE FOURTH GOSPEL

A previous generation of Johannine scholarship considered the ethics of the Fourth Gospel to be negligible, consisting of little more than the vague and generalized "love command" of the Farewell Discourse:[2] "that you love one another" (*hina agapate allēlous*, 13:34, 15:12).[3] While the Farewell Discourse also speaks of keeping the commandment or the commands (*entolē*),[4] these expressions are gen-

---

1. For a critique of this kind of approach, see Normal C. Habel, "Introducing the Earth Bible," in *Readings from the Perspective of Earth*, ed. Norman C. Habel, The Earth Bible 1 (Sheffield: Sheffield Academic, 2000), 25–37.

2. See, e.g. Wayne A. Meeks, "The Ethics of the Fourth Evangelist," in *Exploring the Gospel of John: In Honor of D. Moody Smith*, ed. R. Alan Culpepper and C. Clifton Black (Louisville: Westminster John Knox, 1996), 317–26. Ruben Zimmermann outlines scholarly dismissal of ethics in John's Gospel ("Is there Ethics in the Gospel of John? Challenging an outdated Consensus," in *Rethinking the Ethics of John: "Implicit Ethics" in the Johannine Writings*, ed. Jan G. van der Watt and Ruben Zimmermann, Kontexte und Normen neutestamentliche Ethik/Contexts and Norms of New Testament Ethics 3, WUNT 291 (Tübingen: Mohr Siebeck, 2012), 44–51.

3. English translations, unless otherwise indicated, are my own.

4. The word in singular or plural is found interchangeably at John 10:18; 12:49–50; 13:34; 14:15, 21; 15: 10, 12, 14, 17, being synonymous with the expression "keeping my word/words" (*tērein*, 8:51–52; 14:23–24; 15:20; 17:6). There are other commands in the Gospel, particularly the Farewell Discourse, but they are not usually regarded as ethical (e.g., "abide in me/my love," 15:4, 9; "believe," 14:11; "do not let your hearts be troubled," 14:1, 27, and "be bold," 16:33; "ask and you will receive," 16:24). For a challenge to this assumption, see Chrys C. Caragounis, "'Abide in Me': The New Mode of Relationship between Jesus and His Followers as a Basis for Christian Ethics (John 15)," in van der Watt and Zimmermann, *Rethinking the Ethics of John*, 250–63.

erally regarded as interchangeable, especially given the absence of any other specific, ethical commands. They are read simply as a reiteration of the solitary love command.[5] The conclusion is that John's Gospel is simply uninterested in ethics, beyond the one, somewhat nebulous instruction, which gives no specific guidance and no actual precepts for moral living.[6]

This antiethical reading of John's Gospel tends to go alongside the conviction that the Johannine community is sectarian in character, isolated from the Roman-Hellenistic culture of its environment, from the Judaism in which it was once embedded, and from the rest of the Christian community from which it lives in isolation.[7] Even if not actually sectarian, the Johannine community is viewed as narrow and elitist. One recent study of social identity in the Fourth Gospel, for example, argues that the evangelist encourages the community to erect dualistic barriers against the outside world in order to cement its own, unique and exclusive social identity—even against those groups that have some sympathy and affinity with its own worldview.[8] In either case, in this interpretation the command to love is directed solely at the community of faith behind the Fourth Gospel and is not explicitly enjoined as a responsibility to those beyond it. The Johannine community (in the wider sense that includes the Johannine Epistles) is seen as either sectarian or at least narrow and exclusivist. In this view, there is no overt injunction to, and no expectation of, extramural love.[9]

There are compelling arguments, however, that advocate a very different view: that ethics do play a significant role in Johannine theology beyond the generalities of the love command. These

5. On the love command and Johannine ethics, see Michael Labahn, "'It's Only Love'—Is That All? Limits and Potentials of Johannine 'Ethic'—A Critical Evaluation of Research," in van der Watt and Zimmermann, *Rethinking the Ethics of John*, 3–43.

6. For the view that John's references to the commandments go back to the Decalogue, see Jey J. Kanagaraj, "The Implied Ethics of the Fourth Gospel: A Reinterpretation of the Decalogue," *TynBul* 52 (2001): 33–60.

7. E.g., Wayne Meeks, "The Man from Heaven in Johannine Sectarianism," *JBL* 91 (1972): 44–72, and Fernando F. Segovia, "The Love and Hatred of Jesus and Johannine Sectarianism," *CBQ* 43 (1981): 258–72.

8. See, e.g., Raimo Hakola, *Reconsidering Johannine Christianity: A Social Identity Approach* (London: Routledge, 2015).

9. The perspective of the Johannine Epistles seems to reinforce this interpretation of the Fourth Gospel. The ethical injunctions, particularly in 1 John, focus on the community's love of its own (the brothers and sisters within its own ranks), while apparently eschewing the opponents who have abandoned the community. In this view, Johannine believers appear to have no moral responsibility toward the opponents or anyone else outside the community.

arguments challenge previous assumptions that the Gospel is only marginally interested in ethics or is veering toward a theological but essentially amoral view of the world. The argument for the presence of Johannine ethics is grounded in a number of features of the Fourth Gospel. In the first place, the positive presentation of Moses and the law is itself an indication that ethics is not bypassed or dismissed in the symbolic universe of John's Gospel.[10] Both Moses and the law are pictured as standing on Jesus's side and acting as his symbolic proto-types: indeed, the Johannine Jesus claims that Moses "wrote of me" (5:46). Thus, for example, in defending his Sabbath work against the authorities who accuse him of moral turpitude, Jesus defends him-self not only theologically, in terms of his unique relationship to the Father, but also morally in terms of the law: because his healing is fundamentally life-giving, directed toward the glorification of God and not his own self-aggrandizement (5:39–47). This moral quality of self-giving love, as opposed to the self-promotion and hypocrisy of the authorities, as John portrays them, is confirmed in the Taberna-cles Discourse, where Jesus sees his Sabbath ministry as itself fulfilling the Mosaic law (7:19–24).[11] Law and grace in the Johannine equation stand together, in other words, the one pointing symbolically to the other (1:16).[12] Jesus does not break the moral law in his ministry but, on the contrary, fulfills it in self-giving, other-centered love. What Jesus represents in this Gospel is thus both the acknowledgment and the fulfillment of Moses and what he represents. In its symbolic func-tions, the law is not set aside in the theology of the Fourth Gospel but rather fulfilled and given its authentic place within John's ethical framework.[13]

Johannine ethics, moreover, can be observed and extrapolated from

10. Note that scholarly opinion is divided on the place of the law in John: whether the evan-gelist sees the law as possessing a continuing function or whether Jesus replaces the law entirely. For a review of this material, see William R. G. Loader, *Jesus' Attitude towards the Law: A Study of the Gospels*, WUNT 97 (Tübingen: Mohr Siebeck, 1997), 433–47.

11. Dorothy A. Lee, *Flesh and Glory: Symbol, Gender, and Theology in the Gospel of John* (New York: Crossroad, 2002), 116–18. Severino Pancaro sees the law as having "prepared the way for a correct understanding of the significance of Jesus' Sabbath work" (*The Law in the Fourth Gospel: The Torah and the Gospel, Moses and Jesus, Judaism and Christianity according to John*, NovTSup 42 [Leiden: Brill, 1975], 508).

12. See Ruth B. Edwards, "Χάριν ἀντὶ χάριτος (John 1.16): Grace and the Law in the Johan-nine Prologue," *JSNT* 32 (1988): 3–15.

13. See Dorothy A. Lee, "The Significance of Moses in the Gospel of John," *ABR* 63 (2015): 52–66. Against this view of the ongoing relevance of the law, see William R. G. Loader, "The Law and Ethics in John's Gospel," in van der Watt and Zimmermann, *Rethinking the Ethics of John*, 143–58.

the narrative itself. Jan G. van der Watt demonstrates that, while there may be only a single command in the Fourth Gospel, much may be derived about John's ethics and value system from the narrative of the Gospel: that is, from the behavior of the actors in the drama and Jesus's response to them.[14] Ruben Zimmermann likewise argues that, while there is "a lack of concrete ethical advice in John," at a deeper level there is an "implicit ethics" in John's Gospel.[15] Jesus's own words and actions are obvious examples of ethical being and ethical behavior in self-donating, sacrificial love, which, as the foot-washing demonstrates, consists in Jesus loving "his own," even "to the end" (*tous idious . . . eis telos*, 13:1). The same implied ethics can be found in Jesus's courageous confrontation with the forces of evil, in his patient dialogue with those who misunderstand, in his life-giving ministry of "signs" and works, in his climactic death on the cross, and in his resurrection appearances, which draw the disbelieving and doubting disciples to Easter faith.

Other characters also act as exemplary types of ethical behavior. John the Baptist's readiness to "decrease that he [Jesus] might increase" is an early example (3:30), followed also by the Samaritan woman whose testimony recedes before her fellow villagers' encounter with Jesus (4:42). Similarly, Mary of Bethany's costly and faithful anointing of Jesus's feet is another example of generosity and selflessness (12:1–8). Other ethical models include the disciples' commission for mission as the effecting of reconciliation (20:23) and Simon Peter's restoration to grace after his fainthearted denial of Jesus (18:15–18, 25–27; 21:15–19). The "signs" of the Gospel (*sēmeia*) likewise display an ethic of love, care, and liberation directed toward those in need.[16]

There are negative examples of ethical behavior as well. These are closely tied to the theme of judgment, intrinsic to the role of Jesus as light of the world, illuminating goodness and critically exposing evil. The imagery of walking in the light or walking in darkness expresses the moral sense of a life choice that can be rightly or wrongly made (12:35–36). Judas's betrayal of Jesus is perhaps the

---

14. Jan G. van der Watt, "Ethics and Ethos in the Gospel according to John," *ZNW* 97 (2006): 150–66. See also Ruben Zimmermann, "Is There Ethics in the Gospel of John?," in van der Watt and Zimmermann, *Rethinking the Ethics of* John, 44–80.

15. Zimmermann, "Is There Ethics," 79 (74–79).

16. Christos Karakolis, "*Sēmeia* Conveying Ethics in the Gospel of John," in van der Watt and Zimmermann, *Rethinking the Ethics of John*, 192–212.

most glaring example, a betrayal reiterated throughout the Gospel and interpreted as the result of simple greed and love of money (see 1 Tim 6:10).[17] Its poignancy is emphasized in Judas's venture into the darkness even after receiving the intimate offering of love in the foot-washing as well as the gift of the morsel, the piece of bread dipped in sauce (*to psōmion*, 13:1–30).[18] Despite treading the path of light and goodness in companionship with Jesus and his disciples, Judas chooses the dark night of moral bankruptcy for the sake of money (13:30). Paralleling Judas is Caiaphas's brutal political pragmatism, which leads him to justify judicial murder on the grounds of pro-tecting his people, a classic example of the ends justifying the means (11:49–53).[19] Last of all within the Gospel narrative is the figure of Pilate, the Roman governor, and arguably his cynical indifference to truth and justice (19:16), despite his role to protect them. His moral indifference leads him to ignore his sense of Jesus's innocence and instead use the opportunity to jibe arrogantly at the religious authori-ties, pushing them to extremes, in preference to doing what he knows is morally just and right.[20]

In these and other instances, both positive and negative, John's Gospel displays a distinctive narrative ethics. Through the characters and their actions, the evangelist commends as life-affirming values of humility, costly self-giving, forgiveness and restoration, recon-ciliation, commitment to justice and truth, and the selfless use of power, while exposing as life-denying and destructive the oppression of the vulnerable, political expediency, and treachery. As the Johan-nine Jesus declares at the end of the first narrative in which Nicode-mus appears, the coming of the Light discloses both good and evil in its role of judgment, making visible the truth of the moral heart for good or evil, for life or death (3:19–21).

17. Cornelis Bennema, "Judas (the Betrayer): The Black Sheep of the Family," in *Character Studies in the Fourth Gospel: Narrative Approaches to Seventy Figures in John*, ed. Steven A. Hunt, D. François Tolmie, and R. Zimmermann, WUNT 314 (Tübingen: Mohr Siebeck, 2013), 360–72.

18. Francis J. Moloney, *The Gospel of John*, SP4 (Collegeville, MN: Liturgical Press, 1998), 383–85.

19. Helen K. Bond, *Caiaphas: Friend of Rome and Judge of Jesus?* (Louisville: Westminster John Knox, 2004), 129–40.

20. For this reading of Pilate's character, see David Rensberger, *Overcoming the World: Politics and Community in the Gospel of John* (London: SPCK, 1988), 87–106, and Warren Carter, *John and Empire: Initial Explorations* (New York: T&T Clark, 2008), 289–314.

CREATION AND THE FOURTH GOSPEL

But how far do these examples of Johannine ethics extend, and can they be enlarged to include a moral responsibility for creation on the part of Jesus's disciples? The presence of creation allusions in the Fourth Gospel has long been conceded,[21] but their significance has tended to be ignored or downplayed, largely because of an outlook that assumes the dominance of human well-being and destiny to the exclusion of other living beings. Those studies that have taken a more inclusive perspective on the Fourth Gospel have demonstrated how the evangelist's theological understanding of salvation is grounded in a theology of creation.[22] Indeed, creation is arguably the theological backdrop for all the events of the Johannine narrative: the incarnation, the life and ministry of Jesus, his death and resurrection, and the consequential birth of the community of faith. Creation can be shown to undergird John's understanding of theology, Christology, eschatology, and the life of the church.

This profound connection with creation, as the theological underpinning of the Johannine narrative, is explicit from the beginning of the Gospel. The first section of the Prologue (1:1–5) consists in large part of an interweaving of the first creation account (Gen 1:1–2:3) with John's understanding of salvation.[23] This intertextuality is apparent in the opening words of the Prologue: the phrase "in the beginning" replays the opening words of Genesis in the Greek Old Testament and its initial recounting of creation (*en archē*, Gen 1:1 LXX). The introduction of the Word (*ho logos*) parallels the repetition of "and God said," around which the whole panoply of creation turns (*kai eipen ho theos*, Gen 1:3).[24] The first mention of life, as created by the *logos*, manifests itself in the emergence of light from primordial darkness, light being the first created element on day one of

21. See, e.g., Edwyn C. Hoskyns and Francis Noel Davey, *The Fourth Gospel* (London: Faber and Faber, 1947), 136–54, and Thomas Barrosse, "The Seven Days of the New Creation in St. John's Gospel," *CBQ* 21 (1959): 507–16.

22. For a summary of scholarship on creation in John, see Carlos Raul Sosa Siliezar, *Creation Imagery in the Gospel of John*, LNTS 546 (London: Bloomsbury T&T Clark, 2015), 1–22. Siliezar takes a qualified view of creation imagery in John, seeing its presence aimed solely at bolstering Johannine Christology. For a less qualified view see, in particular, Mary L. Coloe, "Theological Reflections on Creation in the Gospel of John," *Pacifica* 24 (2011): 1–12.

23. Mary L Coloe, "The Structure of the Johannine Prologue and Genesis 1," *ABR* 45 (1977): 40–55.

24. The words are repeated at Gen 1:6, 9, 11, 14, 20, 24, 26, and 29. God's voice also speaks throughout the creation account in naming (Gen 1:5, 8, 10) and blessing (Gen 1:22, 28; 2:3).

creation (Gen 1:3). God's word is enough to bring to birth the vast-ness of the universe and seven times to declare it "good" (*kalon*, Gen 1:4, 10, 12, 18, 21, 25, 31); just as God's *logos*, now in the form of God's self-communication in Jesus Christ, is sufficient to transfigure the same universe. It is the one God, and the one creative, self-donat-ing God, who lies behind both.[25] The Prologue demonstrates that the story about to be narrated is the sequel in the story of God's rela-tionship to the world: created, sustained and re-created by the one gracious, speaking Word.[26] This means that Johannine Christology, strictly speaking, is not the second phase in God's work—the inter-vention for an alienated creation—but rather is present from the start. The one who redeems the world is also the source of its creation (1:3).

The same point is apparent in later stories in the Fourth Gospel that have connections to the second creation account (Genesis 2–3).[27] In the narrative of the man born blind, for example, the miracle Jesus performs is not strictly the restoration of the man's sight, since he is born blind, but rather the creation of his sight (9:1–41). The use of the mud paste that Jesus spreads on the man's unseeing eyes is linked to the dust of the earth out of which Adam is created (9:6; Gen 2:7a) (Irenaeus, *Against Heresies* 5.15.2).[28] Similarly, on Easter Day, the risen Christ's appearance to the disciples in their fear and unbelief (20:19–23) empowers and revitalizes them with the gift of the Holy Spirit that he breathes upon them (*enephysēsen . . . pneuma hagion*, 20:22). Here again, in the similarities of wording, the creation of Adam is echoed, into whose face God "breathed the breath of life," thus making him a "living being" (*enephysēsen . . . pnoēn zōēs . . . phy-chēn zōsan*, Gen 2:7b).[29] And just as Adam is given a commission to till

---

25. A similar notion is present in the prologue to the Epistle to the Hebrews, where the one speaking God addresses the world, first and partially through Moses and the prophets, and then definitively through the Son (Heb 1:1–4).

26. On John's spirituality of Word and words, see Dorothy A. Lee, *Hallowed in Truth and Love: Spirituality in the Johannine Literature* (Eugene, OR: Wipf and Stock, 2010), 31–60.

27. Augustine discerns a close link with creation in several narratives of the Fourth Gospel (*Tractates on the Gospel of John* 8.2.1 [*NPNF1* 7:57, http://www.ccel.org/ccel/schaff/npnf107.iii.ix.html]). The God who changes water into wine is the same God who causes the rain to fall on the grapes to make wine; the same God who causes Lazarus to emerge from the tomb also causes infants to be born from the darkness of the womb each day.

28. Joel C. Elowsky, ed., *John 1–10*, ACCS, NT 4a (Downers Grove, IL: InterVarsity Press, 2006), 324.

29. Cyril of Alexandria, *Commentary on John*, trans. David R. Maxwell, ACT (Downers Grove, IL: IVP Academic), 1:369.

the earth (Gen 2:15), so the disciples are immediately commissioned to bring reconciliation and forgiveness (20:23).

A similar view arises from John's complex use of the notion of the word *sarx* (flesh) throughout the Gospel,[30] a complexity that is set out clearly in the Prologue of the Gospel. The first instance of "flesh" in the Prologue is a neutral one, set in the context of the tragic lack of recognition and rejection of the light (1:10–11). Flesh is created by God, as the opening verses make plain (*panta di' autou egeneto*, "all things were made through him," 1:3), yet it does not of itself possess the "authority" (*exousia*, 1:12) to effect new birth. For all its goodness, it cannot cross the abyss between God and creation (see 1:5) but proves weak and ineffective. Here John assumes—though does not attempt to explain—a rift in the order of creation, a tear in the fabric of the world that has had disastrous consequences, alienating human beings from their Creator and their created identity as children of God, made in the divine image (Gen 1:26–27).[31] Only God can enable human beings to recover their lost identity; only God can restore the image and bring about new birth (1:13; 3:3–8).

Yet the way in which that restoration occurs is precisely, and paradoxically, through the same medium, through flesh. The second instance of *sarx* in the Prologue is entirely positive and constructive. John sees the flesh of the Word as providing that reconciling bridge between God and matter, between the heavenly realm and the fallen world: "the Word became flesh and pitched his tent among us" (*ho logos sarx egeneto kai eskēnōsen en hēmin*, 1:14a). Flesh here signifies the full materiality of the divine Word, a materiality that is both embodied and spirited.[32] In this complex picture, John's point is that, while flesh of itself cannot re-create the lost image, the flesh of the Son can achieve exactly that since, in becoming flesh, the Word "became himself what was his own image" (Irenaeus, *Proof of the Apostolic Preaching* 22.61).[33] As Athanasius expresses it, human beings, already made in the image of the Word, can be restored only by the one

30. On the symbolic role of "flesh" throughout the Johannine narrative, see especially Lee, *Flesh and Glory*, 29–64.

31. Dorothy A. Lee, "Imagery," in *How John Works: Storytelling in the Fourth Gospel*, ed. Douglas Estes and Ruth Sheridan, RBS 86 (Atlanta: SBL Press, 2016), 154.

32. For Tertullian, the paradox in the Prologue is that the Word is "born yet not born, carnal yet spiritual, weak yet strong, dying yet living" (*Treatise on the Incarnation*, ed. Ernest Evans [London: SPCK, 1956], 5.38–40).

33. Irenaeus, *Proof of the Apostolic Preaching*, trans. Joseph P. Smith (Westminster, MD: Newman Press, 1952).

who is the image of the Father: "Therefore the Word of God came through himself, in order that, being the Image of the Father, he might re-create humanity according to the image" (Athanasius, *On the Incarnation* 13.7).[34] In both uses of *sarx* therefore, John in the Prologue is speaking of created reality. The term itself establishes the dynamic connection between creation and redemption.[35]

The same vital yet subtle distinction between "flesh" in one sense and "flesh" in another is also apparent in the long dialogue that follows the feeding narrative. John presents Jesus in this narrative as the "bread of life" (*ho artos tēs zōēs*, 6:35, 48, 51), the host at the table and the food itself, the giver and the gift. It is inevitable that, with this imagery and in the context of the feeding of the five thousand, Jesus begins to speak more explicitly of eating and drinking—and of how sacramental participation gives life to the community of faith that abides in him (6:51–58).[36] Here, in this immediate context, the flesh of the Son of Man is the source of the community's nurture and nourishment, and it is set out uncompromisingly as the necessary precondition for eternal life: "unless you eat the flesh . . . you have no life within yourselves" (*ean mē phagēte tēn sarka . . . ouk echete zōēn en heautois*, 6:53). In the following scene, faced with the crowds' increasing hostility, Jesus speaks of the flesh as being "of no avail" compared with the Spirit who is the source of life (*ouk ōphelei ouden*, 6:63). Once again flesh is distinguished from flesh: creation can do nothing to create life in the face of death, but is powerless and immobilized, since only the Spirit is the source of life. Yet the incarnate flesh of the Son can and does effect that transformation and new life, flesh speaking to flesh particularly through the medium of the senses.[37] God's means of salvation is not by means of a disembodied Spirit but rather through the Spirit operative in the incarnation: in this narrative, through the flesh and blood of the Johannine Jesus.[38]

---

34. Athanasius, *On the Incarnation*, ed. F. L. Cross (London: SPCK, 1957).

35. For this theme, see Lee, *Flesh and Glory*, 29–64.

36. Further on the narrative of John 6, see Dorothy A. Lee, *The Symbolic Narratives of the Fourth Gospel: The Interplay of Form and Meaning*, JSNTSup 95 (Sheffield: Sheffield Academic, 1994), 126–60.

37. Dorothy A. Lee, "The Gospel of John and the Five Senses," *JBL* 129 (2010): 115–27.

38. Ephrem the Syrian (*Commentary on Tatian's Diatessaron* 1.1): "the Word came and clothed itself with flesh, so that what cannot be grasped [divinity] might be grasped through that which can be grasped [flesh]," in Elowsky, *John 1–10*, 42.

THE LOVE COMMAND AND
THE BELIEVING COMMUNITY

Here we reach my central question: Does the inherent Johannine link between creation and salvation imply an ethical responsibility on the part of disciples for the care and protection of the earth? To this the Johannine "answer" is ambiguous. On the one hand, and at face value, the answer is apparently no. John's Gospel occupies a very different context from our own; it does not share the contemporary moral predicament over the abuse of the earth and the depletion of its resources. There is nothing explicit in Johannine ethics, whether prescriptive or narrative, that advocates an ethical responsibility by believers for the guardianship of the earth. Yet there is more to be said than a simple negative, and it concerns precisely the extent of the Johannine moral universe.

As we have seen, the love command at the Last Supper is aimed at disciples and their love for, and service to, one another. It does not address directly the unbelieving world beyond the confines of the community of believers. Not only is this true of the love command, but it is also the case with the related language of belonging that like-wise restricts itself to the faith community. This sense of belonging derives from Jesus himself, just as does the love command: "they are not of [do not belong to] the world, just as I myself am not of the world" (*ek tou kosmou ouk eisin kathōs egō ouk eimi ek tou kosmou*, 17:16). Given this constricted perspective, how is it possible to extend the command to love and its concomitant sense of belonging even further afield to respond to ethical ecological concerns that are, in the narrowest sense, anachronistic? If we were to discern an implicit creation ethics in the Fourth Gospel, in other words, we would need to deal first and foremost with the seemingly exclusive nature of the love command and the accompanying sense of exclusive belonging it implies.

There is no question that Jesus advocates love of believers for one another, nor that he is himself the exemplar of such love (13:15). More than exemplary, this love is transformative because it is the love shared between Father and Son, the love into which believers are born, thereby recovering their true identity as children of God. It is not primarily their own love that believers are to manifest to one another—in acts of sacrificial service such as footwashing—but rather the originating divine love into which they have been drawn through their identification with the Son and through the work of the Paraclete-Spirit. John's ethical focus concerns fundamentally the transformation of the community.[39]

In each case, however, that internal circle of love within the believing community is not an end in itself. On the contrary, love is directed precisely at the unbelieving world. This end goal is captured in the emphatic sense of the phrase "in this" in the initial giving of the love command (*en toutō*, 13:35). The purpose of the love which is to flow among believers is to be a missional sign so that all people may "know" (*gnōsontai*). In John's Gospel, while the idea of knowing can have a more literal sense of fact recognition (e.g., 2:9), its meaning is often associated with a deeper sense of perceptive awareness that, on the part of human beings, is tantamount to faith.[40] This is the sense that the verb *ginōskō* ('I know') has at the beginning of the Farewell Discourse. The purpose of the believing community's love is to act as an irresistible sign that will engage outsiders who are entranced by the manifestation of divine love in the life and love of the believing community. This statement parallels the display of love and glory on the cross, which has a similar goal to "draw all to myself" (12:32).

The same can be said of the language of belonging, nowhere more clearly displayed than in Jesus's prayer at the end of the Last Supper (17:6–26). The Johannine Jesus speaks in characteristic imagery of the oneness and communion which are to flow among believers through the vital connection they enjoy with God. The goal of this communion is its perfection, yet that perfection has itself a further goal, beyond the totality of love within the community: "so that the world may know that you sent me" (*hina ginōskē ho kosmos hoti su me apesteilas*, 17:23). This theme of belonging as itself a sign becomes the basis of the community's mission; because they belong, and because they love, they engage in the mission of God to share that divine love and belonging. Here they act in companionship with the Good Shepherd, who has "other sheep not of this fold" to be gathered

39. Johannes Nissen, "Community and Ethics in the Gospel of John," in *New Readings in John: Literary and Theological Perspectives*, ed. Johannes Nissen and Sigfred Pedersen, JSNTSup 182 (Sheffield: Sheffield Academic, 1999), 199–200.

40. See, e.g., 3:11; 4:10, 42; 6:69; 8:32; 9:25; 10:4, 38; 13:17; 14:7, 20; 15:15; 16:30; 17:3; 19:35; 21:12. The two Greek verbs, *ginōskō* and *oida*, are used synonymously in John's Gospel; see, for example, the footwashing: *ho egō poiō su ouk oidas arti, gnōsē de meta tauta* (what I do you do not *know* at present, but you will *know* after these things," John 13:7).

in (10:16).[41] The Johannine love ethic, therefore, has a further goal beyond the communion of believers. The Gospel makes clear that the Johannine community is not an end in itself but is to direct itself at mission in the unbelieving world, which God desires not to condemn but to save (3:16–17; 12:47).[42]

One complexity in this discussion is John's ambiguous use of the term "world" (*kosmos*), which is not dissimilar to his use of the contentious term "the Jews" (Greek: *hoi Ioudaioi*).[43] In some contexts, "world" seems to have an everyday meaning, referring to the realm of creation (e.g., 9:23), which is also the domain of God's creative and re-creative love (e.g. 9:23; 11:9; 17:24).[44] In other contexts, it seems to refer more narrowly to the realm of unbelief, of death and darkness, a meaning more usually present in the Farewell Discourse, especially as the passion draws near (e.g., 14:17; 15:18–19). This dual sense is well-captured in Jesus's request that the disciples not be transported out of the world but rather delivered "from the evil one" [or "evil"]: *ek tou ponērou* (17:5). The prayer is made in a context where "world" is sometimes used as a shortcut for the realm of evil, though even here the dominant sense is of the world as belonging to God and destined for redemption.

Something similar is happening when Jesus begins praying for his own disciples rather than the world (17:9)—the same motif seen earlier in the Farewell Discourse when Judas asks why Jesus will reveal himself not to the world but to his disciples (14:22). In both cases, we may assume that it is the unbelieving world that is the issue. But Jesus's response to Judas is, in fact, a call to *anyone* to keep his word, with the promise of the abiding love of Father and Son (14:23); there is no actual exclusion here. Jesus's prayer is more exclusively focused on his disciples, but that is precisely in order to strengthen

41. On the "other sheep," see Marianne Meye Thompson, *John: A Commentary*, NTL (Louisville: Westminster John Knox, 2015), 227.

42. Kobus Kok, "'As the Father Has Sent Me, I Send You': Towards a Missional-Incarnational Ethos in John 4," in *Moral Language in the New Testament*, ed. Ruben Zimmermann, Jan G. van der Watt, and Susanne Luther, WUNT 296 (Tübingen: Mohr Siebeck, 2010), 168–93.

43. For different perspectives on this contentious term, see, e.g., Stephen Motyer, "Bridging the Gap: How Might the Fourth Gospel Help Us Cope with the Legacy of Christianity's Exclusive Claim over against Judaism?," in *The Gospel of John and Christian Theology*, ed. Richard Bauckham and Carl Mosser (Grand Rapids: Eerdmans, 2008), 143–67; and Judith Lieu, "Anti-Judaism, the Jews, and the Worlds of the Fourth Gospel," in Bauckham and Mosser, *Gospel of John*, 168–82.

44. Francis J. Moloney, *Love in the Gospel of John: An Exegetical, Theological, and Literary Study* (Grand Rapids: Baker Academic, 2013), 207–9.

and empower them for their all-embracing mission. John's ethical world, in the end, has a far-reaching goal and is not confined to the community of believers living in a sectarian huddle. Their internal and mutual love is to be public enough to act as a magnetic sign of the divine presence (4:23). Others, outsiders, who see this love are invited to share it and to participate in the one circle of love and belonging. Indeed, this participation is the goal of mission, as it is the purpose of the Gospel: "these things are written that you might believe . . . and that by believing you may have life" (*tauta de gegraptai hina pisteu[s]ēte . . . kai hina pisteuontes zōēn echēte*, 20:30).

A JOHANNINE ETHICS OF CREATION

If the love of the believing community is neither introverted nor self-confirming but has a porous quality to it, open-hearted toward those beyond its borders, it puts us in a very different place to assess the creation implications of the Fourth Gospel. The love command, the one overtly stated ethical principle in John, is not an end in itself but looks beyond itself to the community's mission in an unbelieving, sinful, and often violent world. Moreover, if John's ethical stance is implicit rather than explicit, we can answer the question of whether the Johannine text implies a moral responsibility for creation in other ways. We need not seek for overtly avowed principles of conservation that are not explicit in the Johannine text, but can examine more closely the ambience of the text—its theological scope—in order to draw out what is theologically implicit and what trajectories can legitimately be drawn from the implications. We can also uncover the moral principles to be drawn from the Gospel text by concentrating on the kind of commended moral qualities displayed by the principal Johannine characters, especially Jesus himself. Both the implicit theology and the moral principles will be located in the theological underpinnings of the Gospel and its narrative articulation. These two points are worth delineating in more detail.

In the first place, there is an ethical responsibility that can be derived from the Gospel's theology of creation and the manner in which the material world is taken seriously. The Prologue states that "all things became through him" (*panta di' autou egeneto*, 1:3), referring to creation, and that the light came "to his own places" (*eis ta idia*, 1:11), referring now to salvation. The "flesh" that is embraced in the incarnation is the very stuff of creation, the matter made by God in the beginning through the Word. While the Nicene Creed speaks of God becoming "human" (*enanthrōpēsanta*), John's Gospel speaks of God becoming "flesh," forging a vital connection between the Word and all living creatures.

The same language is found in Jesus's prayer at the end of the Farewell Discourse. There the Johannine Jesus speaks of the divine authority, given him by the Father, over *pasēs sarkos* (all flesh, 17:2a).[45] Once again, in the wider sense, "flesh" can be seen as incorporating all living creatures formed by the divine Word, and need not be confined to human beings, although the immediate focus here is on humankind.[46] John's terminology suggests a broader sphere that encompasses the whole of creation within the orbit of the incarnation, as the Son in this prayer is once more turned "toward" the Father, echoing the opening words of the Prologue (*pros ton theon*, see 1:1).[47]

In a number of other contexts, John's Gospel uses the neuter rather than the generic masculine to refer to the scope of salvation. For example, speaking as the bread of life, Jesus says: "so that, with everything you have given me, I should not lose anything of it but will raise it up on the last day" (*hina pan ho dedōken moi mē apolesō ex autou, alla anastēsō auto [en] tē eschatē ēmera*, 6:39). It is true that the neuter can be paired with a masculine generic expression, suggesting to many readers that the neuter is simply stylistic and refers only to human beings—for example (literally), "every*thing* [*pan*] that the Father has given me will come to me, and the one coming to me I will never cast out" (6:37). But need that always be the case? If

45. Speaking of John 1:14, Rudolf Schnackenburg comments: "When it stands by itself, [*sarx*] is not just another way of saying 'man'" (*The Gospel according to Saint John* [New York: Seabury, 1980], 1:267).

46. The meaning is obscured in English translations such as the NRSV and the NIV, which opt for "human beings," as against the RSV and ESV, which translate literally "all flesh." See Rodney A. Whitacre, *John*, IVP New Testament Commentary (Leicester, UK: Inter-Varsity Press, 1999), 404, and Lee, *Flesh and Glory*, 43–45. Augustine connects John 17:2 to Col 1:16: "in him were created all things in the heavens and on earthy, things visible and invisible" *Tractates on the Gospel of John* 105.2; see also R. H. Lightfoot, who comments on this verse: "He, the Son, was given by the Father a position of authority and trust over all creation" (*St John's Gospel: A Commentary* [Oxford: Clarendon, 1957], 297).

47. On the significance of the preposition *pros*, see Ignace de la Potterie, "L'emploie de *eis* dans Saint Jean et ses incidences théologiques," *Bib* 43 (1962): 366–87, and Francis J. Moloney, "'In the Bosom of' or 'Turned towards' the Father?" *ABR* 31 (1983): 63–71; also Xavier Léon-Dufour, *Lecture de l'evangile selon Jean* (Paris: Éditions du Seuil, 1988), 1:68–72.

we take seriously John's use of "flesh," we might equally well conclude that, while human beings are chosen to become God's children (1:12–13), all creation also finds its place within the divine election.

Similarly, when Jesus realizes "the hour" (*hē hōra*) has come with the advent of the gentiles (Greeks), he speaks of his departure as his exaltation on the cross. There is a textual variant at 12:32, however, that is quite as well attested and that reads the neuter rather than the generic masculine (the difference being one letter in Greek): *panta*, "all things," as against *pantas*, "all people."[48] If this reading is authentic, the sense here is that Jesus's outstretched arms on the cross will attract, not only human beings, but also creation itself, to God. It is potentially a further indication that "all things" are incorporated into the incarnation and thus the sphere of God's re-creation.

In the second place, John's Gospel, through discourse and narrative, unfolds a number of qualities, as we have seen, that originate in the heavenly realm (*anōthen*, "from above") and become integral to the life of the community around Jesus. It is not a large step to move from the inclusion of creation in Johannine theology to reconsidering these qualities in their ethical implications. The divine intention in the incarnation arises from God's love for the world (3:16). These ethical qualities, however, include goodness, humility, self-giving love, and life-giving service, and their ultimate goal—which is both missional and ethical—is to disseminate the virtues of the divine domain in living in community a life of love, joy, peace, truth, and harmony. Although John's main concern is with the restoration of human beings to his moral universe, particularly within the emblematic community of faith, it seems a logical implication of John's worldview that creation also receives the benefit of the same ethical qualities, since it too has its source in the one divine creativity and love.

If we put together these two points—the creation backdrop to the Gospel narrative and the ethical qualities of the divine realm evidenced in Jesus's ministry—the result is to see intimations of a renewed world that includes all living things in God's narrative. These living creatures can be drawn into the realm of love, joy, and peace opened by the incarnation; perhaps for them too we are to give

---

48. Commentators prefer *pantas* here on the grounds that the former makes more sense of John's theology (Bruce M. Metzger, *A Textual Commentary on the Greek New Testament*, 2nd ed. [Stuttgart: Deustche Bibelgesellschaft, 1994], 202); that itself is a debatable point.

ourselves in humble service and costly love. If this is the case, then "all flesh" becomes a recipient in that Johannine quality of life in the here-and-now ("eternal life," *hē aiōnios zōē*), which will ultimately cheat death. Not just for human beings but for all creatures, we may suggest, there is a sense in which the Son has become incarnate, the Son has died, and the Son has overcome the powers of violence, sin, and death. Indeed, for the nonhuman world, it may mean, at least in part, that the light shines in the sinful darkness of human exploitation and greed.

I made reference at the beginning of this chapter to presuppositions we bring to the text and the unquestioned assumption that John is concerned purely and solely with human welfare. This assumption leads to certain decisions, as we have seen, around manuscript and translation that are themselves questionable. Another way of reading the Johannine text, however, arises from the conviction that human destiny is always and inextricably linked to the destiny of creation in the biblical world: neither can survive or thrive without the other. This perspective is grounded in the creation accounts of Genesis 1–3 on which, as we have seen, John's Gospel is dependent.

Eastern traditions of Christianity begin with the assumption that salvation for human beings in scripture has a direct and profound effect on creation, for which humankind is given unique, ethical responsibility.[49] Just as Paul makes the link between the ultimate fate of human beings and that of creation (Rom 8:19),[50] so John from the same perspective makes an implicit link between the two realms in his choice of the word "flesh" and the use of the neuter alongside the generic masculine throughout the Gospel. The implication of this presupposition is that human salvation extends by definition to creation and that, for human beings to experience salvation, is to find themselves in community, not only with God and with one another, but also with the whole created domain in which they belong and to which their destiny is tied: "Orthodox theology . . . recognizes the natural creation as inseparable from the identity and destiny of humanity, because every human action leaves a lasting imprint on the

49. John D. Zizioulas argues that the creation stories present an image of human beings as "priests of creation" rather than "proprietors and possessors" of it ("Proprietors or Priests of Creation," in *Toward an Ecology of Transfiguration: Orthodox Christian Perspectives on Environment, Nature, and Creation*, ed. John Chryssavgis and Bruce V. Foltz [New York: Fordham University Press, 2013], 163–71).

50. Bartholomew I of Constantinople, *Encountering the Mystery: Understanding Orthodox Christianity Today*, ed. John Chryssavgis (New York: Doubleday, 2008), 92.

body of the earth."[51] This assumption, so very different from Western anthropocentrism, reads the Gospel of John—and indeed the New Testament itself—as inclusive of creation in human transformation.

This perspective is not just a legitimate trajectory from the theology and ethics of the Fourth Gospel, but rather part of its implicit nature. From that presupposition flows the conviction that all living creatures participate, albeit indirectly, in the restoration of the divine image in human beings. For John, therefore, as we become more fully and more truly "children of God" (*tekna theou*) through the incarnation, our responsibility for the well-being of the earth and its inhabitants, like Adam and Eve in the garden, is once more restored as foundational to what it means to be human (Gen 2:15). To recover that identity restores the human primeval place in the created order, codependent on it and morally answerable for its well-being. It is no accident that the Johannine Jesus is arrested in a garden, buried in a garden tomb, and reveals himself first to Mary Magdalene in the spring garden of the resurrection (18:1; 19:41).[52] Not only human beings but also all living things, in this sense, can be said to recover their original identity and to move toward their final goal in Jesus, who is the Way, the Truth, and the Life (14:6): a destination that mirrors yet also far exceeds the original design. For this design, human beings can be seen to possess a particular, ethical responsibility toward creation that draws on the moral vision embedded in the Gospel of John.

CONCLUSION

Because the flesh of the Word displays the divine glory—to use John's language—the incarnation can be said to become the source of salvation for creation as well as for humankind. It is this sense of flesh, the divine and radiant enfleshment, rather than frail human nature, that restores the divine image in human beings and thus, by extension, in creation. In crossing the gulf between heaven and earth, "above" and "below," the enfleshment of the Johannine Jesus navigates the seas that divide creation from God, forging a vital link between the Word

---

51. Ibid., 94–95.

52. See, e.g., Mariusz Rosik, "Discovering the Secrets of God's Gardens: Resurrection as New Creation (Gen 2:4b–3:24; Jn 20:1–18)," *SBLFA* 58 (2008): 81–96, and Frédéric Manns, *L'Evangile de Jean: à la lumière du Judaïsme* (Jerusalem: Franciscan Printing Press, 1991), 407–29. Against this, see Siliezar, *Creation Imagery*, 174–90.

and all that he has made. The incarnation embraces all that is formed by the generative and regenerative Word of God. This is the basis for the believing community's ethical life and mission, which proclaim that God's re-creative energy envelopes the material world in all its variety and complexity—"all things" created at the beginning (*panta*) and "all things" enlivened by the revelation of divine love and glory at the end. In this sense, the flesh that is replete with glory disseminates the promise, not only of human restoration, but also more broadly of a creation renewed, re-created, immortal. In this hermeneutical trajectory, "love one another" can be extended beyond the bounds of the community of faith into the widest community of God's love and domain.

John's Gospel does not address directly the ecological crisis, nor is its context the same as ours today. Nonetheless, there are profound theological and ethical resources within the Fourth Gospel that can be brought to bear upon the contemporary context, providing that anthropocentric assumptions are not made that have no warrant in the biblical text. These resources do not give us a plan of action or specific suggestions on how to respond, but they do portray a theology grounded in creation and they suggest further trajectories of interpretation that can transform our thinking and actions.[53] Most importantly, they imply that the ethical perspectives within the Johannine narrative can be directed to creation as well as to the life of the community of faith.

53. For a helpful model of interpretation that includes the exegetical and the transformational, see Theodore G. Stylianopoulos, *The New Testament: An Orthodox Perspective* (Brookline, MA: Holy Cross Orthodox Press, 1997), 187–238.

13.

Virtue Ethics and the Johannine Writings

CORNELIS BENNEMA

Ethics as a branch of philosophy generally refers to "a system of moral codes" or "the systematic reflection upon morality." In this case, it would be impossible to speak of ethics in the New Testament. Johannine ethics in particular has long been a problematic area because most scholars contend that John's Gospel contains little or no ethical content, that even its most or only explicit ethic, "to love one another," raises many questions, and that it has an inward or sectarian outlook. In 2012, a landmark study, *Rethinking the Ethics of John*, countered this consensus and provided scholarship with a new impetus to explore Johannine ethics.[1] The topic of this study is virtue ethics in the Gospel of John with occasional references to the Johannine Epistles.[2] Virtue ethics, deontology, and consequentialism are major approaches in normative ethics. While virtue ethics is the oldest form, originating in ancient Greek philosophy (Plato, Aristotle), it became marginalized during the Enlightenment and was only revived in the late twentieth century. Unlike duty to rules (deontology) or the outcomes of actions (consequentialism), virtue ethics

---

1. Jan G. van der Watt and Ruben Zimmermann, eds., *Rethinking the Ethics of John: "Implicit Ethics" in the Johannine Writings*, Contexts and Norms of New Testament Ethics 3, WUNT 291 (Tübingen: Mohr Siebeck, 2012).

2. The term *John* refers to the author of the Gospel and Epistles without making any claim about his identity. In an earlier essay, I explored John's Gospel regarding the cardinal virtues of prudence, courage, justice, and temperance, which were common in Greco-Roman antiquity (Cornelis Bennema, "Virtue Ethics in the Gospel of John: The Johannine Characters as Moral Agents," in *Rediscovering John: Essays on the Fourth Gospel in Honor of Frédéric Manns*, ed. L. Daniel Chrupcała [Milan: Edizioni Terra Santa, 2013], 167–81). Here, I examine virtues that arise more explicitly from the Johannine text.

stresses moral character and the virtues (i.e., traits of moral excellence) that a person embodies as the basis for determining or evaluating ethical behavior. Virtue ethics seeks to answer questions, such as, What is the good life? and, How should I live it?

I seek to argue against the backdrop of Greco–Roman virtue ethics that for John a virtuous life of allegiance to Jesus, guided by the Spirit, leads to and expresses the ultimate moral good of participation in the divine life. Since some Johannine characters display aspects of this virtuous life, an agent-focused approach such as virtue ethics will prove useful. Without claiming that John intentionally draws on Greco–Roman virtue ethics, I use it heuristically (i.e., as an investigative aid) to explore Johannine ethics. I will first explain Greco–Roman virtue ethics and show how it is a useful framework for understanding Johannine ethics. Next, I will explore the two components of Johannine virtue ethics—virtuous behavior and virtuous thinking. After that, I will show that John models virtue ethics to his audience primarily through the personal example of Jesus but also through other characters. Finally, I will suggest that the Spirit-indwelled community of faith promotes virtue ethics for its members. Although ethics usually pertains only to human behavior, I contend that Johannine ethics should be extended to divine–human behavior because the Johannine literature (1) presents God as a moral being who operates at the human level through the incarnation and (2) uses the human category of "family" to explain the divine–human relationship (e.g., God is presented as Father, Jesus as Son, and believers as God's children and Jesus's siblings).[3]

GRECO–ROMAN VIRTUE ETHICS AS A HEURISTIC DEVICE FOR JOHANNINE ETHICS

To make a comparison between Greco–Roman virtue ethics and Johannine ethics manageable, I will focus on Aristotle's *Nicomachean Ethics*, arguably the most important virtue treatise in antiquity. In Book 1 of his *Nicomachean Ethics* (hereafter *NE*), Aristotle seeks to

---

3. I use the term *believer* to refer to people who have devoted themselves to Jesus, and synonymous terms are "disciple," "follower of Jesus," or "child of God." For this study, I suggest that we need not distinguish between the historical disciples and later believers because the observations that the original disciples made about Jesus's life and teaching will resemble those of later believers as they hear or read the Johannine writings.

define the ultimate goal in human life. His premise is that every human activity aims at some end or good, but since there are many activities it follows that there are as many ends. Nevertheless, Aristotle assumes that "the things achievable by action have some end that we wish for because of itself, and because of which we wish for the other things, and that we do not choose everything because of something else—for if we do, it will go on without limit, so that desire will prove to be empty and futile. Clearly, this end will be the good, that is to say, the best good" (NE 1094a18–22).[4] Aristotle then defines this supreme good achievable by action as *eudaimonia* (well-being, happiness, flourishing, welfare) (NE 1095a19–20). Aristotle states two criteria or features of *eudaimonia*: (1) it must be "final" or "complete," in that it must be desired for its own sake and never for the sake of something else; (2) it must be "self-sufficient," that is, it must be that which taken by itself makes life desirable and lacking in nothing (NE 1097a25–1097b22).

For Aristotle, *eudaimonia* is not a mental or emotional state but relates to humankind's function. The function of humankind is a certain kind of life, "an activity of the soul," which refers to human rational activity (NE 1098a3–4). It then follows that the function of a *good* man or woman is "an activity of the soul in accordance with virtue or excellence" (NE 1098a15–18). However, to be happy takes a lifetime; just as one swallow does not make summer, so one day or a brief period of happiness does not make a man blessed and happy (NE 1098a19–20). Aristotle thus views *eudaimonia* teleologically, that is, with the end in mind—*eudaimonia* is a verdict on a person's entire life. This could imply that no one can be truly called happy or know whether they have successfully completed their purpose in life until death. Aristotle objects to this. Since *eudaimonia* is an activity over a lifetime, people can be called happy during their life, provided that they are able to maintain *eudaimonia* until death. Although fortune has an effect, this is usually outweighed by the permanence of a person's virtuous activities (NE 1100a10–1101a21).

As a virtuous activity of the soul, *eudaimonia* is the result of virtue and some process of learning or education (NE 1099b9–20). Virtue is a moral trait, quality, or disposition that contributes toward a person's

---

4. I use the translation by Terence Irwin (*Aristotle: Nicomachean Ethics*, 2nd ed. [Indianapolis: Hackett, 1999]).

being good.[5] Besides virtuous activity, *eudaimonia* requires "external goods" such as friends, wealth, good birth, good children, and beauty (*NE* 1098b13–1099b8). Aristotle distinguishes between intellectual virtues, which involve the rational part of the soul (e.g., prudence, wisdom, comprehension), and moral virtues, which involve the nonrational part of the soul (e.g., courage, justice, generosity, temperance) (*NE* 1102a5–1103a10).[6] While the former owes both its inception and growth to teaching, the latter results from habit, so that a person's moral disposition arises out of corresponding activities (*NE* 1103a15–25). At the same time, Aristotle emphasizes that moral virtue is primarily a quality of a person rather than an act because anyone can perform a virtuous act incidentally. Acts are virtuous not simply because they have a certain quality but when the human agent knowingly does them from a fixed and permanent disposition (*NE* 1105a17–1105b12). Moral virtue is not a passion (e.g., feeling angry) or a faculty (e.g., the ability to become angry) but a disposition or state of character regarding the feelings concerned (e.g., a bad disposition toward anger if one feels it too strong or too weak). Since moral virtue involves choice, it can be defined as a disposition to choose the mean between two vices, one of excess and one of deficiency (*NE* 1105b20–1107a25). Even though the moral virtues involve the nonrational part of the soul, they nevertheless share in or collaborate with reason in that the mean of a moral virtue is determined by correct reason (*NE* 1102b14–27; 1111b5–1113b2). In fact, moral virtues and prudence require each other (*NE* 1144b2–1145a6).[7] As Alasdair MacIntyre explains, prudence is that intellectual virtue without which none of the moral virtues can be exercised, and conversely, prudence requires the presence of the moral virtues.[8] The aim of the rational part of the soul or reason, and hence of the intellectual virtues, is to attain truth (*NE* 1139b11–13).[9] With this in mind, I turn to John.

In John's Gospel, we can identify the ultimate end people should

5. Michael Pakaluk, *Aristotle's Nicomachean Ethics: An Introduction* (Cambridge: Cambridge University Press, 2005), 87.

6. Aristotle expands on the moral virtues in *NE* 2–5 and on the intellectual virtues in *NE* 6.

7. See Irwin, *Aristotle*, 192. Prudence or practical wisdom refers to the ability to judge or decide well *and* to act on it.

8. Alasdair MacIntyre, *After Virtue: A Study in Moral Theory* (London: Duckworth, 1981), 144–45.

9. See also Pakaluk, *Nicomachean Ethics*, 216–18.

pursue for its own sake and not for the sake of anything else as *zoē* (divine life). John's specific purpose for writing is that people may have *zoē* (20:31; 1 John 5:13). John indicates two kinds of life: (1) *psychē* is the transient, destructible human life that can be laid down (12:25; 13:37; 15:13); (2) *zoē* denotes the divine, everlasting life that the Father and Son share and that defines them (1:4; 5:21, 26; 6:57; 14:6). *Zoē* is John's preferred term to refer to salvation: "in him was life" (1:4), and the rest of the Gospel unpacks how Jesus makes this divine life available to people. In the Johannine scheme of things, people do not (naturally) know God—not in the sense that it saves them—and hence the ultimate good or *eudaimonia* (salvation) is to know God and partake in the divine life that the Father and Son share (17:3). "To have life" does not denote that *zoē* has become a human property but that it allows one to partake or have a share in the divine life of the Father and Son. In other words, "to have life" means to be in a life-giving relationship with God, and life is never to be had apart from this relationship. For John, then, *eudaimonia* is to be in a relationship with the Father and Son and share in their life.

Like Aristotle's concept of *eudaimonia*, John's concept of life is an activity over a lifetime (or part of it) rather than an instantaneous event. For John, it is crucial that one does not simply come to Jesus but also remains with him. As long as believers remain "in" (relationship with) Jesus (15:3), they have access to or partake in the divine life. Moreover, just as Aristotle asserted that, in addition to virtuous activity, *eudaimonia* requires "external goods" such as good birth (*NE* 1099b2–5), so for John, the quest for *eudaimonia* must start with a proper lineage—a birth into God's family through the Spirit (1:12–13; 3:5). Such birth brings people into God's family, where they participate in the divine life. This participation in the divine life then becomes a life journey. In 14:6, Jesus indicates that he is the way, the truth, and the life, so that to walk with Jesus becomes the journey of *eudaimonia*. As in Aristotle's account of *eudaimonia*, Johannine *zoē* is both the journey and the destination. *Zoē* is therefore not simply a reward at the end for virtuous living; rather, believers already "have" life as they journey with Jesus, and virtuous living affirms and demonstrates this reality. Aristotle also includes friends among the "external goods" that facilitate *eudaimonia*, and thus it comes as no surprise that Jesus presents himself as a friend to his followers (15:13–15).

If *zoē* is the highest moral good people can achieve, the means for obtaining it is "practicing" a particular Johannine virtue—*pisteuein* (to believe). For John, belief is the singular virtue essential for achieving life (20:31; 1 John 5:13). We see this confirmed in John 6:27–29. When a crowd inquires about "the works of God" following Jesus's exhortation "to work" for food that leads to life, Jesus explains that the singular "work" God requires from them is to believe in Jesus.[10] So, Jesus views belief as *the* virtuous activity that leads to life. Believing is a moral act in that it acknowledges the true identity and work of God and Jesus. Hence, to believe in Jesus is a moral act because it is the sole means by which people attain life, the highest moral good, and because it is the proper moral response that people should render to God.

For John, therefore, the ultimate moral attainment for people is to participate in the shared life of the Father and Son through the moral act of believing in the Son. However, in contrast to Aristotle, for whom a life guided by several virtues achieves *eudaimonia*, John indicates that only the virtue of belief leads to life. Nevertheless, belief itself is informed, expressed, and sustained by other Johannine virtues. In fact, belief is a *meta-virtue* that links the Johannine virtues and the supreme moral good of life. On the one hand, belief is the singular virtuous activity leading to but not of itself the ultimate end; on the other hand, belief is an ongoing activity, informed, demonstrated, and sustained by lifelong discipleship, that is, a virtuous life in allegiance to Jesus. Finally, corresponding to Aristotelian virtue ethics, Johannine virtue ethics has two components: (1) moral virtues that inform virtuous behavior; and (2) intellectual virtues that inform virtuous thinking. I will explore these in the next two sections.

VIRTUOUS BEHAVIOR

John's Gospel presents a narrative world where two mutually exclusive moral realms and rulers are pitted against each other.[11] Immoral categories such as darkness, hate, lies, sin, and murder are related

---

10. Recently, Sigurd Grindheim has argued that "the work of God" in 6:29 is a subjective genitive, referring to the work that God does, rather than an objective genitive, referring to the work that God expects from people ("The Work of God or of Human Beings: A Note on John 6:29," *JETS* 59 [2016]: 63–66). Arguably, both aspects are in view (see Andrew T. Lincoln, *The Gospel according to Saint John*, BNTC 4 [London: Continuum, 2005], 227).

11. See also János Bolyki, who uses the theory of ethical conflicts in ancient drama to argue

to the devil and his realm (including its people). Moral attributes or qualities such as life, light, love, truth, good, righteous, and holy are ascribed to God and Jesus, and those who belong to him. For John, God and Jesus are moral beings, characterized by various moral attributes and behavior. The ultimate moral attainment for people is to participate in the life of God and Jesus through the moral act of believing in Jesus. The dynamics of the relationship between believers and the Father and Son are expressed through the language of family. "Family" (John uses the terms *oikos* and *oikia*) is a major theological category in John. Just as "family" denotes the basic social unit in ancient Jewish and Greco–Roman cultures, so the "family of God" describes the basic unit of the divine society. The nucleus of the divine family comprises God the Father and Jesus the Son, and people can enter God's family through a birth of the Spirit (1:12; 3:5).[12] Within God's family, believers are expected to show virtuous behavior, shaped by the moral attributes or properties that characterize God and Jesus. In other words, virtuous behavior is behavior corresponding to the beliefs, values, and norms of God's world, or, in Aristotle's words, activity in accordance with virtue (*NE* 1098a17).

I differentiate between the intrinsic properties of God in which believers have a share, and the virtues as properties that believers can or should acquire. A stainless steel knife illustrates the difference. Stainless steel is an alloy of iron and chromium, which is an intrinsic property of the knife. Virtue relates to the object's function. The function of a good knife is to cut well, which is achieved when the knife is sharp, so sharpness is a virtue or acquired property of the knife. While the knife cannot lose its "steelness" (for its composition does not change), it can lose its sharpness; by becoming blunt it ceases to be virtuous. In contrast to Plato, Aristotle contends that virtues are not innate but must be acquired and cultivated through right habits, so virtue is an acquired property of the soul (*NE* 1098b13–20). Similarly, in God's family, Johannine believers share in certain divine properties and are expected to cultivate certain moral values, which will inform and direct their behavior.

---

that the conflict in John's Gospel is also ethical in nature and part of John's moral story ("Ethics in the Gospel of John," *Communio Viatorum* 45 [2003]: 198–208).

12. Family language also occurs in 11:52; 19:26–27; and 20:17, indicating that the cross is central or climactic to the Johannine concept of family.

DIVINE INTRINSIC PROPERTIES INFORMING
VIRTUOUS BEHAVIOR

The intrinsic attributes that characterize the Father and Son are primarily life, light, love, and truth. These divine properties are also moral properties because God extends them to people to shape their character and conduct. In other words, when people enter God's family, they partake of these divine properties, which then begin to shape their identity and behavior. I will elaborate.

Zoē is the everlasting, indestructible life that the Father and Son have in themselves and that defines them (1:4; 5:26; 11:25–26; 14:6). While people only have *psychē*, which is transient and destructible, entry into the divine family allows them to share in the divine *zoē* (e.g., 3:15–16; 4:14; 5:24). We noted earlier that divine life, as the Johannine equivalent of *eudaimonia*, is the highest moral good people can achieve. While people only have a *share* in the divine life of the Father and Son and cannot distribute it to others (the verb "to give life" is reserved for the Father, the Son, and the Spirit [5:21; 6:63]), they can become a derivative source of life for others when they testify about Jesus and thus display virtuous behavior (see 7:38b). For example, when the Samaritan woman has drunk from the life-giving water that Jesus offers her,[13] she, in turn, becomes a derivative source of life-giving water for her fellow villagers because her testimony results in their believing in Jesus and thus achieving life (4:28–30, 39). Similarly, believers are to testify about Jesus in order to evoke belief among others (15:27; 17:20). Hence, as believers partake in the life of the Father and Son, they are expected to display virtuous behavior to help others to achieve the supreme moral good.

Jesus is described as the life-giving light of the world (1:4–5, 9; 8:12; 12:46), and God is also described as light (1 John 1:5). Light is a moral quality of the Father and Son because it is associated with life and contrasted with the immoral, epistemic darkness that characterizes the world (1:4–5, 9; 8:12).[14] The divine light illuminates

---

13. This is the probable corollary of her abandoning her water jar, her suggestion that she has met the Messiah, and the Samaritans' confession (which most probably includes hers) that Jesus is the Savior of the world.

14. The darkness in 1:5 can be understood as an epistemic darkness (people do not know God) because both meanings of the verb *katalambanein*, "to overcome, overpower" and "to comprehend, understand," are probably in view here, and captured best by the English "to grasp."

people's minds to provide access to life (1:9, 12–13; 8:12; see also 1 John 2:8). Believers are called "children of light" when they accept the light (12:35–36), and their subsequent behavior should reflect the moral realm of light (3:19–21; 11:9–10; 1 John 1:7; 2:10). An example is John the Baptist. While he was not the light, he nevertheless gave light by testifying to the light in order to evoke belief among his audience (1:6–8). Jesus's description of John as a shining lamp (5:33) is in keeping with John's ability to give light and analogous to the moon's capacity to shine by reflecting the light of the sun. Likewise, enlightened believers who partake in the light can be derivative lights when they show virtuous behavior such as testifying to Jesus as the life-giving light (see 17:20).

Love is an identity marker in that it defines God (1 John 4:8, 16) and Jesus (in 17:26, God's love in the believer is equated to Jesus residing in the believer). The mutual love between the Father and Son (3:35; 5:20; 14:31) is shared with or extended to the believer (14:21, 23; 16:27). Hence, love identifies those who belong to God's family (13:34–35; 14:23; 15:12, 17; 1 John 2:9–11).[15] Love is a moral property because it compels God to act morally—the Father expresses his love for the world by giving up his Son (on the cross) (3:16; 1 John 4:8–10), and love drives the Son to give his life for the life of the world (15:13; 1 John 3:16). Similarly, the love that characterizes believers should be discernible in their behavior (13:34–35; 1 John 3:18). I will return to this discussion below because love is also a virtue to be practiced.

Truth is Johannine shorthand for the reality of God and the world above (see 1:9, 17; 3:33; 8:26, 40; 17:17). Like the other intrinsic properties, truth defines the Father (3:33; 17:3) and Son (14:6; 1 John 5:20). Jesus embodies and defines truth (1:14; 14:6) but also mediates it to people (1:17–18; 3:31–33; 8:31–32, 40, 45). Truth is the defining moral component of Jesus's teaching because it liberates a person from sin and provides moral cleansing (8:31–32; 15:3; 17:17). Those who accept the truth are then "from the truth" (18:37; 1 John 3:19),

---

15. Friendship is a related concept because the noun *philos* (friend) is a derivative of *philein* (to love). For Aristotle, friendship is an external good necessary for happiness, denoting any relationship of reciprocal affection/love between people in a community (see *NE* 8–9). John's Gospel identifies John the Baptist (3:29), Lazarus (11:11), and the disciples (15:14–15) as Jesus's friends, and Jesus's acts of friendship include providing knowledge of God and sacrificing his life for his friends (15:13–15). In 1 John, the community of believers with the Father and Son (1:3–7) is specifically one of love (4:7–21). Friendship naturally nurtures the virtues of love, loyalty, and truthfulness.

and this truth must shape the believers' virtuous behavior. Indeed, John uses various expressions to stress that truth should be demonstrable in virtuous behavior: "to do the truth" (3:21), "to worship in truth" (4:23–24), "to testify to the truth" (15:27; 19:35; 21:24), and "to be guided into the truth" (16:13). Since truth is intrinsic to the virtue of truthfulness and the goal of the intellectual virtues, I will also explain this further below. In sum, the intrinsic moral properties that characterize the Father and Son and direct their actions also govern the believer's character and conduct.

MORAL VIRTUES AS ACQUIRED PROPERTIES FOR VIRTUOUS BEHAVIOR

In addition to these moral properties, believers are expected to practice moral virtues in order to sustain and demonstrate their participation in the supreme moral good of life. Typical moral virtues for John include love, humility, loyalty, truthfulness, obedience, and courage, and these moral virtues inform and shape the believers' behavior. While John does not spell out these virtues explicitly, they can be inferred from the virtuous behavior commended in the text. The following expressions of virtuous behavior, driven by implied virtues, are exemplary rather than exhaustive.

To love one another (13:34; 15:12). This behavior not only expresses the virtue of love but can also express other virtues, depending on the concrete act. For example, the washing of one another's feet expresses both love and humility. In 1 John 3:17–18, John explains that providing tangible help to the needy expresses the virtues of love/care and truthfulness.[16]

To lay down one's life for one's friends (15:13). This is an intensification of the previous activity, to love one another. The virtues of courage, love, and loyalty lie beneath the virtuous behavior of laying down one's life for one's friends: (1) for Aristotle, courage involves doing what is right in circumstances in which death is at hand in battle and when dying would be noblest; (2) to die for one's friends is

16. See also Christopher W. Skinner, who identifies service and sacrifice as essential characteristics of love as the supreme Johannine virtue ("Virtue in the New Testament: The Legacies of John and Paul in Comparative Perspective," in *Unity and Diversity in the Gospels and Paul: Essays in Honor of Frank J. Matera*, ed. Christopher W. Skinner and Kelly R. Iverson, ECL 7 [Atlanta: SBL Press, 2012], 305–15).

the highest expression of love and loyalty. Jesus displays this virtuous behavior on the cross; Thomas hints at possessing this virtue, albeit mixed with misunderstanding (11:16); Peter claims he is capable of such virtuous behavior (13:37–38) but will only be expected to prove his claims later (21:18–19); and John reminds his audience that every believer should exhibit this virtuous behavior (1 John 3:16).

To serve one another (13:14–15). Servanthood expresses the virtue of humility, and no believer is exempt; regardless of status in society, one is to take on a slave identity and role in order to perform virtuous acts of sacrificial service to one another (13:13, 16).

To abide in Jesus, his teaching, and his love (15:4–10). This expresses the virtue of loyalty or steadfast allegiance to Jesus and his cause. The verb "to abide, remain" stresses duration in that loyalty to Jesus is expressed as virtuous behavior over a lifetime.

To testify to Jesus. To testify to Jesus in a hostile world expresses the virtues of courage (not to shrink back from testifying despite the threats and persecution from the world) and truthfulness (to depict accurately the reality of God and his world; see testifying to the truth, below). For example, the man born blind testifies to Jesus while facing persecution from his interrogators (9:24–34). The man's experience approximates what awaits believers when they are called to testify about Jesus in a hostile world (15:18–16:4a).

To keep Jesus's commandments (14:15, 21; 15:10). By keeping Jesus's commandments, believers express the virtues of love (14:15, 21) and obedience. As to what Jesus's commandments are, we can think of the imperatives to serve one another (13:15), to love one another (13:34), to abide in Jesus (15:4), and to testify (15:27). Hence, most forms of virtuous behavior express the virtue of obedience.

To bear fruit (12:24; 15:2–8, 16). Fruitfulness is a mark of virtuous behavior in that it is the outcome of the virtues of loyalty (bearing fruit occurs in relationship with Jesus; 15:4–5) and humility (bearing fruit occurs when one dies to self and displays servanthood; 12:24–26).

To act in keeping with the truth. John lists various virtuous actions: to do the truth, to worship in truth, to be guided into the truth, and especially to testify to the truth.[17] In 18:37, Jesus declares that

---

17. "To do the truth" is to act in keeping with the values and norms of God; "to worship in truth" denotes rendering to God the respect or honor that is due to him; and "to be guided into the truth" refers to obtaining further understanding of Jesus's teaching, which is saturated with

his reason for coming into the world is to testify to the truth, that is, to explain the reality of God and his world (see 1:18; 3:34). Others who testify to the truth are John the Baptist (5:33; 10:41), the Beloved Disciple (19:35; 21:24), and Jesus's followers (15:27). Testifying to the truth counts as virtuous behavior because it cultivates the virtues of (1) belief (1:7; 8:46; 10:41–42; 17:20; 20:31); (2) truthfulness (see 3:33; 10:41); and (3) courage. Regarding the latter, John the Baptist and the man born blind testify to the truth while facing pressure or persecution (1:19–28; 9:24–34), but others refrain from testimony due to fear (the blind man's parents in 9:18–23; the authorities in 12:42; Joseph of Arimathea in 19:38) or provide false testimony ("the Jews" in 8:39–47; Peter in 18:15–27).

To be sent into the world (17:18; 20:21). While believers no longer belong to the world, they are not taken out of it (17:14–15). Instead, Jesus commissions them to be his emissaries, which requires that they testify to the truth/Jesus in order to elicit belief. Hence, to go into the world is a virtuous activity because it requires obedience, courage (one should not shrink back from testifying when facing the world's hate), and truthfulness.

Virtuous behavior thus demonstrates the practice of one or more virtues. While for Aristotle, practicing the virtues over a lifetime results in *eudaimonia*, for John *zoē* is obtained only by exercising the intellectual meta-virtue of believing in Jesus, and then the practice of the moral virtues over a lifetime sustains and attests that one has life. For John, living a virtuous life does not result in *zoē* at the end of one's life; rather, a virtuous life shows that one already shares in the life of the Father and Son. The practice of the intellectual meta-virtue belief admits one into *zoē*, and the practice of the moral virtues affirms one's participation in the divine life.

VIRTUOUS THINKING

Believers or members of God's family are expected to align their thinking to their new environment, the world above, and this new thinking should inform their behavior. Virtuous thinking is reasoning in line with the beliefs, values, and norms of the world above; to think in line with the ethos of God's family. For Aristotle,

truth. In addition, the Johannine Letters exhort believers "to love in truth" (1 John 3:18; 2 John 1; 3 John 1) and "to walk in the truth" (2 John 4; 3 John 3–4).

the function or aim of the rational part of the soul or reason is to attain truth, and to do this well one needs to practice the intellectual virtues (*NE* 1139a19–1139b13). Likewise, for John, virtuous thinking refers to the practice of the intellectual virtues in order to attain truth. Truth or the divine reality is not naturally accessible to people since they are part of the realm below, which does not know God. Jesus, who has open access to the divine realm, mediates truth to people through his revelation/teaching (1:51; 3:31–35; 8:31–32, 40). Hence, Jesus's revelatory teaching forms the basis for the human practice of the intellectual virtues. Virtuous thinking thus aims at the cognitive penetration of Jesus's teaching in order to extract truth. The most prominent intellectual virtues in John that inform virtuous thinking are perception, knowledge/understanding, remembrance, and belief/faith.[18]

Perception/Insight. John's vocabulary for sensory perception, "to see" and "to hear," connotes cognitive perception of what is seen or heard in relation to Jesus's signs and teaching. For example, in 6:36, 40, to "see" Jesus (and believe in him to have life) means to perceive his significance. John 9 shows a play on the dual levels of seeing, where physical sight should lead to insight. In 5:24–25, "hearing" Jesus's words implies understanding them if it leads to life. In 8:43, Jesus laments that his opponents do not "hear," that is, understand, his words. For John, true "seeing" and "hearing" involves perceiving the significance of Jesus's works and words.

Knowledge/Understanding. This virtue, denoted by the interchangeable verbs *ginōskein* and *eidenai* (to know, understand), is rooted in the knowledge of the truth, that is, an understanding of God and Jesus in terms of their identity, relationship, and mission.[19] As we saw earlier, people naturally do not know God and are not from God (8:23, 47, 55), but they can know God through knowing/ understanding the truth as it is revealed in Jesus and his teaching (see the phrase "to know the/in truth" in 8:32; 17:8; 19:35). Such saving knowledge of the truth should then lead to belief in order to attain life.

Remembrance. Mnemonic language is prevalent in John's Gospel —"to remember, recall" in 2:17, 22; 12:16; 15:20; 16:4, 21; "to remind,

---

18. In addition, 1 John 4:1 mentions the virtue of discernment.

19. The single occurrence of *noein* (to comprehend, understand) in 12:40 is perhaps best explained by a conflation of Isa 6:10 LXX (the quoted source of 12:40) and Isa 44:18 LXX (where *noein* occurs).

call to mind" in 14:26—and an examination of these passages reveals that John's concept of memory has two aspects. First, the object of remembrance is the scripture (in relation to what it says about Jesus) or Jesus's own teaching. Second, and following from this, remembrance aims at understanding and belief.[20] Remembrance is not about traveling back in time but refers to a selective reconstruction of the past for the sake of the present. Indeed, the disciples' remembrance of Jesus's teaching, which they had not understood prior to Easter, leads to understanding belief in the post-Easter era (2:22; 12:16).

Belief/Faith. We learned that *pisteuein* is the sole means to attain life and hence a meta-virtue. Belief is an intellectual virtue because it is essentially cognitive. Sensory perception and cognitive perception lead to and inform belief. Hence, what is observed and understood about Jesus's teaching regarding the divine reality constitutes the cognitive component of believing. Thus for John, *pisteuein* is *a knowing belief.*[21] Belief, however, is more than a cognitive act or intellectual assent to propositional truth about God; it also is a volitional act that involves lifelong personal allegiance to Jesus as a disciple. One could thus say that belief is both an intellectual virtue (it has a cognitive component) and a moral virtue (it is an ongoing, volitional act expressing allegiance to Jesus and rendering the honor due to him), and it thus seems right to categorize it as a meta-virtue.[22]

Typically, characters in the Johannine narrative do not display virtuous thinking, which is unsurprising considering people are "from below" and do not have knowledge of the divine reality (see 8:23, 43–47). A few characters, however, do begin to think virtuously, although they struggle and often require Jesus's help. Initially, the Samaritan woman misunderstands the nature of the living water (4:10–15), but starts to think more virtuously when Jesus changes tactics (4:16–26). Her dawning comprehension sees her rushing back to

20. Similarly, Larry W. Hurtado notes that Johannine remembrance is more than recollection and includes "a new understanding of Jesus' pre-resurrection sayings and actions" ("Remembering and Revelation: The Historic and Glorified Jesus in the Gospel of John," in *Israel's God and Rebecca's Children: Christology and Community in Early Judaism and Christianity*, ed. David B. Capes et al. [Waco, TX: Baylor University Press, 2007], 208).

21. See Rudolf Bultmann's concept of "knowing faith" (*The Gospel of John: A Commentary*, trans. G. R. Beasley-Murray, R. W. N. Hoare, and J. K. Riches [Oxford: Blackwell, 1971], 435n4). Yet for Bultmann the cognitive content of faith was minimal—only the (ac)knowledge(ment) that God is revealed through the Son.

22. Elsewhere in this volume, Sherri Brown examines belief as an (explicit) ethical imperative. My focus on belief as virtue does not contradict this because the virtue of belief as the sole means to attain life is implicitly imperative.

the village and testifying to her people that, perhaps, she has met the Messiah—and their belief-response is overwhelming (4:28–30, 39). Hence, the woman's virtuous thinking results in virtuous behavior. In John 9, the man born blind shows a similar tendency to think virtuously about Jesus, followed by the virtuous behavior of believing and worshiping Jesus (9:38).

These examples show that virtuous thinking and virtuous behavior are closely related. Just as for Aristotle, prudence guides the moral virtues, so for John the intellectual virtues inform and direct virtuous behavior.[23] Perhaps this explains why neither John nor Jesus spells out the particulars of virtuous behavior. The directives to serve and love one another lack specifics, which must be supplied through virtuous thinking. Virtuous thinking must guide believers, for example, on how to testify to the truth in a particular context, what bearing fruit looks like, or what constitutes a loving action in a specific situation. At the same time, virtuous behavior supports virtuous thinking. Abiding in Jesus's words, for example, implies having to examine Jesus's teaching, reflect on its meaning, explore possible applications, which, in turn, stimulate and shape various intellectual virtues. The Johannine concept "to testify, do, or be guided according to the truth" connects virtuous thinking and virtuous behavior. Hence, virtuous behavior refers to the practice of moral virtues guided by reason.

JOHANNINE CHARACTERS AS
VIRTUOUS EXAMPLES

John models virtue ethics through the characters in his narrative, where various Johannine characters exemplify aspects of virtuous thinking and behavior for John's audience to emulate. I start with Jesus as the primary example for virtuous living and then look at other characters who exemplify aspects of a virtuous life.

---

23. See Stanley Hauerwas, who argues that character as the "deliberate disposition to use a certain range of reasons for our actions" forms a vital link between a person's identity (who one is) and behavior (what one does), and shapes the person's moral orientation ("Toward an Ethics of Character," TS 33 [1972]: 703, 707, 714 [quotation from 707]).

JESUS AS THE SUPREME VIRTUOUS EXAMPLE

Jesus often sets the example of virtuous behavior for his disciples. The episode that illustrates this best is the footwashing in John 13, where Jesus, after he has washed his disciples' feet, addresses them with a mimetic imperative to wash one another's feet, that is, serve one another in loving humility: "For I gave you an example, that just as I have done to you, you also should do" (13:15, my translation).[24] Besides servanthood, Jesus provides other examples of virtuous behavior for his disciples to imitate. In 13:34a, Jesus issues the well-known love command, and 13:34b expands 13:34a with a mimetic imperative: "Just as I have loved you, you also should love one another" (see also 15:12). It is significant that the love command is not given in a vacuum but is derived from a precedent. That is, the disciples' love for one another is based on their experience of Jesus's love for them. Then, in 15:10, Jesus clarifies that just as he has obeyed his Father and (hence) abides in his love, so the disciples should imitate Jesus. Likewise, the disciples' being sent into the world is patterned after Jesus's being sent into the world by the Father (17:18; 20:21). Just as Jesus testified to the truth (18:37), so believers are expected to testify to the truth (15:27; see also 5:33; 19:35). In his first letter, John even asserts that Jesus's laying down his life for his followers is an example to follow (1 John 3:16). A pattern emerges where Jesus shows an example of virtuous behavior and his disciples can then (and therefore) imitate him.

Jesus's method of teaching by example to move his disciples toward virtuous behavior did not arise in a vacuum. I suggest that Jesus learned this from his Father. The paradigm for the believer–Jesus mimesis is the Son–Father mimesis in 5:19–20, where Jesus says that he does nothing by himself but does what he sees the Father do. While 5:19–20 speaks of the Son–Father mimesis in a broad, general sense (Jesus imitates the Father in everything), other passages mention specific mimetic activities, such as giving life (5:21, 26), speaking (8:26, 28, 38; 12:49–50; 15:15), loving (15:9), honoring (17:22), and sending (20:21). Thus, Jesus sets an example of virtuous behavior for

---

24. Understanding Jesus's example in terms of loving service does, of course, not exhaust its meaning. See, for example, R. Alan Culpepper, "The Johannine *hypodeigma*: A Reading of John 13," *Semeia* 53 (1991): 133–52 (to imitate Jesus's virtuous death); Mary L. Coloe, "Welcome into the Household of God: The Foot Washing in John 13," *CBQ* 66 (2004): 400–415 (to welcome believers into God's family).

believers to follow because he himself follows the example set by the Father. Since Jesus often models the virtuous behavior that he wants his followers to emulate, John's virtue ethics includes mimetic ethics where the believers' behavior is shaped by imitating Jesus.[25]

OTHER JOHANNINE CHARACTERS AS VIRTUOUS EXAMPLES

In my 2013 essay, I examined the extent to which Peter, Nicodemus, the Samaritan woman, the man born blind, and Pilate are virtuous,[26] so here I will explore aspects of the life of the royal official and the Bethany sisters.

Royal official. In 4:46–54, the royal official shows exemplary virtuous thinking. First, he seems to know of Jesus's ability to perform miracles and so approaches Jesus to heal his son who is near death. Jesus challenges him to move beyond a belief that is merely based on miraculous signs or requires his physical presence. The official responds by "believing" what Jesus said (4:50)—probably not a belief that attains divine life but at least shows that he trusts Jesus's word. Finally, when he inquires of his slaves the precise hour of his son's recovery (4:52), his "belief" is attested and becomes knowledge, based on which he reaches an adequate belief in Jesus (4:53). His inquiry and deduction about the efficacy of Jesus's word shows he is meticulous and analytical. The official also displays virtuous behavior by implication: (1) his willingness, as a high-ranking official, to come to Jesus, an itinerant preacher, in person rather than send a slave, and submit to Jesus's authority illustrates humility; (2) the succinct phrase that his whole household followed their master in his belief-response shows he must have testified about Jesus to them—and successfully.

Martha and Mary of Bethany. Following their brother's death, the sisters have identical complaints when Jesus finally arrives (11:21, 32), but their reactions vary. At the risk of oversimplification, I suggest that Martha is primarily characterized by virtuous thinking and Mary by virtuous behavior—and Jesus criticizes neither. Underlying Martha's initial reproach in 11:21 is her belief in Jesus as a miracle worker who could have healed her brother. Jesus's assurance to her

25. See further Cornelis Bennema, *Mimesis in the Johannine Literature: A Study in Johannine Ethics*, LNTS 498 (London: Bloomsbury T&T Clark, 2017).

26. See note 2 above.

that Lazarus will rise again does not startle her, although she does not grasp the full significance of his statement—she simply states her belief in the final resurrection (11:23–24). Jesus's self-revelation that he is the resurrection and the life intends to probe whether Martha can grasp that Lazarus need not wait until the last day but can rise *now* because of Jesus's presence (11:25–26). While 11:27 does not indicate whether Martha understands this completely, her response that she believes Jesus is "the Messiah, the Son of God" echoes the intended belief-response John has in mind in 20:31.[27] While Mary starts from the same epistemic position as her sister (11:32), she is overwhelmed by grief and her thinking does not progress (11:29–33). Be that as it may, at a thanksgiving meal in honor of Jesus, Mary shows remarkable virtuous behavior (12:1–3). Her extraordinary, affectionate act of bathing Jesus's feet with expensive perfume and drying them with her hair foreshadows the kind of virtuous behavior Jesus expects from his followers as described a chapter later.[28]

EMPOWERMENT FOR VIRTUOUS LIVING

Jesus's teaching in John is enigmatic or ambiguous because it contains literary devices such as double entendre, metaphors, symbolism, and irony, which are easily misunderstood. Indeed, various people fail to understand Jesus's teaching about the divine reality and hence to attain life and exercise virtuous living. So, what or who empowers believers for virtuous living? I suggest the answer lies with the intertwined elements of community and Spirit.

COMMUNITY

When Jesus was about to depart from this world, he assured his followers of his ongoing presence with them by means of the indwelling Spirit (14:16–23). The presence of Jesus in the community

---

27. Although Martha flinches when she faces the prospect of a rotting corpse (11:39), it does not nullify her newfound faith. As in real life, people's thinking and behavior are not consistent.

28. In addition to various characters in the Johannine narrative, the author also models virtuous thinking and behavior. For example, in 1 John 3:16–18, John creates a new mimetic ethic from Jesus's saying in John 15:13, and then articulates a practical application of the love command; in 1 John 4:11, the mimetic imperative to love one another seems a conflation of John 3:16 and 13:34; in 1 John 1:2; 4:14, he claims to testify to the truth, and the writing down of his testimony aims at eliciting belief among his audience (1 John 5:13).

of faith provides believers with continued access to his example. For as believers imitate Jesus, they also mediate him. To perform an authentic act of love that imitates Jesus *mediates* the experience of Jesus and his love to the beneficiary. In addition, just as various characters in the Johannine narrative exemplify aspects of the virtuous life, so believers in real life can exemplify the virtuous life to one another. Indeed, the most notable forms of virtuous behavior are to love *one another* and to wash *one another's* feet. Similarly, the understanding of the divine reality gained from abiding in Jesus's words is to be shared among the members of the community for mutual edification. In sum, the practice of the Johannine virtues among believers strengthens the virtuous fabric of the community of faith.[29]

SPIRIT

The Spirit mediates the presence of the Father and Son to the community of believers (14:23), and enables truthful worship (4:23–24). Besides, the Spirit will take over Jesus's teaching role, providing ongoing understanding and recontextualization of Jesus's teaching to aid believers in cultivating virtuous thinking and behavior (14:16, 26; 16:13–15). Hence, in his didactic role, the Spirit shapes the controlling moral story of the believing community.[30] In 16:25a, Jesus refers to his teaching as being "veiled" but promises to speak "plainly" in the future (16:25b), referring to the time of the Spirit, who will explain everything that Jesus has said in such a way that Jesus's words become plain. In 16:26–29, the disciples get a brief glimpse of that coming reality. Thus, while Jesus presents God's life-giving revelation, he does so in a "veiled" way and the Spirit has the task of revealing its meaning and significance. John records a few instances where the disciples are able to grasp Jesus's teaching after the

29. See W. Jay Wood, who asserts that becoming morally and intellectually virtuous occurs within a community context (*Epistemology: Becoming Intellectually Virtuous* [Leicester: Apollos, 1998], 20). For the formation of Christian virtue in community, see Stanley Hauerwas, *A Community of Character: Toward a Constructive Christian Social Ethic* (Notre Dame: University of Notre Dame Press, 1981), esp. chaps. 6–7; Lisa Sowle Cahill, "Christian Character, Biblical Community, and Human Values," in *Character and Scripture: Moral Formation, Community, and Biblical Interpretation*, ed. William P. Brown (Grand Rapids: Eerdmans, 2002), 3–17.

30. See Hauerwas, who argues that what is missing in Aristotle's account of virtue ethics is "the formation of character by a narrative that provides a sufficiently truthful account of our existence" and hence "understanding the story of God as found in Israel and Jesus is the necessary basis for any moral development that is Christianly significant" (*Community*, 136).

resurrection (2:17, 22; 12:26; 16:4), and this virtuous thinking is most likely the result of the Spirit's reminiscence (14:26). Indeed, in his first letter John describes the post-Easter reality, where the frequent use of the phrase "we/you know that" suggests that the Spirit's cognitive function has effectively enabled the community's virtuous thinking (see also 1 John 2:27). The Spirit thus functions as a decoder, decrypting or unlocking Jesus's revelation, thereby enabling virtuous thinking and corresponding virtuous behavior. Jesus mentions in 15:26 that "the Spirit of truth" will testify about him—a testimony in which believers will partake (15:27). "Spirit of truth" is shorthand for the Spirit who mediates the truth that is available in Jesus (15:26; 16:13–15). As such, the Spirit prepares and empowers the believers' testimony of the divine reality by communicating to them the truth that resides in Jesus's teaching (14:26; 16:13). Thus, as a relational and cognitive agent, the Spirit informs and enables the virtuous life of the community. Since the Spirit shapes the moral character of believers in community, we could say that the Spirit is the moral force of the community of faith, shaping its moral vision and directing its actions.[31]

CONCLUSION

The starting point of Johannine virtue ethics is God. The primary moral goods that characterize the Father and Son are life, light, love, and truth. Among these, the greatest moral good is life: light leads to life because it dispels darkness from people's minds; love compels God to give up his Son on the cross and the Son to give up his life for the life of the world; and truth relates to the divine realm where life is available. Believers share in these moral goods when they enter God's family by exercising the virtue of belief. Belief in Jesus is both an intellectual and moral virtue—intellectual in that knowledge or understanding is an essential component of belief; moral in that belief involves life-long loyalty to Jesus as his disciple. In other words, the supreme moral good of life is obtained through the practice of the meta-virtue of belief.

John's virtue ethics has two components: moral virtues that direct virtuous behavior, and intellectual virtues that guide virtuous thinking. The main moral virtues are love, humility, loyalty, truthfulness,

31. See Paul's concept of the Spirit-led life producing various virtues in Gal 5:22–23a.

obedience, and courage, and these virtues are expressed through various forms of virtuous behavior. The main intellectual virtues are perception, knowledge/understanding, remembrance, and belief. The aim of the intellectual virtues is to attain truth, which is available to believers in their relationship with the Father and Son. The intellectual virtues also inform virtuous behavior. Both virtuous thinking and virtuous behavior feed into the meta-virtue of belief and guarantee the believer's access to the divine realm, where they partake in the life, light, love, and truth that the Father and Son share.

The Spirit is vital to this entire process in his role as a cognitive and relational agent. The Spirit facilitates perception and knowledge/understanding of Jesus's teaching, reminds believers of Jesus's teaching and its significance, facilitates entry into God's family, mediates the presence of the Father and Son to the believer, and informs and enables the believer's testimony. While Jesus often models the virtuous behavior he requires of his disciples (e.g., to serve, love, be sent, obey, testify), the Spirit is Jesus's executive power given to believers in order to (1) understand and carry through Jesus's educational program, and (2) imitate his personal example. So, the Spirit-indwelled community of faith promotes and cultivates virtue ethics among its members.

Johannine virtue ethics is a form of narrative ethics in community superintended by the Spirit. John's Spirit-shaped narrative of Jesus's life circulated among various churches and shaped the virtuous thinking and behavior of its members. I arrived at this understanding of John's virtue ethics by using the heuristic device of Aristotelian virtue ethics. I have shown that this Greco–Roman model of virtue ethics finds a close parallel in John's Gospel. In Aristotelian virtue ethics, a life guided by moral and intellectual virtues leads to *eudaimonia*. These aspects have direct equivalents in the Johannine writings. For John, a virtuous life of allegiance to Jesus, guided by the Spirit, leads to and guarantees ongoing participation in the divine life. While Jesus is the supreme example for modeling virtuous behavior, other characters in the Johannine narrative also display aspects of a virtuous life. Hence, an agent-focused approach such as virtue ethics seems a (perhaps the most) conducive approach to Johannine ethics.

Conclusion:
Moving the Conversation Forward—
Johannine Ethics in Prospect

CHRISTOPHER W. SKINNER AND
SHERRI BROWN

Throughout the foregoing chapters our contributors have offered detailed engagements with the three Johannine imperatives (believe, love, and follow), numerous subjects that fall under the category of "implied ethics," and a handful of topics that attempt to move other conversations forward in the area of Johannine ethics. We believe that our coverage of these topics shows that our field is currently open for ongoing dialogue about the presence, nature, and value of ethics within the Johannine literature. Against that backdrop, we want to conclude this volume by briefly enumerating several areas of potential benefit for those interested in further exploring the "moral world" of the Gospel and Epistles of John.

1. JOHANNINE ETHICS AND THE RHETORIC OF CHARACTERIZATION IN GRECO-ROMAN BIOGRAPHY

In recent years, studies of characterization in the Gospels have become increasingly abundant.[1] While this area of inquiry has been

---

1. See, e.g., Frank Dicken and Julia Snyder, *Characters and Characterization in Luke-Acts*, LNTS 548 (London: Bloomsbury T&T Clark, 2016); Christopher W. Skinner and Matthew Ryan Hauge, eds., *Character Studies and the Gospel of Mark*, LNTS 483 (London: Bloomsbury T&T Clark, 2014); Cornelis Bennema, *Encountering Jesus: Character Studies in the Gospel of*

blossoming, little has been done to connect rhetorical patterns of characterization to an understanding of ethics in the Gospels. One enduring insight of Richard Burridge's landmark publication, *What Are the Gospels?* is the awareness that the Gospels participate in the wider genre of Greco-Roman biography (*bios*), and an important function of such writings is to show the virtue and imitability of the work's protagonist.[2] While Burridge has already attempted an ethical analysis of Jesus's imitability in his book, *Imitating Jesus*, more work remains to be done in analyzing Jesus as well as other figures in the Fourth Gospel against the backdrop of the Gospel's participation in the *bios* genre and in light of ethical concerns.[3] In particular, how are we to understand the literary function of minor characters, and in what ways do such figures contribute to an understanding of the ethics implied by the text? This area of inquiry holds numerous prospects for future research.

2. JOHANNINE ETHICS AND RECEPTION HISTORY

Recent years have also seen a rise in studies devoted to the reception history of the Bible.[4] Studies in reception history are technically outside the realm of direct exegesis of biblical texts but are rather more concerned with examining ways in which biblical texts were

John, 2nd ed. (Minneapolis: Fortress Press, 2014); Bennema, *A Theory of Character in New Testament Narrative* (Minneapolis: Fortress Press, 2014); Alicia D. Myers, *Characterizing Jesus: A Rhetorical Analysis of the Fourth Gospel's Use of Scripture in its Presentation of Jesus*, LNTS 458 (London: Bloomsbury T&T Clark, 2012); Steven A. Hunt, Francois Tolmie, and Ruben Zimmerman, eds., *Character Studies in the Fourth Gospel: Narrative Approaches to Seventy Figures in John*, WUNT 314 (Tübingen: Mohr Siebeck, 2012); Christopher W. Skinner, ed., *Characters and Characterization in the Gospel of John*, LNTS 461 (London: Bloomsbury T&T Clark, 2012); Susan E. Hylen, *Imperfect Believers: Ambiguous Characters in the Gospel of John* (Louisville: Westminster John Knox, 2009).

2. Richard Burridge, *What Are the Gospels? A Comparison with Graeco-Roman Biography*, 2nd ed. (Grand Rapids: Eerdmans, 2004; 1st ed., 1992).

3. Richard Burridge, *Imitating Jesus: An Inclusive Approach to New Testament Ethics* (Grand Rapids: Eerdmans, 2007).

4. See, e.g., Emma England and William John Lyons, eds. *Reception History and Biblical Studies: Theory and Practice*, Scriptural Traces: Critical Perspectives on the Reception and Influence of the Bible 6 (London: Bloomsbury T&T Clark, 2015); William John Lyons, *Joseph of Arimathea: A Study in Reception History*, Biblical Refigurations (Oxford: Oxford University Press, 2014); Eve-Marie Becker and Anders Runesson, eds., *Mark and Matthew II: Comparative Readings, Reception History, Cultural Hermeneutics, and Theology*, WUNT 304 (Tübingen: Mohr Siebeck, 2013); Michael Lieb, Emma Mason, and Jonathan Roberts, eds., *The Oxford Handbook of the Reception History of the Bible* (Oxford: Oxford University Press, 2011).

interpreted ("received") in various locales by different interpreters throughout time. However, such an approach has the potential to yield insights into the earliest uses of and approaches to the Johannine literature. The opening chapter of this book includes a quotation that seems apropos here. In the context of a discussion of patristic writers and their preference for the Fourth Gospel in thinking about the development of moral character, Bernd Wannenwetsch writes that there are "powerful and *specifically modern biases* that trigger the suspicion that with John we cannot do the sort of ethics we think we should be doing today."[5] This raises the question: How did the earliest interpreters understand the moral world of the Johannine literature, and what, if anything, can this teach us about Johannine ethics, implied or otherwise? It is our opinion that an appeal to the reception history of the Johannine literature vis-à-vis discussions of ethics, moral formation, virtue, and related topics can prove to be a fruitful exercise in the pursuit of Johannine ethics.

3. JOHANNINE ETHICS, THE HISTORY OF THE JOHANNINE COMMUNITY, AND SOCIAL MEMORY

In an intriguing study from 2006, Tom Thatcher asked why John wrote a Gospel in the first place.[6] His answer focused on the communal memories that were passed on for decades via oral tradition until they were ultimately written down. Thatcher argued that early Christians found themselves in conflict not only over who Jesus was but also over what memories should be retained. Thatcher's insights and the assumptions that generated them have the potential to serve as a helpful launching point for future investigations of the moral world of the Johannine writings. In our examination of John's ethics, we still have a great deal to learn not only from those who have sought to advance our understanding of the oral/aural dynamics of life in the ancient Mediterranean world,[7] but also from those scholars

5. Bernd Wannenwetsch, "Political Love: Why John's Gospel Is Not as Barren for Contemporary Ethics as It Might Appear," in *"You Have the Words of Eternal Life": Transformative Readings of the Gospel of John from a Lutheran Perspective*, ed. Kenneth Mtata (Minneapolis: Lutheran University Press, 2012), 93–94 (emphasis added).

6. Tom Thatcher, *Why John Wrote a Gospel: Jesus—Memory—History* (Louisville: Westminster John Knox, 2006).

7. The foundational work in this area is Werner H. Kelber, *The Oral and the Written Gospel: The Hermeneutics of Speaking and Writing in the Synoptic Tradition, Mark, Paul, and Q* (Bloom-

who have sought to refine our understanding of social memory theory and its relevance for the study of the New Testament.[8] Little has been done in this area, and thus there are literally dozens of avenues to explore.

4. JOHANNINE ETHICS VERSUS OTHER ETHICAL SYSTEMS IN THE THOUGHT WORLD OF EARLY CHRISTIANITY

Finally, it is worth delving deeper into the thought world of early Christianity in order to explore both similar and contrasting systems of ethics. Earliest expressions of Christianity emerged in a complex and variegated world of religious, social, and political ideologies. An analysis of these competing ideological systems can help us arrive at a broader context in which to locate our understandings of Johannine ethics. In particular, comparisons with various forms of Jewish ethics, Stoic ethics,[9] and the pervasive virtue ethics[10] of the Greco-Roman world can provide fodder for fruitful discussions about the presence and value of ethics in the Johannine literature. We hope our own initial engagement with a broader understanding of ethics, the study thereof, and the moral world of the Johannine literature will serve to spur such conversations.

ington: Indiana University Press, 1997). For a recent engagement with advances in this area, see Tom Thatcher, ed., *Jesus, the Voice, and the Text: Beyond the Oral and the Written Gospel* (Waco, TX: Baylor University Press, 2008). See also, Rafael Rodriguez, *Oral Tradition and the New Testament: A Guide for the Perplexed* (London: T&T Clark, 2014). For a foray into this area in Johannine studies that has not yet breached the realm of ethics, see Anthony Le Donne and Tom Thatcher, eds., *The Fourth Gospel in First-Century Media Culture*, LNTS 426 (London: T&T Clark, 2011).

8. See Chris Keith, "Social Memory Theory and Gospels Research: The First Decade Part One," *Early Christianity* 6 (2015): 354–376; Keith, "Social Memory Theory and Gospels Research: The First Decade Part Two," *Early Christianity* 6 (2015): 517–42.

9. We are grateful to Prof. Harold Attridge for turning our attention to this concern. In a breakfast conversation at the 79th Annual Meeting of the Catholic Biblical Association at Santa Clara University in August 2016, Prof. Attridge suggested that a comparison with Stoic ethics might be one of the more fruitful avenues of research for future investigations into Johannine ethics. While this suggestion came too late in the editorial process for us to devote a chapter to its consideration, we wanted, nevertheless, to acknowledge our indebtedness to him. For his own initial study of the integration of the Johannine literature and Stoicism, see Harold W. Attridge, "An 'Emotional' Jesus and Stoic Tradition," in *Stoicism in Early Christianity*, ed. Tuomas Rasimus, Troels Engberg-Pedersen, and Ismo Dunderberg (Grand Rapids: Baker Academic, 2010), 77–92.

10. This is the approach advocated by Cornelis Bennema in chapter 13 of this book. See also, Cornelis Bennema, "Moral Transformation in the Johannine Writings," *IDS* 51 (2017): 1–7.

Bibliography

Alter, Robert. *The Art of Biblical Narrative.* New York: Basic Books, 1981.

Anderson, Hesper, and Mark Medoff. *Children of a Lesser God.* DVD. Directed by Randa Haines. Hollywood, CA: Paramount Pictures, 2000.

The Ante-Nicene Fathers. Edited by Alexander Roberts and James Donaldson. 1885–1887. 10 vols. Repr., Peabody, MA: Hendrickson, 1994.

Aristotle. *The Nicomachean Ethics*, edited by W. D. Ross and J. O. Urmson. Oxford: Oxford University Press, 1980.

Ashton, John. "The Transformation of Wisdom: A Study of the Prologue of John's Gospel." *NTS* 32 (1986): 161–86.

Ashton, John. *Understanding the Fourth Gospel.* Oxford: Clarendon, 1991.

Athanasius. *On the Incarnation.* Edited by F. L. Cross. London: SPCK, 1957.

Attridge, Harold W. "An 'Emotional' Jesus and Stoic Tradition." In *Stoicism in Early Christianity*, edited by Tuomas Rasimus, Troels Engberg-Pedersen, and Ismo Dunderberg, 77–92. Grand Rapids: Baker Academic, 2010.

Augustine. *Lectures or Tractates on the Gospel according to St John.* In *Nicene and Post-Nicene Fathers*, vol. 7, series 1. Edited by Philip Schaff. Christian Classics Ethereal Library. http://www.ccel.org/ccel/schaff/npnf107. iii.ix.html.

Berg, Shane. "Ben Sira, the Genesis Creation Accounts, and the Knowledge of God's Will." *JBL* 132 (2013): 139–57.

Barnes, Jonathan. Introduction to *The Ethics of Aristotle: The Nicomachean Ethics.* Translated by J. A. K. Thomson. London: Penguin, 1976.

Barrett, C. K. "Christocentric or Theocentric? Observations on the Theological Method of the Fourth Gospel." In *Essays on John*, 1–18. London: SPCK, 1982.

———. *The Gospel according to St. John: An Introduction with Commentary and Notes on the Greek Text.* 2nd ed. London: SPCK, 1978.

———. "The Lamb of God." *NTS* 1 (1954–1955): 210–18.

Barrosse, Thomas. "The Seven Days of the New Creation in St. John's Gospel." *CBQ* 21 (1959): 507–16.

Barth, Karl. *Erklärung des Johannes-Evangeliums (Kapitel 1–8).* Edited by Walter Fürst. Gesamtausgabe 2. Zurich: TVZ, 1976.

Bartholomew I of Constantinople. *Encountering the Mystery: Understanding Orthodox Christianity Today.* New York: Doubleday, 2008.

Bauckham, Richard. "For Whom Were the Gospels Written?" In *The Gospels for All Christians: Rethinking the Gospel Audiences*, edited by Richard Bauckham, 9–48. Grand Rapids: Eerdmans, 1998.

Becker, Eve-Marie, and Anders Runesson, eds. *Mark and Matthew.* Vol. 2, *Comparative Readings: Reception History, Cultural Hermeneutics, and Theology.* WUNT 304. Tübingen: Mohr Siebeck, 2013.

Becker, Jürgen. *Das Evangelium nach Johannes.* 2 vols. ÖTKNT 4/1–2. Gütersloh: Mohn; Würzburg: Echter, 1979–81.

Belle, Gilbert van, Michael Labahn, and P. Martiz, eds. *Repetitions and Variations in the Fourth Gospel: Styles, Text, Interpretation.* BETL 223. Leuven: Peeters, 2009.

Bennema, Cornelis. "A Theory of Character in the Fourth Gospel, with Reference to Ancient and Modern Literature." *BibInt* 17 (2009): 375–421.

———. *A Theory of Character in New Testament Narrative.* Minneapolis: Fortress Press, 2014.

———. *Encountering Jesus: Character Studies in the Gospel of John.* 2nd ed. Minneapolis: Fortress Press, 2014.

———. "Judas (the Betrayer): The Black Sheep of the Family." In *Character Studies in the Fourth Gospel: Narrative Approaches to Seventy Figures in John*, edited by Steven A. Hunt, Francois Tolmie, and Ruben Zimmermann, 360–72. WUNT 314. Tübingen: Mohr Siebeck, 2013.

———. *Mimesis in the Johannine Literature: A Study in Johannine Ethics.* LNTS 498. London: Bloomsbury T&T Clark, 2017.

———. "Mimetic Ethics in the Gospel of John." In *Metapher–Narratio–Mimesis–Doxologie: Begründungsformen frühchristlicher und antiker Ethik*, edited by Ulrich Volp, Friedrich W. Horn, and Ruben Zimmermann, 205–17. Contexts and Norms of New Testament Ethics 7, WUNT 356. Tübingen: Mohr Siebeck, 2016.

_____. "Moral Transformation in the Johannine Writings." *In die Skriflig* 51 (2017): 1–7.

_____. "The Identity and Composition of ΟΙ ΙΟΥΔΑΙΟΙ in the Gospel of John." *TynBul* 60 (2009): 239–63.

_____. "Virtue Ethics in the Gospel of John: The Johannine Characters as Moral Agents." In *Rediscovering John: Essays on the Fourth Gospel in Honour of Frédéric Manns*, edited by L. Daniel Chrupcała, 167–81. SBFA 80 Milan: Edizioni Terra Santa, 2013.

Bernier, Jonathan. *Aposynagōgos and the Historical Jesus in John: Rethinking the Historicity of the Johannine Expulsion Passages.* BibInt 122. Leiden: Brill, 2013.

Bieringer, Reimund. "Das Lamm Gottes, Das die Sünde der Welt hinwegnimmt (1,29)." In *The Death of Jesus in the Fourth Gospel*, edited by Gilbert Van Belle, 199–232. BETL 200. Leuven: Leuven University Press, 2007.

Bieringer, Reimund, Didier Pollefeyt, and Frederique Vandecasteele-Vanneuville, eds. *Anti-Judaism and the Fourth Gospel: Papers of the Leuven Colloquium 2000.* Assen: Royal Van Gorcum, 2001.

Birch, Bruce C., and Larry L. Rasmussen. *The Bible and Ethics in the Christian Life.* Minneapolis: Augsburg Publishing House, 1976.

Blomberg, Craig L. *The Historical Reliability of John's Gospel: Issues and Commentary.* Downers Grove, IL: InterVarsity Press, 2001.

Bockmuehl, Markus. *Revelation and Mystery in Ancient Judaism and Pauline Christianity.* Tübingen: J. C. B. Mohr, 1990.

Boersma, Hans. "A New Age Love Story: Worldview and Ethics in the Gospel of John." *CTJ* 38 (2003): 103–19.

Boismard, Marie-Emile. *Du Baptême à Cana (Jean 1:19–2:11).* Paris: Cerf, 1956.

Bolyki, János. "Ethics in the Gospel of John." *ActAnt* 44 (2004): 99–107.

_____. "Ethics in the Gospel of John," *CV* 45 (2003): 198–208.

Bond, Helen K. *Caiaphas: Friend of Rome and Judge of Jesus?* Louisville: Westminster John Knox, 2004.

Bonhoeffer, Dietrich. *Ethics.* Translated by Reinhard Krauss, Charles C. West, and Douglas W. Stott. Edited by Clifford J. Green. Dietrich Bonhoeffer Works 6. Minneapolis: Fortress Press, 2008.

_____. *Letters and Papers from Prison.* Edited by Eberhard Bethge. New York: Macmillan, 1972.

Booth, Wayne C. *The Rhetoric of Fiction.* 2nd ed. Chicago: University of Chicago Press, 1983.

Borgen, Peder. *The Gospel of John: More Light from Philo, Paul and Archae-ology: The Scriptures, Tradition, Exposition, Settings, Meaning.* NovTSup 154. Leiden: Brill, 2014.

Boyarin, Daniel. "The Gospel of the *Memra*: Jewish Binitarianism and the Prologue to John." *HTR* 94 (2001): 243–84.

Brant, Jo-Ann A. *John.* Paideia Commentaries on the New Testament. Grand Rapids: Baker Academic, 2011.

Brown, Raymond E. *An Introduction to the Gospel of John.* Edited by Francis J. Moloney. ABRL. New York: Doubleday, 2003.

———. *The Community of the Beloved Disciple: The Life, Loves, and Hates of an Individual Church in New Testament Times.* New York: Paulist Press, 1979.

———. *The Epistles of John.* AB 30. Garden City, NY: Doubleday, 1982.

———. *The Gospel according to John I–XII.* AB 29. Garden City, NY: Doubleday, 1966.

———. *The Gospel according to John XIII–XXI.* AB 29a. Garden City, NY: Doubleday, 1970.

Brown, Sherri. *Gift upon Gift: Covenant through Word in the Gospel of John.* Princeton Theological Monograph Series 144. Eugene, OR: Pickwick, 2010.

———. *God's Promise: Covenant in John.* Mahwah, NJ: Paulist Press, 2014.

Brown, Sherri, and Francis J. Moloney. *Interpreting the Gospel and Letters of John: An Interpretation.* Grand Rapids: Eerdmans, 2017.

Bultmann, Rudolf. "New Testament and Mythology." In *Kerygma and Myth by Rudolf Bultmann and Five Critics*, edited by Hans Werner Bartsch, 1–44. Translated by Reginald H. Fuller. New York: Harper & Row, 1961.

———. *The Gospel of John: A Commentary.* Translated by G. R. Beasley-Murray, R. W. N. Hoare, and J. K. Riches. Philadelphia: Westminster, 1971.

———. *Theology of the New Testament.* Translated by Kendrick Grobel. 2 vols. London: SCM, 1955.

Burridge, Richard. *Imitating Jesus: An Inclusive Approach to New Testament Ethics.* Grand Rapids: Eerdmans, 2007.

———. "Imitating Jesus: An Inclusive Approach to the Ethics of the Historical Jesus and John's Gospel." In *John, Jesus, and History.* Vol. 2, *Aspects of Historicity in the Fourth Gospel*, 281–90. Edited by Paul N. Anderson,

Felix Just, and Tom Thatcher. Atlanta: Society of Biblical Literature, 2009.

———. *What Are the Gospels? A Comparison with Greco-Roman Biography.* 2nd ed. Grand Rapids: Eerdmans, 2004.

Byers, Andrew J. *Ecclesiology and Theosis in the Gospel of John.* SNTSMS 167. Cambridge: Cambridge University Press, 2017.

Byrne, Brendan. *Life Abounding: A Reading of John's Gospel.* Collegeville, MN: Liturgical Press, 2014.

Cahill, Lisa Sowle, "Christian Character, Biblical Community, and Human Values." In *Character and Scripture: Moral Formation, Community, and Biblical Interpretation*, edited by William P. Brown, 3–17. Grand Rapids: Eerdmans, 2002.

Callahan, Allen Dwight. "John." In *True to Our Native Land: An African American New Testament Commentary*, edited by Brian K. Blount, 186–212. Minneapolis: Fortress Press, 2007.

Caragounis, Chrys. "'Abide in Me': The New Mode of Relationship between Jesus and His Followers as a Basis for Christian Ethics." In *Rethinking the Ethics of John: "Implicit Ethics" in the Johannine Writings*, edited by Jan G. van der Watt and Ruben Zimmermann, 250–63. Kontexte und Normen neutestamentliche Ethik/Contexts and Norms of New Testament Ethics 3. WUNT 291. Tübingen: Mohr Siebeck, 2012.

———. "Jesus, His Brothers and the Journey to the Feast (John 7:8–10)." *SEÅ* 63 (1998): 177–87.

———. "Vine, Vineyard, Israel, and Jesus." *SEÅ* 65 (2000): 201–14.

Carson, D. A. *The Gospel according to John.* Pillar New Testament Commentary. Grand Rapids: Eerdmans, 1990.

Carter, Warren. *John and Empire: Initial Explorations.* New York: T&T Clark, 2008.

———. "'The Blind, Lame, and Paralyzed' (John 5:3): John's Gospel, Disability Studies, and Postcolonial Perspectives." In *Disability Studies and Biblical Literature*, edited by Candida R. Moss and Jeremy Schipper, 129–50. New York: Palgrave Macmillan, 2011.

Cassem, N. H. "A Grammatical and Conceptual Inventory of the Use of κόσμος in the Johannine Corpus with Some Implications for a Johannine Cosmic Theology." *NTS* 19 (1972–1973): 81–91.

Cavallin, H. C. "Leben nach dem Tod im Spätjudentum und frühen Christentum." *ANRW* 1:240–345. Part 2, *Principat.* Edited by Hildegard Temporini and Wolfgang Haase. Berlin: de Gruyter, 1972.

Charlesworth, James H. "A Critical Comparison of the Dualism in 1QS 3:13–4:26 and the 'Dualism' Contained in the Gospel of John." In *John and Qumran*, edited by James H. Charlesworth, 76–106. London: Geoffrey Chapman, 1972.

———, ed. *The Old Testament Pseudepigrapha*. 2 vols. Garden City, NY: Doubleday, 1983–1985.

Clark-Soles, Jaime. *Death and Afterlife in the New Testament*. London: T&T Clark, 2006.

———. "Disability in the Johannine Literature (Gospel of John, 1–3 John, Apocalypse)." In *Disability and the Bible: A Commentary*, edited by Sarah J. Melcher, Mikeal C. Parsons, and Amos Yong. Waco, TX: Baylor University Press, forthcoming.

———. "'The Jews' in the Fourth Gospel." In *John*. Vol. 1, *Chapters 1–9*, edited by Cynthia A. Jarvis and E. Elizabeth Johnson, xi–xiv. Feasting on the Word Commentary. Louisville: Westminster John Knox, 2015.

———. *Reading John for Dear Life: A Spiritual Walk with the Fourth Gospel*. Louisville: Westminster John Knox, 2016.

Coleman, John A. "Catholic Human Rights Theory: Four Challenges to an Intellectual Tradition." *Journal of Law and Religion* 2 (1984): 343–66.

Clarkson, Mary E. "The Ethics of the Fourth Gospel." *AThR* 31 (1949): 112–15.

Cohen, Shaye J. D. *From the Maccabees to the Mishnah*. LEC 7. Louisville: Westminster John Knox, 1987.

Collins, Adela Yarbro. "The Secret Son of Man in the Parables of Enoch and the Gospel of Mark: A Response to Leslie Walck." In *Enoch and the Messiah Son of Man: Revisiting the Book of Parables*, edited by Gabriele Boccaccini, 338–42. Grand Rapids: Eerdmans, 2007.

Collins, Raymond F. *John and His Witness*. Zacchaeus Studies: New Testament. Collegeville, MN: Liturgical Press, 1991.

———. *These Things Have Been Written: Studies on the Fourth Gospel*. LThPM 2. Louvain: Peeters; Grand Rapids: Eerdmans, 1990.

———. "'You Call Me Teacher and Lord—and You Are Right. For That Is What I Am' (John 13:13)." In *Studies in the Gospel of John and Its Christology: Festschrift Gilbert Van Belle*. Edited by Joseph Verheyden, Geert van Oyen, Michael Labahn, and Reimund Bieringer. BETL 265 (Leuven: Peeters, 2014), 327–48.

Coloe, Mary L. *God Dwells with Us: Temple Symbolism in the Fourth Gospel*. Collegeville, MN: Liturgical Press, 2001.

_____. "The Structure of the Johannine Prologue and Genesis 1." *ABR* 45 (1977): 40–55.

_____. "Theological Reflections on Creation in the Gospel of John." *Pacifica* 24 (2011): 1–12.

Conway, Colleen M. "Speaking through Ambiguity: Minor Characters in the Fourth Gospel." *BibInt* 10 (2002): 324–41.

Culpepper, R. Alan. *Anatomy of the Fourth Gospel: A Study in Literary Design.* Philadelphia: Fortress Press, 1983.

_____. "The Johannine *hypodeigma*: A Reading of John 13:1–38." *Semeia* 53 (1981): 133–52.

_____. *The Johannine School.* SBLDS 26. Missoula, MT: Scholars Press, 1975.

_____. "Anti-Judaism in the Fourth Gospel as a Theological Problem for Christian Interpreters." In *Anti-Judaism and the Fourth Gospel*, edited by Reimund Bieringer, Didier Pollefeyt, and Frederique Vandecasteele-Vanneuville, 61–82. Louisville: Westminster John Knox, 2001.

_____. "Nicodemus: The Travail of New Birth." In *Character Studies in the Fourth Gospel*, Edited by Steven A. Hunt, D. Francois Tolmie, and Ruben Zimmermann, 249–59. WUNT 314. Tübingen: Mohr Siebeck, 2013.

_____. "'Children of God': Evolution, Cosmology, and Johannine Thought." In *Creation Stories in Dialogue: The Bible, Science, and Folk Traditions*, edited by R. Alan Culpepper and Jan G. van der Watt, 3–31. BibInt 139. Leiden: Brill, 2016.

_____. "The Johannine *hypodeigma*: A Reading of John 13." *Semeia* 53 (1991): 133–52.

_____. "The Pivot of John's Prologue." *NTS* 27 (1980): 1–31.

_____. "The Prologue as Theological Prolegomenon to the Gospel of John." In *The Prologue of the Gospel of John: Its Literary, Theological, and Philosophical Contexts. Papers Read at the Colloquium Ioanneum 2013*, edited by Jan G. van der Watt, R. Alan Culpepper, and Udo Schnelle, 3–26. WUNT 359. Tübingen: Mohr Siebeck, 2016.

Culy, Martin M. *Echoes of Friendship in the Gospel of John.* NTM 30. Sheffield: Sheffield Phoenix, 2010.

Cyril of Alexandria. *Commentary on John.* Translated by David R. Maxwell. 2 vols. ACT. Downers Grove: IVP Academic, 2015.

Daise, Michael A. *Feasts in John: Jewish Festivals and Jesus' "Hour" in the Fourth Gospel.* WUNT 2/229. Tübingen: Mohr Siebeck, 2007.

Danby, Herbert, trans. *The Mishnah.* London: Oxford University Press, 1933.

Boer, Martinus C. de. "The Depiction of 'the Jews' in John's Gospel: Matters of Behavior and Identity." In *Anti-Judaism and the Fourth Gospel*, edited by Reimund Bieringer, Didier Pollefeyt, and Frederique Vandecasteele-Vanneuville, 141–57. Louisville: Westminster John Knox, 2001.

_____. "Andrew: The First Link in the Chain." In *Character Studies in the Fourth Gospel: Narrative Approaches to Seventy Figures in John*, edited by Steven A. Hunt, Francois Tolmie, and Ruben Zimmermann, 137–50. WUNT 314. Tübingen: Mohr Siebeck, 2013.

_____. "The Original Prologue to the Gospel of John." *NTS* 61 (2015): 448–67.

Dicken, Frank, and Julia Snyder, eds. *Characters and Characterization in Luke-Acts*. LNTS 548. London: Bloomsbury T&T Clark, 2016.

Do, Toan. "Does περὶ ὅλου τοῦ κοσμοῦ Imply 'the Sins of the Whole World' in 1 John 2:2?" *Bib* 94 (2013): 415–35.

_____. *Re-thinking the Death of Jesus: An Exegetical and Theological Study of* Hilasmos *and* Agapē *in 1 John 2:1–2 and 4:7–10*. CBET 73. Leuven: Peeters, 2014.

_____. "Εἰδῆτε, ἴδητε, οἴδατε, and Scribal Activities in 1 John 2:29a." *Babelao* 5 (2016): 77–104.

Dodd, Charles H. *The Interpretation of the Fourth Gospel*. Cambridge: Cambridge University Press, 1953.

Dombrowski, Daniel. "Plato's 'Noble' Lie." *History of Political Thought* 17 (1997): 565–78.

Donahue, James A., "The Use of Virtue and Character in Applied Ethics." *Horizons* 17 (1990): 228–43.

Draper, Jonathan A. "'If Those to Whom the W/word of God Came Were Called Gods . . . '–Logos, Wisdom and Prophecy, and John 10:22–30." *HvTSt* 71, no. 1 (2015): http://dx.doi.org/10.4102/hts.v71i1.2905.

_____. "Ils virent Dieu, puis ils managèrent et burent (Exode 24:11): L'immanence mystique du dieu transcendant dans la creation, la théophanie et l'incarnation dans l'étrange Jésus de l'évangile de Jean." In *Figures del'étrangeté dabs l'évangile de Jean: Etudes socio-historiques et littéraires*, edited by B. Decarneux and F. Nobilio, 237–81. Cortil-Wodon, PA: Editions Modulaires Européennes/FNRS, 2007.

Duff, Tim. *Plutarch's "Lives": Exploring Virtue and Vice*. Oxford: Clarendon, 1999.

Duke, Paul D. *Irony in the Fourth Gospel*. Atlanta: John Knox, 1985.

Edwards, R. B. "Χάριν ἀντὶ χάριτος [Charin anti charitos] (John 1.16): Grace and the Law in the Johannine Prologue." *JSNT* 32 (1988): 3–15.

Eiesland, Nancy L. *The Disabled God: Toward a Liberatory Theology of Disability*. Nashville: Abingdon, 1994.

Elowsky, Joel C., ed. *John 11–21*. ACCS, NT 4b. Downers Grove, IL: Inter-Varsity Press, 2007.

England, Emma, and William John Lyons, eds. *Reception History and Biblical Studies: Theory and Practice*. Scriptural Traces: Critical Perspectives on the Reception and Influence of the Bible 6. London: Bloomsbury T&T Clark, 2015.

Epictetus. *The Works of Epictetus, His Discourses, in Four Books, the Enchiridion, and Fragments*. Edited by Thomas Wentworth Higginson. New York: Thomas Nelson & Sons, 1890.

Fretheim, Terence E. "The Reclamation of Creation." *Int* 45 (1991): 354–65.

Frey, Jörg. *Die johanneische Eschatologie*. 3 vols. WUNT 96, 110, 117. Tübingen: Mohr Siebeck, 1997–2000.

_____. "Love-Relations in the Fourth Gospel: Establishing a Semantic Network." In *Repetitions and Variations in the Fourth Gospel: Style, Text, Interpretation*, edited by Gilbert Van Belle, Michael Labahn, and Peter Maritz, 171–98. BETL 223. Leuven: Peeters, 2009.

Funk, Robert W. *A Beginning-Intermediate Grammar of Hellenistic Greek*. 3rd ed. Salem, OR: Polebridge, 2013.

Furnish, Victor Paul. *The Love Command in the New Testament*. Nashville: Abingdon, 1972.

Garland-Thomson, Rosemarie. *Extraordinary Bodies: Figuring Physical Disability in American Culture and Literature*. New York: Columbia University Press, 1997.

_____. "Politics of Staring: Visual Rhetorics of Disability in Popular Photography." In *Disability Studies: Enabling the Humanities*, edited by Sharon L. Snyder, Brenda Jo Brueggemann, and Rosemarie Garland-Thomson, 56–75. New York: Modern Language Association of America, 2002.

Giblin, Charles H. "Two Complementary Literary Structures in John 1:1–18." *JBL* 104 (1985): 87–103.

Gignac, Francis T. "The Use of Verbal Variety in the Fourth Gospel." In *Transcending Boundaries: Contemporary Readings of the New Testament. Essays in Honor of Francis J. Moloney*, edited by Rekka M. Chennattu and Mary L. Coloe, 191–200. Rome: Las, 2005.

Gill, Christopher. "The Transformation of Aristotle's Ethics in Roman Philosophy." In *The Reception of Aristotle's Ethics*, edited by Jon Miller, 31–52. Cambridge: Cambridge University Press, 2012.

Goedt, Michael de. "Un Scheme de revelation dans le Quatrieme Evangile." *NTS* 8, no. 2 (1962): 142–50.

Gorman, Michael J. *Abide and Go: John, Participation, and Mission*. Eugene, OR: Cascade, 2017.

Goss, Robert E. "John." In *The Queer Bible Commentary*, edited by Deryn Guest, Robert E. Goss, Mona West, and Thomas Bohache, 548–65. London: SCM, 2006.

Grant, Colleen. "Reinterpreting the Healing Narratives." In *Human Disability and the Service of God: Reassessing Religious Practice*, edited by Nancy L. Eiesland and Don E. Saliers, 72–87. Nashville: Abingdon, 1998.

Grindheim, Sigurd, "The Work of God or of Human Beings: A Note on John 6:29." *JETS* 59 (2016): 63–66.

Grönum, Nico J. "A Return to Virtue Ethics: Virtue Ethics, Cognitive Science and Character Education." *Verbum et Ecclesia* 36, no. 1 (2015): 1–6. http://dx.doi.org/10.4102/ve.v36i1.1413.

Gundry, Robert H. *Jesus the Word according to John the Sectarian: A Paleofundamentalist Manifesto for Contemporary Evangelicalism, Especially Its Elites, in North America*. Grand Rapids: Eerdmans, 2002.

Gushee, David P. *The Sacredness of Human Life: Why an Ancient Biblical Vision Is Key to the World's Future*. Grand Rapids: Eerdmans, 2013.

Haddorff, David W. "Can Character Ethics Have Moral Rules and Principles? Christian Doctrine and Comprehensive Moral Theory." *Horizons* 23 (1996): 48–71.

Haenchen, Ernst. *John 1: A Commentary on the Gospel of John 1–6*. Translated by Robert W. Funk. Edited by Robert W. Funk and Ulrich Busse. Hermeneia. Philadelphia: Fortress Press, 1984.

———. *John 2: A Commentary on the Gospel of John Chapters 7–21*. Translated by Robert W. Funk. Edited by Robert W. Funk and Ulrich Busse. Hermeneia. Philadelphia: Fortress Press, 1984.

Hakola, Raimo. *Reconsidering Johannine Christianity: A Social Identity Approach*. New York: Routledge, 2015.

Hartman, David. *A Living Covenant: The Innovative Spirit in Traditional Judaism*. Woodstock, VT: Jewish Lights, 1997.

Harvey, W. J. *Character and the Novel*. Ithaca, NY: Cornell University Press, 1965.

Hauerwas, Stanley. *A Community of Character: Toward a Constructive Christian Social Ethic.* Notre Dame: University of Notre Dame Press, 1981.

_____. *The Peaceable Kingdom: A Primer in Christian Ethics.* Notre Dame: University of Notre Dame Press, 1983.

_____. "Toward an Ethics of Character." *Texts and Studies* 33 (1972): 698–715.

Hauerwas, Stanley, and Charles Pinches. *Christians among the Virtues: Theological Conversations with Ancient and Modern Ethics.* Notre Dame: University of Notre Dame Press, 1997

Hays, Richard B. "Mapping the Field: Approaches to New Testament Ethics." In *Identity, Ethics, and Ethos in the New Testament,* edited by Jan G. van der Watt, 3–19. BZNW 141 Berlin: de Gruyter, 2006.

_____. *The Moral Vision of the New Testament: A Contemporary Introduction to New Testament Ethics.* San Francisco: HarperSanFrancisco, 1996.

Heschel, Abraham Joshua. *The Sabbath.* New York: Farrar, Straus and Giroux, 1951.

Hooker, Morna D. *Beginnings: Keys That Open the Gospels.* Harrisburg, PA: Trinity Press International, 1997.

_____. *Endings: Invitations to Discipleship.* Peabody, MA: Hendrickson, 2003.

_____. "John the Baptist and the Johannine Prologue." *NTS* 16 (1970): 354–58.

Hoskyns, Edwyn C., and Francis N. Davey. *The Fourth Gospel* London: Faber & Faber, 1947.

Houlden, J. L. *Ethics and the New Testament.* Harmondsworth, UK: Penguin, 1973.

Hull, John M. *In the Beginning There Was Darkness: A Blind Person's Conversations with the Bible.* Harrisburg, PA: Trinity Press International, 2002.

Hunt, Steven A. "Nathanael: Under the Fig Tree on the Fourth Day." In *Character Studies in the Fourth Gospel: Narrative Approaches to Seventy Figures in John,* edited by Steven A. Hunt, Francois Tolmie, and Ruben Zimmermann, 189–201. WUNT 314. Tübingen: Mohr Siebeck, 2013.

_____, Francois Tolmie, and Ruben Zimmerman, eds. *Narrative Approaches to Seventy Figures in John.* WUNT 314. Tübingen: Mohr Siebeck, 2013.

Hurtado, Larry W. "Remembering and Revelation: The Historic and Glorified Jesus in the Gospel of John." In *Israel's God and Rebecca's Children: Christology and Community in Early Judaism and Christianity,* edited by David B. Capes, April D. DeConick, Helen K. Bond, and Troy Miller, 195–213. Waco, TX: Baylor University Press, 2007.

Hylen, Susan. *Imperfect Believers: Ambiguous Characters in the Gospel of John.* Louisville: Westminster John Knox, 2009.

Irenaeus. *Proof of the Apostolic Preaching.* Translated by Joseph P. Smith. Westminster, MD: Newman Press, 1952.

Irigoin, J. "La composition rythmique du prologue de Jean (I, 1–18)." *RB* 98 (1991): 5–50.

Irwin, Terence, ed. *Aristotle: Nicomachean Ethics: Translated, with Introduction, Notes, and Glossary.* 2nd ed. Indianapolis: Hackett, 1999.

Johnson, Brian D. "'Salvation Is from the Jews': Judaism in the Gospel of John." In *New Currents through John: A Global Perspective*, edited by Francisco Lozada Jr. and Tom Thatcher, 83–99. RBS 54. Atlanta: Society of Biblical Literature, 2006.

Judge, Peter J. "Come and See: The First Disciples and Christology in the Fourth Gospel." In *Studies in the Gospel of John and Its Christology: Festschrift Gilbert Van Belle*, edited by Joseph Verheyden, Geert van Oyen, Michael Labahn, and Reimund Bieringer, 61–69. BETL 265. Leuven: Peeters, 2014.

Junior, Nyasha, and Jeremy Schipper. "Disability Studies and the Bible." In *New Meanings for Ancient Texts: Recent Approaches to Biblical Criticisms*, edited by Steven L. McKenzie and John Kaltner, 21–37. Louisville: Westminster John Knox, 2013.

Kanagaraj, Jey J. "The Implied Ethics of the Fourth Gospel: A Reinterpretation of the Decalogue." *TynBul* 52 (2001): 33–60.

Kannaday, Wayne Campbell. *Apologetic Discourse and the Scribal Tradition: Evidence of the Influence of Apologetic Interests on the Text of the Canonical Gospels.* Atlanta: Society of Biblical Literature, 2004.

Karakolis, Christos. "Semeia Conveying Ethics in the Gospel of John." In *Rethinking the Ethics of John: "Implicit Ethics" in the Johannine Writings*, edited by Jan G. van der Watt and Ruben Zimmermann, 192–212. Kontexte und Normen neutestamentliche Ethik/Contexts and Norms of New Testament Ethics 3. WUNT 291. Tübingen: Mohr Siebeck, 2012.

Käsemann, Ernst. *New Testament Questions of Today.* London: SCM, 1969.

———. *The Testament of Jesus: A Study of the Gospel of John in the Light of Chapter 17.* Translated by Gerhard Krodel. Philadelphia: Fortress Press, 1968.

Keenan, James F. *History of Catholic Moral Theology in the Twentieth Century: From Confessing Sins to Liberating Consciences.* London: Continuum, 2010.

Keener, Craig R. *The Gospel of John: A Commentary*. 2 vols. Grand Rapids: Baker Academic, 2003.

Keith, Chris. "Social Memory Theory and Gospels Research: The First Decade Part One." *Early Christianity* 6 (2015): 354–76.

_____. "Social Memory Theory and Gospels Research: The First Decade Part Two." *Early Christianity* 6 (2015): 517–42.

Kelber, Werner H. "The Birth of a Beginning: John 1:1–18." *Semeia* 52 (1990): 121–44.

_____. *The Oral and the Written Gospel: The Hermeneutics of Speaking and Writing in the Synoptic Tradition, Mark, Paul, and Q*. Bloomington: Indiana University Press, 1997.

Kellum, Scott E. *The Unity of the Farewell Discourse: The Literary Integrity of John 13:31–16:33*. JSNTSup 256. Sheffield: Sheffield Academic, 2004.

Kennedy, George A., trans. *"Progymnasmata": Greek Textbooks of Prose Composition and Rhetoric*. WGRW 10. Atlanta: Society of Biblical Literature, 2003.

King, Martin Luther, Jr. "The Ethical Demands for Integration." In *A Testament of Hope: The Essential Writings of Martin Luther King, Jr.*, edited by James M. Washington, 117–25. San Francisco: Harper & Row, 1986.

_____. "Transformed Nonconformist." In *Strength to Love*, 11–20. Gift ed. Minneapolis: Fortress Press, 2010.

Klink, Edward W. *The Audience of the Gospels: The Origin and Function of the Gospels in Early Christianity*. LNTS 353. London: T&T Clark, 2010.

_____. *The Sheep of the Fold: The Audience and Origin of the Gospel of John*. SNTSMS 141. Cambridge: Cambridge University Press, 2007.

Knoppers, Gary N. *Jews and Samaritans: The Origins and History of Their Early Relations*. New York: Oxford University Press, 2013.

Koester, Craig S. "Hearing, Seeing, and Believing in the Gospel of John." *Biblica* 70 (1989): 327–48.

_____. *Symbolism in the Fourth Gospel: Meaning, Mystery, Community*. 2nd ed. Minneapolis: Fortress Press, 2003.

_____. "Theological Complexity and the Characterization of Nicodemus in John's Gospel." In *Characters and Characterization in the Gospel of John*, edited by Christopher W. Skinner, 165–81. LNTS 461. London: Bloomsbury T&T Clark, 2013.

_____. *The Word of Life: A Theology of John's Gospel*. Grand Rapids: Eerdmans, 2008.

Kok, Kobus. "As the Father Has Sent Me, I Send You: Towards a Missional-

Incarnational Ethos in John 4." In *Moral language in the New Testament: The Interrelatedness of Language and Ethics in Early Christian Writings*, edited by Ruben Zimmermann, Jan G. van der Watt, and Susanne Luther, 168–96. WUNT 2/296. Tübingen: Mohr Siebeck, 2010.

Koosed, Jennifer L., ed. *The Bible and Posthumanism*. SemeiaSt 74. Atlanta: SBL Press, 2014.

Kysar, Robert. *John*. ACNT. Minneapolis: Augsburg Press, 1986.

Labahn, Michael. "'It's Only Love'—Is That All? Limits and Potentials of Johannine 'Ethic'—Critical Evaluation of Research." In *Rethinking the Ethics of John: "Implicit Ethics" in the Johannine Writings*, edited by Jan G. van der Watt and Ruben Zimmermann, 3–43. Kontexte und Normen neutestamentliche Ethik/Contexts and Norms of New Testament Ethics 3. WUNT 291. Tübingen: Mohr Siebeck, 2012.

Lambrecht, Jan. *The Sermon on the Mount: Proclamation and Exhortation*. GNS 14. Wilmington, DE: Michael Glazier, 1985.

Larsson, Tord. *God in the Fourth Gospel: A Hermeneutical Discussion of the History of Interpretation*. ConBNT 35. Lund: Almqvist, 2001.

Lazure, Noël. *Les Valeurs Morales de la Théologie Johannique (Évangile et Épîtres)*. EBib. Paris: Gabalda, 1965.

Le Donne, Anthony, and Tom Thatcher, eds. *The Fourth Gospel in First-Century Media Culture*. LNTS 426. London: T&T Clark, 2011.

Lee, Dorothy A. *Flesh and Glory: Symbolism, Gender and Theology in the Gospel of John*. New York: Crossroad, 2002.

_____. "The Gospel of John and the Five Senses." *JBL* 129 (2010): 115–27.

_____. *Hallowed in Truth and Love: Spirituality in the Johannine Literature*. Eugene, OR: Wipf & Stock, 2012.

_____. "Imagery." In *How John Works: Storytelling in the Fourth Gospel*, edited by Douglas Estes and Ruth Sheridan, 151–69. RBS. Atlanta: SBL Press, 2016.

_____. "The Significance of Moses in the Gospel of John." *ABR* 63 (2015): 52–66.

_____. *The Symbolic Narratives of the Fourth Gospel: The Interplay of Form and Meaning*. Sheffield: Sheffield Academic, 1994.

Léon-Dufour, Xavier. *Lecture de l'evangile selon Jean*. 4 vols. Paris: Éditions du Seuil, 1988–1996.

Levine, Amy-Jill, with Marianne Blickenstaff. *A Feminist Companion to John*. 2 vols. Cleveland: Pilgrim Press, 2003.

Lévy, Carlos, "Philo's Ethics." In *The Cambridge Companion to Philo*, edited by Adam Kamesar, 146–71. Cambridge: Cambridge University Press, 2009.

Lieb, Michael, Emma Mason, and Jonathan Roberts, eds., *The Oxford Handbook of the Reception History of the Bible*. Oxford: Oxford University Press, 2011.

Lieu, Judith. "Anti-Judaism, the Jews, and the Worlds of the Fourth Gospel." In *The Gospel of John and Christian Theology*, edited by Richard Bauckham and Carl Mossner, 168–82. Grand Rapids: Eerdmans, 2008.

_____. "The Mother of the Son in the Fourth Gospel." *JBL* 117 (1998): 61–77.

Lincoln, Andrew T. *The Gospel according to Saint John*. BNTC. New York: Crossroad, 2005.

Linton, Simi. "What Is Disability Studies?" *PMLA* 120, no. 2 (2005): 518–22.

Loader, William R. G. *Jesus' Attitude towards the Law: A Study of the Gospels*. WUNT 97. Tübingen: Mohr Siebeck, 1997.

_____. "The Law and Ethics in John's Gospel." In *Rethinking the Ethics of John: "Implicit Ethics" in the Johannine Writings*, edited by Jan G. van der Watt and Ruben Zimmermann, 143–58. Kontexte und Normen neutestamentliche Ethik/Contexts and Norms of New Testament Ethics 3. WUNT 291. Tübingen: Mohr Siebeck, 2012.

Löhr, Hermut. "Ἔργον as an Element of Moral Language in John." In *Rethinking the Ethics of John: "Implicit Ethics" in the Johannine Writings*, edited by Jan G. van der Watt and Ruben Zimmermann, 228–49. Kontexte und Normen neutestamentliche Ethik/Contexts and Norms of New Testament Ethics 3. WUNT 291. Tübingen: Mohr Siebeck, 2012.

Lund, Nils Wilhelm. *Chiasmus in the New Testament: A Study in the Form and Function of Chiastic Structures*. Peabody, MA: Hendrickson, 1992.

Lyons, William John. *Joseph of Arimathea: A Study in Reception History*. Biblical Refigurations. Oxford: Oxford University Press, 2014.

MacIntyre, Alasdair. *After Virtue: A Study in Moral Theory*. London: Duckworth, 1981.

_____. *A Short History of Ethics: A History of Moral Philosophy from the Homeric Age to the Twentieth Century*. Rev. ed. London: Routledge, 2002.

Manning, Gary T. "The Disciples of John (the Baptist): Hearers of John, Followers of Jesus." In *Character Studies in the Fourth Gospel: Narrative Approaches to Seventy Figures in John*, edited by Steven A. Hunt, D. Francois Tolmie, and Ruben Zimmermann, 127–32. WUNT 314. Tübingen: Mohr Siebeck, 2013.

Manns, Frédéric. *L'Evangile de Jean: à la lumière du Judaïsme.* Jerusalem: Franciscan Printing Press, 1991.

Marcus, Joel. "*Birkat Ha-Minim* Revisited." *NTS* 55 (2009): 523–51.

Marrow, Stanley B. "*Kosmos* in John." *CBQ* 64 (2002): 90–102.

Martínez, Florentino García, and Eibert J. C. Tigchelaar, eds. *The Dead Sea Scrolls.* Vol. 1, *1Q1–4Q273.* Study ed. Leiden: Brill; Grand Rapids: Eerdmans, 2000.

Martyn, J. Louis. *History and Theology in the Fourth Gospel.* Nashville: Abingdon, 1968.

_____. *History and Theology in the Fourth Gospel.* 3rd ed. New Testament Library. Louisville: Westminster John Knox, 2003.

Matera, Frank J. *New Testament Ethics: The Legacies of Jesus and Paul.* Louisville: Westminster John Knox, 1996.

_____. *The Sermon on the Mount: The Perfect Measure of the Christian Life.* Collegeville, MN: Liturgical Press, 2013.

McClendon, James W. *Systematic Theology.* Vol. 1, *Ethics.* 2nd ed. Nashville: Abingdon, 2002.

McRuer, Robert. *Crip Theory: Cultural Signs of Queerness and Disability.* New York: New York University Press, 2006.

Meeks, Wayne A. "The Ethics of the Fourth Evangelist." In *Exploring the Gospel of John: In Honor of D. Moody Smith,* edited by R. Alan Culpepper and C. Clifton Black, 317–26. Louisville: Westminster John Knox, 1996.

_____. "The Man from Heaven in Johannine Sectarianism." *JBL* 91 (1972): 44–72.

Meier, John P. "Love in Q and John: Love of Enemies, Love of One Another." *Mid-Stream* 40 (2001): 42–50.

_____. *A Marginal Jew: Rethinking the Historical Jesus.* Vol. 4, *Law and Love.* AYBRL. New Haven: Yale University Press, 2009.

Mercer, Calvin, and Tracy J. Trothen, eds. *Religion and Transhumanism: The Unknown Future of Human Enhancement.* Santa Barbara: Praeger, 2015.

Metzger, Bruce M. *A Textual Commentary on the Greek New Testament.* 2nd ed. Stuttgart: Deutsche Bibelgesellschaft, 1994.

Michaelis, Wilhelm. "Joh 1:5, Gen 28:12 und das Menschensohn-Problem." *TLZ* 58 (1960): 561–78.

Michaels, J. Ramsey. *The Gospel of John.* NICNT. Grand Rapids: Eerdmans, 2010.

Mitchell, David, and Sharon Snyder. "'Jesus Thrown Everything Off Balance': Disability and Redemption in Biblical Literature." In *This Abled*

Body: Rethinking Disabilities in Biblical Studies, edited by Hector Avalos, Sarah J. Melcher, and Jeremy Schipper, 173–83. Atlanta: Society of Biblical Literature, 2007.

Mittleman, Alan L. *A Short History of Jewish Ethics: Conduct and Character in the Context of Covenant*. Chichester, UK: Wiley-Blackwell, 2012.

Moloney, Francis J. *Belief in the Word: Reading John 1–4*. Minneapolis: Fortress Press, 1993.

_____. "Can Everyone Be Wrong? A Reading of John 11:1–12:8." In *The Gospel of John: Text and Context*, 214–40. BibInt 72. Leiden: Brill, 2005.

_____. "Εἰς τέλος (v. 1) as the Hermeneutical Key to John 13:1–38." *Salesianum* 86 (2014): 27–46.

_____. "The Fourth Gospel: A Tale of Two Paracletes." In *The Gospel of John: Text and Context*, 241–59. BibInt 72. Leiden: Brill, 2005.

_____. *Glory Not Dishonor: Reading John 13–21*. Minneapolis: Fortress Press, 1998.

_____. "The Gospel of John as Scripture." In *The Gospel of John: Text and Context*, 333–47. BibInt 72. Leiden: Brill, 2005.

_____. *The Gospel of John*. SP 4. Collegeville, MN: Liturgical Press, 1998.

_____. "'In the Bosom of' or 'Turned towards' the Father?" *ABR* 31 (1983): 63–71.

_____. "'The Jews' in the Fourth Gospel: Another Perspective." In *The Gospel of John: Text and Context*, 20–44. BibInt 72. Leiden: Brill, 2005.

_____. *The Johannine Son of Man*. 2nd ed. Eugene, OR: Wipf & Stock, 2007.

_____. "The Literary Unity of John 13,1–38." *ETL* 91 (2015): 33–53.

_____. *Love in the Gospel of John: An Exegetical, Theological, and Literary Study*. Grand Rapids: Baker Academic, 2013.

_____. "Telling God's Story: The Fourth Gospel." In *The Gospel of John: Text and Context*, 93–111. BibInt 72. Leiden: Brill, 2005.

Morris, Leon. *The Gospel according to John*. NICNT. Grand Rapids: Eerdmans, 1995.

Motyer, Stephen. "Bridging the Gap: How Might the Fourth Gospel Help us Cope with the Legacy of Christianity's Exclusive Claim over against Judaism?" In *The Gospel of John and Christian Theology*, edited by Richard Bauckham and Carl A. Mosser, 143–67. Grand Rapids: Eerdmans, 2008.

_____. "The Fourth Gospel and the Salvation of Israel: An Appeal for a New Start." In *Anti-Judaism and the Fourth Gospel*, edited by Reimund

Bieringer, Didier Pollefeyt, and Frederique Vandecasteele-Vanneuville, 83–100. Louisville: Westminster John Knox, 2001.

_____. *Your Father the Devil? A New Approach to John and "the Jews."* Carlisle, UK: Paternoster, 1997.

Myers, Alicia D. *Characterizing Jesus: A Rhetorical Analysis on the Fourth Gospel's Use of Scripture in its Presentation of Jesus.* LNTS 458. London: Bloomsbury T&T Clark, 2012.

Nissen, Johannes. "Community and Ethics in the Gospel of John." In *New Readings in John: Literary and Theological Perspectives; Essays from the Scandinavian Conference on the Fourth Gospel in Aarhus 1997*, edited by Johannes Nissen and Sigfred Pedersen, 194–212. JSNTSup 182. Sheffield: Sheffield Academic, 1999.

Neyrey, Jerome H. "Encomium versus Vituperation: Contrasting Portraits of Jesus in the Fourth Gospel." *JBL* 126 (2007): 529–52.

_____. *The Gospel of John.* NCB. Cambridge: Cambridge University Press, 2007.

_____. *The Gospel of John in Cultural and Rhetorical Perspective.* Grand Rapids: Eerdmans, 2009.

O'Day, Gail. "Gospel of John." In *Women's Bible Commentary*, edited by Carol A. Newsom, Sharon H. Ringe, and Jacqueline E. Lapsley, 517–30. 3rd ed. Louisville: Westminster John Knox Press, 2012.

_____. *Revelation in the Fourth Gospel: Narrative Mode and Theological Claim.* Philadelphia: Fortress Press, 1986.

Painter, John. "The 'Opponents' in 1 John." *NTS* 32 (1986): 48–71.

_____. *The Quest for the Messiah: The History, Literature and Theology of the Johannine Community.* Nashville: Abingdon, 1993.

_____. "Inclined to God. The Quest for Eternal Life—Bultmannian Hermeneutics in the Theology of the Fourth Gospel." In *Exploring the Gospel of John: In Honor of D. Moody Smith*, edited by R. Alan Culpepper and C. Clifton Black, 346–68. Louisville: Westminster John Knox, 1996.

Pakaluk, Michael, *Aristotle's Nicomachean Ethics: An Introduction.* Cambridge: Cambridge University Press, 2005.

Pancaro, Severino. *The Law in the Fourth Gospel: The Torah and the Gospel, Moses and Jesus, Judaism and Christianity according to John.* NovTSup 42. Leiden: Brill, 1975.

Pelling, Christopher R., ed. *Characterization and Individuality in Greek Literature.* Oxford: Clarendon, 1990.

Postell, Seth D. *Adam as Israel: Genesis 1–3 as the Introduction to the Torah and Tanakh.* Cambridge: James Clarke, 2012.

Potterie, I. de la. "L'emploie dynamique de eis dans Saint Jean et ses incidences théologiques." *Bib* 43 (1962): 366–87.

Pippin, Tina. "'For Fear of the Jews': Lying and Truth-Telling in Translating the Fourth Gospel." *Semitica* 76 (1996): 81–97.

Plutarch. *Lives.* Vol. 6, *Dion and Brutus. Timoleon and Aemilius Paulus.* Edited by Bernadotte Perrin. LCL. Cambridge, MA: Harvard University Press, 1918.

Pryor, John W. "Covenant and Community in John's Gospel." *RTR* 47 (1988) 44–51.

Reich, Keith A. *Figuring Jesus: The Power of Rhetorical Figures of Speech in the Gospel of Luke.* BibInt 107. Leiden: Brill, 2011.

Reinhartz, Adele. *Befriending the Beloved Disciple: A Jewish Reading of the Gospel of John.* New York: Continuum, 2001.

———. "Incarnation and Covenant: The Fourth Gospel through the Lens of Trauma Theory." *Int* 69 (2015): 35–48.

———. "'Jews' and Jews in the Fourth Gospel." In *Anti-Judaism and the Fourth Gospel,* edited by Reimund Bieringer, Didier Pollefeyt, and Frederique Vandecasteele-Vanneuville, 213–27. Louisville: Westminster John Knox, 2001.

———. "Judaism in the Gospel of John." *Int* 63 (2009): 382–93.

———. "A Rebellious Son? Jesus and His Mother in John 2:4." In *The Opening of John's Narrative,* edited by R. Alan Culpepper and Jörg Frey, 235-49. Tübingen: Mohr-Siebeck, 2017.

———. "Reproach and Revelation: Ethics in John 11:1–44." In *Torah Ethics and Early Christian Identity,* edited by Susan J. Wendel and David Miller, 92–106. Grand Rapids: Eerdmans, 2016.

———. "The Vanishing Jews of Antiquity." *Marginalia Review of Books.* June 24, 2014. http://marginalia.lareviewofbooks.org/vanishing-jews-antiquity-adele-reinhartz/.

Rensberger, David. "Completed Love: 1 John 4:11–18 and the Mission of the New Testament Church." In *Communities in Dispute: Current Scholarship on the Johannine Epistles,* edited by R. Alan Culpepper and Paul N. Anderson, 237–71. ECL 13. Atlanta: SBL Press, 2014.

———. *Johannine Faith and Liberating Community.* Philadelphia: Westminster, 1988.

_____. *Overcoming the World: Politics and Community in the Gospel of John.* London: SPCK, 1988.

Ridderbos, Herman N. *The Gospel according to John: A Theological Commentary.* Grand Rapids: Eerdmans, 1992.

Robinson, John A. T. "The Relation of the Prologue to the Gospel of John." *NTS* 9 (1963): 120–29.

Rodriguez, Rafael. *Oral Tradition and the New Testament: A Guide for the Perplexed.* London: T&T Clark, 2014.

Rosik, Mariusz. "Discovering the Secrets of God's Gardens: Resurrection as New Creation (Gen 2:4b–3:24; Jn 20:1–18)." *SBFLA* 58 (2008): 81–96.

Sanders, Jack T. *Ethics in the New Testament.* Philadelphia: Fortress Press, 1975.

Schnackenburg, Rudolf. *The Gospel according to St John.* 3 vols. New York: Seabury, 1980.

Schneiders, Sandra M. "Death in the Community and Eternal Life: History, Theology, and Spirituality in John 11." *Int* 41 (1987): 44–56.

Schnelle, Udo. *Antidocetic Christology in the Gospel of John: An Investigation of the Place of the Fourth Gospel in the Johannine School.* Translated by Linda M. Maloney. Minneapolis: Fortress Press, 1992.

_____. "Die Reihenfolge der johanneischen Schriften." *NTS* 37 (2011): 91–113.

_____. "Theologie als creative Sinnbildung: Johannes als Weiterbildung von Paulus und Markus." In *Das Johannesevangeliums—Mitte oder Rand des Kanons" Neue Standortsbestimmungen,* edited by Thomas Söding, 119–45. QD 203. Freiburg: Herder, 2003.

_____. *Theology of the New Testament.* Translated by M. Eugene Boring. Grand Rapids: Baker Academic, 2009.

Scott, Martin. *Sophia and the Johannine Jesus.* JSNTSup 71. Sheffield: Sheffield Academic, 1992.

Segovia, Fernando F. *Love Relationships in the Johannine Traditions: Agapē/ Agapan in 1 John and the Fourth Gospel.* SBLDS 58. Chico, CA: Scholars Press, 1982.

_____. "The Love and Hatred of Jesus and Johannine Sectarianism." *CBQ* 43 (1981): 258–72.

Seim, Turid Karlsen. "Descent and Divine Paternity in the Gospel of John: Does the Mother Matter?" *NTS* 51 (2005): 361–75.

Sharpe, Matthew, "Stoic Virtue Ethics," In *The Handbook of Virtue Ethics,* edited by Stan van Hooft, 28–41. London: Routledge, 2014.

Shepherd, David. "'Do You Love Me?' A Narrative-Critical Reappraisal of ἀγαπάω and φιλέω in John 21:15–17." *JBL* 129 (2010): 777–92.

Sheridan, Ruth. "Identity, Alterity, and the Gospel of John." *BibInt* 22 (2014): 188–209.

_____. *Retelling Scripture: "The Jews" and the Scriptural Citations in John 1:19–12:15*. BibInt 110. Leiden: Brill, 2012.

Siliezar, Carlos Raül Siliezar. *Creation Imagery in the Gospel of John*. LNTS 546; London: Bloomsbury T&T Clark, 2015.

Skinner, Christopher W., ed. *Characters and Characterization in the Gospel of John*. LNTS 416. London: Bloomsbury T&T Clark, 2014.

_____. "Characters and Characterization in the Gospel of John: Reflections on the *Status Quaestionis*." In *Characters and Characterization in the Gospel of John*, edited by Christopher W. Skinner, xvii–xxxii. LNTS 416. London: Bloomsbury T&T Clark, 2013.

_____. *Reading John*. Cascade Companions. Eugene, OR: Cascade, 2015.

_____. "Virtue in the New Testament: The Legacies of Paul and John in Comparative Perspective." In *Unity and Diversity in the Gospels and Paul: Essays in Honor of Frank J. Matera*, edited by Christopher W. Skinner and Kelly R. Iverson, 301–24. ECL 7. Atlanta: SBL Press 2012.

_____. "The World: Promise and Unfulfilled Hope." In *Character Studies in the Fourth Gospel: Narrative Approaches to Seventy Figures in John*, edited by Steven A. Hunt, D. Francois Tolmie, and Ruben Zimmermann, 61–70. WUNT 314. Tübingen: Mohr Siebeck, 2013.

Skinner, Christopher W., and Matthew Ryan Hauge, eds. *Character Studies and the Gospel of Mark*. LNTS 483. London: Bloomsbury T&T Clark, 2014.

Smith, D. Moody. "Ethics and Interpretation of the Fourth Gospel." In *Word, Theology, and Community in John*, edited by John Painter, R. Alan Culpepper, and Fernando F. Segovia, 109–22. St. Louis: Chalice, 2002.

_____. "Johannine Christianity: Some Reflections on Its Character and Delineation." *NTS* 21 (1975): 222–48.

_____. *John*. ANTC. Nashville: Abingdon, 1999.

Smyth, Herbert W. *Greek Grammar*. Oxford: Benediction Classics, 2014.

Spohn, William C. *Go and Do Likewise: Jesus and Ethics*. New York: Continuum, 2007.

Stählin, Gustav. "Zum Problem der johanneischen Eschatologie." *ZNW* 33 (1934): 225–59.

Sternberg, Meir. *Expositional Modes and Temporal Ordering in Fiction.* Baltimore: Johns Hopkins University Press, 1978.

Stylianopoulos, Theodore G. *The New Testament: An Orthodox Perspective.* Brookline, MA: Holy Cross Orthodox Press, 1997.

Swartley, Willard M. *Covenant of Peace: The Missing Peace in New Testament Theology and Ethics.* Grand Rapids: Eerdmans, 2006.

Talbert, Charles H. "Artistry and Theology: An Analysis of the Architecture of Jn 1,19–5,47." *CBQ* 32 (1970): 341–66.

Tannehill, Robert. "The Gospel of Mark as Narrative Christology." *Semeia* 16 (1979): 57–95.

Thatcher, Tom. "Cain the Jew the AntiChrist: Collective Memory and the Johannine Ethics of Loving and Hating." In *Rethinking the Ethics of John: "Implicit Ethics" in the Johannine Writings,* edited by Jan G. van der Watt and Ruben Zimmerman, 350–73. Kontexte und Normen neutestamentliche Ethik/Contexts and Norms of New Testament Ethics 3. WUNT 291. Tübingen: Mohr Siebeck, 2012.

———. "Jesus, Judas, and Peter: Character by Contrast in the Fourth Gospel." *BSac* 153 (1996): 435–48.

———, ed. *Jesus, the Voice, and the Text: Beyond the Oral and the Written Gospel.* Waco, TX: Baylor University Press, 2008.

———. *Why John Wrote a Gospel: Jesus—Memory—History.* Louisville: Westminster John Knox, 2006.

Theobald, Michael. *Das Evangelium nach Johannes.* RNT. Regensburg: Pustet, 2009.

Tertullian. *Treatise on the Incarnation.* Edited by Ernest Evans. London: SPCK, 1956.

Thompson, Marianne Meye. *The God of the Gospel of John.* Grand Rapids: Eerdmans, 2001.

———. *John: A Commentary.* NTL. Louisville: Westminster John Knox, 2015.

Henten, Jan Willem van, and Joseph Verheyden, eds. *Early Christian Ethics in Interaction with Jewish and Greco-Roman Contexts.* STAR 17. Leiden: Brill, 2013.

Virgulin, S. "Recent Discussion of the Title, 'Lamb of God.'" *Scripture* 13 (1961): 74–80.

The Visual Bible: The Gospel of John. DVD. Directed by Philip Saville. Toronto: Think Film, 2003.

von Wahlde, Urban C. *Gnosticism, Docetism, and the Judaisms of the First Cen-*

tury: The Search for the Wider Context of the Johannine Literature and Why It Matters. LNTS 517. London: Bloomsbury T&T Clark, 2015.

——. *The Gospel and Letters of John.* 3 vols. ECC. Grand Rapids: Eerdmans, 2010.

——. "The Terms for Religious Authorities in the Fourth Century: A Key to Literary-Strata?" *JBL* 98 (1979): 221–53.

Vogels, Walter. *God's Universal Covenant.* Ottawa: University of Ottawa Press, 1979.

Watt, Jan G. van der. "Ethics Alive in Imagery." In *Imagery in the Gospel of John,* edited by Jörg Frey, Jan G. van der Watt, and Ruben Zimmermann, 421–48. WUNT 200. Tübingen: Mohr Siebeck, 2006.

——. "Ethics and Ethos in the Gospel according to John." *ZNW* 97 (2006): 147–75.

——. "Ethics of/and the Opponents of Jesus in John's Gospel," In *Rethinking the Ethics of John: "Implicit Ethics" in the Johannine Writings,* edited by Jan G. van der Watt and Ruben Zimmermann, 175–91. Kontexte und Normen neutestamentliche Ethik/Contexts and Norms of New Testament Ethics 3. WUNT 291. Tübingen: Mohr Siebeck, 2012.

——. "Ethics through the Power of Language: Some Explorations in the Gospel according to John." In *Moral Language in the New Testament: The Interrelatedness of Language and Ethics in Early Christian Writings,* edited by Ruben Zimmerman, Jan G. van der Watt, and Susanne Luther, 139–67. WUNT 296. Tübingen: Mohr Siebeck 2010.

——. *Identity, Ethics, and Ethos in the New Testament.* BZNW 141 Berlin: de Gruyter, 2006.

——. "The Gospel of John's Perception of Ethical Behaviour." *IDS* 45 (2011): 431–47.

Watt, Jan G. van der, and Ruben Zimmermann, eds. *Rethinking the Ethics of John: "Implicit Ethics" in the Johannine Writings.* Kontexte und Normen neutestamentliche Ethik/Contexts and Norms of New Testament Ethics 3. WUNT 291. Tübingen: Mohr Siebeck, 2012.

Wagener, Fredrik. *Figuren als Handlungsmodelle: Simon Petrus, die Samaritische Frau, Judas und Thomas als zugänge zu einer narrativer Ethik des Johannesevangeliums.* Kontexte und Normen neutestamentliche Ethik/Contexts and Norms of New Testament Ethics 3. WUNT 2/408. Tübingen: Mohr Siebeck, 2016.

Wannenwetsch, Bernd. "Political Love: Why John's Gospel Is Not as Barren for Contemporary Ethics as It Might Appear." In *"You Have the Words of*

Eternal Life": Transformative Readings of the Gospel of John from a Lutheran Perspective, edited by Kenneth Mtata, 93–105. Minneapolis: Lutheran University Press, 2012.

Weitzman, Steven. "He That Cometh Out: On How to Disclose a Messianic Secret." In *Rethinking the Messianic Idea in Judaism*, edited by Michael L. Morgan and Steven Weitzman, 63–89. Bloomington: Indiana University Press, 2015.

Weyer-Menkhoff, Karl. "The Response of Jesus: Ethics in John by Considering Scripture as Word of God." In *Rethinking the Ethics of John: "Implicit Ethics" in the Johannine Writings*, edited by Jan G. van der Watt and Ruben Zimmermann, 159–74. Kontexte und Normen neutestamentliche Ethik/Contexts and Norms of New Testament Ethics 3. WUNT 291. Tübingen: Mohr Siebeck, 2012.

Williams, David Lay. "Plato's Noble Lie: From Kallipolis to Magnesia." *History of Political Thought* 34 (2013): 363–92.

Woll, Bruce. "The Departure of 'The Way': The First Farewell Discourse in the Gospel of John." *JBL* 99 (1980): 225–39.

Wood, W. Jay. *Epistemology: Becoming Intellectually Virtuous*. Leicester, UK: Apollos, 1998.

Wynn, Kerry H. "Johannine Healings and the Otherness of Disability." *PRSt* 34 (2007): 61–75.

_____. "Second Temple Literature: I & II Chronicles, Ezra, Nehemiah, Esther." In *Disability and the Bible: A Commentary*, edited by Sarah J. Melcher, Mikeal C. Parsons, and Amos Yong. Waco, TX: Baylor University Press, forthcoming.

Young, Stella. "I'm Not Your Inspiration, Thank You Very Much." Filmed April 2014. TED video. 3:10. http://www.ted.com/talks/stella_young_i_m_not_your_inspiration_thank_you_very_much?language=en.

Zimmerman, Ruben "Is There Ethics in the Gospel of John?" In *Rethinking the Ethics of John: "Implicit Ethics" in the Johannine Writings*, edited by Jan G. van der Watt and Ruben Zimmermann, 44–88. Kontexte und Normen neutestamentliche Ethik/Contexts and Norms of New Testament Ethics 3. WUNT 291. Tübingen: Mohr Siebeck, 2012.

_____. "The 'Implicit Ethics' of New Testament Writings: A Draft of a New Methodology for Analysing New Testament Ethics." *Neot* 43, no. 2 (2009): 399–423.

_____. "'The Jews': Unreliable Figures or Unreliable Narration?" In *Character Studies in the Fourth Gospel*, edited by Steven A. Hunt, D. Francois

Tolmie, and Ruben Zimmermann, 71–109. WUNT 314. Tübingen: Mohr Siebeck, 2013.

Zizioulas, John. "Proprietors or Priests of Creation." In *Toward an Ecology of Transfiguration: Orthodox Christian Perspectives on Environment, Nature, and Creation*, edited by John Chryssavgis and Bruce V. Foltz, 163–71. New York: Fordham University Press, 2013.

Zumstein, Jean. *L'Évangile selon Saint Jean*. 2 vols. CNT 4a–b. Second Series. Geneva: Labor et Fides, 2007–2014.

_____. "L'évangile johannique, une stratégie de croire." *RSR* 77 (1989): 217–32.

Author Index